NEVER SAW IT COMING

NEVER SAW IT COMING

Cultural Challenges to Envisioning the Worst

KAREN A. CERULO

THE UNIVERSITY OF CHICAGO PRESS

CHICAGO AND LONDON

KAREN A. CERULO is professor of sociology at Rutgers University and the author of several books, including *Identity Designs: The Sights and Sounds of a Nation*, winner of the American Sociological Association Culture Section's Best Book Award, and *Deciphering Violence: The Cognitive Structure of Right and Wrong*.

The University of Chicago Press, Chicago 60637
The University of Chicago Press, Ltd., London
© 2006 by The University of Chicago
All rights reserved. Published 2006
Printed in the United States of America

15 14 13 12 11 10 09 08 07 06   1 2 3 4 5

ISBN-10: 0-226-10032-4 (cloth)
ISBN-13: 978-0-226-10032-6 (cloth)
ISBN-10: 0-226-10033-2 (paper)
ISBN-13: 978-0-226-10033-3 (paper)

Library of Congress Cataloging-in-Publication Data

Cerulo, Karen A.
    Never saw it coming : cultural challenges to envisioning the worst / Karen A. Cerulo.
        p.   cm.
    Includes bibliographical references and index.
    ISBN 0-226-10032-4 (cloth : alk. paper) — ISBN 0-226-10033-2 (pbk. : alk. paper)
        1. Catastrophical, The. 2. Cognition and culture. 3. Social psychology.
    4. Knowledge, Sociology of. I. Title.

BD375.C47 2006
302'.12—dc33   2006002487

⊗ The paper used in this publication meets the minimum requirements of the American National Standard for Information Sciences—Permanence of Paper for Printed Library Materials, ANSI Z39.48-1992.

TO JAN . . .

with me through best and worst

CONTENTS

ACKNOWLEDGMENTS

So many good colleagues, friends, and family played a role in the development of this work. Their efforts warrant a heartfelt and grateful mention here. In some cases, help came in the form of a keen and critical ear, willingly lent as I described the ideas and concepts that underpin this book. In this regard my thanks go to Joel Best, Jim Beniger, Judith Blau, Marvin Bressler, Deborah Carr, Paul DiMaggio, John Douard, Ellen Idler, Michele Lamont, Joan Manley, Ann Mische, Cliff Nass, Barry Schwartz, Elaine Swingle, John Tabachnik, Ann Swidler, and Chaim Waxman. Some very dedicated colleagues and friends generously gave of their time, reading and carefully commenting on the book prospectus or the finished manuscript. For this, my sincere gratitude goes to Allan Horwitz, Janet Ruane, Robert Wuthnow, Eviatar Zerubavel, and two anonymous reviewers from the University of Chicago Press. All provided me with constructive feedback and welcome encouragement. Thanks also to the many people who offered kindness and support during the always demanding writing process: Mary Jane Blodgett, Al Cerulo Jr., Anne Glassman, Laura Kramer, Joe and Edna Nicastro, Mary Ruane, and Jan Warner. Finally, my appreciation goes to the many wonderful people at the University of Chicago Press who shepherded this project with great care and enthusiasm. Thanks to Timothy McGovern, Monica Holliday, Carlisle Rex-Waller, Joan Davies, Alice Lee, Laura Moss Gottlieb, Peter Cavagnaro, and of course, to Doug Mitchell—the most insightful and erudite editor in the business.

CHAPTER ONE

What's the Worst That Could Happen?

In *The Art of the Deal*, Donald Trump offered his readers the secret to his success: "It's been said that I believe in the power of positive thinking. In fact, I believe in the power of negative thinking. . . . I always go into a deal anticipating the worst. If you plan for the worst—if you can live with the worst—the good will always take care of itself."[1]

Donald Trump is, after all, an American success story. In business circles, he's lauded as the "comeback kid" and more. So if triumph is indeed one's aim, shouldn't Trump's strategy be part of the game plan? . . . Perhaps. But it is important to note that the Trump method holds one unexpected glitch. For the strategy to be effective, one must be able to fully anticipate the worst. And in this book, I propose that envisioning the worst may be a more difficult task than it seems.

The worst outcome, the worst fate, the worst of the lot, the worst of times—at first glance, these concepts seem so stark, so clear. Yet as we will see, when individuals, groups, and communities attempt to detail such instances, they often find that worst cases elude definition. In many situations, the worst simply cannot be pinned down. Why would the worst prove problematic to conceive?

Many would argue that the challenge stems from emotional or psychological forces. For some, envisioning the worst may be frightening, even terrifying. Others may see the exercise as too morose and find the task unreasonably depressing and void of all hope. Envisioning the worst may even prove disabling for some, with dismal ideas keeping them from productive action. To be sure, one cannot deny the psychoemotional pitfalls of imagining the worst. But I suggest that there are additional factors at play. Building on theories and ideas forwarded by both cultural and cognitive sociologists,

I argue that *the inability to envision and specify the worst is, in part, a socio-cultural phenomenon.* I contend that the worst can become a perceptual blind spot, obscured or blurred by a variety of routine and patterned socio-cultural practices—practices that, despite any single individual's intentions, can veil the worst and make it difficult to define.

In *Never Saw It Coming*, I take readers to a wide variety of settings in which the worst is hidden from view, and I investigate the sociocultural prac-tices that sustain this very common perceptual gap. I explore as well the ways in which certain elements of social structure may encourage this biased perspective. Finally, I consider the social consequences and pitfalls that masking the worst can exact. In so doing, I question whether a more symmetrical view of quality is an achievable, or desirable, social goal.

Recognizing the Worst

What's the worst that could happen to you? Can you clearly articulate it?

In the winter of 2000, I suffered an unexpected and extended illness. Fol-lowing what was predicted to be a difficult but uneventful sinus surgery, I developed a series of life-disrupting ailments that, at first, the doctors seemed unable to diagnose accurately. It became difficult for me to swallow, and I was unable to digest and eliminate food properly. I began to experience an irregular heartbeat and periods of blurred vision. I also developed a variety of serious bacterial and viral infections, the origins and recurrences of which were not wholly clear. For more than two years, my days were filled with pain, discomfort, and fear; it seemed as if my body had completely failed me. I had additional surgeries and underwent specialized treatment strategies. I had what seemed like endless tests and took a battery of prescribed medi-cations—each with its own brand of difficult side effects. Through it all, I wrestled with the overwhelming uncertainty that threats to one's health and well-being can pose. What was the worst news the doctors could deliver to me? Cancer . . . an inoperable tumor . . . some other terminal disease? More surgery . . . more medicine? Would a successful treatment emerge? Would that treatment be worse than the disease? Or would the doctors remain unable to tell me what was wrong? Which of these options would be the worst? Frankly, in the midst of this ordeal, I simply wasn't sure.

Explicating the worst can prove difficult in a wide variety of settings. Recently, for example, I polled my classes at Rutgers University and asked my students, What's the best thing that could happen to you?[2] My students' answers were amazingly precise. One person wrote, "The best thing that could happen to me is that Tom and I finish school and get married." Another wrote, "To get all A's this semester." Still another said, "I would win three hundred million dollars instantly." And one student reported, "I would become an NBA franchise player within the next three years." Clearly, my students had very specific definitions of the best things in life.[3] But a few moments later, I asked my classes, What's the worst thing that could happen to you? When faced with this question, the students' precision all but disappeared. Rather than pinpointing the worst, students offered very general, abstract answers such as "maybe, death?" "getting sick," or simply "failure." While these young men and women could itemize the best of events with a high degree of specificity, their articulations of the worst were both vague and terse.

My students are not alone in their confused sense of the worst. In an interesting study of applause and booing, sociologist Steven Clayman crystallized the nebulous quality of the worst, as well as people's shared inability to perceive it definitively. Clayman reported that applause, a collective signal by which audiences acknowledge the best, is typically exerted with concerted assuredness. In general, audiences initiate applause within three seconds of a precipitating event, and they sustain a unified response that lasts about eight seconds.[4] This pattern suggests an intersubjective agreement regarding the "upper end" of quality; it implies a widely shared definition of the best, one that garners a swift and standard response. But Clayman found a notable difference in audiences' execution of booing. Booing, he reported, lacked the concerted spontaneity of applause. Clayman uncovered a substantial time lag between the completion of a precipitating event and a full blown "boo." "This time lag allows mutual monitoring to guide the onset of booing," with certain isolated responses such as mumbling, moaning or heckling needed to trigger a unified audience response.[5] The disorganization of booing suggests that audiences are not always sure as to what constitutes the worst, and this vagueness seems to preclude their discharging a unified negative response.

One could, of course, argue that the inability to see the worst is a product of the "untrained eye." Surely, in settings characterized by the systematic evaluation of quality, the best and worst are studied with equal vigor. The issue is easy to explore. Contemporary American society suffers no shortage of performance standards and assessment criteria. In the United States, we grade everything from students to steaks, wines to Web sites, movies to mutual funds to minivans. We are not unique in this regard. Indeed, ranking and grading is a longstanding and widespread historical phenomenon. More than a century ago, sociologist Emile Durkheim noted the importance of standards and rankings. Indeed, Durkheim believed that without such standards human beings would be unable to maintain a functioning social collective. According to Durkheim, human beings are endowed with limitless desire, an aspect of human nature that leaves human beings in a precarious position, for if desires are not capped, frustration may run too high. In Durkheim's words, "One does not advance when one walks toward no goal, or—which is the same thing—when his goal is infinity." Thus, in order for human beings to achieve any productive result, Durkheim believed that a society must provide standards that will limit human desires. "Only then can the passions be harmonized with the faculties and satisfied."[6]

The creation of standards and rankings implies a dual focus—a consideration of both ends of the performance scale. But despite intentions to delineate both the best and the worst of people, places, objects, and events, conceptions of quality often remain an asymmetrical affair. Durkheim himself, while arguing adamantly for a balanced regulatory scale, had little to say about what constitutes the worst. His writings on the subject repeatedly explore examples of appropriate "upper limits" and "rewards," yet his work is nearly silent regarding the itemization of unacceptable quality. His single reference to the worst describes it as a "limit below which [the social actor] is not willingly permitted to fall unless he has seriously bemeaned himself."[7]

Durkheim's inattention to the specification of the worst alerts us to a pattern that persists in present-day thinking. In contemporary contexts, where official standards of quality guide all manners of assessment—manufacturing, healthcare, education, for example—scales of quality often display the same type of asymmetry exhibited in Durkheim's work. Standard makers purport to consider the full range of quality. Yet standards are constructed in such a way as to eliminate the worst people, places, objects, and events from an active frame of reference. Many quality gauges, for example, are guided by "standards of best quality." In such cases, the criteria for production or achievement completely ignore the worst, directing participants solely toward dimensions of excellence.[8] Similarly, many quality gauges operate according to "minimum standards of excellence." To be sure, this technique considers a somewhat broader segment of the quality scale than does the "standards of best quality" approach. However, the notion of minimum standards still forgoes considerations of the worst, as the technique diverts attention from any object or performance that is below a specified cutoff point. In the minimum-standards approach, the very worst quality need not be delineated, for the worst is treated exactly the same as those entities that just miss the stated benchmark.

It appears that the trained eye is not protected from perceptual bias. Indeed, even among agencies designed to anticipate and combat disaster, envisioning the worst often proves an elusive task. The September 11 terrorist attacks on New York and Washington taught us much about this. At the time of the attack, official terror warnings were certainly in the air. In 2000, for example, Congress's General Accounting Office reported that "the threat of terrorism against the United States is an ever-present danger."[9] During the same period, the FAA commissioned a number of secret studies that revealed U.S. airport security to be hopelessly ineffective.[10] Note too that the CIA and other government security agencies reportedly "received information suggesting that Osama bin Laden was increasingly determined to strike on U.S. soil."[11] These agencies were aware that potential terrorists lived and trained in the United States. Indeed, several of the September 11 attackers apparently appeared on various government security watch lists. Despite precedents and clues, our nation's protectors were unable to see the worst approaching.[12] Perhaps former FBI investigator James Kallstrom best captured the intelligence community's collective state of mind. In an interview with WCBS News in New York on the day of the attacks, Kallstrom noted, "We always knew this day was coming; at some level, we knew that something like this could happen . . . *and yet, no one ever clearly imagined* the enormity of the disaster that occurred" (emphasis added).

My personal health crisis, my students' ruminations of the future, audience judgments of quality, formalized performance standards, official responses to national security—each of these instances describes a situation in which people seem unable to conceptualize the worst. Can these failures of imagination—failures that traverse a variety of social profiles and sociocultural settings—really be attributable to psychoemotional forces alone? In this book, I suggest that the answer to this question is no, and I propose an alternative to such individual-oriented explanations.

Failing to conceptualize the worst is not simply a hallmark of particular individuals who cannot or will not imagine calamity, catastrophe, or ruin. The phenomenon proves much broader in scope. The inability to conceptualize the worst happens in corporate boardrooms across the world, when organizational planners routinely prove unable to articulate a worst-case scenario.[13] It happens among scientists and engineers who seem nearly blind to the most negative of experimental outcomes.[14] The inability to conceptualize the worst happens when governments fail to anticipate the most devastating foreign attacks or natural disasters, or when schoolteachers and officials fail to foresee the very worst reactions of troubled students.[15] It happens when couples or newlyweds plan their futures, clearly envisioning the best of fates and typically disregarding signals of danger and destruction. And it happens among risk takers who visualize triumph while all but ignoring potential failure.[16] Indeed, in a broad array of social situations, conceptions of the worst can constitute a gap in a group's or a community's shared frame of reference.[17] For when sociocultural practices focus our sights on excellence, they can simultaneously divert our gaze from the imperfect, the deficient, and the flawed. In this way, the notion of quality—of the way things are—takes on an asymmetrical character, as reality is evaluated using an "unbalanced" conceptual continuum.

Positive Asymmetry as a Dominant Way of Seeing

When I say that an individual, a group or community, an organization, even a society, conceptualizes quality in ways that emphasize the best, I do not mean to accuse that entity of deviant or clouded thinking. Rather, I argue that these skewed visions of quality represent a normal phenomenon—one that I call "positive asymmetry."[18] Positive asymmetry is a powerful convention of quality evaluation. It is a way of seeing that foregrounds or underscores only the best characteristics and potentials of people, places, objects, and events. I argue that this biased perspective is well embedded in many groups and communities. Further, it can be found in a broad array of sociocultural contexts and historical periods. The widespread presence of positive asymmetry stems from both standard patterns of human cognition and central lessons of cultural socialization. In the sections to follow, I carefully unpack this fascinating interaction.

The Asymmetry of the Mind

In reviewing the basic processes involved in the act of thinking, one thing becomes quite clear: some of the human brain's standard operations are characterized by asymmetry. To illustrate this point, let us briefly consider the trail of a thought from beginning to end.

Every minute of every day information enters the mind. That information may enter through one's eyes or ears; it may enter in the form of a scent or touch; it may even present itself as an idea or a memory. Thinking begins when the brain "takes hold" of such information and centers it in conscious awareness—when it sorts and organizes the information in a meaningful way.[19] According to cognitive scientists, this process of apprehending, centering, and organizing data relies largely on two things: the brain's warehouse of representational constructs, or what we typically call "concepts," and the brain's capacity to integrate new information into its warehouse of concepts.

Concepts are simply critical to thinking, and thus critical to this discussion, for concepts provide the fuel for evaluation.[20]

We can think of concepts as mental categories. These categories allow human beings to partition or cluster information in the brain according to certain essential attributes or prototypical properties. Cognitive scientists have identified three key ingredients of these vital neural building blocks. First, concepts possess certain "critical features," that is, essential components or definitional attributes. Ludwig Wittgenstein best elaborated this idea. According to Wittgenstein, members of a conceptual category share a "family resemblance." Thus, when we review a concept's members, there may be no single feature that is universal to all of them. Yet the overlap of their features proves so striking and so significant that the members' "blood ties" soon become apparent and unmistakable. A second key ingredient of concepts rests in the rules that relate or connect a concept's critical features. Such "similarity rules" help us to understand how things as different as rocket ships and jaguars can share membership in a category; the rules connect them with reference to elements such as motion and speed. "Distinction rules" represent the third key ingredient of concepts; such rules distinguish one concept's features from those that define other concepts. Distinction rules make clear, for example, that while dogs, cats, chairs, and tables all have legs, dogs and cats are conceptually different from chairs and tables; while dog and cat legs can instigate movement, chair and table legs cannot.

Critical features, similarity rules, and distinction rules: with these three ingredients, concepts push the process of thought along. Consider the functions they enable the brain to perform. Concepts, for example, become a benchmark by which to measure and assess new information. Thus, armed with the concept "dog," the healthy functioning brain can correctly classify an encounter with a neighbor's German shepherd, a colleague's mutt, or a passerby's Chihuahua. Similarly, the concept "automobile" directs the healthy functioning brain to the shared attributes of Volkswagen Beetles, Honda Accords, and Chevrolet Corvettes. Concepts also enable interpretation. For example, if the brain recognizes a neighbor's pet as a wolf rather than a dog, one can interpret the situation as dangerous and tailor one's actions accordingly. In the same way, recognizing the differences between a child and an adult allows the brain to interpret behaviors in terms of an individual's true capacities. Concepts perform yet a third function, one that involves generalized prediction. For when a new object or event is interpreted with reference to a particular concept's defining features, it becomes possible to anticipate outcomes and likelihoods. Thus, if one knows that dogs respond positively to affection and defensively to aggression, one can predict any dog's likely response to a menu of possible overtures. Similarly, if one knows the defining features of the concept "wedding," one can anticipate the outcome of any particular marriage ceremony. Finally, the use of concepts allows the brain to produce specific instances of a class. As a result, the brain can convert general properties to particular cases. For example, when a friend expresses the desire for a "warm and cuddly pet," one might accurately respond with a puppy, a kitten, or a rabbit. In the same way, a call for a "rich and decadent dessert" might reasonably result in a hot fudge sundae, a creamy cheesecake, a pecan pie, or a dark chocolate mousse.

With these examples, we can see concepts' importance in identifying and organizing information. The question now becomes how do concepts contribute to evaluation and assessment? Cognitive scientists tell us that the answer is quite straightforward, for in identifying and organizing people, places, objects, and events, the brain generally does not stop with distinguishing sameness or difference. It also orders or grades entities with reference to others in their class. Cognitive scientists refer to this phase of conceptualization as "graded membership." In exercising graded membership, the brain performs a type of "goodness-of-fit" calculation. Beyond considering whether or not an entity falls within a conceptual category, the brain considers the degree to which an entity belongs to the concept. In this regard, the brain not only groups Volkswagen Beetles, Honda Accords, and Chevrolet Corvettes in the category of automobile; it also organizes these entities in a relative fashion. In dealing with automobiles, for example, the brain might grade the cars on the basis of their monetary, symbolic, instrumental, or aesthetic value.[21] Thus, the brain may grade the Honda Accord as a better fit than the Chevrolet Corvette when it comes to the concept of practical function; it may grade the Chevrolet Corvette as a better fit than the Volkswagen Beetle when it comes to the concept of sleekness of form.

The process of graded membership follows from the very structure of concepts. The most central theories on concept structure tell us that concepts are built on a prototype or best-example premise.[22] This means that, at their core, concepts amplify or exaggerate the critical features of a category and focus our brains exclusively on a category's "ideal" or best-case specimen.[23] As one performs graded membership, the brain targets the center of a conceptual category—the ideal prototype—and works its way outward. If an observation lacks all of the concept's critical attributes, the brain will likely exclude that observation from membership in the category. If the observation includes some of the concept's attributes or if it approximates those attributes, the brain will likely include the observation in the category.

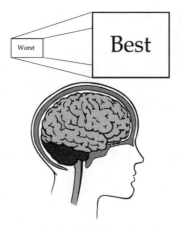

Figure 1.1. The mind's asymmetrical quality continuum

However, in such cases, the brain will mentally distance such an observation from the category ideal, treating it as too fuzzy or hazy to match the category prototype fully. The more attributes an observation shares with the conceptual ideal, the more likely it is that the brain will include the observation in the category. Further, the more attributes an observation shares with the conceptual ideal, the closer the brain will rank that observation to the category's core ideal.[24] Cognitive scientist Daniel Reisberg summarizes the process in everyday language: "Not all cups are equal. Instead, some are 'cupier' than others, namely the ones near the prototype. . . . Some dogs are better dogs than others, according to how close they are to the prototype."[25]

The process of graded membership has obvious results for the way in which we evaluate the world around us. Graded membership quite forcefully establishes asymmetry as the brain's modus operandi. Best-case examples of a concept are overemphasized and highly detailed; anything less than the ideal becomes increasingly nondescript. Because a concept's worst-case examples display only minimal similarity to the category ideal, the brain routinely distances them from active consideration. In this way, the links between worst and best are present yet weak, the character of the worst imprecisely defined. In many ways, the worst case stands as a mere shadow of the category ideal, a best-case example that is missing critical elements.

Figure 1.1 presents a visual depiction of graded membership in practice. The figure suggests that in evaluating input, the brain makes use of a rather unique quality continuum. The continuum contains two poles: the best example and the worst example of a category. Note that the process of graded membership foregrounds the best-case pole, enunciating and highlighting in consciousness the attributes of a concept's ideal. As the brain moves along a quality continuum toward the worst-case example, it does not simply proceed toward another well-articulated pole of meaning. Rather, movement results in a marked loss of definition. In this way, proceeding toward the worst requires an adjustment of both relativity and clarity, of both position and accessibility. The worst-case pole of the quality continuum is simultaneously oppositional and remote. Backgrounded in this way, the worst becomes vague and muted. Absent the articulation of the category ideal, the worst-case is relegated to the fringes of consciousness.[26]

From Asymmetry to Positive Asymmetry: Cultural Completion

Neural mechanics such as graded membership form the basis of evaluation. But extraneural elements—culture, in particular—are critical to the process as well. Cognition does not occur in a vacuum. Clearly, individuals do not take hold of all available stimuli and center them in awareness. Rather, what catches one's eye may be strongly related to one's prior experience or the established cultural agenda of a situation or historical period. Similarly, individuals may organize and grade information with reference to mental concepts. Yet the concepts in one's mental data banks depend on the cultural repertoire of one's group or community.[27] This point—culture's role in the creation of conceptual data banks—proves vital to my inquiry, for I argue that culture harnesses the brain's propensity toward asymmetrical thinking and encodes that process into a much more targeted and specialized experiential bias. In lived experience, groups and communities interpret observations not simply with reference to concept ideals. Rather, these entities consider the world around them with an overwhelming reference to *ideal concepts.* Thus, asymmetry (the tendency to emphasize only the ideal or best-case example of *any* concept) is transformed to positive asymmetry (the tendency to emphasize *only examples of the best or most positive cases*). In this way, the natural workings of the brain are used to support or essentialize something quite unnatural, namely, a socioculturally constructed definition of quality and value, one that quite actively excludes a large array of potential entries.

Culture's role in establishing positive asymmetry requires further explanation. Sociologists Peter Berger and Thomas Luckmann provide a starting point for such an inquiry. In their classic work on the social construction of reality, Berger and Luckmann argue that individuals' perceptions of quality are formed with reference to a group's or society's "stock of knowledge," that is, "the facts a group or society recognizes, the beliefs it espouses, and the routine performances, logics, and symbols by which these facts and beliefs are created and sustained."[28] This stock of knowledge is akin to a pocket dictionary of culture, for it provides the basic cultural elements we use continually as we negotiate the everyday world. And it is here, in the stock of cultural knowledge, that individuals find the criteria they need to assess the people, places, objects, and events of their everyday lives.

In guiding individuals' perceptions, cultural knowledge can direct social action and thus mold social structure. But in order for cultural knowledge to exert such influence, individuals must internalize it; they must become accustomed to invoking and applying the elements of their knowledge base. Here the work of Pierre Bourdieu helps us continue the story. Bourdieu argued that as individuals are socialized to cultural knowledge, they acquire "a system of durable, transposable dispositions" that organize social fields of action and enable individuals to understand, negotiate, and recreate such fields. In essence, this system, which Bourdieu calls "habitus," allows individuals to practice culture without "in any way being the product of obedience to rules." It bids individuals to be "collectively orchestrated without being the product of the orchestrating action of a conductor." In short, the habitus makes the enactment of culture seem second nature.[29]

Bourdieu believed that one's social location played a role in the acquisition of habitus.[30] Different social sectors render different cultural knowledge, thus producing different habitus in the minds of a sector's members. Considered in this way, one might say that in acquiring a habitus, individuals come to join "thought communities"; they enter spaces of shared meaning, spheres of interpersonal understanding that are tied to their social locations.[31] But most important, a thought community provides what philosopher Maurice Merleau-Ponty referred to as a perceptual "point horizon." Membership in a thought community locates individuals at a common "porthole"; it allows them to view and interpret the broader dimensions of social action from a similar vantage point.[32]

While members of thought communities may stand at a common porthole, it is important to remember that a community's view is generally not an objective picture of the group's "natural" setting or concrete circumstance. The habitus possessed by the members of a thought community generally provides a biased or specialized view of the world. We can look to any social arena and see this bias in action. For example, when the Bush administration proclaimed "mission accomplished" in Iraq, their view of reality, while strongly shared by the group, was not fully supported by events on the

ground. Similarly, terrorist communities such as al Qaeda define all westerners as infidels. But their perceptions, while fervent, may not be confirmed
by westerners' actual behaviors. On the home turf, consider that your child's
soccer team may believe they are the best in the league; yet the box scores
produced at the season's end may contradict that sentiment. And fox terrier
owners may contend that the breed represents the smartest of all canine varieties, but German shepherd owners or poodle lovers would vehemently dis-
agree. Community vision is always biased. Such biases occur because the
cultural knowledge from which the habitus is derived is organized in terms
of "relevances."[33] In other words, every community's cultural knowledge
base contains a variety of facts and beliefs, but certain items are emphasized
and prioritized over others. Certain categories of people, places, objects, and
events are underscored for attention, and entities within these categories are
ranked in order of importance. These priorities and rankings can be linked to
a variety of factors, including, for example, the community's survival needs,
its goals and values, its relative station in the broader society, its internal
power structure. But regardless of the source of such "relevance structures,"
the priorities they define become institutionalized via the habitus.

As we move through the chapters of this book, we will see that community ideals differ significantly across time and space. Different thought communities prioritize and attend to different categories of people, places, objects, and events. But amid such differences, a significant majority of thought
communities also hold one thing in common, namely, the relevance of best
quality. Overwhelmingly, *most* thought communities define the best people,
places, objects, and events as highly relevant, highly important, and worthy
of intense focus. In contrast, *most* communities relegate the worst to a
remote position of little or no importance or relevance.[34]

How do thought communities accomplish this? How does the best maintain its dominance in a community's field of vision? We will see that many
thought communities develop elaborate cultural practices that fortify and
concretize the central position of excellence. As these practices become
institutionalized, they function to redirect the cognitive asymmetry that
fuels brain activity. Cultural practices functionally limit the concepts accessed during neural assessment, thus allowing images of the best to guide
and dominate the evaluative process. By centering positive ideals in this way,
cultural practices powerfully establish positive asymmetry as certain communities' dominant "optical tradition."[35] The best is continually defined as
the most immediate and familiar dimension of quality. In contrast, the worst
is distanced and blurred, perhaps completely blocked by images of perfection
and excellence. Thus, the worst evolves as a minimal presence to seemingly

myopic community members. While members know the worst is "somewhere out there," it remains too remote to capture sustained attention.[36]

Are Emotions Involved?

Is it sufficient to frame this inquiry in the fields of culture and cognition? No doubt some would argue that the inability to envision the worst is more strongly rooted in emotions. According to some, fear of the worst, as well as hatred or disgust for its consequences, is the primary reason why groups and communities distance the worst from active consideration.

Emotions may indeed be involved in the process of positive asymmetry. Yet I would argue, they are not the primary triggers of the phenomenon. For while emotions are physiologically grounded, and often activated before the brain's more rational operations, emotions are also culturally elaborated.[37] Sociologist Theodore Kemper contends that the attachment of sociocultural definitions and labels to emotions—the meanings that arise from "the differentiated conditions of interaction and social organization"—is the factor that truly endows emotions with social import, particularly at the collective level.[38] The cultural elaboration of emotions allows groups and communities to establish emotional vocabularies, emotional beliefs, and emotional norms.[39] In this way, emotions, while physiological in origin, are experienced in sociocultural space; they are aroused or subdued with reference to ongoing events, historical periods, power structures, economic organizations, and reigning ideologies.[40]

When we consider the cultural side of emotions, we realize that they may not prove the most fruitful starting point for the present inquiry. For example, in order to experience hate or disgust toward a terrorist such as Osama bin Laden, an ideologue such as Rush Limbaugh, or an activist such as Ralph Nader, one's community must first define that individual as a viable threat. In order to evoke fear of a pandemic disease, a job-related risk, or an economic crisis, the potential for disaster must first be centered in a community's perceptual porthole. Thus, in most cases—particularly those involving collective sentiment—I suggest that emotions do not provoke perception, but rather, link perception to action.[41] Members of groups and communities attend to the elements centered in their perceptual porthole. And only in apprehending those elements do positive or negative affects emerge. If we wish to unpack the role of emotions in the positive-asymmetry phenomenon (indeed, an important goal for subsequent research), I contend that we must first determine the ways in which groups and communities command attention to and sustain the centrality of the best.[42]

Documenting Positive Asymmetry: A Map of Things to Come

For some, positive asymmetry may seem a difficult argument to accept. Critics will contend that all too often we seem to focus on nothing but the worst. Every day we encounter rampant media violence, economic crises, and political scandals. Every day we face looming environmental disasters and pending terrorist threats. Indeed, apocalypse tenders and Armageddon soothsayers seem to be everywhere we turn. In such an environment, the notion of positive asymmetry simply does not jibe with real world experience.

Despite the initial attractiveness of such critiques, systematic analysis will reveal them to be flawed. Indeed, in chapter 2, I document the sheer cultural dominance of positive asymmetry. The chapter takes readers to diverse realms of everyday experience, including life's most intimate relationships, key events in the life cycle, the many sites of work and play, and the organizations and bureaucracies that structure social life. Using a variety of data—interviews, fictional accounts, survey data, media reports, journalistic commentaries, observations, and official records—I illustrate the frequency with which individuals, groups, and communities blatantly disregard the worst-case scenario. The wide variety of social contexts and historical moments in which positive asymmetry occurs provides strong evidence of the phenomenon's widespread presence. Readers will see the variety of social arenas in which group and community members routinely emphasize the best of people, places, objects, and events while failing to fully grasp the worst.[43]

I have argued that cultural practices institutionalize positive asymmetry, making it the dominant mode by which groups and communities evaluate quality. Given the centrality of cultural practices in the evaluative process, it seems critical to dissect the workings of these routines. Toward that end, in chapter 3 I unfold a trio of practices that both initiate and sustain positive asymmetry: "eclipsing," "clouding," and "recasting." Eclipsing practices render the worst people, places, objects, and events invisible. Clouding practices keep the worst vaguely defined. And recasting practices redefine the worst as something positive and good. In chapter 3, we journey through religious scripture, art, and popular culture, through mythology and fairy tales; we review penal codes, military rules of conduct, and norms of financial exchange; we examine the treatment of the mentally ill, the poor, the criminal, and the downtrodden. In traversing these very different arenas, readers will witness the ways in which cultural practices can hide the worst from view. Readers will witness as well the ways in which cultural practices transform the worst, even when it must be directly encountered.

If cultural practices systematically obscure the worst, can we ever accurately gauge the full range of quality? Chapter 4 brings this question to the foreground, focusing readers on the ways in which positive asymmetry can affect formal measurements of quality. As we examine various areas of standardized quality assessment—academic grading, ratings of consumer goods, evaluations of professional services, the scoring of athletic performances, for example—readers will note a clear contradiction between the rhetoric and the practice of quality assessment. Rhetoric suggests that measurement strategies strive for a balanced, accurate examination of quality. Practice, however, boasts a wide array of biased measurement techniques.

Cultural practices affect more than the ability to see the worst. In chapter 5, I explore the ways in which both cultural and social factors influence the consequences of the label "worst." Specifically, I examine a number of key elements, including the durability of a label, the labeler's power vis-à-vis the target, and the normative reactions to criticism at work in the labeling context. When it comes to designating the worst people, places, objects, and events, readers will learn that variability in these conditions can lead to different outcomes. In some cases, being labeled the worst can be especially dire, with targets being stigmatized and often physically harmed or destroyed. Yet in other cases, the label of worst seems to exact a lesser penalty. Indeed, there are instances in which entities identified as worst are often treated no differently than entities defined as simply bad or even average.

The book's first five chapters emphasize the patterned and persistent ways in which the worst people, places, objects, and events are routinely obscured. But here it is important to state that this phenomenon is *not* universal. There are times and places in which the worst is both consciously recognized and extraordinarily well specified. And interestingly, in such arenas, it is often the best that remains a hazy and unfocused concept. To better understand such instances of cultural deviance—a phenomenon to which I refer as "negative asymmetry"—chapter 6 visits two well-known prototypes of the behavior. Medical practitioners and computer technicians represent two communities that vigorously reverse dominant evaluative routines. Taking these communities as case studies, I examine the modus operandi of those working in these sectors. Via such analyses, we can begin to understand the factors associated with the rather deviant practice of attending to and focusing on the worst-case scenario.

Readers will leave chapter 6 with certain insights on negative asymmetry; they will learn that communities that routinely adopt negative asymmetry share certain social characteristics. Such communities, for example, maintain a service orientation; they display porous community boundaries; they are fueled by formal knowledge bases and provide their members with high levels of autonomy. I argue that these traits are not simply a checklist of elements comprised by certain professional identities. Rather, these characteristics, when occurring in concert, create a distinct type of social structure. I dub this structure an "emancipating structure," and I argue that such structures provide a necessary condition for the deviation from well-entrenched perceptual conventions. To illustrate my argument, chapter 7 compares four historical events. Each event is a high-profile case involving a worst-case scenario: The SARS outbreak of 2003, the Y2K millennium bug, the FBI's handling of the "Phoenix memo" in 2001, and the 1986 *Challenger* disaster. Of course, two of these potential catastrophes (SARS and Y2K) were successfully resolved; as we know all too well, the other incidents ended in catastrophe. In the two success stories, negative asymmetry dominated problem-solving efforts; in the two failures, positive asymmetry ruled the day. How did negative asymmetry break through in the case of SARS and Y2K? And what role did emancipating structures play in the process? Using a variety of data sources, including media coverage of these events, official protocols, and previously published scholarly research, I probe these questions in chapter 7. In analyzing the data, I demonstrate that emancipating structures loosened the hold of dominant cultural practices, freeing groups and communities to pursue both unanticipated problems and creative solutions.

As my argument draws to a close, I raise one final point. Seeing the best to the exclusion of the worst has both benefits and costs. In the final analysis, one must ask whether the benefits of positive asymmetry outweigh its costs. If the answer to that question is no, should groups and communities work to revamp collective patterns of thought, to change the cultural practices of centuries? Can we realistically hope to succeed in such a mission? In chapter 8, I explore the question of costs and benefits. I examine as well whether the practices and structures that support positive asymmetry can ever really be successfully transformed.

CHAPTER TWO

The Breadth and Scope of Positive Asymmetry

It has been seven hours since the worst attack ever made on American mainland soil. — *Todd McDermott, news anchor for WCBS Television New York, September 11, 2001*

It is hard to dispute Todd McDermott's characterization of the September 11 tragedy, for on that day, many contend that the United States experienced its worst hour. Even now, years after the fact, the media images are burned into our minds: common passenger planes transformed into targeted attack missiles; a peaceful, majestic skyline turned hellish with raging flame and billowing smoke; the slow, deliberate collapse of two iconic spires of trade; the faces of could-be neighbors and friends smothered in terror and despair. Clearly, the day's events earned their status as modern America's darkest day.

Reporters, rescue workers, and survivors alike characterized the attack as "unthinkable." And as analyses and investigations of the event unfolded, it appears as if the September 11 strike was just that—unthinkable. The worst assault in modern American history was, in all too many ways, unanticipated.

Unanticipated . . . at first, the very idea seems implausible. To be sure, precedence suggested such an attack. Terrorism had struck the United States before: the World Trade Center bombing on February 26, 1993, the bombing of U.S. embassies in Africa on August 7, 1998, and the assault on the USS *Cole* on October 12, 2000. Recall too that U.S. soil had previously been attacked in war. Indeed in 2001, images of Pearl Harbor were fresh in our minds as we commemorated the sixtieth anniversary of the bombing.[1]

The summer of 2001 also brought clues to a looming catastrophe. In chapter 1, I reported that official warnings of a terrorist attack were circulating widely. Yet many government agencies—in some cases, the very same agencies that issued the warnings—seemed unable to see the signs of impending disaster. The INS, for example, failed to stop hijacker Mohamed Atta from entering the United States despite the fact that he had known ties to terrorists and was using an expired visa. Similarly, the FAA, neglecting its own warnings, failed to investigate hijackers Mohamed Atta and Marwan al-Shehhi "after they abandoned a small plane on a busy taxiway at Miami International Airport in December 2000."[2] Indeed, the *New York Times* reported that *the very day of the attack* nine of the terrorists had actually been singled out for special scrutiny at the airport. But since none of the men possessed explosives, officials could see no particular reason to detain them.[3]

The FBI was equally inattentive to clues of impending disaster. Despite warnings from flight instructors and local FBI agents in Minnesota, for example, FBI central overlooked Zacarias Moussaoui, who reportedly wanted to learn how to "fly a plane but didn't care about landing and takeoff."[4] And, of course, there was the now notorious "Phoenix memo." According to *Newsweek* reporters Michael Hirsch and Michael Isikoff, in July of 2001, FBI agent Bill Kurtz, a man described by his colleagues as the most reliable of sources, was involved in the surveillance of a group of suspected Islamic terrorists. Based on his team's discoveries, Kurtz "fired off a lengthy memo raising the possibility that bin Laden might be using U.S. flight schools to infiltrate the country's civic-aviation system." But much like its reactions to the Minnesotan agents, FBI central ignored these ardent warnings from its Phoenix operatives.[5]

Hirsch and Isikoff suggest that "a whole summer of missed clues, taken together, seemed to presage the terrible September of 2001."[6] Yet, despite precedents and hints, our government was unable to connect the dots to see the worst approaching. Who is to blame? Was the government's blindness an aberration, a mistake . . . a horrible, unusual fluke? Was someone asleep on the job—a worker, a supervisor, an entire agency? Or is our government hopelessly fragmented and disorganized, an unwieldy bureaucracy that cannot focus on the information before it?

Each of these scenarios has been adopted by one or another journalist or political pundit. Yet for some, none of the scenarios represents a satisfying explanation of the tragedy. In reflecting on the September 11 disaster for "Inside the Terrorist Attack," a PBS *Frontline* investigation of the catastrophe aired on WNET in January of 2002, journalist Hedrick Smith dismissed notions of flukes, incompetence, and confusion. Rather, Smith described the government's blindness to the terrorist attack as a "failure of the imagination":

People who are in decision-making positions are not mentally precondi-
tioned to think in terms of what happened. So that's what I mean about a
failure of imagination. The evidence comes in, *but your mental reactions
are not geared to thinking in these kinds of terms.* When a guy calls from
a flight school and says they could take a 747 with fuel and plow it into a
building and that's a bomb, you hear it but you say, "Ah, that's a wacko
idea." You don't say, "Holy Jesus, that's what we've got to worry about."
. . . [You] fail to imagine what the danger is. [You] fail to understand the
world we live in and the nature of the enemy.[7]

Several months later, *New York Times* columnist Thomas Friedman made a
similar observation:

The failure to prevent September 11 was not a failure of intelligence or
coordination. It was a *failure of imagination.* . . . Imagining evil of this
magnitude simply does not come naturally to the American character,
which is why, even after we are repeatedly confronted with it, we keep
reverting to our natural, naively optimistic selves. . . . Someone drives a
truck bomb into the U.S. embassy in Beirut, and we still don't really protect the marine barracks there from a similar, but much bigger, attack a
few months later. . . . Someone tries to blow up the World Trade Center
in 1993 with a truck bomb, and the guy who did it tells us he had also
wanted to slam a plane into the CIA, but we still couldn't imagine someone doing just that to the Twin Towers on 9/11.[8]

A failure of imagination—it was an idea that several commentators put forward to their readers. Indeed, upon the one-year anniversary of the 9/11 attacks, journalist Milton Viorst invoked the notion with some urgency:

During the Cold War, the futurists who studied world conflict had devised a clever name for such an event: the "worst-case scenario." Implied in the phrase, however, was the sense that the event was unlikely to
happen. Government and policy professionals hypothesized less severe
outcomes, dismissing the doomsayers. But on September 11 we all learned
that even disasters can be of an unexpected magnitude. *Forthrightness
now demands that we gird not for some tepid end to our conflicts but for
the catastrophes hitherto unimaginable.*[9]

Most recently, members of the 9/11 Commission adopted the concept, listing the failure of imagination as one of four government deficiencies related
to the attacks.[10]

These observations are provocative and worthy of our attention, for as we review the events leading up to the September 11 attacks, it becomes clear that a failure indeed occurred. But that failure was not an aberration or a fluke, and it was not simply a weakness of any one person or any single agency. The failure was indicative of a wider-reaching phenomenon—the surprisingly routine practice that I have described as positive asymmetry.

Just how "routine" is positive asymmetry? In this chapter, I document the phenomenon's widespread presence. The pages that follow examine the myriad of places and times in which positive asymmetry has informed groups' and communities' perceptions of the world. Via this review, readers will learn that the inability to see the worst is not confined to any particular context or any single person or personality type. Rather, this orientation is quite sweeping, and can be found at all levels of interaction—interpersonal, group, organizational, and cultural.

Positive Asymmetry in Interpersonal Interactions

In 2000, Neil Simon wrote a play called *The Dinner Party*.[11] It was a tale of four divorced couples purposely brought together for an evening of emotional exchange. In the play's closing scene, Gabrielle, the hostess of the party, poses the first of two critical questions to her guests:

> I would like to ask each one of us here to tell us the worst thing your ex-spouse ever did to you during your marriage.

The characters in the play are the survivors of four very bitter divorces. Under these circumstances, one might expect each character to have an arsenal of responses at the ready. Yet, despite the animosity between the characters, Gabrielle's question gives each of them great pause. One by one, the dinner guests try to describe their worst experience. But as each character speaks, it becomes clear that the worst moments of their marriages are difficult to conceptualize. Gabrielle is the first to answer the question; her response is quite vague and abstract:

> The worst thing that Andre ever did to me during our marriage was to make me love him unconditionally.

Unconditional love . . . isn't that an element upon which the best of relationships are built, an admirable sentiment? Why is it the worst that could happen? It seems an answer in need of unpacking. And Neil Simon's stage directions underscore the vagueness of Gabrielle's answer: *They all look a little disappointed.*

The response of Albert in the next line of dialogue spells out that disappointment:

That's it? . . . We got locked up to hear that?

The playwright makes it clear that Gabrielle's specification of the worst is obscure and unsatisfying. And the play's other characters don't fare much better. Indeed, after noticeable pauses, the others, now desperate to give an answer, reference events most would consider trivial, somewhat flip, and hardly the worst aspects of a relationship. Witness Albert's complaint:

She burned all my ties. That was the worst thing she ever did to me.

Or Claude's:

At a book party in her honor, Mariette was about to introduce me to her publisher and forgot my name.

When the characters complete their brief reflections on the worst, Gabrielle poses her second question to the group:

What is the nicest thing your spouse ever did for you during your marriage?

Here, the dinner guests seem much more comfortable and assertive. Their answers take on a level of detail missing in the first round of discussion. Gabrielle recalls:

He would bring me a warm croissant and hot tea every morning. Then he would sit on the bed and look at me. Lovingly. His eyes were warmer than the croissant and his hands touching mine were more soothing than the honey he stirred in my tea.

Specifics permeate the other characters' descriptions of their best marital moments as well. Mariette, for example, remembers every dimension of an experience early in her marriage:

On our third anniversary, Claude took me to the restaurant where we first met. He gave me an exquisite pair of earrings from Cartier . . . but as beautiful as they were, it was the note that touched me. I remember every word. "To My Dearest Mariette . . . If I were never born, I would have still found a way to love you . . . If we never met, I would have kept on looking, *hoping* to find you . . . If I died, I would sit on some distant cloud, ignoring my heavenly duties, to watch over you . . . and if I lost you, through my own foolishness, I would forfeit my eternal peace, to win your forgiveness . . . Your loving husband, Claude."

Of course, *The Dinner Party* is a work of fiction—the musings of one playwright and not those of a real group of people. Yet the distinctions Simon makes between his characters' memories of the worst and best of their married lives—the haziness of the former, the detailed elaboration of the latter—corresponds to a real cultural pattern. Research shows that when it comes to some of the most primary and intimate relationships of our lives, most of us anticipate, depict, and recall our experiences in ways akin to Simon's characters. We savor every detail of the best, while either blocking, blurring, or minimizing the worst. Whether at the brink of intimacy or in love's throes, we seem to stand at the same point horizon, with the best case centered in our porthole on the world and the worst at its farthest fringes.

Positive Asymmetry in Love

One study of courtship, conducted by social scientists Cathy Greenblat and Thomas Cottle, followed scores of couples as they moved from engagement through the early days of marriage. The researchers questioned subjects regarding their decision to take the plunge, and they found that the choice to marry was almost always motivated by detailed images of best-case scenarios. Subjects' visions of the future were heavily tipped in favor of bliss and contentment and curiously void of the potential for disaster. Consider, for example, Linda, one of the subjects in the study. As she discusses her expectations for the future, note the detail and assuredness with which she describes a joyful life ahead:

> I want to begin to think of having a family. I want to make myself more a member of the so-called established class. . . . I'm going to wear my makeup and I'm going to have my hair fixed as often as I want. . . . And I'd love to have a summer house on the island, and I'd like to have a sailboat, and there's lots of things I'd like to do. And I want to go with my husband. . . . I want to go various places with my husband . . . and I want him to introduce me as his wife.[12]

As one reads Linda's imaginings of marriage, it becomes clear that disaster is simply not part of her game plan. Worst-case scenarios are blocked by an almost exclusive attention to the good times she believes will follow. Linda is not alone in this perception. Indeed, the same positive asymmetry characterizes the comments of Sam, another of the study's subjects. Sam is a seventy-plus-year-old, marrying for the second time. In Sam's case, we learn that there is clear reason to anticipate disaster in his marriage. He is aging and facing the maladies that old age can bring. Further, his adult daughter, adamantly opposed to the wedding, represents a real and long-term obstacle to future bliss. Yet, despite these concrete problems, clearly fodder for a worst-case scenario, Sam effectively ignores the potential for disruption and stress. Instead, he offers a convincing picture of a best-case future:

> I'll arrange my financial matters and then I'll discuss it [with my daughter]. I'll simply say "Sara, look Bess loves me and I love Bess and for the short life that I've got, I want to be with her and I want to enjoy it and she wants to enjoy me too. And that's all there is to it." . . . We will make a good life. . . . I won't be dependent. I exercise in every respect and I keep in good physical strength. . . . I know that Bess will love me as much as possible and I will love her as much as possible. . . . We'll care for each other. . . . All she has to do is give me her love. And I'll give her all that I can and do all that I'm supposed to do.[13]

Linda and Sam represent prototypes of the Greenblat and Cottle sample. When envisioning the future, most of the study's subjects are seemingly myopic, with the best-case scenario forming the only focused part of their reality.

Of course, there were a few of the study's subjects who truly tried to see in their futures the potential for the worst. These individuals are equally compelling to my argument. For despite their best efforts, these subjects' visions of the worst were enigmatic. Unlike the detailed and well-articulated dreams of the best, thoughts of the worst proved problematic. Cloudy and indecipherable, worst-case images simply could not be brought into focus. Consider the comments of John, a groom to be. While John wants to consider the worst-case scenario of married life, he struggles to articulate what it would be:

> I was wondering and wavering [about the marriage] for a month or two. I became really scared about whether it was the right thing to do or not. It was the idea of just being married. *I don't know how to explain it. . . . It's*

hard to describe—it's not anything you can put your finger on, it's just
like a big scary thing.[14]

Harriet, a young bride to be, had a similar problem. In her interviews, she reports a period in which she considered the potential for a failed marriage. But like John, she cannot fully define these fearful images: "The day after I got the wedding gown," reports Harriet, "I was like a zombie." She reports fearing some disaster, yet when she tries to concretize her fears and visions, she cannot. "I remember calling Sam [her fiancé] and saying 'What's wrong? I don't know what's happening here, it's something really strange.'" For subjects like John and Harriet, a worst-case scenario may be lurking, but such imaginings are too distant to take clear form in the foreground of consciousness.[15]

Nearly twenty-five years after the Greenblat and Cottle study, sociologist Ann Swidler interviewed eighty-eight middle-class men and woman from suburban San Jose, California. Her book, *Talk of Love*, documents these subjects' feelings about love, the things that make it grow, and the factors that sustain it. Like the couples interviewed by Greenblat and Cottle, Swidler's subjects' had definitive perceptions of romantic relationships—perceptions that overwhelmingly favored positive futures and outcomes. Indeed, for Swidler's subjects, "successful" relationships were dominated by visions of the best, with certain cultural myths—in particular, myths of "happily ever after"—most prevalent in their interpretations of romance. Within these subjects' comments, the best-case scenario is crisp, close, and immediate. But like the disappearing ship, like the racing locomotive, the worst-case scenario absents itself from subjects' immediate reality; it resides in horizons knowable yet poorly articulated.

Consider the comments of subject Nora Nelson. According to Swidler, the happily-ever-after myth dominates Nelson's perceptual field. She simply "loves her husband, and does not anticipate that their love will change." When asked if disaster could destroy her relationship, Nelson fails to acknowledge the possibility. She dismisses disaster as a distant enigma, noting simply, "I don't think you fall out of love that fast." The same asymmetry dominates the vision of subject Thomas DaSilva. In Swidler's words, "Thomas DaSilva's youthful image of love combined idealistic expectations with a 'purely glandular' excitement." Swidler continues:

> When he married, he was certain the marriage would last. "It was great. . . .
> I was elated. I am going to provide for this person. I am going to go out and
> set the world on fire. . . . It just *appeared* to me while I was married to my
> first wife that, boy, we had the *ideal* relationship. This was *perfect*."[16]

Throughout her book, Swidler returns to DaSilva's views and opinions because he is so representative of the sample at large. DaSilva sees the lemonade and not the lemons of love; he has dropped anchor in the safest of har-
bors. Indeed, DaSilva's vision of his marriage was so asymmetrical that its
eventual failure took him completely by surprise. Because he focused solely
on the best-case scenario, DaSilva remained functionally blind to the problems that ultimately led to the relationship's demise.

This tendency toward positive asymmetry is, in Swidler's words, a critical "element of the traditional love myth: the ideal that true love lasts forever." Indeed, Swidler notes that studies of love conducted over the past forty
years reveal literally hundreds of research subjects who fervently believe
that "real love *must* last forever." In subjects' musings of "ever after," the
best-case scenario prevails. And when that conception is disrupted—when
the worst occurs and love dies—it is important to note that subjects do not
explain the event by acknowledging the reality of disaster and ruin. Rather,
they deny the occurrence of the worst by redefining the field of experience.
For those who fail in love, love did not die—the worst never occurred.
Rather, a failed relationship indicated that love was not truly present.[17]

The positive asymmetry of romantic vision is perhaps best articulated
in the work of sociologist Diane Vaughan. Vaughan's book *Uncoupling* is important to this discussion because it chronicles not the rise of love, but rather
its demise. Vaughan followed more than a hundred individuals through marital and relationship breakups. In these interviews, subjects tell Vaughan
that their emotional "splits" were never realistically anticipated. Rather, the
potential for a breakup—a worst-case scenario of relationships—became real
only after the fact.

Consider, for example, one respondent's description of her husband's reaction to their breakup:

> When I told him I wanted a divorce, he said, "What do you mean?" *He
> was shocked.* I had been yelling and nagging and complaining about the
> quality of the marriage for years. *It's like he didn't have ears.*

Another subject offers a similar perception:

> I tried for better than a year to persuade him I was unhappy—and *we just
> don't discuss it.* . . . We just go on like there is nothing wrong. We talk
> about the kids, we eat dinner, we go places.

Yet another of Vaughan's subjects articulates the positive asymmetry of love
quite blatantly: *"I had this power to only see the things I wanted to see."*[18]

According to Vaughan, "partners often report that they are unaware, or only remotely aware, even at the point of separation, that the relationship is deteriorating. . . . Typically, partners comment, 'I believe that once you're married, you're married. . . . The idea of divorce *never occurred to me.*'" This suggests that positive asymmetry is embedded in a "life-as-usual" script. Signals of the worst are thus swallowed up by an existing routine. Vaughan argues that "bad news may be so inconsistent with the partner's sense of self and the world, that it is heard but denied." Only *after* the worst occurs—that is, after the relationship has disintegrated beyond repair—can partners retrospectively recognize the signals of failure concealed on the perceptual horizon.[19]

These three studies highlight certain routine visions of love. When it comes to romantic relationships, most individuals are riveted to the best-case scenario. Is it any wonder, then, that when asked about the state of their relationships, 64 percent of married Americans say that they are "very happy," and an additional 33 percent say that they are "pretty happy"?[20] (This, in a nation where approximately one in every two marriages ends in divorce.) Even contemporary American teens, a group directly affected by the high U.S. divorce rate, overwhelmingly report positive expectations for their future relationships. Recent national polls show that 61 percent of American teens believe that they will stay married to the same person for life and 85 percent feel that they will make a "good" or a "very good" spouse. Such positive asymmetry may explain why only 2 percent of Americans give the potential disasters of marriage sufficient credence to secure prenuptial agreements. More commonly, Americans feel the "prenup"—in essence, an acknowledgment of the worst—can doom a marriage. As a result, they feel too uncomfortable to broach the topic with their fiancées.[21]

Positive Asymmetry in Parenting

The positive asymmetry that colors our visions of romantic intimacy also permeates another of life's most central relationships, that of parent and child. When it comes to their children, research documents that the best-case scenario dominates parents' porthole on both the present and future. Parents strive, consciously or not, to keep the worst that their children may encounter distant and remote—from imposed disasters such as economic downturns, sexual predators, or crime, to elected disasters such as alcoholism, drug addiction, or sexual disease. According to psychologist David Strahley, parents—yes, even the best of parents—fall prey to a type of halo effect, identifying with their children to such an extent that they can see only their best qualities.[22] As a result, although parents understand the risks and dangers that face children *in general,* and that *some* kids can go horribly wrong, the disastrous potentials that might befall their *own* children remain at the far horizons of thought.

A study by social scientists Steven Farkas, Jean Johnson, and Ann Dufett illustrates this phenomenon. In *A Lot Easier Said Than Done,* Farkas and his colleagues surveyed a nationally representative sample of 1,607 American parents.[23] Respondents reported on their personal parenting skills, the behaviors of their children, and their views of American families in general. In reviewing the data, it becomes clear that parents' considerations of the worst—either in their own parenting behaviors or in the behaviors of their children—are largely abstract and typically other-oriented. Consider, for example, that the study's respondents overwhelmingly bemoaned the state of American parenting. A full 61 percent of respondents said that today's parents are doing a poor or merely fair job of raising children. And 53 percent, more than half the respondents, said that today's parents were doing a worse job of raising children than had parents of the past. Thus, many of the respondents believed the quality of parenting to be at its worst. However, when questioned about their *personal* parenting skills, only 7 percent of respondents felt that *they themselves* were doing a worse job than their parents.

In a related issue, note that 58 percent of respondents contended that, in general, parents are to blame for a child's bad behavior. Yet, when questioned about their own children, 58 percent of respondents felt that their children are "born with their own personality, and that, as a parent, there is only so much they can do." Note too that while some children may commit the worst behaviors, most parents believe that their own children are quite well behaved. For example, 76 percent of respondents worry about the negative effect that "troubled" peers can have on a child, yet only 45 percent feel this issue is at all relevant to their child. Similarly, 73 percent worry about the negative impact of the media on young people in general, yet 85 percent feel that "there's nothing wrong with my child relaxing for a while in front of the television." Seventy-seven percent of the study's respondents said their child *never* stays out too late; 73 percent said their child *never* uses bad language; 68 percent said their child *never* wears clothes that are sloppy and revealing; 64 percent said their child *never* does poorly in school. Indeed, the overwhelming majority of the survey's respondents saw only the positive side of their children. These findings paint a clear (albeit troubling) picture. When it comes to the worst that a child can encounter or the worst that a child can do, respondents believe that *some* parents may contribute to a child's unfortunate plight. Yet few parents believe that *they themselves* are guilty of such action. Respondents believe that, overall, they are doing a good job of parenting. Obviously, the worst-case scenarios of childcare happen on other parents' watch.

Other surveys have researched parents' visions of their children's futures. Here, too, parents seem unshakably riveted to the best-case porthole on the world. Research shows, for example, that when parents consider their children's economic futures, the potential for economic failure seems nothing more than a blur on the perceptual horizon. Consider the issue of upward socioeconomic mobility. Economists tell us that in the 1950s, the average American male worker enjoyed a 50 percent income increase over the course of his work life. Today, more than fifty years later, that same worker can expect only modest income increases, if that. Indeed, many sociologists and economists feel that economic opportunity in America is fast shrinking. Current figures on intergenerational elasticity and intergenerational mobility suggest that the majority of male American workers are not "doing better" than their fathers. Our economic reality contradicts the ideals of the American Dream and paints a troublesome picture of the future. Yet, despite these projections, most American parents do not see the potential for their children's economic slippage.[24] According to the General Social Survey, 61 percent of the survey's respondents believe that their children will fair "much better" or "better" than they in the future. Despite well-publicized figures to the contrary, only 25 percent believe that their children will be at an economic disadvantage.[25]

Like economic environments, many of the worst things that face children are beyond parental control. Disease, disorders, or criminal violence can strike a child at any time. Like it or not, parents must acknowledge the potential for catastrophe. Yet surveys and polls repeatedly show that parents are far from prepared. Indeed, in most cases, the worst must actually happen before parents adjust their vision. Parents' lack of readiness does not make them deviant or uncaring. Quite to the contrary, positive asymmetry represents the "normal" parenting stance. Indeed, as one examines the advice of parenting experts, it becomes clear that, intentionally or unintentionally, childrearing experts foster parents' inattention to the worst.

To illustrate my point, I offer my analysis of several best-selling manuals on childrearing, considering the types of issues that the experts address.[26] It seems reasonable to think that in "training" a parent, childrearing manuals would offer balanced descriptions of the parenting experience—information on high points, average days, and potential catastrophes and problems. Like the best experiences of childrearing, the worst-case scenarios would be articulated and specified, enabling parents to recognize such events and deal with them effectively even if their occurrence is unlikely. Balanced coverage seems reasonable to expect, but it is not what my analysis showed. Without exception, the childrearing manuals I analyzed minimized the catastrophes and disasters that can befall one's child, thus painting a picture of parenting that was overwhelmingly positive.

Consider, for example, the best-selling *What to Expect* series, with separate volumes devoted to pregnancy, the first year of childhood, and the toddler years. In each volume, the authors Arlene Eisenberg, Heidi Murkhoff, and Sandee Hathaway guide readers in great detail through the month-by-month expectations of childrearing. But are these expectations balanced? Do they suggest both best and worst cases? A content analysis of these manuals reveals that "smooth sailing" is the authors' default expectation. Indeed, each chapter consciously trains parents in best-case vision. For example, the authors start each chapter with a list of the joyful benchmarks parents can expect with each passing month of infancy and each passing year of childhood. To cite just a few of these milestones, in month one, parents are encouraged to anticipate baby's lifting its head, laughing out loud, squealing in delight. In month five, baby will sit without support, say "ah-goo," razz, work to get to a toy out of reach. In month fourteen, the toddler will wave bye-bye, stand alone, and intentionally use the words "mama" and "dada." While the authors meticulously itemize the best developmental experiences, they give minimal emphasis to babies who don't meet these benchmarks. Consistently skirting the reality of poor development, chapters typically include only one gentle disclaimer: "If your baby seems not to have reached one or more of these milestones, check with the doctor. In rare instances the delay could indicate a problem."[27] *Dr. Spock's Baby and Child Care Manual* is similar in tone, leaving even less room for considerations of the worst:

> Remember that your child's early pattern of development is unique and usually due more to the child's nature than to her nurture. . . . She is just growing and developing at her own normal pace. So look at development timetables to your heart's content, but be sure to *take them with a large grain of salt. . . . The odds are on your side* that your baby's development is perfectly normal. *It's a shame to worry about insignificant developmental variations when you could be celebrating them instead.*[28]

My analysis shows that, on average, only 5 percent of a manual's pages explicitly address the worst-case scenarios of childrearing. These topics are rarely prioritized, but rather, are relegated to the end of chapters or the end of the manual itself. And in such sections, authors are often cautious, almost dismissive. Most authors suggest that focusing on the worst represents a bad investment of time. Therefore, although they may state the worst, they also immediately blur the potential with quick rationalizations. Consider, for example, this excerpt from William and Martha Sears's *The Baby Book*. The authors make reference to the fact that every newborn's physical condition is rated using an "Apgar score." According to the Sears manual, "the Apgar score was devised primarily for nursery personnel to determine which babies need more careful observation. . . . It is sort of a which-baby-to-worry-about score." In their book, the authors instruct parents on interpreting the score, directing parents to all but ignore a low rating:

> Some of the healthiest babies I have seen are in a state of quiet alertness at five minutes (after birth), but they lose points on their Apgar for not "crying lustily." . . . If your baby has pink lips and is breathing normally, chances are he or she is a healthy newborn.[29]

William and Martha Sears are not alone in encouraging positive asymmetry. For example, Arlene Eisenberg and her colleagues raise some worst-case scenarios in the realm of baby's digestion. However, in discussing such problems (specifically, the unusual appearance of baby's stools), the authors neutralize the worst before the reader can bring it to the forefront of awareness: "Before you panic at the sight of what's filling your baby's diaper, think about what's been filling her."[30] Experts Gary Ezzo and Robert Bucknam take a similar tact in *On Becoming Baby Wise*. These authors devote a full chapter to crying—why it happens and what to do about it. Of course babies cry for a variety of reasons, and generally those reasons are benign. However, when the worst does happen and something is seriously wrong with an infant, crying is the baby's only means of alerting its caretaker. Despite the importance of crying in this regard, Ezzo and Bucknam devote only four lines of text (less than 1 percent of the chapter) to worst-case scenario crying. Indeed, their mention of worst-case crying is obligatory and tempered:

> *Some crying is normal. You need to expect it.* However, you also need to stay alert to certain identifiable cries. For example, a high-pitched, piercing cry may be a signal of either internal or external bodily injury. Such a cry, if persistent, should be brought to the attention of your pediatrician.[31]

Five percent of a manual—the space is truly minimal. Yet childrearing experts apparently see the space as sufficiently adequate to address everything from improper development to life-threatening diseases, including abnormally high fevers, AIDS/HIV, cerebral palsy, contagious disease and inoculations, cystic fibrosis, frostbite, heart irregularities, household safety, poison control, SIDS, spina bifida, and much, much more. Such space constraints demand that most discussions of the worst remain short and vague. Thus some authors provide parents with nothing more than a brief checklist of potentially problematic symptoms. Consider this excerpt from Steven Shelov and Robert Hannemann's *Caring for Your Baby and Young Child:*

> Alert your pediatrician if your baby displays any of the following signs of *possible* developmental delay in the eight-to-twelve month range:
> • Does not crawl
> • Drags one side of the body while crawling (for over one month)
> • Cannot stand when supported
> • Does not search for objects that are hidden while he watches
> • Says no single words ("mama" or "dada")
> • Does not learn to use gestures, such as waving or shaking head
> • Does not point to objects or pictures[32]

In addition to their brevity, note that these warnings fail to include any discussion of what the symptoms might mean. Beyond calling a physician, parents are left completely in the dark.

If ignorance is impossible—if the worst must be brought into focus—one might expect that authors would provide candid and detailed instructions for parents. But in such cases, childrearing manuals often try to put a positive spin on the worst. In so doing, authors recast current circumstance, returning parental focus to the best-case interpretation. For example, in discussing the very serious disease of cystic fibrosis, Shelov and Hannemann note, "Children with cystic fibrosis now live much longer than previously." Eisenberg and her associates leave parents on a similarly positive note: "If researchers find the gene (they have already located a genetic marker, a gene that seems to be inherited with CF), a cure may be possible." Sears and Sears follow suit in their discussion of sudden infant death syndrome (SIDS). Their manual provides an extensive section on this topic. The authors tell their readers, "By understanding the details of this grim mystery, parents will worry less." However, in the Sears manual's ten-page treatment of the subject, only one page is devoted to defining and explaining the disease, while nine pages are devoted to a more positive topic, namely, reducing a baby's risk of succumbing to SIDS.[33]

Online sites proved similar to advice manuals in their approach to dealing with the worst. Indeed, in searching online sites designed for parents whose children have physical, mental, or emotional disabilities, I found that 72 percent of these sites described positive asymmetry as a normal (and sometimes useful) parental response to the worst conditions.[34] In many ways, these sites encouraged positive asymmetry as an important part of a recovery toolkit. For example, social worker Maureen Brownlow describes her experiences with parents of chronically ill children and adolescents. When the worst happens and parents realize that something is seriously wrong with their child, they "frequently experience a period of shock and denial. *This can be a helpful protective mechanism* until they're ready to absorb the information."[35]

⌒∞⌒

The worst-case scenarios discussed heretofore are typically the product of circumstance. Economic downturns and childhood diseases are generally the luck of the draw. But for many parents, worst-case scenarios are not a matter of chance. For some, the worst occurs because children actively adopt risky behavior (for example, drug and alcohol abuse, anorexia, unprotected sex). Yet, even when dealing with these "elected" problems, the perceptual pattern remains the same; the worst-case scenario seems far removed from most parents' porthole on reality.

In recent years, some segments of the popular media have grappled with this form of positive asymmetry. Consider, for example, widespread coverage of the spring break phenomenon. The most recent concentration of coverage on this issue began when a series of high-profile videos called *Girls Gone Wild* became a best-selling media attraction. These films depict the uninhibited antics of college girls on spring vacation. The popularity of *Girls Gone Wild* triggered a flurry of media coverage, both on spring break and on related issues such as graduation bingeing, sports team initiation rites, and fraternity and sorority hazing. Nightly news broadcasts, television news magazines (for example, *Dateline, 48 Hours, 20/20*), talk shows, and TV dramas placed the topic center stage. In such coverage, two issues were key. Television shows underscored the potentially disastrous outcomes of such rituals; they also emphasized an all too common parental blindness toward such dangers.

Psychological guru and contemporary pop icon "Dr. Phil" McGraw was among the first to cover the issue in detail. His television special *Kids Gone Wild* documented parents' positive asymmetry in harrowing detail.[36] Dr. Phil arranged for the videotaping of scores of college students on their spring break in Texas. He then united the children with their parents so they could view the videotapes together.

> Drinking, stripping in public, setting themselves on fire. . . . Do you really know what's happening when [your children] go off somewhere? . . . I recently sent my son Jay down to South Padre Island in Texas, one of the biggest spring break scenes in the entire country, to find out what goes on when y'all aren't there.

Dr. Phil's comments were followed by tapes of students stripping, drinking heavily, fist fighting, using drugs, jumping from hotel roofs, and similar behaviors. He was especially interested in the parents' reaction to this footage. After airing the tapes, he pursued parents' blindness toward the dangers facing young "spring breakers." How, for example, did students talk their parents into letting them "make the scene"? Dr. Phil asked one student if she had to make any deals with her dad in order to attend spring break. The student's reply illustrates the fact that worst-case scenarios were far from the center of her father's visual field: "No, he was like, 'Here's 360 bucks. Go have fun.'" Another mother, after viewing a tape of her nearly naked and very drunk daughter, was asked for her reactions:

MOTHER: I don't approve of drinking. I don't approve of drinking and driving.
DR. PHIL: But you gave her the money.
MOTHER: Gave her the money; mm-hmm.
DR. PHIL: . . . to go to the biggest drunk-out in America.
MOTHER: Right.
DR. PHIL: And I—I'm really just really curious if you would send her down there now knowing what you know?
MOTHER: Um . . .
DR. PHIL: That's answer enough. That's answer enough . . . So could you please square that up for me?
MOTHER: She knows better than to go to Padre and go drinking.
DR. PHIL: Apparently she doesn't!

The parents of spring breakers illustrate a broader phenomenon. Consider those parents who rent hotel rooms—rooms with fully equipped bars—for their children's use on the night of a high school prom; or parents who, desperate for their child to gain a spot on a sports team, encourage the use of steroids. There are parents who, despite statistics to the contrary, permit their newly licensed children to drive with a carload of friends; and parents who, ignoring guidelines and warnings on age appropriateness, buy extremely violent video games for their children. Each of these scenarios, and others like them, illustrates positive asymmetry. For parents do these things, not out of malice or disregard, but out of an inability to envision catastrophe. Despite the frequency with which most children enter high-risk settings, positive asymmetry routinely keeps their parents from seeing the potential for danger.[37]

Positive Asymmetry at Key Life Events

Just as positive asymmetry guides us through life's most important relationships, so too does this perspective frame life's most important transitions. Many of life's pivotal moments hold the potential for disaster. Yet, at such junctures, the worst-case scenario is often blurred beyond recognition. In this section, we visit some of life's key moments and note the cognitive distance most individuals maintain from the worst case that lurks on the perceptual horizon.

Early Sexual Encounters

One's initiation to sex stands as an important marker in the life cycle. For many, the "first time" signals a leap to adulthood, to independence, to a new level of experience. To be sure, early sexual encounters can present concern, tension, and anxiety. Is this the one? Is now the right time? Will it be wonderful? Or will I do it all wrong? But sexual intercourse carries with it issues larger than timing or skill. Unwanted pregnancy is, of course, always a hazard. And in the contemporary world, serious, even deadly, disease is a grim possibility. Yet, despite the worst-case scenarios involved in one's entry to the sexual arena, research shows that disasters and catastrophes are typically the furthest things from participants' minds.

Two-thirds of U.S. teenagers have sexual intercourse by their eighteenth birthday. Given these levels of sexual activity, it is not surprising that the United States continues to have one of the highest teenage pregnancy rates in the developed world. Currently, nearly one million U.S. teens become pregnant each year, a rate twice as high as that of England or Canada, and nine times as high as rates in the Netherlands or Japan.[38] Experts confirm that positive asymmetry contributes to this dilemma, for 80 percent of teenage pregnancies are unplanned. Indeed, research shows that only 40 percent of sexually active teens report worrying about the possibility of pregnancy. Only about half of sexually active teens practice birth control *at all*, and only 15 percent of sexually active teens report *faithful* birth control use, that is, protection in every encounter.[39] Teens' positive asymmetry has clear consequences. According to the Web page of the American Academy of Pediatricians, a sexually active teen who fails to consider the worst and thus refrains from active contraception "has a 90 percent chance of pregnancy within one year."[40]

Becoming pregnant certainly represents one of a teenager's worst nightmares. The contraction of a serious disease constitutes another. But like pregnancy, sexually transmitted diseases (STDs) remain at teens' far horizons of perception. Teens' positive asymmetry certainly cannot be tied to the issue of prevalence, for each year, approximately one in four sexually active U.S. teens contracts an STD.[41] Much like the figures on pregnancy, U.S. teenagers have higher STD rates than teens in most developed countries (such as Canada, England, France, and Sweden). But despite the prevalence of STDs, only about half of American teens consider the issue upon entering the sexual arena. Further, some studies suggest that the more serious the disease, the less likely teens are to think about the risk of contraction. Such positive asymmetry is especially prevalent when it comes to HIV-AIDS. The number of HIV-infected teenagers in the United States increases annually, yet teens continue to believe that *they themselves* are less likely to contract the virus than are their peers.[42] In a conference jointly sponsored by the National Center on Addiction and Substance Abuse (CASA) and the Kaiser Family Foundation, one teen's words captured this sentiment with chilling realism:

> A teenager is gonna think about STD probably like one of the last things. It's probably gonna be the last thing on anybody's mind, you know, until a situation happens. In my community it's the same way as any other, you know. People tend to think about the outcome of things later.[43]

Teens' positive asymmetry toward sex can place them in harm's way. Thus, a number of child and family advocate groups have tried to lead teens to a more realistic porthole on sexual activity. Through Web sites, research foundations, policy organizations, and formal education, these groups attempt to foreground both the worst-case scenarios of unprotected sex and strategies for avoiding those scenarios.[44] But because positive asymmetry is such a well-entrenched phenomenon, these initiatives typically meet with limited success. Consider that teen advocate groups have rallied for school-sponsored sex education programs that would prepare teens for the risks

inherent in sex. However, one-third of U.S. public school systems refuse to
implement such curricula. And among districts that permit sex education,
more than a third adopt an amended curriculum (generally, one that presents
abstinence as the *only* protection against pregnancy and STDs).[45] Teen advocate groups argue that this head-in-the-sand approach to sexuality only distances teens from the dangers of sex. Further, official silence on the use of
contraception simply reinforces teens' biased perspective. Thus, teens tend
to wait until after the fact to talk with someone about sexual worst-case scenarios. And in many cases such talks never occur. The Kaiser Family Foundation reports that only about half of teens *ever* discuss their sexuality with
their parents and less than a third discuss their sexuality with a physician or
like professional.[46]

Early sexual experience is not necessarily an appointment with calamity
and ruin. However, positive asymmetry leaves sexually active teens unable
to take in the full scope of the playing field. If the worst remains on the horizons of perception, planning for disaster can easily be abandoned, for if something remains vague and unspecified, planning for it is akin to planning for
the unknown.

Childbirth

The National Center for Health Statistics tells us that by age forty, more
than 80 percent of women have had at least one child. While most deliveries
result in a healthy baby, childbirth is not disaster free. Approximately 2 percent of all pregnancies result in the death of the fetus, the infant, or the
mother, and roughly 4 percent of births result in birth defects. Birthing complications occur with some frequency as well. For example, over 3 percent of
births involve fetal distress; nearly 4 percent involve breech or malpresen-
tation, and almost 3 percent involve the premature rupture of membranes.
These statistics tell us that troubled pregnancies are more common than one
might guess.[47] And while parents-to-be certainly worry about such issues,
research suggests that they probably invest more energy in deciding their
baby's name or the color of baby's new nursery. Indeed, the culture surrounding pregnancy and childbirth has a direct impact on parents' ability to see the
calamities that may be waiting on the horizon.

To examine the ways in which positive asymmetry might dominate pregnancy, I analyzed a sample of pregnancy and healthcare manuals, and a
sample of pregnancy and health care Web sites.[48] The results of that analysis
show that the blurring of the worst occurs from the earliest stages of pregnancy, and healthcare experts play an active role in the process. It is not that

experts completely ignore worst-case scenarios, (although one-third of the manuals devoted less than five pages to such topics). Rather, most experts give momentary glimpses of the worst, but then quickly refocus their readers on the best-case alternative. For example, in *The Mother of All Pregnancy Books,* Ann Douglas presents her readers with a chapter called "The Worry Zone," where she tackles the top ten worries of each pregnancy trimester. To be sure, this chapter identifies several worst-case scenarios (for example, miscarriage, premature labor, birth defects). But it simultaneously directs readers to the positive side of each problem. With regard to miscarriage, for example, Douglas states:

> While the majority of pregnant women will go on to have a healthy baby, between 15 [and] 20% will have their hopes and dreams shattered. Although it is easy to fixate on this figure, *it's important to turn it on its head and look at it from another perspective.* You have an 80 to 85% chance of not miscarrying.

Similarly, in addressing fears of a difficult labor, Douglas emphasizes the positive:

> Don't underestimate your abilities. Labor is indeed a trial by fire, but you're up to the challenge. Generations of other women have walked this path before and lived to tell. (Heck, some of them even went back and had more babies!)

Indeed, Douglas is so intent on promoting best-case interpretations that she ends her chapter on worry with a section entitled "the joys of pregnancy" lest her readers forget to leave the worst behind them.[49]

The positive asymmetry found in Douglas's pregnancy manual is certainly not unique. Glade Curtis and Judith Schuler take a similar tack in *Your Pregnancy Week by Week.* For example, the authors discuss the risk of delivering a Down syndrome baby. They begin by reporting the statistical odds of such an occurrence. After reporting the odds, however, they tell readers:

> But there is also a positive way to look at these statistics. If you're 45, you have a 97% chance of *not* having a baby with Down syndrome. If you're 49, you have a 92% chance of delivering a child without Down syndrome.[50]

Similarly, in *What To Expect When You're Expecting,* Heidi Murkhoff, Arlene Eisenberg, and Sandee Hathaway discuss abdominal pain—a potentially serious problem during pregnancy. But here too, they divert the reader's gaze to the best-case outcome:

> As long as it is occasional and not persistent—and is not accompanied by fever, chills, bleeding, increased vaginal discharge, faintness, or other unusual symptoms—there's no cause for concern. Getting off your feet and resting in a comfortable position should bring some relief. You should, of course, mention the pain to your practitioner at your next visit, so that he or she can reassure you that this is just another normal, if annoying, part of pregnancy.[51]

The message of these manuals is clear: Don't worry . . . be happy! And it is a message that dominates pregnancy Web sites as well. Indeed, most sites confine themselves to routine matters—choosing an obstetrician, finding a midwife, taking vitamins, fetal development, and so forth. Only 5 percent of the sampled sites were devoted solely to pregnancy complications. The remaining sites either mentioned complications in brief (typically, at the conclusion of the site) or provided a "complications" link that only interested parties might access.

Distancing individuals from pregnancy's worst-case scenarios can carry costs. Consider, for example, the issue of amniocentesis, a common tool for detecting abnormalities in a fetus. In the United States, approximately half of all pregnant women elect to have this test. The test presents a fair amount of risk to a patient. Indeed, one out of every two hundred cases results in the miscarriage of the fetus, with a greater risk for women over the age of forty. While nearly all of the manuals and Web sites I analyzed reported the test's probability of miscarriage, more than half of these sources (61 percent) attempt to "spin" the numbers.[52] For example, the Web site of the American Academy of Physicians downplays the test's dangers by underscoring its routine nature:

> Amniocentesis and CVS carry a small risk of miscarriage. . . . The baby will not be hurt during the procedure. Some women feel mild cramping during or after the procedure. Your doctor may tell you to rest on the day of the test, but usually you can resume normal activity the next day.[53]

The authors of *What To Expect When You're Expecting* take a similar tack:

> Most women experience no more than a few minutes to a few hours of mild pain or cramping after the procedure. Some doctors recommend

resting for the remainder of the day, while others don't. Rarely, there is slight vaginal bleeding or amniotic fluid leakage. In very few cases, women experience infection or other complications that may lead to miscarriage.[54]

And in *The Girlfriend's Guide to Pregnancy*, which received a favorable review from the American Medical Association, Vicki Iovine actively minimizes the dangers of amniocentesis. Indeed, she suggests that the test's risks would not be discussed but for legal obligations: "Our genetics counselors or doctors have been legally obligated to tell us that there is a very small chance of causing the miscarriage of a healthy fetus through amnio."[55]

It is interesting to note that amniocentesis is routinely recommended for women with an increased risk of delivering a "defective" fetus. Yet most of the conditions the test can detect present a lower rate of risk than does the test itself. Again, the risk of amnio-stimulated miscarriage is 1 in 200. However, Down syndrome carries a risk of only 1 in 1,250 among women in their twenties, and a risk of 1 in 385 for a woman thirty-five years of age. Similarly, sickle cell disease carries a risk of 1 in 400; spina bifada, 1 in 1,000; and Tay Sachs, 1 in 3,600.[56] Why, then, do so many women opt for amniocentesis? One cannot dismiss the possibility that experts and caretakers have successfully relegated the worst-case scenario, namely, fetal death, to the patient's far horizon.

Widowhood

My father died ten years ago. The illness that led to his death was a difficult one. Stricken with cancer, he immediately started chemotherapy. But in a violent reaction to the medication, he suffered a heart attack and a stroke after several of the treatments. My father remained in a coma for more than five months. Miraculously, he did regain consciousness. But as one might imagine, he was never the same man. Mental deterioration made communication difficult; physical deterioration generated an endless number of problems. For three years, he traveled in and out of the hospital, until, one day, he never came home. When I think of my father's death, I am always struck by my mother's initial reaction. "It's such a surprise," she said. *Such a surprise*—her words puzzled me. A terminally ill man, grasping life so precariously. How could my father's death surprise my mother?

I have never forgotten my mother's reaction, and in recent years I have come to learn that it was not at all unusual. Just as positive asymmetry surrounds the birth of a new life, research shows that it can surround the loss of a life as well—particularly, the loss of one' spouse. In *The Widowed Self*, sociologist Deborah Kestin van den Hoonaard comments on the phenomenon: "Widowhood is an 'expectable event' for older women. Nevertheless, when it does come, it usually comes as a shock, whether their husbands were ill for a period of time or died completely unexpectedly."[57] This sentiment is clear in the words of Kestin van den Hoonaard's research subjects. In discussing their husbands' deaths, one after another of the widows verbalized utter disbelief. "I just couldn't believe it, you know, it was so unbelievable," said one. "I was just stunned, numb," said another.[58] For these elderly widows, the inevitable seemed impossible.

Sociologist Helena Znaniecka Lopata, the foremost expert on widowhood, tells us that the failure to imagine the death of one's spouse is not simply a characteristic of the elderly. Lopata suggests that positive asymmetry proves true for widows of all ages. According to Lopata, the inevitability of death does not necessarily prepare one for the event. Most individuals recognize, at some remote level, that the death of a spouse could happen. (Indeed, 75 percent of all women experience the death of a spouse.) But like other worst-case scenarios, individuals allow the potential to fade to the horizon of daily experience. Sociologist Deborah Carr and colleagues confirm this finding, documenting that even when people know their spouse is dying, they seldom acknowledge, discuss, or prepare for the event.[59]

Sociologist Joan Baily provides some insight on the matter. In her research on widowhood, Baily did intensive interviews, exploring the thoughts and feelings of women anticipating the death of a spouse as well as of those who were recalling the experience. In reviewing her data, Baily raises an interesting point. Many of life's most significant events—whether it be the first day of school, a first date, one's first day on the job, marriage, or the birth of child—involve some form of anticipatory socialization. Rituals and routines prepare individuals for the pivotal moment and its aftermath. But when it comes to widowhood, no such socialization occurs. Baily argues that the lack of anticipatory socialization helps to explain why many of her subjects seemed unable to grasp widowhood even in the abstract. It explains why well over half of her subjects could not estimate the proportion of married women who become widows. (Note that one-fourth of Baily's sample believed that only 20 percent of women are eventually widowed!) Indeed, only 30 percent of Baily's subjects said they gave the idea of widowhood any serious or regular thought, and less than half of the women she interviewed engaged in preparatory activities such as talks with a spouse, talks with friends, or meetings with financial advisors.[60] Thus, just as newlyweds seem unable to imagine failure of a relationship, the long married fail to imagine their relationship's inevitable end. Without cultural preparatory practices connected to widowhood, the experience remains undefined, unarticulated, and thus seemingly highly unlikely.

Aging

In the year 2000, more than 12 percent of the U.S. population—some 35 million people—were age sixty-five and older. By the year 2030, that number is expected to double, with more than one in five Americans being over age sixty-five. In 2002, the U.S. Administration on Aging released "A Profile of Older Americans." This report, along with ongoing studies of the National Center for Health Statistics give us a glimpse into the realities of old age.

To be sure, there are many good things to be said about aging in America. Life expectancy has increased. Older Americans are more active. And, in many ways, older Americans are healthier overall than they were in past decades. Yet aging in America still brings certain unpleasant realities. For example, more than a third of those sixty-five or older have at least one serious disability, including problems such as arthritis, asthma, blindness, diabetes, heart disease, and hypertension. And more than half of those with disabilities report difficulties in carrying out basic daily activities such as bathing, cooking, dressing, eating, shopping, and walking. (When one examines the segment of the population older than eighty, these figures double.)

The median income for U.S. households is about $42,000. However, for those sixty-five and over, that figure drops to about $34,000. Further, approximately 10 percent of older households live below the poverty line, reporting a household income of less than $15,000. This group also experiences a disadvantage in home ownership. About 80 percent of the elderly own their own homes, and three-quarters of that group own a home that is free and clear. But by age seventy-five, nearly 5 percent of the elderly leave those homes for long-term care facilities; by age eighty-five, the proportion is 20 percent. Finally, the median value of homes owned by the elderly is about $108,000, much less than the national median of $124,000. This means that, upon the sale of their homes, the elderly are left with a smaller sum for the future.[61]

Do people see the worst-case scenarios of aging? That is what the Association of Retired Persons (AARP) wanted to know. In 2003, the AARP conducted a nationally representative survey entitled "These Four Walls." In this study, more than two thousand Americans aged forty-five and older discussed their visions of growing old in America. The survey suggests that positive asymmetry colors our visions of aging. Remarkably few of the respondents seriously considered the worst that might happen to them.

Consider respondents' views of physical health. When asked, "How opti-mistic or pessimistic are you that you will be in good physical health in your later years?" only 5 percent said "very pessimistic" and only 9 percent said "somewhat pessimistic." The overwhelming majority saw a best-case sce-nario awaiting them in the future. Indeed, two-thirds of respondents were so optimistic about health that they believed they would *always* be able to drive.

Subjects in this study also saw the economic best-case scenario. Three-quarters felt confident that they would be able to cover their basic expenses and two-thirds anticipated having enough money to do whatever they wanted in their later years. Three-quarters of respondents believed that they would stay in their current home for the rest of their lives—a belief that increased with age. So riveted to the best were these subjects that they seemed unable to prepare for the worst. While the large majority of respon-dents said that they were good planners, less than half had actually executed a plan for old age, whether it involved long-term or catastrophic health care, locating a place to live, or planning for amendments to their current living situation.[62] According to Matthew Greenwald, the author of the AARP re-port, "The lack of forethought does not appear to be intentional; many con-sumers are simply . . . exhibiting what may be an unrealistic sense of opti-mism about the future." But, as he later observes, "The probability of being poor at some point in old age remains high, and many people underestimate the costs associated with aging; similarly, respondents' views reflect unreal-istic expectations about their physical abilities as they grow older."[63]

A similar perspective emerged from a 2001 national survey conducted by the Alliance for Aging Research. In a striking display of positive asymmetry, the findings showed that 60 percent of Americans expect to live past the age of eighty, enjoying life more, not less, as they age. Less than 10 percent of Americans "worry very much about the future," and 80 percent believe that medical science will find cures for life-threatening or debilitating diseases during their lifetimes.[64]

Death

When it comes to considering the worst, the subject of death must rank high on the list, for there are few negative events that have a 100 percent proba-bility of occurrence. Yet, despite the certainty of death, statistics show that few Americans consider or plan for the event. Only about one-third of Amer-icans have wills, a condition many financial experts attribute to Americans' inability to focus on "the dark side" of life.[65] Similarly, although the Patient

Self-Determination Act was passed in 1990, less than 15 percent of Americans have prepared Advanced Directives.[66]

Of course, distancing ourselves from death is, in part, a psychoemotional phenomenon. Individuals tend to avoid what they fear. Yet our failure to imagine death is also a sociohistorical phenomenon. As the realities of death have changed over time, so too have our feelings about it. Consider, for example, that a century ago, more than half of all deaths involved people under the age of fifteen. Today, less than 5 percent of death's victims are young. Medical and social advancements have drastically changed the issue of mortality, transforming death into a phenomenon of the old. As a result, young people are rarely confronted by the death of their chronological peers. For the young, death is an event of the distant future.

The work of scholars like Philippe Ariès and Norbert Elias reminds us that our feelings toward death are also steeped in cultural change. Indeed, culture has effectively clouded death in modern perception—even the death of the elderly.[67] Contemporary practices shelter all but the dying themselves from the phenomenon. Most elderly die in institutions that remove them from the home and their extended community. Michael Darwin reflects on this change:

> So long as death was an everyday reality, people inevitably developed coping mechanisms. By contrast, most of us in the Western world today have had little or no experience with death either as children or as adults. The drop in infant mortality, coupled with the great increase in average life expectancy, have created the illusion that death is now the exception rather than the rule.[68]

Death's inevitability seems beyond the view of most Americans, and so too are death's most likely causes. Consider the case of cancer.[69] The American Association for Cancer Research reports that 75 percent of voting Americans have had a close friend or relative that died from cancer. Yet that reality apparently does little to focus Americans on this worst-case scenario. Only 48 percent of voting Americans fear contracting or dying from cancer. For many, the threat of cancer seems an unlikely end. The same biased perception pertains to heart disease. While 32 percent of Americans die each year of heart-related diseases, only 15 percent of Americans believe they will suffer such a fate. When it comes to mortality, the trend seems clear. Our true "Achilles heels" stand at the most distant perceptual horizons.[70]

In many ways, the issue of death underscores culture's ability to rivet the attention of groups and communities upon the best-case porthole. Indeed, in efforts to highlight the best, contemporary culture has effectively rendered death a "nonterminal" condition.[71] Many central and powerful institutions have encouraged redefinitions of death. In 1996, for example, the Vatican officially "blessed" contact with the dead:

> Roman Catholics were given the Church's blessing yesterday to "contact" loved ones beyond the grave. Leading Vatican theologian Father Gino Concetti said it was no longer a sin, providing mediums, fortune-tellers and palmists were not involved. . . ."We can pray for our loved ones. They will respond in dreams and inspiration. In one example, a grandmother advised a girl about her marriage choice in a dream. The girl did not heed the counsel and a grave problem developed. If we pray seriously in a quiet place, with our hearts and our voices, the departed will express themselves and advise us."[72]

The mass media have also contributed to death's newfound popularity. Indeed, during the past twenty years, several top-rated TV shows have introduced the dead as part of the regular cast (for example, *Ally McBeal, Dead Like Me, Evergreen, Ghost Whisperer, Joan of Arcadia, Medium, Providence, Thirty-Something, Touched by an Angel, Tru Calling*). On such shows, the dead are literally a part of life as usual. Such treatments of the dead are not simply the trappings of fiction. Death has come alive in television's nonfiction programming as well. The shows of psychics such as George Anderson, John Edward, and James Van Praugh—men devoted to connecting you with those on "the other side"—are now a regular feature of each season's television schedule.

   The role of the dead in popular culture is inescapable. Whether it be Alice Sebold's *The Lovely Bones* (a tale of a murdered girl who returns to earth and helps to solve her own killing), Terry Pratchett's *Mr. Reaper* (a book in which Death questions his vocation), or Garth Nix's *Sabriel* (the story of a girl who leads disgruntled spirits to the other side), fictional best-sellers assure us that the dead are not really gone. And nonfiction blockbusters such as Dannion Brinkley's *Saved by the Light*, Betty J. Eadie's *Embraced by the Light*, or Raymond J. Moody Jr.'s *The Light Beyond* describe life after death in the greatest detail, thus legitimating our newfound comfort with the event. Motion pictures too forward stories that blur the distinctions between the living and the dead. Films such as *Afterlife, Always, Chances Are, Defending Your Life, Death Becomes Her, Dragonfly, Ghost, Meet Joe Black, The Sixth Sense, Truly Madly Deeply, What Dreams May Come,* and *White Noise* merge the living and dead in loving friendships and relationships. In this way, films actively deny death's worst-case status.[73] Journalist Roger Rosenblatt comments on this cultural turn: "Today, the element of fantasy is played down and we are meant to believe that something like *Ghost* could really happen. The closeness of death is made tantalizing, the passage from life to death a stroll in the park."[74]

Sociologists Andrew Greeley and Michael Hout tell us that approximately 75 percent of Americans believe there is a life after death.[75] Given current depictions of death, it is no wonder that the ultimate worst-case scenario seems beyond our perceptual grasp.

Positive Asymmetry in Everyday Routine

Routine activities may be the most frequent site of positive asymmetry. For when groups and communities stand at the best-case porthole, positive asymmetry effectively transforms the must-dos of a day into can-dos. Indeed, from that lookout, one cannot detect the undercurrent of calamity and danger running beneath the apparent calm of the everyday. To prove the point, let us consider the times and places in which positive asymmetry dominates the mundane experiences of our lives.

The Workplace

Approximately 65 percent of the U.S. population reports to work each day. Few of us assume that our office or plant could evolve into a worst-case scenario. And yet for many Americans, the workplace becomes just that. Each year, nearly 4 million people are killed or seriously injured at work.[76] Indeed, the Harvard Center for Risk Analysis estimates that Americans face a 1 in 3,000 chance of being involved in a work-related accident. It may happen while you are driving from one location to another or when equipment at your job site malfunctions. You may be killed or injured when struck by a fallen object or attacked by another employee. You may even be hurt or killed in a fall or suffer exposure to a dangerous toxin. Whatever the cause, your workplace can pose a serious threat to your well-being.[77]

Despite their frequency, occupational hazards are one of the furthest things from Americans' minds. Indeed, when we examine surveys and polls devoted to our most common fears, workplace dangers *never* emerge as a common concern.[78] Knowing this, we should not be surprised to learn that most Americans fail to plan for the worst. For example, the Health Insurance Association of America notes that a large majority of American workers (60 percent) fail to secure disability insurance. Similarly, the National Institute for Occupational Safety and Health documents scores of cases in which workers fail to take adequate safety precautions. Employees often ignore warning signs of danger; they fail to wear protective safety equipment or follow safety guidelines. Of course, employers contribute to workers' asymmetrical visions of risk. Because workers compensation often fails to create sufficient incentive, employers fail to invest in safety and health insurance for their workers. Thus, taken together, employees' and employers' positive asymmetry may be responsible for between 20 and 50 percent of work-related accidents.[79]

So blind are Americans to the worst-case scenarios of work that we may be working ourselves to death. Research shows that we work more hours than anyone in the industrialized world. Many of us simply refuse to take vacations. Indeed, last year, Americans returned 175 million vacation days. (Others officially took vacation days, but continued to work while away from the job.) In general, we wear our long hours like a badge of courage. We fail to see the dangers inherent in overwork. What are these dangers? Studies reveal that people who take vacations are actually more productive than those who do not vacation. Further, workaholics who fail to see the risks of overwork tend to die younger than alcoholics. But changing perceptions of how much work is enough proves a difficult task. Americans' visions of the subject are an institutionalized part of the American workplace. Perhaps this explains why the United States is the only industrialized nation without legally mandated vacation time for its workforce. France, Spain, and Sweden require twenty-five vacation days for workers. Britain, Italy, and the Netherlands require twenty. China has fifteen, while Canada and Japan have ten.[80]

Sports and Leisure

Americans work hard, and we play hard as well. Over 500 million rounds of golf were played in the United States last year. More than 40 million Americans ran the bases in local softball leagues, and over 90 million went bowling. More than two-thirds of us tried our hand at games of chance. A similar number chose to bake, barbecue, cook, or dine out for fun. About a fourth of us headed to the beach for some sand, sea, and sun. And almost 7 million of us took it to heart when someone told us to "go fly a kite."[81] One thing is for certain, when Americans take time off, we enjoy it—so much so that considerations of the worst rarely invade our leisure.

Consider the area of sports. According to the Centers for Disease Control

(CDC), participation in recreational sports and exercise is becoming more and more popular. While such activities can contribute to good health, the risk of injury is always present. "More than 10,000 people receive treatment in the nation's emergency departments *each day* for injuries sustained in sports, recreation and exercise."[82] And it is worth noting that approximately 10 percent of those injuries are traumatic brain injuries. The CDC reports that effective preventive mechanisms exist for sports-related injuries, but many individuals simply fail to adopt them. Despite the growing frequency of bicycle and motorcycle injuries, for example, only about a fourth of riders wear helmets and other protective gear. Similarly, despite the grave dangers one can encounter in scuba diving, few divers acknowledge the risk of decompression illness (the bends), and despite the ever-increasing cancer risks involved in sunbathing, only about a third of sunbathers wear protection.[83] The list goes on and on.

In many ways, positive asymmetry is built into athletic "training." Serious athletes are coached to distance themselves from the potential for dangerous injury. The voices of college athletes give testimony to this bias. Melody Fairchild, for example, a track and field star of the 1990s, told the press: "Being healthy has a lot to do with [my success]. I expect to be healthy. I don't expect to be injured." North Carolina Tarheel star Sean May expressed a similar sentiment. Upon an injury in the field, May told the press: "I never thought I'd get hurt."[84] Professional athletes prove no better at seeing the worst-case scenario. Each year thousands of athletes are sidelined because of injury. For the professional, a serious injury can translate to the loss of a season, a permanent departure from play, or in some rare cases, death. Yet, despite the cost and frequency of injury, professional athletes rarely report focusing on the possibility. Tennis great Serena Williams, for example, spoke with the press following the 2002 Italian Open. When asked if she worried about injuries, Ms. Williams replied: "I don't think so, no." Williams referred to injuries as "freak accidents," that "can't happen to me"—this despite the fact that she had twisted her ankle in a match *immediately prior* to the interview, and a short time earlier, she had been forced out of the Australian Open by injury. The worst-case scenario proved equally distant to soccer star Gareth Ainsworth. In an attempt to come to terms with groin and ankle injuries, Ainsworth penned a letter to his fans. The athlete's positive asymmetry could not have been more pronounced: "I've said this before," wrote Ainsworth, "but prior to Wimbledon, *I never thought about injuries.*"[85]

One might be tempted to think that positive asymmetry levels off in sports that pose the greatest risk. Perhaps boxers, for example, are more realistic in their visions of the worst. Not according to journalist Pete Hamill. In his essay "Blood on Their Hands," Hamill offers a scathing commentary on the positive asymmetry of boxers:

> The most obvious hazard to the prizefighter is the one that is most un-avoidable: Brain damage. Fighters know that when they engage in a box-ing match, they are risking everything, up to and including their lives. . . . [Yet fighters like] Riddick Bowe and Lennox Lewis are still young enough to believe in the lie that swears, *It can't happen to me.*[86]

Racecar driving represents another sport in which risk seems hard to ignore. Yet former racecar driver Alison Hine explains most drivers' failure to imagine catastrophe: "You need to be able to condition yourself to ignore the risk of physical harm, to yourself and to your car. You cannot drive to the limit if you are thinking about what will happen if you crash."[87] On the racing circuit, critics contend that the worst must actually occur before it is considered. As a result, preventive measures remain insufficient. Consider, for example, Associated Press writer Mike Harris's comments following the death of racing legend Dale Earnhardt: "There was an uproar over the earlier deaths [of Adam Petty and Kenny Irwin Jr.], but it took the demise of the sport's biggest star to get NASCAR, which has been criticized by media and fans of dragging its feet on safety issues, to act."

And so it goes—individuals playing hard before the brilliant scenery of the best-case porthole, with the worst nothing more than a distant cloud.[88]

Gambling

Gambling (casino games, horseracing, lotteries, sports pools, and the like) represents an especially popular form of leisure entertainment. Indeed about 70 percent of Americans gamble each year. Statistics show that American gamblers spend over $630 billion per year, nearly 50 percent more than the annual price tag for groceries![89] In gambling—both the legal and illegal varieties—the house banks on the positive asymmetry of players. Indeed, gambling requires that one firmly anchor oneself before the best-case porthole and diligently weather all reference to failure. Psychologists Richard Gonzalez and George Wu describe the phenomenon this way: gamblers "overweight" the very small probability of winning and "underweight" the very likely probability of losing.[90]

Positive asymmetry can be found in all forms of gambling. Consider the most widespread form of wagering—government-sponsored lotteries. Between 50 and 90 percent of state populations (depending on the state) regularly purchase lottery tickets. In such drawings, the odds of winning are often greater than a million to one.[91] Yet Americans' belief in this best-case scenario far outweighs worries about life's more likely catastrophes. Residents of California, for example, are nearly twice as likely to invest in the lottery than they are to invest in earthquake insurance for their homes. Similarly, North Carolina, a state hit with an average of three major hurricanes per year, finds its residents more likely to invest in lottery tickets than they are to invest in flood insurance. And in New Jersey, one of the most densely populated states in the Union, residents are nearly equally likely to invest in the lottery as they are to invest in auto insurance. Yet, because of New Jersey's notoriously high accident rate, the probability of being involved in an auto accident is far, far greater than the probability of winning the state lottery.

Positive asymmetry dominates most games of chance. Studies on horseracing, casino gambling, poker playing, and even day trading find that most gamers enter a wager believing that they will "cash in." The inability to imagine failure seems especially strong when gamers perceive some sense of control in the wagering context. Thus, dice rollers in craps, handicappers at the track, and dealers in a poker games are likely to make the riskiest of bets. For those in apparent control, positive asymmetry is especially pronounced. The worst is something that happens to someone else—someone who knows less or has been poorly prepared.[92]

Lest we forget the sociocultural nature of positive asymmetry, it is important to note the ways in which such perceptions vary among those in different social locations. Men, for example, appear far less likely than women to envision the worst-case scenarios of gambling. Thus, men gamble far more than women, and male gamblers take far more risks. Similarly, gambling's worst-case scenario appears far more distant to some class, ethnic, or religious groups than to others. Research shows, for example, that groups with fatalistic traditions are especially blind to the pitfalls of gambling. For these groups, gambling presents a pathology of hope, a chance to overcome the worst.[93] Note too that the longer one is involved in gambling, the more skewed one's vision becomes. For the lifetime gambler, "no one can convince them that their great schemes will not someday come true."[94]

Eating

Eating is a part of everyone's day. Like it or not (but most of us like it), it is a must-do routine. As I have mentioned, approximately two-thirds of Americans find entertainment in eating-related activities (cooking, baking, barbe-

cuing, dining out). These large numbers illustrate a sad fact. Enjoyable as eating may be, Americans are simply doing too much of it.

The U.S. surgeon general reports that 61 percent of Americans are overweight. Indeed, 20 percent of Americans are so obese that their life spans will
likely be cut short from excess body fat. According to the surgeon general,
300,000 deaths each year are attributable to obesity—a number fast approaching the levels posed by smoking and heavy alcohol consumption. The
fattening of America is not really new. As a group, our weight has been increasing for some time. The problem cuts across all age, ethnic, gender, and
racial groups, but it is particularly stark among children and the poor. The
rate of obesity among American children has doubled in the past thirty years.
And among the working poor, rates of obesity and related diseases (diabetes,
heart disease, etc.) can be up to 90 percent higher than the rates for middle-
and upper-class workers.[95]

Research shows that Americans have effectively distanced themselves
from the risks of poor eating habits. In his book *Fatland: How Americans
Became the Fattest People in the World*, Greg Critser reports:

> Doctors and health care providers remain either in ignorance or outright
> denial about the health dangers. . . . A few years ago, the Centers for Dis-
> ease Control surveyed twelve thousand obese adults to find out what,
> exactly, doctors are telling them. Fewer than half reported being advised
> to lose weight. A separate study sharpened the indictment: Patients with
> incomes above $50,000 were more likely to receive such advice than
> those with incomes below.

But, according to Critser, doctors are not the only ones to blame for America's obesity problem:

> Get a group of boomers together and, within minutes, the topic of obesity
> shifts not to medical issues but, rather, to aesthetic and gender issues, to
> the notion—widely held in the urban upper middle class—that "talking
> too much obesity just ends up making kids have low self-esteem." Or that
> it "might lead to anorexia."[96]

Oblivious to the pitfalls of eating, the majority of us are "supersizing" our
way to heart attacks, strokes, diabetes, and other life-threatening illnesses.
In this regard, the surgeon general identifies positive asymmetry as the greatest impediment to collective weight loss, and urges Americans to realign
their views of the proper diet. But contemporary culture makes this realign-

ment difficult to accomplish. An institutionalized diet of condiments, candy, snacks, and baked goods, a routine of grab, eat, and run, supports Americans' failure to imagine the worst-case scenario of a fast food existence. Few of us envision a hospital bed or a coffin as we reach for the fries and coke.[97]

As we eat our way through steak houses, pizza joints, and the temples of deep-fried delights, Americans show little tolerance for *any* reminders of eating's potential disasters. Consider, for example, that the law requires all restaurants to post instructions on the Heimlich maneuver in a prominent area, for if the worst occurs, and a patron starts to choke, the correct execution of the maneuver may save that patron's life. Despite the usefulness of the instructions, most restaurant owners seek a less obvious place to display them. Apparently, the disaster these instructions address can disrupt customers' comfort level. When it comes to eating, worst-case scenarios can deaden the appetite. Thus, if references to disasters are out of sight, it is hoped they will remain out of mind.

On the Road

In modern American society, it is almost impossible to exist without a car. More than 90 percent of American households own at least one car, and 87 percent of Americans over the age of fifteen are licensed drivers.[98] What with taking the kids to school, driving to work, getting to soccer games, to the mall, or to the nearest fast food restaurant, Americans spend a lot of time in their cars. Indeed the U.S. Census Bureau reports that the average American household clocks over 20,000 miles of auto travel per year.[99]

In the United States, automobiles can prove a dangerous place to be. "Every nine seconds someone in America is injured in a traffic crash, and every 13 minutes someone is killed." Indeed, motor vehicle accidents constitute the fifth leading cause of death in the United States.[100] There are, of course, a number of things one can do to avoid the worst-case scenarios of driving. However, in order for these precautions to be effective, one must recognize the worst and be willing to prepare for it.

Advocates of auto safety note that this is easier said than done. Positive asymmetry among American drivers greatly obscures the dangers of the road. Consider, for example, the notion of alertness. Over half of American drivers (51 percent) admit to driving while sleepy, and approximately 20 percent of drivers report actually falling asleep behind the wheel. Clearly, this problem poses a huge health risk to both the driver and others on the road. Indeed, Richard Gelula, the executive director of the National Sleep Foundation, contends that "driving while drowsy is no different than driving under the influence of alcohol or drugs. Sleepiness slows reaction time, decreases awareness and impairs judgement." Do drivers consider the worst-case scenario of driving while drowsy? Far from it. According to Gelula, "We're finding that sleepy drivers are more tense and impatient and may even be speeding up when they should be stopping to rest." Indeed, only 22 percent of drivers say they pull of the road when drowsy.[101]

Positive asymmetry emerges with regard to drivers, passengers, and their use of seatbelts. Research shows that seat belt usage could dramatically reduce driving disasters. Some estimates suggest that the mere act of "buckling up" could reduce motor vehicle fatalities by nearly 20 percent and motor vehicle injuries by nearly 50 percent. Despite these figures, well over a fourth of Americans fail to use their seat belts.[102] In fact, two-thirds of those killed in auto accidents were not wearing a seatbelt at the time of impact. Why, one might ask, are drivers and passengers so blind to the worst-case scenarios of the road? In this regard, Michael Prestipino of Lowell, Massachusetts, notes the power of positive asymmetry. In a *USA Today* story on seatbelt usage, Mr. Prestipinio, now a quadriplegic as the result of an automobile accident, noted, "You never think something like this could happen to you." Mr. Prestipinio's doctors believe that a seat belt would have saved the use of his limbs, but by the victim's own admission, he simply never saw the potential for the worst.[103]

The same asymmetry characterizes decisions regarding drinking, driving, and disaster. Organizations such as the American Prosecutors Research Institute, MADD, and SAMHSA (an agency in the Department of Health and Human Services) have done much to raise the public consciousness to the worst-case scenarios of drunk driving. At some level, these groups have achieved great success. At present, 97 percent of Americans acknowledge that drinking and driving is a threat to their personal safety. Yet more work on this issue remains to be done. For in some groups and communities, behaviors suggest that positive asymmetry on the issue persists. Consider that slightly more than 11 percent of Americans report driving a car while under the influence of alcohol. (And during holiday seasons, this statistic more than doubles.) Research also shows that, for heavy drinkers, the worst-case scenarios of drinking and driving are especially distant. Apparently, the heaviest drinkers believe they can control both their vehicles and their alcohol. And as alcohol consumption increases, so too does that sense of control. This relationship is especially unfortunate because heavy drinkers actually prefer to drink at multiple locations. This preference increases their time on the road and the potential for disaster.[104]

Given the sociocultural foundations of positive asymmetry, we should not be surprised to learn that perspectives on driving and disaster vary greatly by social location. When we examine safety perception among various age groups, for example, clear differences emerge. Note that teens and young adults between the ages of eighteen and twenty-five are the group least likely to buckle up and the group most likely to die in traffic accidents. Volkswagon America Inc. conducted a nationwide survey designed to explain this age group's reluctance to adopt auto safety measures. The company's results suggested that many young people experience heightened levels of positive asymmetry. Nearly 20 percent of respondents described feelings of invincibility on the road; an additional 20 percent expressed skepticism toward risk, especially during short-distance trips.[105] Heightened asymmetry may also explain young people's approach to drinking and driving. The National Household Survey on Drug Abuse found that one in four teenagers drives while under the influence of alcohol, a rate 2.5 times higher than that of the driving population at large.[106] Do teens consider the dangers that such actions may invoke? Interviews with teens suggest that many do not. In a recent study of high school–aged drivers, one subject noted, "Most students realize the statistics, but choose to disregard them. They don't think *they'll* get caught or in trouble." Only when the worst occurs do teens' views of reality seem to change. In the words of one respondent who recently lost a schoolmate to drunk driving, "This incident brought it to reality and changed my perspective."[107]

Youth represents a powerful engine in the often cavalier attitude of teens and young adults toward driving. But note that many other sociocultural factors have a similar effect. Research shows, for example, that perceptions of auto safety vary with regard to regional cultures. In states like New Hampshire and Massachusetts, where the "live free or die" mentality is strong, drivers resist seatbelt usage and vehemently reject arguments on risk. Indeed, New Hampshire is the only state in the union that lacks a mandatory seatbelt law. And among the remaining forty-nine states, Massachusetts displays the lowest rate of seatbelt usage (51 percent). States with low population density, wide-open spaces, and frontier traditions resist seatbelt usage as well. Alaska, Idaho, the Dakotas, and Wyoming display rates of seatbelt usage well below the national average.

The regional traditions that discourage seatbelt safety apply to other facets of driving as well. There is, for example, a strong association between a state's seatbelt usage rate and its rate of alcohol-related fatalities. Sixty-nine percent of the states with the *lowest* seatbelt usage rates also display the *highest* rates of alcohol-related fatalities. Do such states see the worst-case scenarios playing out within their borders? Statistics suggest not. In states where alcohol-related fatalities are 50 percent or higher, safety laws remain difficult to enact. Indeed, only 20 percent of such states have laws whose statutory language allows the drunk driver to be prosecuted for more serious crimes such as homicide or reckless endangerment.[108]

Working, playing, eating, driving—these activities are a part of most people's everyday routine. And as we have seen, visions of the worst often hold little or no place in these fields of action. During the course of our day, most of us remain at the best-case porthole of perception, allowing the potential for the worst-case scenario to remain at the far reaches of active consciousness.

Positive Asymmetry in Groups and Organizations

Thus far, we have examined the ways in which positive asymmetry can influence individual cognition. We have noted that members of many groups and communities, people at similar sociocultural junctures, often prove unable to focus on the worst. In this section, we consider another level of analysis. We visit the literature that addresses thinking as a small-group phenomenon. In this area (the specialty of social psychologists as well as certain organizational sociologists), a fascinating argument emerges. Scholars contend that the structure of a small group, its developing group culture, and the interaction patterns of its members can bring about a single perceptual script—a script that all the group members embrace as their own. From this viewpoint, perception is not just a process enacted by an individual within a group. Rather, perception is the product of the group itself.

Perception in Small Groups

Perception as a group phenomenon—the idea is central to the study of small-group dynamics. And within that literature, scholars identify three specific processes that are relevant for our purposes: groupthink, risky shift, and bystander intervention. Here, I discuss each of these phenomena in turn and explore their relationship to positive asymmetry.

GROUPTHINK Social psychologist Irving Janis proposed the notion of groupthink more than four decades ago. Janis defined groupthink as a deteriorated and biased view of facts and circumstances. According to Janis, this bias results from a group's excessive desire to reach consensus. Further, the desire for consensus drives group members to link certain strategies to the best-case outcomes of action. In so doing, the group fails to fully explore the potential for the worst-case scenario.

Janis's theory of groupthink arose from his analysis of several historical fiascoes. He studied, for example, the devastating 1941 attack on Pearl Harbor, noting that military commanders had information to suggest the invasion, but decided as a group against taking precautions to protect the U.S. fleet. Similarly, Janis analyzed the 1961 Bay of Pigs invasion. In planning the attack, the group failed to see the obvious flaws that led to a military disaster. Janis also analyzed several strategic decisions to escalate the U.S. military presence during the Vietnam War. He found that intelligence experts and U.S. allies urged President Johnson to contain U.S. involvement. Yet Lyndon Johnson and his policy advisors failed to see the worst-case scenario of escalation. As a result, fifty-eight thousand American and a million Vietnamese lives were lost, dividing American public opinion on the war and driving Johnson from office.[109]

Janis contends that these real-world events illustrate groups in the clutches of groupthink. In each case, an excessive sense of optimism distanced the worst from group members' view. According to Janis, each group's local culture prevented it from seeing beyond the best-case perceptual porthole. This position insulated the group from those with a more balanced vision. The positive asymmetry of groupthink promoted a sense of moral superiority that encouraged each group to assume complete success.

RISKY SHIFT   Risky shift refers to a group level phenomenon in decision making. The term describes the tendency for groups to make riskier decisions than individuals who are left to their own devices. Thus, when groups are faced with a dilemma and must collectively decide on a course of action, they tend to exaggerate the best-case outcome of their decisions and distance the worst in their perceptual field. The risky-shift phenomenon means, for example, that a football team will devise a game strategy that casts caution to the wind—injuries and penalties be damned—in an effort to win at all costs. Risky shift means that investment groups acting in the marketplace will put enormous amounts of money at risk; they will assume profit and fully dismiss the potential for significant loss.

Risky shift was first documented in the experimental laboratories of social psychologist James Stoner.[110] During the past four decades, Stoner's work has been replicated in over three hundred experimental studies—studies conducted with people of varying ages and occupations across dozens of nations.

To be sure, not all group decisions are plagued by risky shift. Local culture is key to the phenomenon. This is because group decisions tend to be an extreme or exaggerated version of the group's initial preferences. Thus, if a group is embedded in a context that values caution, its discussions and ultimate decisions may be quite balanced with regard to best and worst cases. But if a group is embedded in a risk-oriented context, risky shift is likely to emerge in the decision-making process.[111]

BYSTANDER INTERVENTION   Bystander intervention, or the bystander effect, refers to the propensity for one individual to help another in the event of an emergency, for example, when the other is under attack, trapped in a smoke-filled room, or has fallen from a ladder. Research on bystander intervention was prompted by the murder of a woman named Kitty Genovese on March 13, 1964. Many readers may recall this sad and gruesome tale. Kitty Genovese was walking home from work one night when she was approached and viciously stabbed by a stranger. Genovese screamed for help, and indeed, many of those in a nearby apartment building came to their windows. Fearful of apprehension, the attacker started to flee. But when the attacker realized that none of the neighbors was coming to the victim's aid, he stayed at the scene and continued the assault. The attack went on for forty-five minutes, and Genovese screamed continuously, hoping for rescue. She was stabbed multiple times before finally succumbing. Thirty-eight people witnessed her murder. Not one intervened or called for help.

Why were people so hesitant to help Genovese? That was the question posed by social psychologists John Darley and Bibb Latane. In their initial studies, as well as in the hundreds of experiments that followed, Darley and Latane found that, in part, positive asymmetry contributed to people's "reluctance" to respond. When an emergency occurs in a crowd as opposed to a one-on-one situation, research shows that social actors are less likely to notice it; they are less likely to assume the responsibility of aid and less likely to interpret the event as an emergency. This final point is especially key to my inquiry. Studies show that individuals who witness an emergency typically hide their concern more than they realize. And as they look at other bystanders, they see the same masked expressions. Amazingly, bystanders tend to cognitively emphasize the calm of other bystanders, allowing it to obscure the worst-case scenario that is unfolding before their eyes (a mugging, burglary, accident, or assault). In essence, the best-case scenario suggested by onlookers' expressionless demeanor takes overwhelming precedence over the violence or unpleasantness that is clearly occurring before the group.[112]

Groupthink, risky shift, and bystander intervention—these processes are important to any discussion of positive asymmetry. Research on these phenomena makes clear that even here, beyond the level of the individual, perception depends on vantage point. If the group's cultural script positions members at the best-case porthole on reality, then the failure to imagine the worst will prove part of a group's dominant routines.

From Groups to Organizations

Organizations are, of course, much more complicated than the small groups addressed in the research on groupthink, risky shift, and bystander intervention. In contrast to such groups, we can think of an organization as a large, complex network of positions formed with specific goals or purposes in mind. As these positions interconnect, they form a definitive structure, which is often hierarchical in design.

While organizations are more complex than small groups, they hold one important thing in common with such groups. Most organizations also develop a culture—what sociologists refer to as an organizational culture—a set of values, beliefs, and assumptions that guide the thinking and action of the organization's members. Is positive asymmetry a part of organizational culture? Often the answer to that question is yes. As a result, organizational theorists devote much of their energies to studying the ways in which biased perceptions become part of an organization's modus operandi.[113]

Organizations are, in part, constituted by plans, routines, and standard operating procedures. Thus, when organization-related disasters occur—design flaws, nuclear accidents, oil spills, toxic dumping—one is tempted to assume that the organization must have seen the disaster coming; its members must have anticipated and planned for the worst. Under such conditions, it is not uncommon for people to suspect a conspiracy of sorts, to assume that the organization saw the potential for danger, yet plowed ahead, simply covering up any prior knowledge of danger.

To be sure, there are certain disasters that fit this model. The Ford Motor Company (the Pinto), Firestone Tires (exploding tires), the Tobacco industry (tar and nicotine cover-up), Union Carbide (toxic waste dumping), and the U.S. government (Tuskegee, Agent Orange, etc.) are just a few of the organizations that have been involved in notorious cover-ups. But organizational sociologists suggest that such cases are more the exception than the rule. In organizations, the worst case is more likely uncertain, unrealistically articulated, and hence unanticipated, leaving organizations scrambling when catastrophes actually occur.

Nearly twenty-five years ago, sociologists Martha Feldman and James

March suggested that organizations are "systematically stupid." In assessing a situation, organizations often follow a methodical but ineffective course of action. The stupidity begins with information collection. According to Feldman and March, organizational actors collect more information than they need. Indeed, the collection of information often becomes more central than the problem at hand. Drowned in data, decision makers may fail to review pertinent information prior to making a decision; they may make a decision on the basis of irrelevant data, or ignore information that is counter to the organization's desired plan.[114]

The systematic stupidity of which Feldman and March speak is strongly tied to positive asymmetry. Research shows that organizations often gravitate to data that supports the best-case outcome of action. Organizational scholars reference this trend under various analytic labels: the appeal to ignorance, the disqualification heuristic, failed vision, and microscopic vision.[115] Each of these concepts suggests a decision embedded in a biased perceptual location, for when organizations and their members have focused their gaze through the best-case porthole, when the worst is unarticulated and backgrounded in consciousness, disaster plans simply prove unrealistic. Decision makers are, in essence, planning for what they cannot conceive.

What factors place an organization at the best-case vantage point? In reading the work of sociologist Charles Perrow, for example, we learn that the failure to imagine the worst may be rooted in certain types of technical and organizational systems. Perrow contends that two qualities in particular—"interactive complexity" and "tight coupling"—can make it difficult or impossible for decision makers to envision the worst-case scenario. Interactive complexity occurs when a system's parts serve multiple functions—functions that are executed in the absence of a predictable production sequence, thus producing unfamiliar or unintended feedback loops. Tight coupling occurs when there is no slack or give between system units. Under such conditions, one unit's effect on another is direct and rapid. Lest these definitions make trouble seem too abstract, Perrow provides a concrete description of interactive complexity and tight coupling in action:

> We start with a plant, airplane, ship, biology laboratory, or other setting with a lot of components (parts, procedures, operators). Then we need two or more failures among components that interact in some unexpected way. No one dreamed that when X failed, Y would also be out of order and the two failures would interact so as to both start a fire and silence the fire alarm. Furthermore, no one can figure out the interaction at the time and thus know what to do. The problem is *just something that never occurred*

to the designers. . . . Suppose the system is also "tightly coupled," that is, processes happen very fast and can't be turned off, the failed parts cannot be isolated from other parts, or there is not a way to keep the production going safely. Then recovery from the initial disturbance is not possible; it will spread quickly and irretrievably for at least some time. Indeed, operator action or the safety systems make it worse, since for a time, it is not known what the problem really is.[116]

Perrow reviews a variety of organizational and technical systems, including air and water transport, dams, mines, petrochemical plants, and weapon systems. He contrasts systems dependent on interactive complexity and tight coupling with systems that are not. In so doing, Perrow demonstrates that system designs prioritize certain vantage points on reality. In this way, system design and structure plays a powerful role in what the organization acknowledges and what it fails to recognize.

System structure is vital to our understanding of positive asymmetry in organizations (so important, in fact, that we will revisit this issue in chapter 7). But, as mentioned above, organizations also develop their own culture. Indeed, sociologists Paul DiMaggio and Walter Powell tell us that organizational structure is always associated with a set of cultural schemata and practices that both constrain options for action and "establish the very criteria by which people discover their preferences."[117] In establishing evaluative criteria, organizational culture proves pivotal in positioning an organization before the best-case perceptual porthole. Diane Vaughan was among the first to explicate that fact as she explored the role of organizational culture in conceptualizing potential disasters. In her acclaimed book *The Challenger Launch Decision,* as well as in her recent work as a NASA consultant on the *Columbia* disaster, Vaughan analyzed NASA's failed missions in brilliant detail.[118] Her research is important to any discussion of positive asymmetry, for she shows that this bias is not simply a product of certain system structures. Rather, positive asymmetry is a product of the cultures that inhabit system structures. The phenomenon, like all forms of cognition, is mediated by cultural beliefs and conventions, making it an unreflexive, routine way of seeing the world.

Through Vaughan's work, we learn that the worst-case scenarios surrounding both the *Challenger* and *Columbia* missions were known to NASA prior to their occurrence. The potential failure of the O-rings, the problems of breaking foam—these were not surprises or flukes. Indeed, some at NASA attempted to flag these issues for the notice of key NASA decision makers. Why, then, did NASA managers, "who not only had all the information on the eve of the launch but also were warned against it, decide to proceed?" According to Vaughan, the managers' inability to see the worst was "a mistake embedded in the banality of organizational life and facilitated by an environment of scarcity and competition, elite bargaining, uncertain technology, incrementalism, patterns of information, routinization, organizational and interorganizational structures." But along with these organizational factors—indeed, embedded in them—was "a complex culture . . . that normalized signals of potential danger and re-aligned action with organizational goals." Vaughan's study of the NASA disasters unfolds a dynamic motivated by positive asymmetry—a way of seeing that, within organizations, is more common than we suspect, more routine than we dare discuss.[119]

The organizational theorists I have discussed in this section remind us that, despite its inaccuracy, positive asymmetry is "normal" to organizations. It represents what sociologists Roger Friedland and Roger Alford call an "institutional logic," that is, "a set of material practices and symbolic constructions" that configure an organization's worldview.[120] To be sure, positive asymmetry may lead an organization to an ill-fated decision. But as an embedded convention, positive asymmetry will continue to guide organizations as they enact plans, mold strategies, interpret pasts, and anticipate futures.

Positive Asymmetry: Part of the American Cultural Fabric

Remember the old song? "You've got to acc-en-tu-ate the positive / E-li-mi-nate the negative . . ." Apparently, many groups and communities have taken its lessons to heart, particularly in the United States. Indeed, positive asymmetry represents an important dimension of American national culture.[121]

The inability to see the worst is nestled in the very language we speak. One need only consider the healthy number of entries corresponding to the term "best" in *Roget's A–Z Thesaurus*. When it comes to the best, we are simply never at a loss for words:

Best, *modif* 1. [Generally excellent]—*Syn.* Choicest, finest, greatest, highest, first, transcendent, prime, premium, supreme, optimum, incomparable, culminating, preeminent, leading, crowning, *sans pareil* (French), paramount, matchless, nonpareil, unrivaled, unparalleled, unsurpassed, second to none, in a class by itself, nonesuch, unequaled, unexcelled, inimitable, beyond compare, superlative, foremost, peerless, champion, top, prize, most desirable, most suitable, most favorable, most advantageous, outstanding, tip-top.

2. [Applied especially to things]—*Syn.* Choice, premium, highest-quality, top-of-the-line.

3. [Applied especially to people]—*Syn.* Of the elite, belonging to the upper classes, socially preferred, aristocratic.

4. [Applied especially to actions]—*Syn.* Noblest, sincerest, most magnanimous, most creditable, most illustrious, most glorious, most honorable, most praiseworthy, greatest, kindest, nicest.

n.—*Syn.* First, favorite choice, finest, top, pick, prime, flower, cream, elite, *crème de la crème* (French), utmost, salt of the earth, pick of the crop, cream of the crop, tops.

But when it comes to "worst," we have considerably less to say. Note the meager number of synonyms associated with the word:

Worst, *modif*—*Syn* most terrible, most harmful, poorest, lowest, least, most ghastly, most horrible, most pitiful, least meaningful, meanest, least understanding, least effective.

n.—*Syn.* Calamity, catastrophe, ruin.[122]

The linguistic differences in the expression of quality are indicative of a broader cultural message. American culture encourages Americans to "look for the silver lining" and "make lemonade out of life's lemons." "Don't think the worst," we are warned, for focusing on it is destructive and self-defeating. Indeed, those who recognize the worst risk being dismissed as nothing more than "sad sacks," "sourpusses" or "wet blankets."[123]

Cognitive scientist N. D. Weinstein contends that American culture's obsession with the best has created a land of "Pollyannas." Americans suffer from what Weinstein calls the "optimism bias." Is it any wonder, then, that whatever the negatives life throws at Americans, we tend to view the future as unequivocally positive.[124] While some worry that the optimism bias may carry hidden costs, others contend that it may be an invaluable cultural trait. Noted economist Robert Reich, for example, argues that American optimism may be behind the long-term success of the American economy:

American optimism carries over into our economy, which is one reason why we've always been a nation of inventors and tinkerers, of innovators and experimenters and why we're the most productive economy in the world. Optimism also explains why we spend so much and save so little. . . . Our willingness to go deep into debt and keep spending is intimately related to our optimism and our deepest assumptions about future peace, stability and progress.[125]

Could Reich be right? Opinion polls certainly confirm Reich's depiction of American attitudes on the economy. Consider, for example, a critical moment in recent American experience. In 2000–2001, despite a serious downturn in the U.S. stock market and despite the tragedy of the September 11 attacks, the worst-case scenario seemed absent from most Americans' vision of the economic future. A CNN/Money poll showed that Americans' view of the economy had reached an eighteen-year high.[126] Similarly, an AARP poll noted that 68 percent of Americans were optimistic about the economy, both in the short and long term. That figure was even higher among blacks and Hispanics (80 percent and 81 percent respectively), two groups that, overall, have been harder hit than whites in the most recent recession. The same trend characterized Americans' reactions to the economic climate of late 2005. Despite the destruction of Katrina, the billions spent on the Iraqi war, and rising gas prices, the Gallup poll showed that only 27 percent of Americans viewed economic conditions as poor—a figure on a par with ratings from 2003 and 2004.[127]

Because we tend to look to the sunny side, Americans, as a whole, take forecasts of doom in their stride. Recall the predictions of the Y2K catastrophe. Most Americans reacted to the warnings with measured calm. In March of 1999, for example, only about 50 percent of Americans expressed concern about a Y2K disaster. And in December of 1999, just weeks before the critical moment of transition, polls showed that only 26 percent of Americans worried about Y2K or an associated terrorist attack.[128] The same can be said for the Social Security "emergency" raised by George W. Bush in 2005. Recall that the president traversed the nation warning of impending economic disaster. Indeed, Bush argued that the children of the baby boomers would likely retire to a bankrupt system. But despite the doomsday scenario painted by the president, polls showed that less than 35 percent of Americans proved willing to abandon their position at the best-case porthole on the future.[129]

Clearly, positive asymmetry is one of American culture's most prevalent resources. And perhaps the most jarring proof of that fact rests in Americans' ability to rebound after the September 11 terrorist attack. Polls show that in the weeks immediately following the attack, many Americans worried about additional disasters—an errant plane, an anthrax attack, a dirty bomb. But "even as Attorney General John Ashcroft was issuing news alerts on Oct[ober] 11 and 29, fears of terrorism were dissipating. By early November

2001, only 13 percent of people said they were 'very worried' about terrorism, the same number as in July 1996, according to a Pew poll."[130]

Expect the best—that stance is central to the "American way." Indeed, in the United States, an entire industry has been built upon these values and beliefs. "Down with stinkin' thinkin'" is the mantra of the self-help industry.[131] In fact, self-help gurus, a group currently central to American popular culture, insist that a "healthy" life requires one to actively eliminate considerations of the worst. Consider the advice of Deepak Chopra, a frontrunner in the field. Chopra demands that his followers relentlessly shun thoughts of the worst, refusing to allow "the creation of negativity in your environment." For Chopra, a balanced vision of best and worst sets the stage for personal failure. Success demands that only the best remain in the center of consciousness:

> B stands for better and best. Evolution implies getting better in every way with time, ultimately getting for ourselves the best of everything. People with wealth consciousness settle only for the best. This is called the principle of highest first.[132]

"Dr. Phil" McGraw, another star of the self-help market, promotes a similar idea. Dr. Phil explicitly urges his followers to "realign" their vision. He argues that one's view of the world should be measured by positive potential rather than actual behavior. Thus, Dr. Phil instructs his followers to release any destructive and negative internal rhetoric, to distance themselves from the worst events of the past, and to "get on with it," embracing only positive accomplishments and goals.[133] Of course, positive asymmetry has been at the core of America's most popular contemporary icon of success, Oprah Winfrey. Winfrey makes no bones about her self-defined mission to help her followers realize their best selves. How does she guide her flock to this goal? Winfrey believes in what social psychologists call an "availability bias." This concept suggests that the sentiment most prominent or available to us is the one that has the most powerful impact on our perceptions of reality. She urges her followers to keep the best "at one's fingertips," while rendering the worst inaccessible and far from reach. Making this bold move, according to Winfrey, "is the only way to truly advance toward the grandest vision the universe has for you." Indeed, Winfrey contends that making the worst available in one's consciousness can "jeopardize one's legacy." According to Winfrey, worst-case scenarios breed fear, "and if you allow fear to touch you, it will fight to keep you from ever becoming your best self."[134]

Be all that you can be. Expect the best. These sentiments are woven into
the fabric of American culture. Risk-perception theorists suggest that such a
widespread bias is not at all unusual. Indeed, according to risk researchers,
cultures, as a whole, often attend to the wrong things.[135] In this way, members of a culture engage in collective miscalculations. Collectives often see
relationships where there actually are none (what scientists call the type 1
error), and they often fail to see relationships that actually exist (what scientists call the type 2 error). Type 1 errors become errors of optimism, for individuals, groups, and communities are much more likely to see positive connections or best-case relationships where none exist. In contrast, type 2
errors become dangerous omissions, as individuals, groups, and communities ignore existing negative connections or worst-case relationships.[136]

Kooks, Jokers, and Villains

Positive asymmetry may dominate mainstream American culture, but there
are, of course, exceptions to the rule.[137] Indeed, one must acknowledge that
certain individuals, groups, and communities seem to see nothing but the
worst. In many ways, however, the existence of those who hold such negative attitudes only strengthens the broader collective's optimistic bias.
Indeed, those who are fixated on the worst are often treated as lost and misguided. Labeled as abnormal or deviant, these naysayers are thought to be
standing at the wrong perceptual porthole. Viewed in this way, naysayers
become a tool that keeps the rest of us correctly positioned.

In contemporary American society, for example, those who prioritize the
worst may be characterized as "troubled" and, from a psychiatric standpoint,
unequivocally dysfunctional and abnormal. Individuals who show signs of
such behavior are quickly referred for diagnosis and treatment. Thus, those
who consistently see themselves as the target of danger or conspiracy will
likely be diagnosed with "delusional disorder of the persecutory variety"
(DSM IV diagnosis 297.1). People who routinely focus on the worst-case
scenario, those who cannot seem to sustain any real optimism, will likely
be diagnosed with dysthymic disorder (commonly known as depression,
DSM IV diagnosis 300.4) or generalized anxiety disorder (DSM IV diagnosis
300.02).[138] According to psychiatrists, focusing on the worst is clearly a disease. And lest the general public forget it, pharmaceutical companies aggressively underscore the point, relentlessly "educating" the public regarding
such maladies and their cures. Consider this popular ad for Paxil, one of many
drugs prescribed for such disorders:[139]

PATIENT 1: It's your worst fears . . . the what ifs . . . and I can't control it.

PATIENT 2: It's like I never get a chance to relax. I worry all the time. . . . When I'm at work, I worry about stuff at home. When I'm at home, I worry about stuff at work.

NARRATOR: If you've been suffering from any of these symptoms for six months or more, you may have general anxiety disorder and a chemical imbalance could be to blame. Talk to your doctor about Paxil.[140]

By showing individuals that their perceptual vantage point is flawed, such ads claim to hasten treatment and recovery. "Talk to your doctor," because therapy, medicine, or both, will help you rediscover the positive. Only then can you journey back to the broader community, back to the best-case porthole on reality.

When those fixated on the worst cannot or will not be "cured," they will likely be distanced from the broader community, their deviance underscored. Consider, for example, individuals and groups devoted to an almost exclusive fixation with the worst—apocalyptists. Such groups populate the historical landscape and many social scientists, historians, and journalists have studied them extensively. From such accounts we learn that, when brought to the attention of the broader community, the claims of apocalyptists are rarely taken seriously. Indeed, researchers themselves, while claiming objectivity in studying such groups, make clear their assessments of apocalyptists as deviant or misguided. We see this pattern in the work of noted social psychologists Leon Festinger, Henry Riecken, and Stanley Schachter. Their classic book *When Prophecy Fails* brought readers inside the mind of a group of people who believed that on December 21, 1955, a substantial part of the western hemisphere would be destroyed by a massive flood. While Festinger and his colleagues studied the phenomenon of doomsday cults with the utmost seriousness, and while they forwarded important theories in an effort to explain how such groups are sustained, their assessment of the group's claims were never in question. The proselytizers were outsiders and useful for research only by virtue of their deviance. Indeed, the authors wrote of their subjects:

> A man with a conviction is a hard man to change. Tell him you disagree and he turns away. Show him facts or figures and he questions your sources. Appeal to logic and he fails to see your point. . . . We have all experienced the futility of trying to change a strong conviction, especially if the convinced person has some investment in his belief. . . . How and

why does such a response to contradictory evidence come about? That is
the question on which this book focuses.[141]

It was their subjects' very refusal to recognize "reality" that captured the
minds of Festinger and his colleagues. In short, the group's deviance was
never *in* question, it was *a* question for study, the group's marginal location
nothing more than the likely fate of misguided pessimists.[142]

The stance of Festinger and his colleagues is hardly unusual. In American culture, worst-case junkies are routinely "put in the proper perspective."
And the more visible the group, the more scathing the review.[143] Consider
the coverage on the Heaven's Gate cult in Rancho Santa Fe, California. Readers will recall Heaven's Gate as a well-publicized cult whose members believed that on March 24, 1997, they would "converge upon a spaceship following the comet Hale-Bopp, their true home. . . . Members of the Kingdom
of Heaven would be aboard a craft, awaiting them."[144] As the rest of the world
perished in the coming Armageddon, cult members would bask in the dawn-
ing of the Golden Age. In journalistic accounts of the Heaven's Gate cult, the
groups' deviance is a constant theme. Indeed, most reporters characterized
the cult as the epitome of the lunatic fringe. Peter Klebnikov, for example,
described the cult thus: "Within their walls I found a mix of the scary and the
farcical under the cloak of spirituality. Unlike millions of fundamentalist
Christians who quietly accept the possibility of the apocalypse, doomsday
sects seek to accelerate Armageddon for personal and often twisted reasons."[145] Taking a similar tone, journalist Stephen Hedges and his colleagues
described the cult in this way:

> For more than 20 years, Applewhite [the group's leader] had recruited a
> small number of followers and indoctrinated them in his ersatz sci-fi reli-
> gion that borrows heavily from Christianity, Gnosticism, theosophy, and
> a belief in extraterrestrials and life in outer space that Heaven's Gate
> members called the "Next Level." . . . The X-Files, Star Trek, Jesus—it
> had all been part of Applewhite's catechism as he crisscrossed the coun-
> try trying to sell the promise of an otherworldly existence.[146]

The treatment of Heaven's Gate within the media illustrates a broader phenomenon. When worst-case naysayers win the cultural spotlight, response is
swift and sure. The group's deviance is immediately established, the group's
oddities immediately displayed, the group's dogma labeled as foreign to the
concerns of a culture that champions only the brightest scenarios.

The propensity to marginalize those fixated on the worst is not simply a phenomenon of modern American culture. In *Apocalypses,* historian Eugen Weber puts this reaction in perspective. Weber's review of apocalyptists spans Old Testament writings such as the book of Daniel and the prophecies of Amos, Isaiah, and Joel. He discusses New Testament works such as St. Paul's epistles, John's revelations, writings by John's contemporary Esdras, as well as those of Montanus, an Anatolian prophet who followed shortly after John. Weber examines Renaissance and Enlightenment apocalyptic movements, and the apocalyptic writings of several nineteenth-century seculars. In this sweeping review, Weber shows that cultural norms have always discouraged apocalyptists from foregrounding their views. In Daniel 8:26, for example, the prophet is warned by the archangel Gabriel to keep his visions to himself. More worldly figures such as St. Augustine adopted the same position, warning that the Apocalypse was as much about salvation as it was destruction. According to St. Augustine, fixating on doom—predicting its nature and arrival—was an unworthy cause, for it simply distracted believers from reconciling with the Lord. St. Augustine's marginalization of apocalyptists was a practice that grew stronger in subsequent generations. "Before the eighteenth century ended, *The Holy Bible Adapted to the Use of Schools and Private Families* (Birmingham, 1783) had omitted most of Paul's epistles and the whole of Revelation as too incendiary."[147]

Along with rejection, the routine reaction to purveyors of the worst-case scenario, it should come as no surprise that doomsayers who manage to achieve some success are actively ridiculed—even ostracized—by their peers. Consider, for example, one of the most famous of contemporary apocalyptists, radio personality and author Art Bell. Art Bell is best known for his talk radio program *Coast to Coast AM.*[148] Broadcast seven nights a week from one to five in the morning eastern time, the program covers a wide variety of worst-case scenarios: alien abductions, takeovers of the U.S. government, demonic possession, ghost hauntings, natural disasters, nuclear demise. One night a guest may predict the explosion of the sun. Another night discussion may turn to "Planet X," a newly discovered planet that will collide with the earth in the next few years. On still another night, the show may feature those boasting routine contact with Satan and other assorted "shadow people." Is it any wonder that journalist Don DeLillo calls Bell "a purveyor of doom and gloom." The title is fitting, for Bell's goal is to convince his listeners and readers that things are bad, very bad, and that denying the fact will only doom the human race.

During Art Bell's tenure, *Coast to Coast AM* reached more than four hundred radio stations nationwide and well over ten million listeners, a number topped only by radio legends such as Paul Harvey or Rush Limbaugh. But while Bell has assembled a "respectable" following, (both for his radio show and his similarly themed books), his persona and that of his followers is anything but respected. Most reviewers and commentators make it their mission to marginalize Bell's work, attempting to relocate the doomsayer to the far horizons of perception. Thus, Tim Cuprisin, media reviewer for the *Milwaukee Sentinel*, refers to Bell as that "spooky overnight radio guy."[149] Similarly, note the ridicule that infuses this piece by journalist Ken Layne as he explains Art Bell's 1998 decision to retire from *Coast to Coast AM* (one of three retirements and counting):

> Art Bell ran into something big: Martians, the Secret World Government, the Return of the Devil, etc. He either hinted at the scope of the horror or was about to bring it to the airwaves. And that's when the unmarked helicopters landed at his desert home and the men in civilian suits knocked on his studio door. "Mr. Bell," one of the spooks said. "Your time is up. Either get off the air or die like one of those mutilated cattle." . . . You are a weird case . . . a talented radio host who knew how to bring strange tales from your loony guests and callers.[150]

In the same mocking fashion, the *Daily Hog*, an Internet satire site, ran this story about Bell:

> A newfound object orbiting the earth has now been confirmed not to be a new earth moon as first thought. NASA released satellite images confirming the object is Art Bell's head. . . . Speculation over the past several months that Art Bell was abducted by Alien beings is now being taken more seriously.[151]

Reviewers are equally harsh in their dismissal of Bell's "research," including *The Source*, *The Quickening*, and *The Coming Global Superstorm*. For example, in reviewing *The Quickening*, psychologist Robert Baker comments:

> We've long known that Art Bell, night radio's paranoid propagandist knows how to rave and rant. What we didn't know was whether or not he could read and write. An organized rumor that he is, indeed, literate comes to us in the form of an "alleged" book entitled *The Quickening: Today's Trend, Tomorrow's World.*

Baker dismisses the book in no uncertain terms, describing it as a series of "doom and gloom themes" and a litany of errors and misinformation." In so doing, Baker reinforces the broader cultural tendency to write off those who attempt to move us from the best-case porthole on the world.[152]

When worst-case promoters profit from their rhetoric, the public's disdain for them is particularly pronounced. Perhaps this explains the constant criticism leveled at the mass media, for according to some scholars, the media has made a rather lucrative career of sensationalizing the worst.[153] Indeed, sociologists such as David Altheide, George Gerbner, and Barry Glassner contend that, by centering the worst-case scenarios in the minds of media users, the media challenge American optimism and promote a "discourse of fear"—an expectation that danger and risk are a central feature of everyday life.[154]

In an effort to sanction the media for promoting the worst, some have turned to the courts. For example, family members of school shooting victims (including the "prayer circle" shootings in Kentucky's Heath High School and the Columbine massacre in Colorado) are suing video game makers and movie studios, charging that the violence in these media products spurred the murder of innocent children. Similarly, a Connecticut women sued a video game manufacturer when her daughter was killed by a "Mortal Kombat" gaming aficionado. According to police, the murderer was recreating a fight scene from the arcade game. Short of lawsuits, many groups and communities are organizing to marginalize violent media. Grassroots movements such as the Lion and the Lamb Project and the National Institute on Media and Family are actively organizing to block the marketing of violence to children. (Indeed, the U.S. Senate has heard testimony in this matter.) In 1996, the V-chip became available to TV viewers, and a short time later Congressman Joe Baca of California introduced a bill to make it illegal to rent violent video games to minors. (Joseph Lieberman of Connecticut spearheaded a similar movement in the Senate.)[155] Surveys suggest that these attempts to distance violent media from everyday experience enjoy widespread support. A recent Gallup poll showed that approximately two-thirds of Americans believe that the entertainment industry must do more to protect children and teenagers from exposure to violence. Further, 70 percent link violent action to media exposure. Respondents are so strongly opposed to the media's tendency to promote the worst that they would support explicit government intervention in the control of Internet violence (65 percent), video-game violence (58 percent), and TV violence (56 percent).[156]

In contemporary American culture, there appears to be only one acceptable way to foreground the worst-case scenario, and that is to satirize it. Witness the popularity of horror movies ranging from traditional slasher films such as *Halloween* and *Friday the 13th*, to classic monster flicks such as

Frankenstein or *The Mummy,* to black comedies such as the *Scream* series. Most moviegoers would be unwilling, perhaps unable, to focus on the torture and gore so standard to these films. Yet in the campy fantasy arena of horror films, where individuals are encouraged to suspend reality and belief, we become able to consider, momentarily, the unthinkably dark side of life. Indeed, the entertainment factor woven so well into these worst-case scenarios allows one to dismiss the horror of a film upon exiting the theater.[157]

Foregrounding the worst in the confines of satire: we find more support of the point in the contemporary bad-news phenomenon *The Worst-case Scenario Survival Handbook.*[158] What's the worst that could happen? Joshua Piven and David Borgenicht suggest a variety of answers to the question. And in so doing, their readers learn, for example, how to escape quicksand, how to fend off a shark, how to escape from killer bees, how to survive if your parachute doesn't open. Indeed, Piven and Borgenicht encourage their readers to live their life at the intersection of Murphy's law and the Boy Scout motto: anything that can go wrong will, so be prepared.

The worst-case scenarios presented in the book represent serious events. But it is clear that the authors approach each topic with a wink and a smile. Literary critic Jacqueline Blais explains their success:

> The authors have enough perspective to acknowledge the campy appeal of an armchair guide for the anxious. "We thought it would be funny to people," Borgenicht says. They were, he says, "inspired by pop culture as much as by paranoia—most of the scenarios we talk about were a TV or a movie scene."[159]

Readers' reactions to *The Worst-case Scenario Survival Handbook* are appropriately tongue-in-cheek. Consider this comment from an online reviewer at Amazon.com:

> This book is tremendously enjoyable, although it's hard to explain why that should be so. . . . Somehow it's endlessly amusing to imagine oneself in various dire circumstances, performing James Bond stunts to come out on top. . . . Perhaps it tickles our survival instincts to play out these scenarios in our heads, but regardless of the reason, this book is a blast!

A reviewer at BarnesandNoble.com echoes the sentiment: "We laughed so hard just thumbing through the topics. . . . It completely cracks us up." Lighthearted and entertaining—that's the way Americans like their worst-case scenarios. Light enough, perhaps, to float out of sight and mind, leaving us free to focus on the more uplifting issues of the day.

⟨∞⟩

Home and office, work and play, love and war, life and death—we have examined the moments and contexts dominated by positive asymmetry. But illustrating this particular way of seeing and documenting its widespread occurrence represents only the first of this book's many tasks. Having established the prevalence of positive asymmetry, one is prompted to ask how—*how* has this biased view become such a well-entrenched dimension of quality assessment and perception? In chapter 3, I explore this issue in detail, with the inquiry leading to the realm of cultural practices.

CHAPTER THREE

Practicing Positive Asymmetry

In chapter 2, I documented the overwhelming presence of positive asymmetry in everyday life. I showed how this way of seeing dominates perceptions of quality in vast numbers of social and cultural contexts and at various levels of social interaction. Such a widespread sociocultural phenomenon does not arise spontaneously. Rather, it is the product of what social scientists refer to as cultural practices.

Cultural practices—the term is widely used in the literature. But sociologist Ann Swidler provides us with perhaps the most succinct definition of the concept. For Swidler, cultural practices are means by which individuals, groups, and communities "reproduce, resist, or change social structures and rules." They do so not in a vigilant or fully cognizant way, but by invoking "unconscious, embodied, or habitual actions." Thus, cultural practices are not openly articulated plans. Rather, they are "the routines of institutions and actors."[1]

In elaborating on practices, Swidler raises two additional points that are especially relevant to my argument. First, while unconscious or habitual, cultural practices are nevertheless highly directed action. Thus, in the context of this study, one can say that the practices used to distance the worst from our perceptual portholes are not haphazard or accidental. Rather, they are strategic and oriented to practical outcomes—outcomes, I would argue, of shared relevance to the group or community in which they occur, outcomes often reflecting the core interests of that group or community. Second, practices involve both doing and thinking. While they are behaviors, they are behaviors that are systematically organized by the habitus, the internalized system of durable, transposable dispositions that arises from the patterns of action that structure social domains—a kind of master blueprint that outlines the ways things are or the way things work. It is critical to recognize this link between thinking and behaving, for it is this sociocognitive element that makes the execution of practices seem intuitive or automatic. In the pages to follow, we will see that cultural practices are integral to our understanding of positive asymmetry and its prevalence. Readers will witness a variety of ways in which such practices distance the worst, foreground the best, and thus entrench a perceptual bias within groups and communities. Given their importance to the evaluative process, it seems critical to identify and dissect these cultural strategies. But that task will demand a focused effort. Because cultural practices are routine, they often seem second nature. As a consequence, they can disappear into the fabric of everyday life. Like most routines and conventions, we must step back from action before we can appreciate the scope, true workings, and the impact that practices can have on the life of a group or community. Toward that end, this chapter adopts a wide-angle analytic lens, allowing us to isolate and carefully unpack three sets of practices that both initiate and sustain positive asymmetry. The first set involves what I call "eclipsing practices." Eclipsing practices render the worst of people, places, objects, and events functionally invisible. The second set comprises "clouding practices"; these are routines that keep the worst visible but vaguely defined. The third set involves "recasting practices." Recasting practices redefine the worst as something positive and good. Examples will help me both explicate these practices and illustrate them in action. And when this review is complete, readers will see the mutually constitutive nature of cultural practices and the cognitive categories they create and sustain.

Eclipsing Practices: The Functional Invisibility of the Worst

Across cultures and throughout history, one can identify recurring strategies designed to distance the worst from a group's or community's vantage point. Such "eclipsing practices" hide the worst in a community's perceptual field; they render it functionally invisible—obliterated in the normal range of sight. Eclipsing practices establish positive asymmetry in the extreme. By virtually eliminating a group's "sins," these practices vigorously prioritize the body's "virtues."

It is important to note that eclipsing practices involve much more than simple denial.[2] For unlike denial, where the very existence of a person, place, object, or event is immediately and completely repressed, eclipsing demands—indeed, is initiated by—a moment of clear acknowledgment. The collective avowal of the worst is critical to the practice, for identification is integral to the worst's eventual partitioning or removal. Thus, eclipsing rests on the premise that groups and communities know the worst when they see it; but upon acknowledging it, they will disavow it; after recognizing it, they will release it from focus. In this way, eclipsing dismantles any notion of a quality continua, for the practice ensures that quality "lows" are truncated in actual experience.

In this section, I highlight three common eclipsing practices, strategies so well entrenched in groups and communities that their execution seems automatic and natural: banishment, physical seclusion, and shunning.

Banishment

Banishment is an age-old eclipsing practice executed in both myth and reality. The strategy has one clear objective, namely, to completely expunge the worst from a group's or community's everyday consciousness. By so doing, the practice frees a community from regularly encountering its least admirable or least productive elements. In defining banishment, it is important to note that the practice is, indisputably, a sociocultural phenomenon, for the process relies on interactive affirmations and agreements. Further, the practice demands a collective "thrust." Members of a group or community must come together to acknowledge the worst, ritualistically strike it from view, and then, together, obliterate it from memory.

Some of the world's earliest religious teachings actively promote banishment. Such scriptures and parables forward this eclipsing strategy as the social control mechanism of choice. Consider, for example, one of Greek mythology's primary stories—the story of Zeus. Here banishment proves central to the god's rise to glory. According to myth, Zeus is the son of Cronus, an evil power monger.[3] Disgusted by his father's wickedness, Zeus battles Cronus and eventually captures his throne. With this victory, Zeus emerges as the god of the sky and the ruler of the Olympian gods. But despite his supremacy, despite his power to annihilate, Zeus chooses not to destroy Cronus or his Titan warriors. Rather, Zeus banishes those he has conquered. In sending his enemies to Tartarus, the lowest, darkest, most obscure region of the underworld, Zeus, like other mythical gods, establishes an evaluative convention. He concedes the presence of evil but then quietly eclipses it from view. Stripped of execution's fanfare and martyrdom's glory, banishment precludes evil from mesmerizing the active considerations of the righteous.

This same tactic is espoused in another of the Greeks' most famous myths: the story of Oedipus. Oedipus kills King Laius, and he takes the king's widow as his wife. But he later discovers that Laius was his father, and that he has married his own mother. Upon realizing his sins, Oedipus pronounces himself the most heinous of men. He sees only one resolution to his dilemma. He does not take his life; he does not seek repentance. Rather, he decides to "purge Thebes of his pollution."[4] Oedipus blinds himself and asks the elder Creon to banish him to the wilderness. With this action, Oedipus reifies the eclipsing strategy as a "normal" response to evil.

The Greeks were not alone in choosing to banish the worst of people, places, objects, and events. We read of the practice in the core stories of Judeo-Christian teachings as well. Recall the tale of Lucifer, the fallen angel. Tradition describes Lucifer as one of God's most brilliant creations, an angel with the "brightness of the morning star."[5] But Lucifer's magnificence proves the seed of his demise; he becomes too enamored of his own beauty and power. Driven by pride, he commits the worst of sins—pronouncing himself superior to his creator.[6] After declaring himself supreme, Lucifer attempts to take control of heaven. He initiates a war against the forces of good, vying for dominion over water, air, earth, and fire. Ultimately, Lucifer loses his fight with righteousness. And for our purposes, it is interesting to note the manner in which the worst of all angels is punished. God neither destroys nor forgives Lucifer, both clearly options in resolving the angel's offense. God does not place Lucifer on display so as to encourage others to avoid Lucifer's path. Rather, in punishment for his unspeakable pride, God banishes Lucifer from heaven. As we read in Ezekiel 28:15–16, Michael the Archangel casts Lucifer into the fires of hell, where he is eternally eclipsed from the community of heaven.

The practice applied to Lucifer's worst-case offense represents a biblical routine, a common method of eclipsing the worst in the perceptual porthole of the righteous. Thus, in Genesis 3:23–24, when Adam and Eve question the supremacy of their creator, God demands not death, but a severance from his divinity. In retribution for their most dire transgression, God banishes the couple from paradise, forcing them to live outside his grace.[7] Even biblical characters with longstanding records of righteousness routinely fall victim to banishment. Throughout the Bible, a single act of defiance can elicit this normative response. Recall, for example, that Moses, God's beloved and chosen messenger, is banned from entering the Promised Land, "presumably because of a momentary lack of trust in God at the Water of Contradiction."[8] Similarly, Jesus banishes his once cherished apostle Judas Iscariot from the Passover supper when he learns of Judas' treasonous plans. This act is especially symbolic, for Christianity teaches that the Last Supper established the rite of the modern Eucharist. Thus, to be exiled from this event was to be expunged from Christianity itself.

Like the rulers of mythical Greece, like the God and prophets of Jews and

Christians, the laws of Islam prescribe banishment for the very worst offenders, most notably, those who question Allah and his teachings. In this regard,
the Qur'an commands, "Because they resisted Allah and His Messenger . . .
Allah has decreed banishment for them." Similarly, the book of Al-Ahzab
recommends that communities wipe themselves clean of those who question Islamic prophets: "On the Day when their faces will be tossed about
in the Fire, they will say, 'Woe to us! Would that we had obeyed Allah and
obeyed the Messenger!' . . . Our Lord! Give them double suffering, and banish them utterly from Your Grace!" A similar directive comes from Surah An
Nisa 34, where women are warned that defying one's husband is equal to
defying Allah's supremacy. And in committing such an act, women should
automatically expect to be rendered invisible: "Good women are the obedi-
ent, guarding in secret that which Allah hath guarded. As for those from
whom ye fear rebellion, admonish them and banish them to beds apart, and
scourge them."[9]

The stories and scriptures of all these religions establish a system that
plucks out sinners, rids the community of evil, and abolishes evil's presence
in daily experience. In so doing, religious doctrine works to initiate and sustain positive asymmetry. For in banishing the worst, evil is acknowledged
but never scrutinized, present but never articulated, eclipsed in conscious
consideration. In its wake, the best remain centered in the community's perceptual field. Hailed, exalted, and uncontested, the best lay the path to follow, the action to emulate, the primary model of human experience.

⌒∞⌒

Early religious teachings established banishment as a conventional response
to the worst. And subsequent legends and fairy tales reinforced and sustained
that message. These "lighthearted" cultural products carried religious lessons to new contexts and new arenas, weaving asymmetrical visions of moral
quality into the broader fabric of communal knowledge. As one reviews
medieval, Renaissance, and modern tales, banishment easily emerges as an
automatic, seemingly natural response to a community's worst entities.

The brothers Grimm, keepers of Germany's traditional fairy tales, provide perhaps the clearest evidence of this trend. Indeed, I analyzed the fifty-
five tails published in the first English translation of the Grimm brothers'
work, stories that represented centuries of German folklore.[10] In the thirty-
two tales in which punishment was involved, 60 percent of the guilty were
banished rather than killed. The same trend characterizes the stories of

Hans Christian Andersen, a near contemporary of the Grimms'. Andersen's tales are more lighthearted than the Grimms' and do not generally dwell on punishment. Yet, when punishment occurs, banishment proves the most popular form. "The Ugly Duckling" provides a prototypical example. Recall that in this story, a mother duck patiently awaits the hatching of her brood. But one of the mother's eggs fails to hatch with the rest. When the latecomer finally arrives, its appearance shocks its mother. "So large and gray! Even his mother had to admit that he was rather ugly."[11] While the mother duck tries to tolerate her newborn's "differences," others in the community are far less kind:

> Everyone was mean to the ugly duckling. Some ducks bit him. Some made fun of him. The chickens and geese teased him and bullied him. And the turkey cock, who acted as if *he* were king of the barnyard, said, "That duckling is so ugly I can't bear to look at him." Then he flew at the duckling and scratched him with his claws. The ugly duckling's brothers and sisters were not kind to him either. "Oh, you ugly creature," they scoffed whenever they saw him. "How we wish the cat would get you!"

The ugly duckling represents the worst example of the species. And eventually, even the duckling's mother comes to wish that "he would just disappear." And so begins the ugly duckling's banishment. Moving from marsh to countryside, he is routinely eclipsed from each new community because of his loathsome appearance.

The routinization of banishment as a response to the worst is not simply a western phenomenon. The practice emerged in Middle Eastern fairy tales as well. Consider "The Enchanted Stork," a popular story that recounts the experiences of the Islamic ruler Calif and his trusted vizier Ali ben Manzar. As the story goes, Calif's evil brother Omar plots to steal Calif's throne. He hires a sorcerer to cast an evil spell on Calif and Ali ben Manzar. The sorcerer offers his victims magic snuff, which turns them into storks and forces them into the wild. Eventually, Calif and Ali ben Manzar discover a way to break this curse. They then reclaim their human forms and recapture Calif's throne in Baghdad. Ruler once again, Calif must bring his brother to justice. What does Calif choose as a punishment for this worst of crimes? "For your treason, I should behead you," proclaims Calif. "But instead I will banish you by shipping you to the farthest end of the earth."[12] In the world of Islamic make-believe, Calif's response is predictable. Like the rulers of other tales, the Islamic king views banishment as his most powerful tool. In eclipsing

any remnant of Omar's existence—including his corpse, grave, or memory—
Calif renders his brother's actions invisible as well.

⸎

Banishment proves the punishment of choice in the world of fiction and
myth. But to be sure, it is a real-world practice as well. Indeed, banishment
predates modern incarceration as a form of punishment. The ancient Greeks
and the ancient Hebrews automatically applied banishment for those offenses considered the most heinous in nature—homicide chief among them.
The early Romans espoused a similar philosophy. Historical records indicate
that the Romans favored banishment over all other forms of punishment
(including execution).[13] In Roman society, torture and execution were
thought to prolong the evildoer's presence and, thus, to pollute the community. Such punishments often involved rituals that inadvertently spotlighted
criminals, perhaps raising them to the level of martyrs, centralizing them in
collective memory. But for the Romans, banishment represented an act of
purification. Divorced from the retribution of an "eye for an eye," banishment ensured a complete severance and immateriality. Rather than holding
the worst up to scrutiny, allowing it to be studied and itemized, banishment
allowed the Romans to eclipse the culprit as a potential reference point of
moral action.

   We may be tempted to think of banishment as an ancient eclipsing practice, but the strategy exhibits true staying power. Until 1776, for example,
some of England's worst criminals were banished to the American colonies.
(Note that the loss of the colonies did not dampen England's enthusiasm for
the practice. After 1776, England's criminals were simply redirected to Australian penal settlements.) In its early years, the U.S. government adopted
banishment as well, reserving the treatment for those deemed the worst
political threats. Traitors and seditionists were routinely isolated offshore
and barred from material or symbolical links to the nation. Halfway across
the world, both the Russian czars and the Communist leaders who succeeded
them adopted banishment as well. Indeed, banishment to Siberia was the
routine punishment for those who threatened the social order. Popularized
in 1858 when Russia regained control of the Siberian territories, the practice
escalated during the Russian Revolution, and peaked under the reign of
Stalin (1928–53), when tens of millions of criminals and political dissenters
were deported to brutal Siberian detention camps.[14]

   Given the longstanding practice of banishment, we should not be surprised to find contemporary communities that favor the practice in their

treatment of the worst. Many Native American tribes, for example, retain banishment as a viable form of justice. Of course, the practice is used sparingly, reserved for especially heinous crimes, particularly those of a cross-cultural nature. (Cross-cultural crimes are treated as "double-loaded" actions, because they bring both adversity to the victim and shame to the perpetrator's nation.) Like the rituals exercised in earlier historical eras, Native American banishment begins with a clear acknowledgment of the offender and deed. The practice concludes with a collective dismissal of the worst, a condemnation to an eclipsed existence. Robert Ward discusses the end result: "The banishment inmate is not greeted in any fashion. There are no buildings, no telephone lines, basically there is a complete notice of isolation from the lack of any evidence of civilization."[15]

In practice, banishment destroys an individual's viability in the community. Thus, those wishing to retain either presence or power must fight this sentence above all else. Historians tell us, for example, that Napoleon Bonaparte welcomed death in battle, calling it "an elevation," a vehicle to a permanent place in collective memory. But he referred to the St. Helena banishment as the worst of fates, describing it as both a physical and historical death sentence.[16] We witness the same sentiment among the participants in many of the world's contemporary political conflicts. Consider, for example, Yasser Arafat's response when, in 2002, Israeli prime minister Ariel Sharon revealed a plan to banish him from the region. (In essence, the plan harkened back to a previous policy. Sharon had forced Arafat out of Beirut in 1982; Arafat remained exiled in Tunisia until 1994.) Arafat's reply to the proposal was strong, immediate, and unmistakably clear: "I am telling them, I prefer to be martyred."[17] For Arafat, banishment could never be an acceptable resolution to conflict. For unlike death in battle, banishment carries the potential for irrelevance. When one is not seen, one is not heard, and silence is rarely an effective weapon of political combat.

Saddam Hussein surely understood that point, for he voiced similar sentiments at the onset of the 2003 Iraqi War. When Bahrain, Libya, and North Korea offered him exile, when France, Russia, Saudi Arabia, Turkey, and the United States offered to mediate his banishment from Iraq, Saddam and his government "vociferously rejected" the option, "angrily dismissing the diplomats" who proposed it.[18] In an interview with Dan Rather of CBS News, Saddam explained his decision:

> We will die here in Iraq. We will die in this country and we will maintain our honor. The honor that is required of our people. I believe that whoever asks Saddam to or, offers Saddam asylum in his own country, is in

fact a person without morals because he will be directing an insult to the Iraqi people.[19]

Clearly, Saddam's acceptance of banishment might have prevented war; banishment certainly would have assured his safe relocation. Yet Saddam also understood banishment's potential to eclipse not just his power but his legacy. For those fighting for political viability, life on the perceptual fringe is far less valuable than death in a burst of glory.[20]

꒰∞꒱

Thus far, I have confined my remarks to the banishment of people. But when objects or events exemplify the worst in a group, banishment is often used to eclipse these entities in a community's perceptual field. In past research, I have noted this phenomenon in the treatment of national symbols.[21] At particular historical moments, national governments define existing symbols as detrimental to the goals of their regimes. In such cases, leaders ban these signifiers, eclipsing "evil" ideologies that may threaten governmental control. After the French Revolution, for example, the new French government banned "La Marseillaise," fearing its potentially dire effects "on the passions of the excitable French people." Years later, Napoleon III outlawed the anthem as well, deeming it too dangerous for public consumption. And in Germany, both Bismarck and Hitler banned the German tricolor flag, linking it to the worst defeats and shames of the nation's past.

When declaring independence, new nations often banish the symbols of their former colonial rulers. Colonial symbols can signify grave oppression, and banishment becomes a means of eclipsing the colonial experience in collective memory. Romanian revolutionaries, for example, adopted this practice throughout the 1989 uprising. Years later, Croat and Slovenian revolutionaries followed suit. Readers may recall that these protestors literally cut Communist ornaments from their national flags. By banishing these remnants, revolutionaries hoped to eclipse the worst of their Communist pasts from their new governments' political fields. Similarly, with the fall of the Soviet Union in 1991, Soviet symbols were linked with the worst of times. Such symbols were necessarily banished by many of the reconstituted national governments. In Lithuania, citizens danced on a toppled statue of Lenin; in Russia, plans were made to dismantle Lenin's burial shrine; at the United Nations, the Russian flag replaced the Soviet flag. With these acts, the Soviet Union was driven from active focus while the reinstated nations were brought to the foreground of the international stage.

It is also quite common for invading forces to banish the symbols of the countries they occupy. With such action, invaders erase the old national order from collective vision. The Japanese, for example, invoked this strategy during their occupation of Korea (1910–45). Initially, the Japanese banished the Korean flag and Korean currency. Later, their efforts grew more dramatic as they outlawed the Korean language and traditional Korean surnames. Via banishment, the Japanese tried to obliterate Korea's very history. In so doing, they hoped to move Koreans to the new Japanese regime's perceptual port-hole. The Americans invoked similar thinking during the 2003 invasion of Baghdad. Recall that as American soldiers entered the city, they encircled a prominent statue of Saddam Hussein. Before the statue was toppled, a U.S. soldier climbed up and covered the face of Saddam with an American flag. This brief but powerful action literally eclipsed the image of the "evildoer." But more important, the action signaled an active campaign designed to expunge Saddam from the Iraqi landscape.

⌒∞⌒

The banishment of undesirable objects is not confined to the national stage. This practice occurs in local contexts as well. Consider, for example, the very common phenomenon of banishing books from local schools and libraries. For centuries, book banning has been promoted as a means to protect communities from exposure to the era's worst sins. Thus, after its banning of *Hansel and Gretel*, California's Mt. Diablo school district defended its actions, arguing that it was necessary to counter a harmful attitude—namely, "that it is acceptable to kill witches and paint witches as child-eating monsters."[22] In Minnesota, Michigan, New York, California, and South Carolina, several schools banned *Of Mice and Men*, fearing that the book's presence in consciousness would encourage unthinkable behaviors—"triggering kids to pull out guns and kill their friends."[23] In Rockford, Illinois, city council members banned *Always Running*, a book about life in Los Angeles street gangs. Council member Ed Sharpe commented, "I challenge anyone who knows how the mind works, after reading this book, not to be more likely to assume the lifestyle of a gang person and not to be more likely to have sex in the back of a car." In banishing the book, the city council openly embraced the belief that "out of sight," would indeed mean "out of mind."[24]

It is worth noting that the U.S. Senate has been known to adopt such logic. In 1954, the Senate investigated links between comic books and growing rates of juvenile delinquency. Based on their investigation, Senate committee members drafted a set of quality standards for the comic book industry, standards that called for the complete banishment of "evil" actions and thoughts. The Senate standards demanded that "scenes of excessive violence shall be prohibited"; that "scenes of brutal torture, excessive and unnecessary knife and gun play, physical agony, gory and gruesome crime shall be eliminated"; that "no comic magazine shall use the word 'horror' or 'terror' in its title"; that "all scenes of horror, excessive bloodshed, gory or gruesome crimes, depravity, lust, sadism, masochism shall not be permitted"; and that "all lurid, unsavory, gruesome illustrations shall be eliminated." In essence, the Senate banished all references to the worst of human behaviors.[25]

Before we close this section, it is worth noting the lighter side of banishment. Some use the practice to eclipse what they consider to be the worst trends in popular culture. Consider, for example, that since 1976 Lake Superior State University has issued a "List of Words Banished from the Queen's English for Mis-Use, Over-use, or General Uselessness." Each year, the college accepts open nominations and ultimately selects a group of the worst English words and phrases—language, they argue, that should be permanently banned from the lexicon. Here are a few of the entries (along with their year of banishment): "I know where you're coming from" (1978), "paying my dues" (1981), "live audience" (1983, 1987, 1990), "minor emergency clinic" (1986), "free gift" and "networking" (1988), "forced relaxation" (1989), "almost exactly" (1990), "win-win" (1993), "He/she just doesn't get it" and "threepeat" (1994), "information superhighway" (1995), "Been there, done that" and "dialoguing" (1996), "Don't go there," "multi-tasking," and "You go girl" (1997), "Yadda yadda yadda" (1998), "You da Man" (1999), "Thinking outside the box" and "24/7" (2000), "fuzzy math" (2001), "friendly fire" and "no-brainer" (2002), "undisclosed secret location" (2003), "sanitary land fill" and "bling" (2004), "flip-flopper" and "fishizzle" (2005).[26] Of course, there is a tongue-in-cheek element to the group's efforts, but the positive asymmetry they promote is nevertheless familiar. By eclipsing intolerable words and phrases within the language, the group aims to purify the lexicon and focus users on the linguistic ideal.

Physical Seclusion

There are, of course, other means by which to eclipse the worst, particularly when we look to the traditions of Western Europe. As opposed to the harsh permanence of banishment, the worst entities may be temporarily distanced in a community's awareness. Consider, for example, that since the late eighteenth century, those designated as the worst specimens of humanity—the insane, the downtrodden, the criminal, and the diseased—have been physically sequestered, deliberately hidden from public view. Initially in the West, institutions such as the insane asylum, the almshouse, and the penitentiary provided a new approach to dealing with society's worst, one considered less drastic than banishment and less vengeful than older rituals of degradation and punishment. By the end of the nineteenth century, institutional seclusion had become a popular and convenient option for eclipsing evil in the eyes of the righteous.

Physical seclusion, like banishment, is a two-stage process. It begins with the acknowledgment of the worst, and is followed by the worst's suppression. Yet, in contrast to banishment, physical seclusion involves an element of organized control. This is because seclusionary vehicles such as the insane asylum, the almshouse, and the penitentiary were designed to separate a "vessel" from its "contents." Such institutions were not intended to permanently eclipse worst-case entities. Rather, they worked to expunge the thoughts and behaviors, the motives and desires, that defined and drove "deviant" individuals. In essence, physical seclusion offered the potential for a "cure." Thus, the target's isolation was presumed temporary. Grounded in the hope of reform, seclusion promised to return a member in good standing to the community.

In his classic book *The Discovery of the Asylum*, social historian David Rothman recounts the painstaking care with which early asylum patients were deliberately separated from the community. According to Rothman, asylums were "built at a distance from centers of population." Further, "the institution was to have a country location with ample grounds, to sit on a low hillside with an unobstructed view of a surrounding landscape." To reinforce this isolation, the asylum was to ban "casual visitors and patients' families."[27] These design directives were never intended to be cruel or punishing. Rather, reformers believed that submersion in settings of strict, protected order would stimulate patients' rehabilitation. Behind the closed doors of the asylum, hidden from the sight of the community, the imposed physical order would breed mental order.

Reformers' positions were admirable, but their goals were rarely realized. Indeed, as Rothman indicates, in practice, physical seclusion proved no better than the strategies it was designed to replace: "Institutional programs (such as the asylum) had a pragmatic quality . . . they were workable substitutes for the stock and edicts of banishment." In his view, "the promise of reform had built up the asylums; but the functionalism of custody perpetuated them."[28] Thus, asylums persisted, indeed became a routine treatment. But, in truth, they came to fill a social need that reformers had not anticipated. The isolation so vital to the organization of mental care provided a surprisingly handy vehicle by which a community could completely eclipse the most imperfect of its members.

Social historian William Staples makes a similar case in chronicling the establishment of almshouses in America. Staples recounts a vision of the poor as a scourge to city streets, and he reviews seventeenth-century Americans' struggle to remove this group from their perceptual field. In the early 1800s, laws prohibiting public begging became increasingly popular, with many advocating prison as a means for secluding the poor from view. But reformers of the era proposed a "kinder, gentler solution," establishing almshouses as a remedy for the growing numbers of homeless and downtrodden. Almshouses were touted as a humane gesture to those "down on their luck." At the same time, such institutions offered clear, and less noble, advantages for those addressing societies' worst economic problems:

> [Almshouses] isolated the dependent from the growing middle-class community, who increasingly considered the pauper an idler and a troublemaker. Rather than having the indigent scattered around town in private dwellings, or worse yet, begging on street corners, the almshouse centralized relief administration and provided more effective surveillance of their activities by one overseer."[29]

Almshouses emerged none too soon. For as the nineteenth century progressed, economic depressions and rising immigration multiplied the number of U.S. poor. Hiding this group from sight became an increasingly pressing need. As a result, almshouses became more numerous and, ostensibly, more specialized. In keeping with the reformist philosophy of the period, the poor were assigned to specific institutions on the basis of their particular "defects," a strategy designed to increase the institutions' usefulness. But even with the increased specialization of the almshouse system, charity of heart gave way to the pragmatic needs of the day. In the final analysis, almshouses proved largely ineffective at solving the poverty problem. They lived on, however, because they proved fabulously successful at eclipsing the poor within growing middle-class communities.

Secluding the poor is, of course, not simply a practice of old. This approach to poverty persists in contemporary times. In the United States, present-day politicians often make seclusion a routine response to the urban poor. Recall that Rudy Giuliani, New York City's controversial mayor (1994–2002), ordered numerous sweeps of the city during his two terms in office. Giuliani's policy rested on his "declaration of war" against those he called "public nuisances." (For Giuliani, the term encompassed prostitutes, the homeless, panhandlers, squeegee men, graffiti artists, drunkards, and noise-makers.)[30] During the winter holidays, a period of increased tourism, Giuliani believed it was especially important to eclipse such groups. Thus, he intensi-fied the sweeps, in an admitted effort to protect the wealthy and middle classes from the very sight of the poor. Giuliani was certainly not alone in this regard. Reporter Brad Smith recounts similar efforts made by mayors across the country:

> Miami was sued by the American Civil Liberties Union and 500 vagrants 12 years ago for sweeping its streets before major national events, some-times burning vagrants' properties in bonfires. . . . Other cities, with tol-erant images, such as Seattle, are accused of conducting police sweeps, especially before high-profile events such as last fall's protester-disrupted World Trade Organization convention.[31]

Civil protests aside, seclusion remains the treatment of choice for the ranks of the urban poor. And modern means of seclusion are growing more and more creative. For example, during a campaign designed to bring the 2012 Olympic Games to New York City, Giuliani's successor, Michael Bloomberg, pro-posed collecting the city's homeless and "relocating" them to several retired cruise ships docked off Manhattan. There, afloat beyond the city's solid bor-ders, the poor would simply be eclipsed from everyday urban experience.

⌀∞⌀

The physical seclusion of a society's worst is, perhaps, most obvious when we look to the practice of criminal incarceration. Since the eighteenth cen-tury, the United States has routinely sequestered its legal offenders, effec-tively eclipsing criminals from the daily experience of the law abiding. His-torian Orlando Lewis documents this shift, as he traces the treatment of criminals in U.S. cities.[32] Philadelphia offers a particularly illustrative case. In 1786, Philadelphia enacted the "wheelbarrow law," a precursor of sorts to modern-day prison-work programs. The statute allowed prisoners to labor in city streets, working under the surveillance of armed guards. Initially, the program was lauded as a productive arrangement for the state. But before long, Philadelphians objected vociferously to the prisoners' immediacy. City residents complained that the very sight of the criminals was too offensive to bear; they demanded that the wheelbarrow law be overturned. It was. A new law, enacted on March 27, 1789, confined criminals to private punishment, and sentences were served in seclusion at the Walnut Street Jail.[33]

Over the next thirty years, isolated incarceration emerged as routine justice. By 1821, for example, Pennsylvania moved to a formal prison system, with state laws establishing elaborate institutions in the eastern and western sections of the state. Connecticut converted an old mine near Simsbury to a state prison, and there, the most dangerous of criminals were sequestered from the law-abiding community. Massachusetts imprisoned its most violent criminals at Castle Island, an isolated military post in Boston Harbor. Indeed, by the middle of the nineteenth century, most U.S. states had well-established penal systems in which the worst were automatically isolated from the community at large.[34]

As the eclipsing of criminals grew in popularity, so too did the eclipsing of their deaths.[35] During the 1800s, state after state outlawed public execution. By the 1930s, only a handful maintained the tradition. Rainey Bethea, the last person publicly executed on U.S. soil, was killed in Owensboro, Kentucky, before a crowd of some twenty thousand. The Bethea story is interesting because the circumstances of his death convinced "straggler" states to seclude the execution ritual.

Sheriff Florence Thompson, a widow and mother of four, was responsible for carrying out Bethea's hanging. The event garnered enormous public attention as newspapers from across the country rushed to cover the first female-performed execution in U.S. history. But reporters' efforts were foiled. At the last minute, Thompson, worried about her place in the community, relegated the grisly task to her deputy Arthur Hash:

> Journalists were livid that Thompson had ducked the task. Wielding their pens like clubs, they turned their wrath on the crowd and on the town, exaggerating an event that needed no embellishment. Stories portrayed Owensboro as "The Center of Barbarism," and as the proud sponsor of a "Picnic Hanging" and a "Roman Holiday." Headlines screamed: "Children Picnic as Killer Pays," and "They Ate Hot Dogs While a Man Died on the Gallows."[36]

In essence, journalists thrust capital punishment's worst possible images before the eyes of the public, and the public response was fierce—so fierce, in fact, that the Kentucky General Assembly voted to abolish public execution. The few U.S. states clinging to public execution quickly followed Kentucky's lead. Thus, in 1936, secluded execution became an American universal. The worst of criminals were now quietly "erased," generally in the dark of night. (Indeed, U.S. law requires that executions occur between midnight and sunrise—regulations dubbed in certain locations as the "midnight assassination" laws.)[37]

In the years that followed the Bethea execution, U.S. courts and prisons embraced secluded executions with a newfound enthusiasm. Historian Francis Allen tells us that the U.S. legal system became quite fixated on routinizing the technique:

> Remarkable legislation, clearly invalid by modern constitutional standards, not only barred reporters from attending executions, but also provided fines for newspapers that published any accounts of executions going beyond mere announcements of their occurrence. Even today the sensitivity of officials to close media scrutiny of the conduct of executions is often acute, sometimes bordering on paranoid. . . . There has developed in this country a system sometimes consciously calculated to foster ignorance of the realities of capital punishment.[38]

In essence, secluded executions have proved a satisfactory solution for American communities. On the one hand, the absence of public ritual keeps the worst of criminals eclipsed in a community's consciousness. But secluded execution provides an additional benefit. Cloaking executions in darkness and secrecy also allows the community to avoid the knowledge of its own actions—to completely distance itself from the barbaric nature of its punishment of the worst.[39]

In commenting on the physical seclusion of criminals, two related points bear mentioning. First, note that those intent on centering the worst in a community's perceptual porthole (whistleblowers, consumer watchdogs, and the like) may well find themselves eclipsed along with the crimes and perpetrators they address. In groups and communities dedicated to distancing the worst from view, challengers to the practice become threats to order, and thus they too may be punished for violating the community's established view of reality. Similarly, those who, intentionally or not, put a face on the worst of crimes—victims of heinous acts such as murder, rape, and child molestation, for example—are often eclipsed along with their attackers. Thus the press routinely withholds the names of rape victims. Victims of child molestation generally remain anonymous. And in the case of taboos such as suicide, many newspapers refuse to report the very commission of the crime. Without a face, without a tangible persona, the horror of heinous crimes remains abstract and vague. By keeping such victims anonymous and invisible, groups and communities also keep victims' horrific fates unavailable for conscious scrutiny.

∽◯◯∽

Asylums, poorhouses, and prisons are the most familiar vehicles of physical seclusion. But the practice emerges in other domains as well. Consider the frequency with which seclusion is invoked in the treatment of physical illness. Patients who suffer the worst of medical fates—a fatal or highly debilitating disease—are typically clustered together and separated from patients with more positive prognoses. The eclipsing of worst-case patients can be traced to the ancients' establishment of leper colonies. Note, for example, the directives provided in Leviticus 13:45–46:

> The leper who has the disease shall wear torn clothes and let the hair of his head hang loose, and he shall cover his upper lip and cry, "Unclean, unclean." He shall remain unclean as long as he has the disease; he is unclean; he shall dwell alone in a habitation outside the camp.

The spontaneous healing of leprosy was extremely rare. Thus, most lepers lived in isolation in the wilderness. Even now, thousands of years later, this treatment strategy persists. Leper colonies in places such as Carrville, Louisiana, or the Hawaiian island of Molokai isolate the afflicted; only caregivers are permitted to establish physical contact. Such seclusion marks the presence of the worst, acknowledging the horror of the disease. Yet the practice also ensures that group or community members can avoid seeing, hearing, or touching someone they consider an abomination.

In contemporary settings, seclusion often surrounds issues of death and dying. Witness the remoteness of any hospital morgue. Morgues are rarely identified to the general public, and they are quite deliberately secluded in low-traffic areas of the hospital complex. Removed from the foreground of everyday experience, the dead are eclipsed in the land of the living; they constitute the invisible inhabitants of the hospital community. Similarly, patients with terminal prognoses are typically relegated to secluded hospital wards—intensive care sections, oncology units, AIDS wards, and so forth. Such patients are denied general access and are often separated by visible barriers. And terminal patients often report psychological barriers as well. Indeed, research reveals a significant difference in caretaker-patient interactions. For example, hospital caretakers exhibit greater detachment toward terminal versus nonterminal patients; they also make less eye contact, hold less conversation, and respond more slowly to terminal patients. Family interactions between the living and the dying prove quite different as well. Research shows that family visitations to the terminally ill are less frequent and shorter in length than visits to those with less serious ailments.[40]

Secluding the worst—it is a system that occurs in nursing homes and long-term care facilities as well. Indeed, inhabitants of nursing homes are frequently assigned or located with reference to their degree of malady. The result, of course, means that the healthiest patients are located on the lower, most public floors of the facility. Those with the worst maladies are relegated to the higher, less public floors. And just as in hospitals, nursing homes and long-term care facilities keep death from the eyes of the living. In this regard, sociologist Timothy Diamond recounts some standard procedures:

> Under the dominance of the medical model, death takes on a particular social form. It is whisked away, covered, unspoken, treated in hushed tones as if the subject were taboo. "The Spanish man must have died last night," whispered Mrs. Dobbins. "That's the only time they close the doors around here. . . . Many residents . . . were spending the last years of their lives in an environment with no public forum to mourn together. Praying permeated the homes as a private act, but except for an occasional mass when a priest stopped in, not a public ritual expressing mourning.[41]

As a society, we do not commonly equate our treatment of the dead and dying with practices applied to our society's insane, downtrodden, and criminal. Yet, upon closer examination, it is clear that these groups share a similar fate. Once certified, the worst of each community are quickly eclipsed in common space, placed outside the bounds of routine experience.

Shunning

Shunning represents one final means by which groups and communities eclipse the worst. And like banishment and seclusion, the strategy has its own unique characteristics. Indeed, shunning may be the most demanding of the eclipsing practices heretofore reviewed. For while shunning is designed to extract the worst from a community's perceptual field, the strategy also demands that the shunned remain physically present in the community at large. How can something be eclipsed without completely segregating it? The prescription is quite straightforward. In shunning, community members must commit to a shared blindness. When someone (or something) is shunned, individuals must actively disavow those with whom they physically coexist. Further, they must reify that disavowal with overt behaviors. Thus, members of a community cannot eat, work, talk to, or live with a shunned individual. Family members may be forced to exclude blood relatives from their daily activities. In this way, the shunned remain in a group, but not of it—physically present yet functionally invisible.

The unique nature of shunning may rest in the logic that fuels the practice. For in essence, shunning takes the hopes of reform that drive the practice of physical seclusion and restates those hopes in the extreme. Eclipsing individuals within community life (a life those individuals can still see, hear, and feel) routinely bathing the shunned in the shame of neglect, conferring communal disdain via ostracism of the offender—such conduct becomes a powerful tool in eliciting repentance and reintegration. Communities committed to the practice of shunning firmly believe that this type of intense social pressure will discourage both the condemned behavior of the shunned and its imitation by others.

Like the other eclipsing practices reviewed thus far, shunning is typically reserved for the gravest infractions, in particular, those involving the rejection of a community's most sacred or central tenets. This pattern proves especially clear in highly traditional communities organized around a homogeneous system of values and beliefs. Consider, for example, the use of shunning in Judaism. In the early days of Judaism, classical Jewish law prescribed a variety of punishments for the worst of sinners and criminals—punishments that included stoning, burning, slaying, and strangling.[42] But for the past two thousand years, Jewish law has forbidden such violence, forwarding shunning and excommunication as more appropriate modes of control. On the surface, these changes in Jewish law seem quite humane. But one cannot underestimate the impact of shunning as it was practiced in the Talmudic era and the Middle Ages. Jewish law stripped the shunned offender of all communal rights; further, community members were instructed to regard the offender as dead. "In a closed and tightly knit community, surrounded by a general hostile society, exclusion from community life was a very severe matter." Indeed during the Talmudic era and the Middle Ages, "flogging was perceived as a more merciful punishment" than shunning.[43]

What offenses were sufficiently serious to require shunning or excommunication? The classical Jewish code lists a number of specific acts (the Talmud specifies twenty-four). But according to legal scholar Michael Broyde, the final imposition of shunning depended on more than the offense itself. The decision to shun was largely tied to the "publicness" of the offender's actions and the level of defiance with which the action was performed:

Adultery, polytheism, Sabbath violations, ritual violations and other central tenets of the faith were never subject to shunning by the Jewish tradition unless the person engaged in this conduct in a public manner intended to indicate defiance of the Jewish tradition. . . . [Shunning was reserved for] violations that appear to hinder the creation or maintenance of a community, and which can destroy the community if not stopped.

Since shunning was a matter of community preservation, the practice always involved a constructive element. And here lies the importance of retaining the shunned in the community's ranks. Indeed, Broyde tells us that "the purpose of the shunning . . . is to serve notice to the members of the community that this conduct is unacceptable, and also, secondarily, to encourage the violator to return to the community." Thus the presence of the offender is integral to the punishment's effectiveness. Her or his daily experience of shame and irrelevance forms the basis of possible repentance and core of community control.[44]

Shunning plays a similar role in many close-knit Christian denominations. Such groups couple ostracism with the community's hope for the offender's repentance and renewal. Among Jehovah's Witnesses, for example, shunning awaits those who break the religion's core beliefs (abandoning the fellowship, engaging in adultery or drunkenness, authorizing a blood transfusion, or communicating with a shunned community member):

> If . . . someone unrepentantly practices serious sins, . . . the congregation needs to be protected from their influence. . . . He will be disfellowshipped and such an individual is avoided by former fellow-worshipers . . . for the Bible clearly states: "Remove the wicked man from among yourselves." (1 Corinthians 5:13)

But as was true for Jews, the shunned Jehovah's Witness holds the power to reverse her or his fate:

> Every effort is made to help wrongdoers. . . . Disfellowshipped individuals may continue to attend religious services and, if they wish, they may receive spiritual counsel from the elders with a view to their being restored. They are always welcome to return to the faith if they reject the improper course of conduct for which they were disfellowshipped.[45]

The Old Order Amish, another Christian sect, forwards a similar position. Individuals who formally join the church and then violate their baptismal vows are shunned in accord with religious doctrine in a process the community refers to as "meidung." As in other religions, the practice is undeniably serious. Community members must sever routine contact with the offender; family members cannot welcome the shunned at their table. But like Jehovah's Witnesses, the Amish believe that the "invisible" shunned serve as conductors of good faith. According to church elders, "shunning is meant to be redemptive. It is not an attempt to harm or ruin the individual and in most cases it does bring that member back into the fellowship again."[46]

We may be tempted to think of shunning as a remnant of earlier times or a practice associated with society's most marginal groups. But in the contemporary era, many mainstream communities vigorously adopt the strategy. Recall, for example, the case of David Cash. In 1998, Cash witnessed his friend Jeremy Strohmeyer rape and kill a seven-year-old girl in a Las Vegas casino bathroom. By his own admission, Cash did nothing to stop the crime. He kept silent once it occurred and never reported the rape or murder to the police. Despite his negligence, prosecutors in the case saw no legal grounds for charging Cash; he was never prosecuted as a criminal accessory or for obstructing justice. But while the legal system failed to hold Cash culpable, those in Cash's local community had other ideas. A student at UC Berkeley, Cash found himself the victim of a campus shunning. His fellow students refused to talk with him, eat with him, or share dormitory space with him. Indeed, the social pressures of the shunning were so severe that "police at UC Berkeley quietly shadowed . . . Cash. . . . Bill Cooper, police captain at UC Berkeley, said authorities were concerned for Cash's safety."[47]

In their studies of the homeless, sociologists David Snow and Leon Anderson note that shunning is also quite commonly practiced on contemporary urban streets. The researchers note the routine ways in which most domiciled community members actively shun the homeless that sit or lie on the streets that both groups must share:

> Pedestrians frequently avert their eyes when passing the homeless on the sidewalk, and they often hasten their pace and increase the distance between themselves and the homeless when they sense they may be targeted by a panhandler. Pedestrians sometimes go so far as to cross the street in order to avoid the anticipated interaction with the homeless.[48]

Newly forming communities on the Internet also make ample use of shunning. Most group organizers identify the technique as a powerful tool for maintaining order. Because of its popularity, the practice of shunning is quite explicitly discussed in most chat room membership guidelines. For example, the moderators at Christian Chat, a group devoted to religious discussion, issue the following warning to their users: "All rooms are monitored by a staff of 150 volunteer cybercops who have the ability to boot and ban anyone whose conduct is not rated G (for Godly)."[49] Similarly, the administrators of BigDob's, a chat group for those interested in big Dobsonians telescopes, provide their users with active criteria for shunning:

1. Link a porno group. Sorry BigDob is not about that kind of heavenly body.
2. Make a post whose only purpose is to link a non-astronomy advertising site.
3. Threaten anyone. There's just no civil way to do that.
As a free bonus, we extend this service to emails sent directly to moderators.[50]

And the administrators of Embracing Mystery, a discussion board devoted to otherworldly experiences, are just as explicit in their cautioning:

The Administration can and will at its discretion, ban any member who is deemed to be a disruption to the forum, including, but not limited to, excessive rudeness, hostility, vulgarity, and attempts to interrupt the flow of the board. . . . The Administration runs this forum with a desire for fairness but in the end, has final say. If you do not find this acceptable, please find another board now. The Administration works hard here and will not put up with bullshit because some poster feels they have a "right" to be an asshole.[51]

When members are shunned, the reasons for the action are usually shared with the rest of the chat group. Indeed, in many cases, members in good standing can comment on the offender's actions. And like shunning as it is practiced in offline settings, offenders can be reinstated to the group if they show appropriate remorse. Indeed, many groups have elaborate warning systems that give offenders a chance to avoid this ultimate sanction.[52]

∽∞∾

As previously mentioned, shunning represents the trickiest of the eclipsing practices, for it requires community members to disavow someone or something that remains physically present. Thus shunning, unlike banishment and physical seclusion, often becomes a three-stage process. The worst are acknowledged, but before they can be rendered functionally invisible, they must be "marked" for diversion. (Hester Prynne's scarlet "A" offers, perhaps, the most infamous example of this.) According to sociologists Peter Berger and Thomas Luckmann, marking makes it easier for a community to "nihi-late" the shunned. Marking places community members on heightened alert, directing them to withhold the "respect and regard which the uncontami-nated aspects of [the shunned one's] social identity have led them to antici-pate extending." Thus, marking serves as a catalyst between identification and disavowal. It helps community members convert their worst to "a not to be taken seriously cognitive status," making it less difficult for them to deper-sonalize and "conceptually liquidate" what the worst represents.[53]

Marking is critical in settings where the shunned are integral to opera-tions and hence not realistically removed. Consider, for example, the set-tings *within* seclusionary institutions—mental health care facilities, pris-ons, and the like. Such settings force the "normal" staff to coexist with those labeled the worst. In such situations, the staff relies on marking to aid them in nihilating those they are responsible for. Years ago, psychologist David Rosenhan gave us a firsthand glimpse of this phenomenon when he and seven of his colleagues infiltrated the world of mental asylums. (Recall that Rosenhan and his colleagues faked symptoms of schizophrenia, gaining entry to several mental hospitals.) Rosenhan noted the power of diagnostic labels in marking the "insane." He noted as well the physical markings—clothing and ID bracelets, for example—that reinforced the patients' worst-case status. According to Rosenhan, these marks ensured that the staff would make no mistakes, thus enabling them to disavow and depersonalize patients who might otherwise present as normal:

> At times, depersonalization reached such proportions that pseudopa-tients had the sense that they were *invisible*, or at least unworthy of account. Upon being admitted, I and other pseudopatients took the initial physical examinations in a semipublic room, where staff members went about their own business as if *we were not there*. . . . [In another in-stance,] a nurse unbuttoned her uniform to adjust her brassiere in the presence of an entire ward of viewing men. One did not have the sense that she was being seductive. Rather, she *didn't notice us*.[54]

Charles Derber makes a similar point in studying the ease with which the wealthy can shun those who serve them. By marking servants via special at-tire and assigned routines, communities facilitate the attention deprivation so central to shunning:

The sweeper in the restaurant, for example, carries out his work in full view without anyone else noticing him and remains *unseen* unless he commits an offense which violates his role. . . . A cleaning lady, or other domestic servants, may glide through the house performing her duties *almost as a ghost*, without family members taking any note of her presence.[55]

Marking explains as well our ability to shun objects and places that are nevertheless concretely present in a social setting. This, after all, is the logic behind red-light districts. By highlighting areas of a city in which the worst moral behaviors occur, we allow the virtuous to avoid such places and disavow their existence. Similarly, combat or war zones, crime scenes, and disaster sites are duly designated, allowing the public to avoid the locations of worst-case scenarios. The same logic underpins both the CARA movie rating system and the recent ratings devised for television shows and videogames. The constitutional protection of free speech requires that R-, X-, or M-rated products remain on the social landscape. But by marking such images, rating systems allow potential viewers to avoid exposure.

Clouding Practices: Keeping the Worst Vague

Eclipsing practices—banishment, physical seclusion, and shunning—represent extreme reactions, for they functionally expunge target entities from conscious consideration. At certain times, however, such radical responses are neither viable nor possible. In such cases, clouding practices provide groups and communities with another means of distancing the worst from view.

Like eclipsing, clouding practices involve a moment of distinct identification, a time when group members acknowledge the worst and distinguish it from the best. But in clouding, identification is never followed by disavowal. Rather, the blocking and hiding so critical to eclipsing are systematically replaced by efforts that simply minimize and distort the worst.

Clouded entities are detectable, but blurred in their details. Indeed, one might say that clouding permits "nearsightedness" in a community. The practice makes the worst fuzzy and incomplete, and encourages groups and communities from pursuing the "correction" that would bring the worst into focus. Thus, clouding adjusts the impact of the worst, making its territory difficult to inhabit. Via clouding, the worst becomes the latent element of consciousness—present, but at play beneath the surface. Like static on a radio that makes it difficult to draw in certain sounds, clouding encourages us to abandon the worst-case signal, turn the dial, and tune in the clearer, more manifest best-case alternative.

In this chapter, I highlight two clouding strategies quite common to the perception of quality: impressionism and shadowing. Like the eclipsing practices earlier discussed, these strategies are institutionalized tactics that help to distance the worst in a community's perceptual field. Thus, just like banishment, seclusion, and shunning, the clouding practices discussed here have at their core one important component—the ability to establish and sustain positive asymmetry.

Impressionism

Impressionism, of course, is a word we generally associate with an artistic movement. The movement is famous for art that projects subtle suggestions rather than detailed reflections. For impressionists, the subject matter is "not an object, but an object as it is described by light."[56] Thus, the real center of a painting might be, not a bridge, but the fog that surrounds it, not a haystack, but the sun that dances upon it. This focus gives impressionist paintings a miragelike quality; they provide the viewer with patches of color and light that intimate the subject rather than define it.

Impressionism, as a clouding practice, mirrors the artistic technique. It provides a very subtle treatment of the worst people, places, objects, and events. Rather than explicating the details of such entities, impressionism supplies only broad strokes or patches of meaning. This unfocused presence makes it difficult, almost futile, for groups and communities to dwell on the worst. Despite one's best efforts, impressionism ensures that the characteristics of the worst fail to gain clarity.

To get a sense of the way impressionism works as a clouding practice, try this simple task. Take a moment, right now, and try to imagine being buried alive, or being brutally murdered, or being told you have an inoperable brain tumor. At Rutgers, I teach a course in the sociology of deviance and often give my students this challenge. I am betting that your response to the assignment will be similar to theirs. No doubt, you will conjure up an image, but it will be a hazy, frenetic idea. You may, for example, picture an attacker, but the figure will be shadowed or nondescript. Or you may sense, even smell, the sterile ambience of your physician's office, but you will be unable to construct the specifics of the conversation. In imagining the worst, you will be unable to elaborate your thoughts. As a consequence, those thoughts will probably fail to sustain you for more than a few brief seconds. Your inability to complete my assignment in no way indicates some deficiency on your part. It is a normal reaction. The culture in which you were socialized has encouraged you—indeed, provided you with tools—to cloud the gory details of such worst-case scenarios. Thus, horrible events can be acknowledged; one can have some vague notion of them and can confirm their potential to occur. But one rarely permits these images to become more than an impression in active consciousness.

Groups and communities, both past and present, provide us with numerous illustrations of impressionism in action. In religious communities, for example, impressionism has been central to theological treatments of eternal life. This is perhaps most obvious in Christian depictions of heaven and hell—two places we might denote as the best and worst of final destinations. Consider, for example, the book of Revelation, usually attributed to John the Divine. Here, in this final section of the Bible, we find John's renowned descriptions of the two locales. Note that John devotes a substantial portion of Revelation's twenty-two chapters to descriptions of heaven. Chapters 4 and 5, along with significant portions of chapters 6 through 8, provide us with painstaking detail of heaven's substance. We learn of a throne suspended on a rainbow with "four and twenty seats" surrounding it. We learn of elders "clothed in white raiment" with "crowns of gold" on their heads. John paints a setting that includes "seven lamps of fire," a "sea of glass like unto crystal," and four beasts, each with six wings and each with a distinctive face—a lion, a calf, a man, and an eagle. He recounts the songs and chants of heaven, the rituals of worship. He introduces us to lambs and lions, to angels and horsemen, to seals and books of reckoning.

To be sure, John's descriptions of heaven are elaborate and full of color. And they are strikingly more plentiful than the references to hell. Indeed, in describing hell, in chapter 9, for example, John provides only brief, vague strokes: "He opened the bottomless pit; and there arose a smoke out of the pit, as the smoke of a great furnace; and the sun and the air were darkened by reason of the smoke of the pit. And there came out of the smoke locusts upon the earth." In chapter 14, he offers another abbreviated observation: "And the smoke of their torment ascendeth up for ever and ever; and they have no rest day nor night, who worship the beast and his image, and whosoever receive the mark of his name." John's treatment of hell is noteworthy, both for its brevity and its lack of substance. Indeed, one cannot help but note that his descriptions of hell present an intentionally hazy impression, a veil of smoke that hides hell's specific tortures and miseries.

A similar pattern emerges in modern Christian writings. In the *Catholic*

Encyclopedia, for example, theologian Joseph Hontheim provides readers with a discussion of both heaven and hell. Like John the Divine, Hontheim discusses heaven with incredible specificity. He defines heaven as "the roof of the world," and actually attempts to plot its location, placing it at "the blue firmament, or the region of the clouds that pass along the sky." Heaven resides above the space in which birds fly, in "the region of the stars that shine in the sky." Heaven is, moreover, "a definite dwelling place . . . not within the earth . . . but beyond its limits." It is a "special and glorious abode, in which the blessed have their peculiar home and where they usually abide, even though they be free to go about in this world."

In addition to offering a specific description of heaven's location, Hontheim provides incredible detail regarding the substance of heaven. He tells us for example that "in heaven, the just will see God, clearly and distinctly . . . they see Him as He is, after the manner of His own Being." Further, those who enter heaven will gain access to a beatific vision that "comprises everything the blessed may have a reasonable interest in knowing." With this vision comes the "impossibility of sinning. . . . The blessed have no longer the power of choosing to do evil actions; they cannot but love God; they are merely free to show that love by one good action in preference to another." Hontheim goes on to specify the surroundings of the blessed, noting that they "delight greatly in the company of Christ, the angels, and the saints, and in the reunion with so many who were dear to them on earth . . . those whom death separated from them." Further, he notes that "very special joys are granted to the martyrs, doctors, and virgins," who will wear special crowns called "aureolas or glorioles, by which these three classes of blessed souls are honoured beyond the rest."[57] Hontheim even itemizes the demeanor of heaven's occupants: "In heaven, there is not the least pain or sadness . . . the will of the blessed is in perfect harmony with the Divine will; they feel displeasure at the sins of men, but without experiencing any real pain."[58]

Hontheim's description of hell is far less specific, its substance minimized and poorly articulated. He describes hell only as "a place within and below the earth . . . an invisible, hidden, and dark place." Hontheim is quite forthcoming about the impressionistic way in which hell is conceived:

> It has been suggested that hell is situated on some far island of the sea, or at the two poles of the earth. . . . Some fancied it was in the sun; some assigned it to the moon, others to Mars; others placed it beyond the confines of the universe. . . . *The Church has decided nothing on this subject;* hence we may say hell is a definite place; but *where it is, we do not know.*

Note too that while Hontheim has much to say about the concrete characteristics of heaven, he provides little detail on hell beyond the presence of fire. Quite openly, he writes of the church's haziness on this matter:

> The fire of hell is repeatedly called eternal and unquenchable. . . . The nature of hell-fire is different from that of ordinary fire; for instance, it continues to burn without the need of a continually renewed supply of fuel. *How we are to form a conception of that fire in detail remains quite undetermined;* we merely know that it is corporeal.

And while Hontheim's descriptions of heavenly comrades and demeanor were quite detailed, the theologian offers only one comparable observation on the ambiance of hell: Occupants will suffer "a separation of all the powers of the soul from God that it cannot find in Him even the least peace or rest." Again, admitting the vagueness of hellish existence, he writes, "the demons suffer the torment of fire, even when, by Divine permission, they leave the confines of hell and roam about on the earth. *In what manner this happens is uncertain.*"[59]

According to the catechism of the Greek Orthodox Church, the variable itemization of heaven and hell is perfectly understandable.[60] Greek Orthodox scholars remind us that heaven was detailed to St. Paul in a divine revelation, an experience he later reported in 1 and 2 Corinthians.[61] This siting, according to scholars, gives heaven an empirical foundation; it makes heaven something tangible and knowable. But the catechism teaches that hell is a mystery and hence impossible to itemize. Indeed, the catechism warns its readers regarding the futility of capturing hell's true essence: "Let us be careful here. . . . St. John Damascene writes that 'eternal fire . . . is something that only God comprehends.' The fire of hell is not physical as we know it, but will be fire as God knows it."

The impressionistic descriptions of hell so common to theological discussions are also evident in artistic renditions. Indeed, drawings and paintings of heaven and hell present a stark contrast. Heavenly scenes tend to be highly detailed, bringing the specifics of theological descriptions alive. Hellish scenes, in contrast, often present vague images that leave much to the imagination of the viewer. Consider, for example, *Mary, Queen of Heaven,* painted between 1485 and 1500 by the Master of the Saint Lucy Legend (fig. 3.1).[62] The painting crystallizes all of the elements found in traditional descriptions of heaven. Mary sits enthroned in heaven, high above the earth. (In fact, portions of the earth are visible at the very bottom of the painting.)

Figure 3.1. Master of the Saint Lucy Legend, *Mary, Queen of Heaven*, ca. 1485.
Samuel H. Cress Collection, National Gallery of Art, Washington, D.C.
© Board of Trustees.

The painting shows Mary, amid heavenly clouds and hosts of angels as she
is crowned before the Holy Trinity that constitutes heaven's core: God the
Father, Son, and Holy Spirit. It is one of the most famous scenes in Christian
theology. And note the specificity with which the artist depicts this heavenly ceremony. As the art historians at the U.S. National Gallery write:

Figure 3.2. Depiction of heaven, German woodcut by anonymous hand. Fine Arts Museums of San Francisco, Achenbach Foundation for Graphic Arts, 1963.30.35896.

The painting . . . depicts Renaissance instruments with great accuracy and also reflects contemporary performance practices in the arrangement of music-making angels. At the top, a full orchestra plays before the three figures of the Trinity. The ensemble around the Virgin is a mixed consort composed of "loud" instruments (trumpets and shawms) and "soft"

Figure 3.3. "Sinners in Hell," one of a series of eleven sixteenth-century
German woodcuts by anonymous hand(s). Fine Arts Museums of San Francisco,
gift of Julius Landauer, acquired by Julius Landauer from Jackie Vetter
in Augsburg, ca. 1915, 1975.1.237.

instruments (vielle, lute, and harp). Two of the singing angels hold books
bearing legible lyrics and notations. This music, which is the source of
the painting's title, has been identified as derived from a setting of the
Marion antiphon, *Ave Regina Caelorium*, by Walter Frye (d. 1474/1475).[63]

The same specificity characterizes a medieval illustration of heaven by
an anonymous German artist (fig. 3.2). Note that, again, heaven is intentionally pictured with reference to the earthly firmament, with a glimpse of
the earth below. In this picture, we can clearly see the saints and the hosts of
angels that surround God; we can see the martyrs, doctors, and virgins with
their heavenly crowns. In this celestial palace, heaven's citizens face their
God as he sits on his elaborate throne. God is robed and crowned in splendor,
the ruler of all before him.

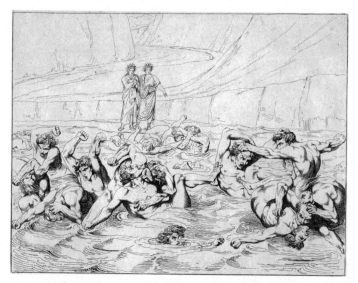

Figure 3.4. Barolomeo Pinelli, "Canto VII, pl. 22 from L'Inferno di Dante," 1824.
Etching 28.4 × 36.2 cm. Fine Arts Museums of San Francisco,
Achenbach Foundation for Graphic Arts, 1963.30.37215.

Contrast these detailed depictions of heaven with artists' renderings of hell. Figure 3.3, for example, reproduces "Sinners in Hell," one of a series of sixteenth-century German woodcuts. The artist's approach to the subject is quite typical, for the woodcut reveals nothing more than the entrance to hell. We witness seven sinners entering a crevice in the earth. At the top of the picture, there is a scant impression of flames. Beyond these two images, the artist provides no further detail of hell's character.

The same can be said for an etching by Bartolomeo Pinelli inspired by Dante's *Inferno* (fig. 3.4). In this image, hell is merely implied as sinners seep through cracks in the earth, presumably on their way to a fiery demise.[64]

The differences captured by these four examples are indicative of a broader pattern. I searched the online collections of the Art Institute of Chicago, the Fine Arts Museums of San Francisco, the Hermitage, the Metropolitan Museum of Art, the National Gallery, and the Vatican Art Museum, and I examined all holdings that specifically depicted either heaven or hell—106 pictures in all.[65] It is worth noting that these museums housed more than twice as many images of heaven than hell (73 renderings of heaven versus 33 of hell). And the depictions of heaven were overwhelmingly more concrete and detailed than those devoted to hell. While only 3 percent of heavenly art was abstract or impressionistic, over 50 percent of hellish pictures fit this description.[66]

These patterns in depictions of heaven and hell persist in contemporary culture. For example, in examining popular literature, I found a number of books (both nonfiction and fiction) devoted solely to the specification of heaven's true nature. Anthony DeStefano, for instance, offers his readers a kind of "Disneyland in the Sky" in his *Travel Guide to Heaven*. Maria Shriver forwards familiar visions of cloudbursts and angels in her child-friendly manual entitled *What's Heaven?* In best-selling fiction such as Mitch Albom's *The Five People You Meet in Heaven* or Alice Sebold's *The Lovely Bones*, readers' curiosity toward heaven is satisfied as they tour heaven's back roads and highways with each novel's protagonist. And author Cynthia Rylant goes one step further as she provides her readers with detailed pictures of *Dog Heaven* and *Cat Heaven*. While literary excursions on heaven's characteristics are too numerous to itemize here, similar treatments of hell are notably absent from contemporary titles—unless, of course, one counts the *Cliffs Notes* for Dante's *Inferno*.[67]

The comparative detail attached to the best and worst of eternal destinations—both historically and in the present—may help to explain contemporary reports of Americans' otherworldly beliefs. Current polls by firms such as Gallup, Fox News, and Roper show that 92 percent of Americans believe in God, 85 percent of Americans believe in heaven, and nearly two-thirds of Americans believe that they are heaven-bound. Those numbers drop noticeably when Americans are queried on heaven's worst-case counterpart. Only 71 percent of Americans believe in the devil, 74 percent believe in the existence of hell, and less than 1 percent believe that they are hell-bound.

⸎

Treatments of heaven and hell illustrate the ways in which religious institutions' use of impressionism can cloud the worst in members' perceptual porthole. Note that the military, another large and regimented institution, has adopted this practice as well. We gain a good sense of this in examining military discharge practices. The military issues discharge papers to all soldiers leaving the armed services (DD Form 2-14). Departing soldiers are discharged at one of five levels in declining degrees of honor—that is, from best to worst:

Honorable Discharge: The honorable discharge announces satisfactory completion of military service. It is conferred to soldiers who meet or exceed the required standards of duty performance and personal conduct. With an honorable discharge, soldiers receive all available benefits.

Under Honorable Conditions (General) Discharge: This discharge denotes "normally" faithful service. But it also indicates a record marred by some negative aspect of duty performance or personal conduct. With the general discharge, a veteran receives most (but not all) available benefits.

Under Other than Honorable Conditions Discharge: This type of discharge indicates that a soldier's conduct fell significantly below acceptable military standards. The designation can result from one or more acts; it can also result from a failure to act. The UOTHC is given only after a soldier has the opportunity to request a hearing by an administrative discharge board (unless requested in lieu of trial by court martial). This discharge denies significant veteran benefits.

Bad Conduct Discharge: This discharge can be adjudged by a court-martial when the court believes the offense warrants severe punishment. Such a discharge deprives one of substantially all veteran benefits (with the exception of vested benefits from a prior period of honorable service).

Dishonorable Discharge: This is the most severe available discharge. It is reserved for those who, in the opinion of the military court, should be released under conditions of dishonor after conviction for a serious offence. A dishonorable discharge deprives one of substantially all veteran benefits and can negatively influence one's desirability in the marketplace in post-military experience.[68]

The honorable discharge represents the best method of separating from the military, particularly if it is accompanied by an award such as the Medal of Honor or the Medal of Good Conduct. When such best cases occur—and indeed, they are the most frequent mode of discharge—the military underscores the event and elaborates the conditions. For example, one's discharge status is not only listed on the official paperwork, one receives an accompanying citation called the "Honorable Discharge Certificate." The impressive certificate looks very much like a diploma and is decorated with the symbols of the relevant military branch. Its text reads:

Honorable discharge from the Armed Forces of the United States
This is to certify that [name, rank, serial number] was honorably discharged from the United States [service branch] on [date]. This certificate is awarded as a testimonial of honest and faithful service.

When one has received the Medal of Honor or the Medal of Good Conduct, the honorable discharge certificate also elaborates the conditions for which the award was bestowed.

Contrast this pageantry with the treatment bestowed on those who are dishonorably discharged—the worst form of military separation. One might guess that those who dishonor the uniform would be publicly shamed or disgraced. But the dishonorable discharge is a surprisingly quiet event. No designation is made beyond a code contained on the DD Form 2-14, no further record, no itemized citation, no statement of the dissatisfaction and shame that the dishonorable discharge conveys. In essence, the dishonorable discharge is treated as a secret, something referenced or discussed in veiled, impressionistic terms.

I spoke informally with several discharge officers about the military's handling of both honorable and dishonorable discharges.[69] In these discussions, the impressionistic treatment of the latter became abundantly clear. One navy officer told me, for example, "We just don't direct attention to the dishonorable discharge in our written documents; we don't itemize the conditions under which it is bestowed." Similarly, an air force officer told me, "The dishonorable discharge is taboo. Everyone knows it's there, but we just don't discuss it." And what about the consequences associated with the dishonorable discharge? An army officer told me, "Well . . . there's lots of things . . . with jobs and pensions and stuff . . . I don't know exactly. I just know it's all bad." Indeed, every soldier knows the potential for a dishonorable discharge, but the specifics of the process are another matter. Beyond the knowledge that a dishonorable discharge is decidedly serious, the details of the sanction are effectively clouded.

⁂

In religion and in the military, impressionism, as well as the positive asymmetry it sustains, provides a lubricant for orderly action. Groups and communities maintain a balance by striking a perceptual imbalance. This strategy is often adopted in the economic realm as well. Indeed, impressionism provides the grease that keeps investment machinery running smoothly and profitably. During the stock market boom of the late 1990s, we saw this practice in action. Recall that during this period most investment experts routinely offered clear, precise predictions regarding the market's best-case scenario. In a November 1999 interview, for example, Robert J. Lucente of Salomon Smith Barney predicted that the Dow would "top 12,000" by the spring of 2000. In 2000, Stuart Freeman of A. G. Edwards told investors to "look for the Dow to reach 13,000 by December 2001." Similarly, Paine Webber's Edward Kerschner forecasted "a year end Dow up 9% from Friday's close to 12,500.[70] Short term, long term—it did not seem to matter. Predicting the Dow seemed so very possible, with regard not only to precise point levels, but to the time frames in which those levels would occur. Art Bonnel of the Bonnel Fund stated that the Dow would reach 20,000 by 2006, while Charles W. Kadlec of J&W Seligman "predict[ed] that the Dow w[ould] reach 100,000 in 21 years if certain political, social and economic conditions remain[ed] favorable."[71]

When it came to worst-case scenarios, however, experts had much less to say. Many acknowledged that the market could eventually turn around. But when pressed to predict the burst of the stock market bubble more precisely, experts veiled their insights in the rhetoric of uncertainty. For example, when the market began to dive in early 2000, Philip Roth of Morgan Stanley Dean Witter would provide nothing more than a broad range of "worst levels." He suggested a NASDAQ low "in the 1,800 to 2,000 range by April or May 2001." Others were even more elusive. "Are we at the absolute bottom?" asked Jeffrey M. Applegate, chief U.S. strategist at Lehman Brothers. "*Who knows.* I wouldn't say this is it." Staff writers at *Barton* conveyed similar impressions: "It is therefore likely that we are going to see some more falls before a bottom comes *at who knows where.*"[72] And Christopher Byron, economic analyst for MSNBC, summed up their collective dilemma:

So, does this mean we are approaching what Wall Streeters like to call "capitulation?" That's the moment contrarians watch for; it's when the last die-hard bull throws in the towel and the market effectively bottoms out because there simply aren't any sellers left. *No one can know for sure.*[73]

In all of these cases, speculators acknowledged the worst in impressionistic terms. They seemed unable—or unwilling—to articulate what the worst might actually be.[74] Thus, in the world of economics, as in the religious and military arenas, impressionism works to blur and distort, making worst-case scenarios difficult for groups and communities to pinpoint and engage.

Shadowing

Can you name the first *American Idol* winner? Millions of Americans can correctly identify Ms. Kelly Clarkson. But while most know the winners of this pop culture competition, only a handful of people can name the first contestant voted off the show. How about the 2005 World Series winner? Most Americans would confidently name the Chicago White Sox. But who was the worst team in the league? That answer is much harder to elicit.[75] If you are like most people, your knowledge of these issues is decidedly one-sided. Shadowing, a second method of clouding the worst, helps us to understand why.

Shadowing is somewhat different from the strategies heretofore reviewed, for the practice manipulates the best rather than the worst. In essence, shadowing spotlights and exaggerates the best, amplifying seemingly endless information on a group's or community's finest. In so doing, the practice generates an overpowering image of excellence. And as the best looms large, it casts the worst into perceptual darkness. Lost in the shadows, the worst remains present, but dim and indistinct, and thus easy for group and community members to ignore.

We can look to any number of groups and communities, any number of social settings and situations. And in each arena, best-case ideals tower over their worst-case counterparts. Often, symbols and rituals facilitate this shadowing process, as groups and communities magnify the best with kudos and awards. Gold medals, blue ribbons, silver cups, and bronzed plaques alert us to the best athletes, cooks, spellers, or livestock in a competition. Sprays of roses mark each year's beauty queens, top singers, or winning racehorses. Among the young, gold stars adorn the best test papers and essays. And when the young mature, Nobel, Pulitzer, and MacArthur Prizes decorate those who embody excellence in the sciences, arts, and letters. From local soccer and little league trophies to World Cups and World Series rings; from the "Employee of the Month" to the "Person of the Year," awards spotlight the best with vigor and enthusiasm; they mesmerize the public with the image of excellence. And in so doing, such awards quietly cast the worst into the shadows.

Awards are so critical to the shadowing process that they are typically bestowed in excess. Consider, for example, the world of the performing arts. In any given year, many competitions will measure performance quality, with each providing an image of perfection and grandeur. The Tonys, the Oscars, the Golden Globes, or the Screen Actors Guild—all will present the public with a bevy of bests. So too will the People's Choice, Kids' Choice, MTV, Grammy and Emmy Awards (both nighttime and daytime versions!). For the best black entertainers, consult the Ebony or Soul Train Awards; for the best Latinos, look to the Latin Grammy or the Latin Music Awards. Indeed, most ethnic groups have now developed awards designed to spotlight the best artists among them.

Beyond the glitter of stage and screen, awards increasingly punctuate the terrain of most professional groups and communities. In my own profession, for example, the American Sociological Association sponsors an amazing number of awards. There is a prize for a career of distinguished scholarship, one for the best book of the past three years, and one for the year's best dissertation. The association awards the year's best teachers and practitioners, those whose work best contributes to our understanding of women, and those who best study issues of discrimination and inequality. Further, the association supports forty-three "sections," that is, subgroups of the organization that reflect various specializations. Each of these sections sponsors competitions that name the best books, articles, and dissertations of the year. When one combines the national association's prizes with those offered by regional sociological societies, well over 160 awards spotlight the community's best works.

Places and things receive abundant awards as well. Week after week, in both local and national venues, the victors cast shadows on anything or anyplace that, according to judges, fails the test of quality. In my home state of New Jersey, for example, each issue of our statewide magazine, *NJ Monthly*, sponsors a variety of "best of" lists. Restaurants, bars, shore spots, weekend getaways, doctors, lawyers: name it—there's a best of it. Our New York neighbors do much the same. *New York* magazine, for example, regularly alerts its readers to the best burgers, martinis, plastic surgeons, apartment buildings, art galleries, and so on, in the city. In contemporary culture, we even note the best of cyberplaces. The Golden Web Awards, the Webby Awards, the Médaille d'Or Award, the Best of the Planet Award, the Webmaster Award, the Surfers' Choice Internet Award, and the World Best Website Award are all designed to recognize the best the Internet has to offer.[76]

Awards are certainly integral to the practice of shadowing, but the strategy demands something more as well. Once the best has been identified and centered in the spotlight, an organized public dialogue must maintain its towering presence. In this regard, media reports, advertising, and the resulting "buzz" prove vital to the process. To elaborate this point, let us return to the motion picture arena. I have already noted that the film industry sponsors several competitive awards—coveted prizes that mark the year's best movies, actors, actresses, directors, writers, and so forth. But in addition to establishing these prestigious awards, the industry makes sure that each competitive ceremony is steeped in public dialogue. There is much critical speculation on worthy nominees, much fanfare when the nominees are announced. There is nonstop media coverage of the voting and endless fawning on the victors. Such dialogue provides year-round attention for the industry's best. It also ensures that the industry's worst never invade the winners' circle of light. Note, for example, that in any given year, it is indeed possible to be named the worst film, actor, or actress of the year. "The Razzies," according to John Wilson, the award's creator, salute the worst that Hollywood has to offer each year—"the movies and actors who really stink up the big screen."[77] But most people don't know about the Razzies, and few follow the nominations and awards. Indeed, the dialogue surrounding the Oscars and other positive-minded awards keeps the Razzies safely in the shadows. This point becomes especially clear in press coverage devoted to the Oscars versus the Razzies. According to Lexis/Nexis, the premiere newspaper and magazine abstracting service, well over a thousand Oscar stories were published in the past year, shadowing the thirty stories devoted to the Razzies.

The story is much the same in other arenas. In the year 2004, for example, thirty-five media stories were devoted to the Clio Awards, an annual honor bestowed on the year's best television commercials. That dialogue effectively shadowed the single press story devoted to the Schmio Award, an honor (or perhaps a dishonor) bestowed on the worst television commercials of the year. Similarly, the twenty-eight stories reporting on the coveted "International Best-Dressed List" kept the four stories reporting "Blackwell's Worst-Dressed List" from the spotlight. The same pattern is being recreated on the Internet. Web sites devoted to the worst of people, places, objects, and events dim in comparison to those addressing the best. For example, I used Google to identify sites devoted to the "ten best" of anything. The search engine yielded 120,000 sites: the ten best running routes in the twin cities, the ten best articles on teaching and learning, the ten best magazine editors, the ten best Arizona resorts, the ten best tips for fearless flying, the ten best-researched herbs, the ten best airport lounges, the ten best art galleries in Washington, D.C., the ten best ways to hide your valuables, and so on. When I searched for "ten worst" sites, the results were far less impressive. Only 22,800 such sites existed, less than a fifth of those devoted to the best.[78] I repeated this exercise using Yahoo, another popular search engine. The results were even more dramatic. While my "ten best" prompt yielded 140,000 sites, my "ten worst" prompt provided only 14,300.

In essence, public dialogue on quality involves a system of weighting. The quantity of talk and narrative devoted to best versus worst ensures that images of perfection and excellence rule the day. This simple element can facilitate the practice of shadowing even in arenas we believe to be resistant to such bias. Consider, for example, public opinion polls. Recently, I visited both Gallup and Roper's online archives.[79] And in searching these data, I found both polls were heavily skewed to researching best-case issues. During

2002, for example, Gallup posed 384 different questions concerning the best of people, places, objects, or events; these questions included items on the best U.S. president, the best athlete, the best economic era, and the best American college. During the same period, the Roper poll asked 148 different survey questions about the best, including queries about the respondent's best quality and the best year of a respondent's life. Both polls, however, were relatively silent regarding the worst. During the period in question, Gallup posed only thirty-five questions addressing the worst. Roper asked only one. More important, questions about the worst were generally "tagged on" to a series of questions about the best. Note too that when asked to identify the worst of people, places, objects, and events, respondents were four to six times more likely to have "no response" than they were when assessing the best. Such data suggest that the best so dramatically overshadowed the worst that individuals experienced difficulty in even articulating the worst.

⌒∞⌒

Governments are, perhaps, the most prolific agents of shadowing. The practice is especially common during times of war. Thus, government spokespeople routinely emphasize the highpoints of military performance—successful strikes, for example, or the destruction of targets and the surrender of enemy personnel. Amplifying these victories helps to overshadow worst-case scenarios such as misfires, retreats, casualties. Historian Frank McLynn tells us that wartime shadowing dates back to ancient regimes. Armies across space and time show a tendency to spotlight their best-case military moments:

> In the Iliad, we are told off-handedly that Achilles and Hector slew thousands in a single day. In the Bible, we learn that Samson tied together the tails of 300 foxes and killed 1000 men with the jawbone of an ass. The Psalms boast: "Saul hath slain his thousands and David his 10,000s." Lest it be thought that this is mere poetic license, it is worth establishing that the ancients always had an irritating habit of describing anything more numerous than they could shake a stick at as "10,000."

Exaggerate the highs and you effectively shadow the lows. By following this simple rule, governments can easily relegate their own casualties to the gray areas of perception. According to Mclynn, such stories of glory allowed the Argentinean government to shadow the casualties of the 1970s military regimes, claiming only 5,000 victims when in fact the toll was closer to

30,000. The same strategy enabled Soviet officials to hide the true number of World War II casualties. Amid tales of victory, the government shadowed its 38 million victims. The U.S. government has been guilty of wartime shadowing as well. Historian Doris Kearns Goodwin notes, for example, that Lyndon Johnson's "constant reference to 'the progress' made in Vietnam . . . drowned the black and ominous analysis of dissenters." By amplifying the best, Johnson was able, for a time, to shadow the losses of money and men that surrounded the Vietnam War.[80]

Knowing the historical effectiveness of shadowing, it should not surprise us to learn that the practice continues in contemporary warfare. Consider Iraqi officials' use of the strategy in the 1991 Persian Gulf War. The Iraqi government regularly shadowed their losses beneath exaggerated reports of victorious aircraft strikes. According to journalist David Bar-Illan, if Iraqi claims were true, the whole coalition air force should have been destroyed in the first week of the war.[81] Shadowing continued in the war of 2003 under Iraq's minister of information, Mohammed Saeed al-Sahaf. The minister proclaimed the complete rout of the coalition forces: "Whenever we attack, they retreat. When we pound them with missiles and heavy artillery, they retreat even deeper." The minister maintained that the reports of American advances were part of the Iraqi strategy to entrap the invaders.[82] Al-Sahaf's statements should not be mistaken for out-and-out lies. Rather, the minister quite predictably shadowed Iraqi defeats by exaggerating Iraqi military capabilities and amplifying isolated instances of victory. According to CNN, the Middle Eastern "man on the street" recognized the minister's statements for exactly what they were. Hazem, a twenty-five-year-old security guard in Cairo, had this to say: "I believe [al-]Sahaf exaggerates a little, but he needs to do that to reassure his people."[83] Citizen Hazem clearly understood the benefits of shadowing in keeping one's public at the best-case porthole. Rear Admiral Richard Cobbold, director of the Royal United Services Institute think-tank, echoed Hazem's assessment: "With regard to the information coming out of Baghdad," he noted, "spin is all very well and to be expected."[84] Cobbold could really say nothing else, for in its dealings with Iraq, his own government made ample use of shadowing. During the 1991 war, for example, press reports suggest that the British government shadowed information on nerve gas casualties. The government sanitized and aggressively downplayed its defeats, allowing victories to dominate the public's perceptual field.

꜒∞꜓

Tracking the use of shadowing in these varied arenas shows the power of the practice in everyday action. And before closing this section, it is worth noting shadowing's potential to command the past. For just as the practice ensures that the worst is veiled in lived experience, so too does it dim the worst in the commemoration of past experience. Indeed, attempts to spotlight the worst in historical accounts—to bring the worst out of the shadows—can meet with substantial resistance. Consider, for example, the case of *Time* magazine's "Person of the Century." In 1999, the editors at *Time* initiated a search for the individual who, "for better or worse, most influenced the course of history over the past 100 years."[85] Despite *Time*'s evenhanded intentions, the magazine's search clearly resulted in a positively skewed vision of the century. Few of the century's top one hundred could be considered scoundrels or villains. And while editors reported that Adolf Hitler was considered for the top position, they noted that he was ultimately rejected as *the* representative of the era. According to the editors, it seemed inappropriate to commemorate a century with someone best noted for acts of hatred and aggression.[86] Sociologist Gary Alan Fine helps us understand the editors' decision. Fine contends that commemorating worst over best can stigmatize the speaker. The worst "can rub off on the [speaker's] identity," causing a loss of moral credibility. Thus, failing to shadow the worst "is tantamount to rejecting the social order."[87] Stability demands that evil be cast to the shadows rather than permitted to bask in the light.

Only the light may prevail in memory—so too said the jury selecting designs for New York City's Ground Zero memorial. "Garden of Lights," "Inversion of Light," "Passage of Light: The Memorial Cloud," "Votives in Suspension": such designs, all finalists in the competition, use light to shadow the dark reality commemorated by the memorial. *New York Times* columnist Maureen Dowd summarized the message of the finalists:

> All ambient light and transient emotion—nothing raw or harsh or rough on which heart and mind can collide. . . . There is no darkness in these designs, literally or metaphorically. They have taken death and finality out of this pulverized graveyard.[88]

Many, including Dowd, were disappointed in the contestants' transcendence of the horror and pain of September 11. Yet the designers were guilty only of adhering to conventional practice, centering in light the order and meaning that the best-case scenario embodies and relegating to the shadows all that contradicts our society's highest hopes and ideals.

Recasting Practices: Redefining the Worst

Thus far, we have addressed two types of practices that facilitate the centering of the best. Eclipsing practices render the worst invisible, thus freeing social actors to concentrate on the best. Clouding practices blur and obscure the worst, making it a poor competitor for best-case images and references. At times, however, the worst may be too blatant or even too tremendous to eclipse or cloud from view. When this occurs, the worst sustains a presence that threatens positive asymmetry. In order to protect the unbalanced perception so "normal" to quality evaluation, groups and communities must engage in a practice I call "recasting."

Recasting redefines the meaning of the worst. The practice allows a group or community to reconstruct calamity or catastrophe, making such entities positive, valuable, and critical to collective well-being. When recast, the worst need never be distanced from consciousness. Inverted and refashioned, stripped of its ugliness, the worst now embodies the vital and noble dimensions of existence. In this way, it can remain centered in a group's or community's perceptual porthole.

In this final section of the chapter, I examine two ways of recasting the worst: rhetorical recasting and prescriptive recasting.

Rhetorical Recasting

Recasting is often a rhetorical practice. Language or image become vehicles that engulf the worst in greatness and splendor. We witness this strategy quite often in historical treatments of catastrophic moments or events. Historians adopt grandiose exaltations, refashioning worst-case scenarios as momentous, centrally important, indeed critical, to a group's development. In such cases, the worst becomes the proverbial "best medicine."[89]

Consider, for example, the Great Schism. Despite the majestic label, the Great Schism refers to the two worst periods of flux in the Catholic Church. In 1054, the world witnessed a break between the eastern and western churches, and from 1378 to 1417 three different popes fought for the right to lead the western church. There is no doubt, objectively speaking, that the Great Schism was destructive to Catholicism. Indeed, many believe that this era planted the seeds for the Protestant Reformation. Nevertheless, historians cloak the period in the language of greatness. This linguistic frame recasts the Great Schism as a watershed moment, one that was unpleasant, yet nevertheless, triggered vital and necessary growth in the Catholic Church.

In a similar vein, recall the Great Northern War (1700–1721). While described in the language of grandeur, the Great Northern War proved one of the worst defeats in Sweden's history. The Battle of Poltava (1709) marked both Sweden's loss of Baltic dominance and the rise of Russian power in the region. Although the Great Northern War stands as a stunning loss for Sweden, the majesty rhetorically granted to this war recasts defeat into honor and resolve. Indeed, the language of greatness frames the Great Northern War not as Sweden's final defeat but as its final shining moment.

Finally, note that World War I (1914–18) has long been dubbed the Great War. That acclamation often distracts us from the war's massive destruction. The Great War involved thirty-two nations and, at its close, was considered the worst conflict of modern times. Direct war costs amounted to about $186 billion, and military casualties topped 37 million, with close to 10 million additional civilian deaths. Viewed by the facts, there seems little to warrant World War I's image of majesty. Yet the label quite effectively distracts us from the war's actual carnage and destruction. The Great War conjures memories of doughboys' youthful enthusiasm, of rousing Irving Berlin victory tunes, of liberated nations. The rhetoric of greatness burnishes the war in a folklorish glow of freedom and triumph.

Some of the biggest catastrophes in U.S. history have been masked in the language of grandeur. Consider, for example, the Great Diamond Hoax of 1872, an event historians consider the worst mining swindle of the nineteenth century.[90] This ruse, perpetrated by Phillip Arnold and John Slack, found unsuspecting victims investing in a mythical diamond mine. Before their hoax was finally exposed, Arnold and Slack had successfully swindled tens of millions of dollars from unsuspecting speculators. Were the hoax not so "great," we might feel more pity for the victims. But engulfed in linguistic brilliance, the hoax seems more like a Hollywood "sting" than a horrendous crime. Similarly, recall that we commonly refer to the worst depression in U.S. history as the Great Depression. This period, one of America's true economic disasters, brought hundreds of bank failures, hundreds of mill and factory closings. Farms and houses were foreclosed in large numbers, and more than ten million workers were left without jobs. "Great"—the word seems a mismatch for these events. Yet attaching the term to the depression enables us to concentrate on the "silver lining" of the era. People were poor, yet gentle and helpful. Times were hard, and yet curiously communal. The period gave birth to unmatched creativity—golden eras in film, radio, and music. Attaching grandeur to an otherwise disastrous time allows us to incorporate the worst into collective perception without threatening an otherwise optimistic stance.

Like historians, theologians often use recasting to establish both standards of morality and visions of hope. In religious scriptures, for example, the worst frequently undergoes a metamorphosis of sorts; evil and destruction are carefully recast in language of glory and redemption. Thus, in many religions, death is recast as eternal life. Similarly, martyrdom—from crucifixions to suicide bombings—become supreme sacrifices that embody the salvation of both the martyrs and the groups for which they die. (Both Catholic and Islamic doctrine instruct that martyrs will be given a special place in heaven.) And one of Christianity's most central verses—the Beatitudes—linguistically transposes the worst of fates to the greatest of blessings. As we read in verses 20–23 of the sixth chapter of Luke:

> Blessed be ye poor, for yours is the kingdom of God. Blessed are ye that hunger now, for ye shall be filled. Blessed are ye that weep now, for ye shall laugh. Blessed are ye when men shall hate you and when they shall separate you from their company, and shall reproach you, and cast out your name as evil, for the Son of man's sake. Rejoice ye in that day and leap for joy: for, behold, your reward is great in heaven.

Here, in the scriptures, language does more than transform curse into fortune. The worst is recast not simply as asset, but as a cherished opportunity.

The worst as opportunity—I have found no better example of this than in considerations of the Black Plague. Norman Cantor, a respected historian of the Middle Ages, argues that despite its massive devastation, the Black Plague was a catalyst to a new and improved Europe:

> The Black Death was the trauma that liberated the new. . . . [It] accelerated the decline of serfdom and the rise of a prosperous class of peasants called yeoman in the fifteenth century. . . . The Black Death was good for the surviving women. Among the gentry, dowagers flourished. Among the working-class families both in country and town, women in the late fourteenth and fifteenth century took a prominent role in productivity, giving them more of an air of independence. . . . The Black Death provided an activating psychological context for privatization of late medieval religions. . . . [It] weakened faith in traditional medieval Catholic spirituality and set off a quest for a deeper naturalistic understanding of human psychology and behavior and the expression of a more personal sensibility.[91]

For Cantor, the plague's dissolution of the old European order allowed scientific thinking to flourish. In the wake of devastation, the Black Plague created an intellectual revolution. With such claims, Cantor frames the plague in concert with the sentiments of Samul Daniel, the English poet: "The greatest works of admiration, and all the fair examples of renown, out of distress and misery are grown."[92]

Prescriptive Recasting

Practices that define the worst as opportunity rather than obstacle encourage prescriptions for action that can temper one's encounters with tragedy and disaster. We see this phenomenon quite often in the treatment of physical and psychological maladies. Consider, for example, the case of migraine headaches. I have been a migraine sufferer for many years. And in researching the subject, I was quite amazed at the positive way medical experts frame the problem. On the one hand, doctors acknowledge that migraines are the worst of headaches, involving "pain like no other" headache.[93] Yet many address the occurrence of migraines as an opportunity in disguise. For example, Andrew Weil, a contemporary holistic guru, tells migraine sufferers to "try to change the way you think about the headaches." He then sets up an analogy that is intended to enable the sufferer to begin that recasting:

> [A] migraine is like an electrical storm in the head, violent and disruptive but leading to a calm, clear state at the end. It is not so bad to let yourself have a headache once in a while. It is a good excuse to drop your usual routines and go inward, letting accumulated stress dissipate. . . . Come to accept the migraine this way and see it serving a purpose in your life.[94]

Dr. Lawrence Robbins, one of the country's foremost headache specialists, gives similar advice. He encourages headache sufferers to redefine their pain by employing positive thinking strategies: "Deep relaxation can change your perception and experience of pain and your response to it . . . [and it] may also boost your hope and optimism and make you less conscious of your pain." Morevoer, he continues, "Learning to focus on the bright side rather than the worst-case scenario can help you view the circumstances in perspective."[95]

As health problems increase in severity, one finds more and more evidence of practitioners who advise us to treat the worst as a positive opportunity. It is in this spirit that holistic physician Bernie Siegel urges his readers to be "thankful for their problems." Indeed, Siegel tells patients that dying, which many consider the worst possible fate, can actually be a blessing in disguise:

A woman in one of our groups wanted to quit chemotherapy because it was making her feel horrible. Her doctor had grumbled, "Well, you know you could die, because cancer has side effects too." She told us, "I went home and learned about cancer's side effects, and found that some of them are wonderful." The side effects of the cancer were the faith she rediscovered, the work she did on herself and the relationships she repaired after cancer gave her a wake-up call. Another man said, "Thank God I have cancer. I could have dropped dead from a heart attack and would have died without learning about love and kindness."[96]

Dr. Stephen Strum, of the Prostate Cancer Research Institute in Marina del Rey, California, offers similar advice:

> You may not believe this, but prostate cancer is an opportunity. As the Chinese say, there is a seemingly small but important opportunity that comes out of a situation that at first glance appears only as crisis. Prostate cancer is a path, a model, a paradigm, of how you can interact to help yourself, and another. By doing so, you evolve to a much higher level of humanity. In the decades of my involvement with cancer patients, I have seen again and again a higher spirit emerge out of situations laden with fear and depression.[97]

Healers are not alone in urging individuals to focus on the best of the worst. Many victims of disease openly promote this practice as well. Such behaviors gain special attention when high-profile personalities recast their diseases in public venues. Lou Gherig epitomizes this attitude. Diagnosed with ALS and forced to leave the game of baseball, Gherig nevertheless proclaimed to Yankee fans on the day of his retirement, "Today, I am the luckiest man in the world." Actor Christopher Reeve adopted a similar strategy— a practice he maintained until his death in 2004. Recall that Reeve suffered near total paralysis after injuring his spinal cord in a riding accident. Yet shortly after the accident, in an ABC interview with Barbara Walters, Reeve labeled himself as an incredibly lucky man. Rather than viewing his disability as a tragedy or a liability, Reeve actively defined it as an amazing opportunity, an opened door leading him to new and exciting possibilities in the service of others. Consider too the story of actor Michael J. Fox. Although forced to restructure his career when diagnosed with Parkinson's disease, Fox has chosen to acknowledge only the positive elements of his condition. One need hardly look beyond the title of his 2002 autobiography to see recasting in action: *Lucky Man: A Memoir*. Similarly, Kirk Douglas, after suffering a debilitating cerebral hemorrhage, discussed this "good fortune" in his 2002 book, *My Stroke of Luck*.

⌒∞⌒

Recasting empowers those who routinely adopt the practice. The strategy allows individuals, groups, and communities to reconstruct their environment, providing an opportunity for change and improvement. It is no wonder, then, that recasting represents the foundation of the "self-help" industry. Indeed, some of the area's most popular manuals champion the technique. Consider, for example, Harold Kushner's monster best-seller, *When Bad Things Happen to Good People*. Kushner's book was inspired by one of life's worst events—the death of one's child. In reflecting on this tragic experience, Kushner notes the countless ways in which onlookers attempt to recast such a loss:

> The family's clergyman had said: "This is not a time for sadness or tears. This is a time for rejoicing, because Michael has been taken out of this world of sin and pain with his innocent soul unstained by sin. He is in a happier land now where there is no pain and no grief; let us thank God for that."[98]

According to Kushner, the practices that support positive asymmetry—especially prescriptive recasting—help individuals persuade themselves that a tragedy is not really bad. Enduring the worst demands that individuals move beyond negativity, redefining their experiences as life's best opportunities:

> We may not ever understand why we suffer or be able to control the forces that cause our suffering, but we can have a lot to say about what the suffering does to us, and what sort of people we become because of it.
>
> All we can do is rise above the question "why did it happen?" and begin to ask the question "what do I do now that it has happened?" . . . *[One must] see the tragedy in the context of a whole life, keeping one's eye and mind on what has enriched you and not only on what you have lost.*[99]

Susan Taylor, author of the best-seller *Lessons in Living*, expresses a similar message. In comforting those who experience the death of a loved one, she writes: "The pain of losing a loved one is a reminder of how blessed we are to have loved. . . . *We can give positive value to our most painful experiences.*"[100]

Prescriptions for a "happy ending" represent the bottom line of the self-help industry. Popular self-help author Gary Zukav preaches this advice almost exclusively: "Your pain is not to be avoided. It is your avenue to spiritual growth. It is the blessing of your life descending upon you."[101] The ability to embrace the best of the worst becomes the core of survival. This sentiment was, perhaps, most starkly expressed by Viktor Frankl in his classic treatise *Man's Search for Meaning.* When Frankl, an Auschwitz survivor, reflected on his experiences, the product was a philosophy underpinned by amazing positivity:

> We must never forget that we may also find meaning in life even when confronted with a hopeless situation, when facing a fate that cannot be changed. For what then matters is to bear witness to the uniquely human potential at its best, which is to *transform a personal tragedy into a triumph,* to turn one's predicament into a human achievement.[102]

Prescriptive recasting equals empowerment. Our politicians know it, and they thus adopt the practice with frequency and conviction. History is ripe with examples of leaders who used the practice to extricate themselves from political disasters. For example, when U.S. involvement in Vietnam reached overwhelming proportions, the late Senator George Aiken (a Republican from Vermont) advised both Presidents Johnson and Nixon to recast the war. Aiken counseled the two presidents to simply declare victory and withdraw U.S. troops from the region. Of course, Johnson failed to heed Aiken's advice. But many historians contend that, eventually, Richard Nixon followed the prescription. By withdrawing U.S. troops and leaving the conflict in the hands of the South Vietnamese, Nixon recast a foreign policy disaster as a long-awaited triumph. President George W. Bush adopted a similar strategy in the early phases of the war with Iraq. In April of 2003, the president declared victory and cited an official end to the conflict—even as the American casualty count grew larger by the day. Members of his cabinet, including Secretary of Defense Donald Rumsfeld and National Security Advisor Condoleezza Rice, told the media, "We are winning the war." Each day, as American soldiers died, as museums were looted, as Iraqi prisoners were mistreated, members of the administration stood firm. The administration actively chided those who questioned their positive interpretations of the

war, for the Bush administration believed that recasting all setbacks was critical to establishing a best-case ending in Iraq.

⟨∞⟩

Our perceptions of the worst people, places, objects, and events are elusive
and fleeting. And in this chapter I have shown that such elusiveness is neither natural nor accidental. Our inability to see or imagine the worst stems
from institutionalized cultural practices, practices that routinely eclipse,
cloud, or simply recast our conceptions of quality. With the worst distanced
from view so systematically, groups and communities are left with a brighter
vantage point on the world, a place where the best-case scenario remains
centered in their gaze.

In identifying and exploring the practices that sustain positive asymmetry, we learn something about the constitutive rules by which quality is
defined. We learn something as well about the scope and consistency of culture's impact on cognition and resulting action. For the practices that support
positive asymmetry, while not universal, remain strikingly consistent across
social situations and equally recalcitrant through time. Indeed, in chapter 4,
we will see that positive asymmetry, so subjective and so clearly constructed,
can be found in domains and arenas that claim immunity from such biases,
namely, in the very "objective" world of measurement and science.

CHAPTER FOUR

Positive Asymmetry and the Subjective Side of Scientific Measurement

In chapter 3, we focused on the ways in which cultural practices promote and sustain positive asymmetry. But surely, in arenas where quality assessment is well developed and standardized, such practices lose their power. When measures are specifically designed to provide fair and balanced assessment, to capture the full gamut of quality, surely one finds specific safeguards and strategies that preclude positive asymmetry—or perhaps not.

In his recent book *Damned Lies and Statistics*, sociologist Joel Best reminds us that statistics and measurements are not objective tools. Rather, they are the *products* of subjective judgments:

> We sometimes talk about statistics as though they are facts that simply exist, like rocks, completely independent of people, and that people gather statistics much as rock collectors pick up stones. This is wrong. All statistics are created through people's actions: people have to decide what to count and how to count it, people have to do the counting and the other calculations, and people have to interpret the resulting statistics, to decide what the numbers mean. All statistics are social products, the results of people's efforts.[1]

In the spirit of Best's comments, this chapter explores a vast array of scientific gauges—measures designed to capture the broad range of quality. We will visit a variety of arenas from academic grading to consumer ratings, from psychological assessments to the scoring of athletic performances, and more. In so doing, I direct readers to one consistent finding. Positive asymmetry is so deeply entrenched in most groups and communities that it affects a variety of carefully crafted quality-assessment tools—scientific tools that we commonly assume to be objective and accurate measures. This influence

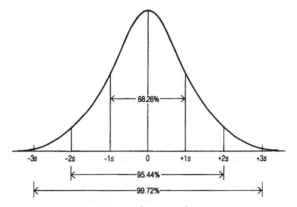

Figure 4.1. The normal curve

is not always immediately apparent, for the rhetoric of quality assessment suggests that formal gauges are equally sensitive to quality highs and lows. Yet upon closer scrutiny, it becomes clear that the rhetoric of assessment does not always translate to practice. Indeed, in many arenas, the measurement of quality falls prey to the practices heretofore discussed, diverting groups and communities from the true magnitude and meaning of the worst.

What We Say: The Rhetoric of Quality Assessment

Simply stated, measurement involves the assignment of numbers. Assigning numbers allows us to quantify people and objects, concepts and ideals; it allows us to represent both the presence and the magnitude of a particular attribute. We tend to think of measurement as an exact science. This is because contemporary measurement techniques emerge from the discipline of statistics, a field that translates abstract theories of probability into useful, concrete applications.[2] Case in point: the normal curve.

The normal curve is a theoretical distribution defined by a mathematical equation.[3] In approximately 1720, mathematician Abraham de Moivre devised the normal curve as a tool for solving problems connected to games of chance. More than 150 years later, another mathematician, Adolph Quetelet, suggested one could use this curve as an ideal by which to compare various distributions of data.

The normal curve has several defining features (see fig. 4.1). First, it is unimodal, meaning it has a single high point or peak. The normal curve is also bell shaped, meaning that the curve peaks in its absolute center and tapers downward as one moves to its right and left extremes. Finally, and most

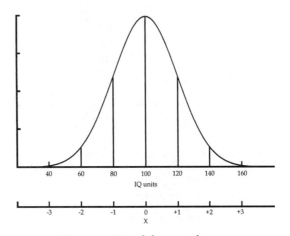

Figure 4.2. IQ and the normal curve

important for our purposes, the normal curve is symmetric about its center. The curve's center is generally represented by the Greek letter mu (μ) or the Arabic numeral zero (o). Thus, the shape of the curve to the right of zero mirrors the shape of the curve to the left of zero.

Statisticians use the normal curve to measure objects and attributes. In this process, statisticians are especially interested in the numeric value or score assigned to an observation and that score's distance from zero. Distances from zero are expressed in standard units. And statisticians have shown that approximately 68 percent of the scores or observations in a normal distribution fall within one standard unit above and below zero; approximately 95 percent fall within two standard units above and below zero; and approximately 99 percent fall within three standard units above and below zero.

How do the properties of the normal curve translate to the measurement of everyday phenomenon? The case of the intelligence quotient (IQ) provides a prototypical example (see fig. 4.2). A person's IQ is generally defined as the ratio of mental age to chronological age multiplied by 100. IQ is typically measured via a tool such as the Stanford-Binet test or the Wechsler intelligence scale. Using these tools, statisticians assign a number or score to an individual's intellectual capacity.

Research shows that when one reviews IQ scores across a population, those scores are normally distributed, and 100 represents the average score. We can say, then, that 100 signifies the center of the normal curve of intelligence (that is, it corresponds to μ or o). Using the logic of the normal curve, we can also say that about two-thirds of men and women will display scores within one standard unit of the average (in the case of IQ, ±15 points). About

95 percent will display scores within two standard units of the average (±30 points), and about 99 percent display scores within three standard units of the average (±45 points). IQ scores also allow one to gauge one's intelligence with reference to the population at large. A score of 104, for example, suggests average intelligence. A score of 146 is more than three standard deviations above the population average, indicating phenomenal intelligence.

The normal curve dominates the thinking of those who develop standardized measures. Indeed, it is one of the most commonly used tools in statistics. This is because occurrences of many real-world phenomena approximate the normal curve. (We can thank people like Quetelet and English scientist Sir Francis Galton for providing this useful insight.) Height, weight, chest size, visual acuity, IQ, political orientation, the melodic structure of national anthems, wear patterns resulting from the traffic in doorways—when measured and graphed, these things and thousands more prove normally distributed. Is this true for issues of quality? The logic of the normal curve tells us that in measuring quality, best and worst—the extremes of a quality distribution—will be equally represented in anything we assess. Thus, standards and measures of quality must be designed in ways that capture both ends of the quality curve.

In theory, measurement tools are constructed with this goal in mind. And in practice, this goal is sometimes met. However, it is equally likely that the measurement of quality will be skewed by positive asymmetry. In the section to follow, we will see that certain cultural practices can invade the measurement process, functioning to create serious biases—biases that taint even the most carefully constructed assessment tools.

What We Do: The Practice of Measuring Quality

Earl Babbie, one of the social sciences' foremost methodological teachers, often talks about the problems that can invade the practice of measurement. Consider this example:

> Suppose you're interested in people's attitudes toward the use of nuclear power generators. You'd anticipate that some people consider nuclear power the greatest thing since the wheel, whereas other people have absolutely no interest in it. Given that anticipation, it would seem to make sense to ask people how much they favor expanding the use of nuclear energy and to give them answer categories ranging from "Favor it very much" to "Don't favor it at all." This operationalization, however, conceals half the attitudinal spectrum regarding nuclear energy. Many

people have feelings that go beyond simply not favoring it: They are, with greater or lesser degrees of intensity, actively opposed to it. . . . In this instance, there is considerable variation on the left side of zero. . . . To measure the full range of variation, then, you'd want to operationalize attitudes toward nuclear energy with a range of favoring it very much, through no feelings one way or the other, to opposing it very much. . . . Unless you're careful, *you may end up measuring only half an attitude.*[4]

Measuring half an attitude, a behavior, a problem—the error is more common than one might think. And in writing on the issue, Babbie reminds us of the ways in which positive asymmetry can creep into measurement. If a researcher's initial perspective is biased or unbalanced, if operationalization (that is, the translations of empirical phenomenon to numbers) fails to incorporate the symmetry demanded by the normal curve, then even the most carefully crafted of measures can provide us with an inaccurate image of reality.

What factors preclude the incorporation of measurement symmetry? In chapter 3, I reviewed several cultural practices that work to create and sustain positive asymmetry. And here, I will show that even in the careful work of formal measurement, two of these practices—eclipsing and clouding—often invade the process.

Eclipsing: The Best-Case Prototype

Recall that eclipsing strategies expunge the worst from a group's or society's active consciousness; these practices relocate the worst to the far reaches of a community's perceptual field, rendering it invisible—outside the range of normal sight. Such a practice seems misplaced in measurement and assessment. Indeed, it contradicts the assumption of symmetry so central to the logic of the normal curve. Nevertheless, many measurement scales evolve in ways that establish a "best-case prototype"—that is, a detailed and absolute standard of best that completely eclipses the specification of worst. Best-case prototypes treat quality as a one-condition variable. While the best of a person, place, object, or event is exhaustively articulated, all other levels of quality are functionally ignored.[5]

Consider, for example, the evaluative tools used by judges in sporting competitions. These tools are quite layered and complex—designed to ensure fair and balanced assessment. Yet upon close reflection, it becomes clear that most of these evaluative tools lack the symmetry that balanced measurement demands, for in sporting assessment, strict criteria define the best athletic performances, but the notion of a worst performance simply does not exist. In most sporting venues, contestants are assessed *relative only to* a best-case prototype.

The grading scale applied in both the International Figure Skating Association and the United States Figure Skating Association illustrates this point. Skating judges begin their work with a definition of the "ideal skate." Such definitions speak to the types of tasks performers must render: for example, skaters must execute a specified number of triple toe loops and double axle jumps; they must include in a routine certain spins or certain types of footwork. The definitions also address the level of mastery with which the tasks must be executed: for example, jump landings must be one-footed and clean, and leg extensions must be perfectly straight and of a certain height. In skating, it is the job of the athlete to meet the performance ideal. And when tasks are executed in accord with the criteria of perfection, skaters receive the maximum point value (usually 6.0). But when skaters fail to meet the best-case prototype, they are not relegated to categories that define average or worst quality. Rather, skaters receive deductions, often of mandatory values, for the flawed components of their routines. A fall incurred during a jump may receive a mandatory deduction of 0.3 points; touching the ice with one's hand may receive a mandatory 0.1-point deduction. In this way, a skater's performance is either perfect or a specified distance from perfection. The best is the only criterion utilized in the evaluative process.[6]

Diving associations utilize a very similar assessment method. The ideal dive is defined with reference to starting position (forward or back-/inward), execution position (pike, tuck, straight, or free), approach (number of steps and position), takeoff (form and height), flight (posture and trajectory), and entry (posture and verticality). Judges then grade each diver's performance with reference to this prototype of excellence:

> Every diver starts with an award of 10. In your analysis of the dive, you subtract from the 10 everything you consider a detriment to the dive, i.e. sloppy approach, gracelessness, leaning, crow hop, knees spread, toes not pointed (flat footed), entering too far out, finishing the execution of a somersault below the board, diving to the side of the board, the moving of arms during the flight to save the dive, poor approach/hurdle/execution or entry, etc.

Thus, symmetry plays no role in the measurements of diving quality. Indeed like skating, assessment tools contain no category for the worst: "If you can say 'That was a good dive,' it is worth a 6–7; 'A very good dive' is worth a 7½–

10; and a 'fair dive' (satisfactory), is worth 4½ to 5½." The worst dive? Evaluation criteria never mention it. And while judges are working with a ten-point scale, divers never receive a score of zero.[7]

The story is much the same in the measurement of beauty. In contests such as Miss America, Miss Universe, or Miss USA, the tools used to assess each candidate are purely asymmetrical. In the Miss America Pageant, for example, the rules demand that judges evaluate contestants in four predetermined categories: talent, interview skills, on-stage personality in evening wear, and physical fitness in swimsuit. To guide judges in their deliberations, contest rules define excellence in each category. Thus, scoring a contestant as a "10" (the highest possible score) in the category of "on-stage personality in evening wear" implies that she has mastered certain core elements of this activity (including posture, poise, ease of movement, elegance, and fashion taste). In essence, the score 10 signifies perfect conformity to an established prototype of best quality. All contestants are evaluated with regard to their distance from perfection. Contestants are either perfect or something less than perfect. Not surprisingly then, the pageant names a fourth, third, second, and first runner-up for the crown, but never identifies the ugliest or least graceful woman in the competition.[8]

Sports performances and beauty pageants: positive asymmetry's role in measurement does not stop there. The best-case prototype also governs manufacturers' assessments of consumer goods such as foods, automobiles, and pharmaceuticals. For manufacturers, the measurement of production quality is tied to predefined standards—standards that specify the best or ideal product even before production begins.[9] These standards may be set with reference to government requirements as forwarded by agencies such as the EPA, the FDA, or the U.S. Pharmacopoeia. Standards may also be set with reference to specific corporate goals, product placement considerations, or consumer preferences. But once in place, quality standards dictate strict manufacturing specifications regarding both a product's desired attributes and the levels or intensities with which those attributes must be present. In essence, quality standards demand a final product that meets or surpasses a manufacturer's best-case prototype. Thus if Quaker Oats defines 98 percent rolled oats to be the ideal content level of its oatmeal, then the best Quaker Oats product will have 98 percent *or more* of that ingredient. Similarly, if Lever Brothers defines 25 percent moisturizing lotion as the ideal content level for Dove soap, then the best production samples will meet or surpass that criterion.[10] When products fail to meet standards of excellence, they may still be good but they are not "good enough." In the business of quality control, there is no distinction made between products that miss the standard by a degree or by "a mile." Thus, *all* substandard products are discarded or destroyed.[11]

This method of quality measurement for products of all varieties—the setting of best-case standards—ensures that the worst remains completely undefined. Indeed, several quality-control agents told me that a worst case is impossible to specify because, functionally speaking, the worst *is an unknown.* The worst is the problem or flaw that was *never considered* in conceptualizing an ideal product; as a consequence, it goes unseen or undetected by one's quality-control methodology. The worst cannot be anticipated or defined in abstraction. It must appear as a concrete disaster before it can even be acknowledged. And once it does occur, it is rarely scrutinized. Rather, it is pulled from production and treated as a failure in the achievement of an ideal.

From athletes to beauty queens to consumer goods, the worst people, places, objects, or events are easily eclipsed by the best-case prototype. When measurement criteria highlight only one extreme of quality, we are forced to view final products as either perfect or something less than perfect. In essence, entities that stray from the quality ideal become invisible in the assessment process.

Eclipsing: Oppositional Measurement

Eclipsing can lead to other measurement problems as well. When the worst is eclipsed, measurement scales may mark or acknowledge poor quality, but fail to specify that level of quality in its own *unique* terms. In this way, the worst is stripped of its sui generis characteristics and comes to be defined simply as the opposite of the best—the flip side of excellence and thus reversible in meaning. This is important, for like the best-case prototype, such oppositional measurement can violate the logic of the normal curve as well.

By way of illustration, we have only to recall the normal distribution of IQ scores shown in figure 4.2. Consider the misinterpretations that would result if we treated symmetrical IQ scores as oppositional entities. In the intelligence distribution, scores 115 and 85 are each one standard deviation away from the average IQ of 100. Thus, these scores are symmetrical, but are they reversible? The meaning of 85 is not simply the opposite of a score of 115. Each number designates a very different quality, a very different level of intelligence. Most important, *each score designates a certain distance from the average or mean of the intelligence distribution.* Thus, the logic of the normal curve encourages us to consider both best and worst *relative to the average.* To consider and define qualities of intelligence solely with reference to the best would provide a flawed interpretation of mental ability. Such a strategy would maintain the integrity of excellence at the expense of all other levels of quality.

Although oppositional measurement taints objective measurement, it is surprisingly common in the science of quality assessment. Consider, for example, a recent survey sponsored by the National Mental Health Association. In the "Best and Worst Practices in Private Sector Managed Mental Healthcare," researchers designed measurement tools that would distinguish the finest and poorest private mental health facilities in the United States.[12] The measurement tool contained forty-five criteria to gauge the best of private sector care. Consider the first three of these criteria:

Best Practices [Involve]
1. Truly making the level-of-care criteria available to the public.
2. Including detailed bibliographies and literature reviews.
3. Basing criteria on the American Psychiatric Association's *DSM* IV and/or practice guidelines developed by the APA and the American Academy of Child and Adolescent Psychiatry.

These criteria begin to unpack and explicate the meaning of best care in the private sector. And in the study, researchers claimed to do the same for the meaning of worst care. But in reviewing their criteria, it becomes clear that the worst bore no independent identity. Rather, the worst practices were operationalized as the opposite of the best practices:

Worst Practices [Involve]
1. Limiting public access to the level-of-care criteria.
2. Failing to including detailed bibliographies and literature reviews.
3. Failing to reference the *DSM* IV and/or practice guidelines developed by the APA and the American Academy of Child and Adolescent Psychiatry.[13]

In reviewing this study, one can see that considerable effort was taken to establish the parameters of the best. Clear thought was given to the qualities that would represent the finest in services and offerings. But these criteria then became the driving force in the construction of the measurement scale. As a result, the worst was never articulated or fully specified. It became nothing more than the antithesis of the best, gauged only by reversing positive aspects of quality.

Despite its flaws, oppositional measurement guides quality assessment in many contemporary fields of study. Consider "educational rubrics," a tool currently the rage in the field of education. Educational rubrics are scoring guides used to evaluate the quality of students' performance. They are typically reserved for significant and demanding intellectual tasks and may be applied in a variety of arenas, including written compositions, oral presentations, science projects, and art projects. Rubric construction is a well-specified process. Yet as one unfolds this technique, it becomes quite clear that oppositional measurement has invaded the procedure.

An educational rubric consists of three specific features: evaluative criteria, quality definitions, and scoring strategies. Let us consider each feature in turn. Evaluative criteria provide educators with specific assessment categories, and educators review these categories in determining acceptable versus unacceptable student responses. For example, in evaluating a written composition, one might attend to categories such as organization, mechanics, or word choice. In an oral presentation, one might attend to categories such as main idea, vocabulary, or voice and style. Once evaluative criteria are stated and defined, they are subject to quality definitions. Quality definitions help educators gauge and rank differences in students' responses. Thus, if mechanics constitutes one of the evaluative criteria used to assess a written composition, a quality definition will, in theory, specify varying levels of that skill—that is, it will itemize the meaning of excellent, good, fair, and poor mechanics. (In concrete terms, a quality definition might state that a composition will be designated as excellent *only if* it contains no mechanical errors; it may be designated as good *only if* it contains no more than three mechanical errors, and so forth.) Armed with both evaluative criteria and quality definitions, educators can turn to a scoring strategy. A scoring strategy may be either holistic or analytic. Holistic strategies systematically aggregate all of a rubric's evaluative criteria, forming a single overall quality score. Analytic strategies allow educators to grade a student's performance criterion by criterion.[14]

On the surface, the design of educational rubrics seems highly balanced and precise. With attention paid to strict evaluative criteria, explicit quality definitions, and systematized scoring, the rubrics should be equally sensitive to quality highs and lows. Yet in examining some of the rubrics currently in use, one finds that oppositional measurement renders many problematic. Consider, for example, this excerpt from the "Multimedia Mania 99 Rubric," a tool developed for the assessment of entries to a national multimedia competition.[15] The rubric establishes "originality" as an evaluative criterion; it also specifies originality's quality definitions. Note that the definition for "best originality" is pointed and precise: "The product shows significant evidence of originality and inventiveness. The majority of the content and many of the ideas are fresh, original, inventive and based upon logical conclusions and sound research." When it comes to the quality definition for "worst originality," however, the rubric fails to establish a distinct definition. Rather, the worst is described as nothing more than the opposite of the best: "The work is a minimal collection or rehash of other people's ideas, products, and inventions. There is no evidence of new thought."

The same problems plague the criterion of "screen design." The "best screen design" is specified in crisp, unique terms: "The screen contains all necessary navigational tools and buttons. Users can progress intuitively through screens in a logical path to find information." But the quality definition of "worst screen design" is nothing more than a reversal of best-case ideas: "Buttons or navigational tools are absent or confusing. Screens are either confusing and cluttered or barren and stark."

We can turn to a completely different area—high school composition—and find that oppositional measurement plagues that field's rubrics as well. Consider a rubric used to score written essays at the Thomas O'Brien Academy of Science and Technology in Albany, New York. "Detail" is one of the rubric's evaluative criteria. Note the quality definition for "best detail": "[The writer] uses interesting details that add to the overall clarity and organization of the essay." In contrast, the quality definition of "worst detail" offers no new material, no unique characteristics by which to judge the worst. The definition of "worst detail" simply states: "Details are missing or inaccurate."

One might think that the more systematic the rubric, the less likely the presence of oppositional measurement. But I found that even the most intricate of rubrics fell prey to this measurement flaw. For example, those who rate the quality of Internet sites (including the Best of the Planet Awards, the Golden Web Awards, the Médaille d'Or Awards, the Webby Awards, and the World Best Website Awards) use rubrics quite liberally, and these rubrics are among the most systematic that I encountered. Yet in every case, judgment criteria provide strict definitions of the best, while definitions of the worst are nothing more than the best turned upside down. Consider that judges for the Webby Awards consider six specific categories in assessing the quality of a site: content, structure and navigation, visual design, functionality, interactivity, and overall experience. For each category, the Webby Awards organization forwards explicit criteria, quality blueprints that aid judges in their quest to identify the best entries. Take, for example, the criteria for structure and navigation:

Structure and navigation refers to the organization of information on the site and the method in which users move through the sections. Sites with good structure and navigation are *consistent and effective.* They allow you to *form a mental model* of the information provided, where to find things, and what to expect. Good navigation *gets you where you want to go quickly* and *offers easy access* to the breadth and depth of the site's content. (emphasis added)

We find similar requirements in the organization's criteria for functionality:

Functionality is the use of technology on the site. Good functionality means that the *site loads quickly,* has *live links,* and any *new technology used is functional and relevant* for the intended audience. The site *should work cross-platform* and *be browser independent.* Good functionality is technology you can't see. (emphasis added)

In evaluating entries, judges review each of the six main categories. They score sites on a ten-point scale, where 10 represents the best and 1 represents the worst. When all criteria have been evaluated, the judges calculate a summary score. This technique carries with it certain implicit assumptions. Specifically, it assumes that the worst Web sites are neither exclusive nor unique, but simply oppose the marks of true quality. To score a site with a 1 on the quality of its structure and navigation indicates that the site is "inconsistent and ineffective; it is slow and access is laborious, etc." To score a site with a 1 on the quality of its functionality means that "its links are dead or it does not work cross-platform." In other words, the site is scored as worst not for its own special characteristics. Rather, it earns the rank of worst because it accomplishes the very opposite of excellence.[16]

Clouding: Decreasing Rigor

In chapter 3, I noted that some cultural practices do not completely obliterate the worst. Clouding practices, for example, acknowledge the worst and maintain it in the evaluative field. But clouding greatly blurs the details of poor quality, keeping the worst present but ill defined, outlined rather than articulated.

When clouding invades the measurement process, it results in flawed evaluative tools. Such flaws, however, are somewhat different than those reviewed heretofore in this chapter. "Cloudy" measures do indeed consider both extremes of quality, but the rigor applied to capturing quality highs and

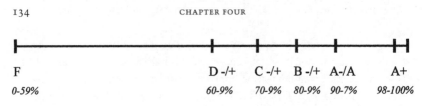

Figure 4.3. The traditional academic grading distribution

lows varies considerably. Attention to best quality is meticulous and involves stringent measurement criteria. In contrast, the measurement of worst quality is imprecise, involving far less care and accuracy.

In the world of assessment, cloudy measures are more common than one might think. Consider, for example, a measurement tool that most of us have experienced firsthand: the system of letter grades in the world of academic grading. In nearly all school systems, A+ represents the very best grade a student can earn. And the meaning of that grade is very strictly defined. An A+ is typically awarded to students who master 98–100 percent of the material at hand.

As figure 4.3 shows, the meaning of letter grades becomes less rigorously defined as one moves across the quality continuum. And when we arrive at the grade of F, we arrive at the system's least precise indicator. Note than an F can signify an extremely wide margin of performance. Indeed, in most institutions, the grade generally denotes a mastery of anywhere from 0 to 59 percent of the material. Thus, while A+ students can rightfully claim to be the *crème de la crème*—hovering within a mere point or two of perfection, F students represent a mixed bag, running the gamut from "clueless" to "halfway there." In many ways, traditional grading scales forward an unspoken relinquishment of the F student. For once students fall below a certain level of mastery, the system lumps them together, making no further distinctions regarding their distance from excellence.

Grading is only one of the areas in which cloudy measures prevail. I found the strategy used quite frequently in the world of finance as well. Financial pundits are constantly rating the quality of investment brokers. And when one examines these rankings, a clear pattern emerges. Those financial players ranked the best of their kind typically display unique quality scores—scores that are significantly higher than those of their nearest competitors. In contrast, players ranked the worst of their kind generally yield indistinct scores. Indeed, the worst of players may rate no lower than other poor-quality entities.

The data in table 4.1 illustrate this phenomenon. The table displays summary quality ratings from an online survey executed by *Money.com*. The

Table 4.1. Summary satisfaction scores for the fifteen largest e-brokers of 1999

Broker	Level of Satisfaction
Charles Schwab	20
National Discount	18.5
DLJ Direct	17.5
Suretrade	17
Datek Online	16.5
E*Trade	16
Fidelity	15.5
TD Waterhouse	5
Quick & Reilly	14.5
ScoTTrade	14
Discover	14
A. B. Watley	13
Ameritrade	13
Web Street Securities	11.5
Brown & Co.	11.5

Data derived from CNN/Money, http://www.money.com/money/broker (accessed May 9, 2000).

survey measured the quality of the fifteen largest "do-it-yourself" online brokers.[17]

Charles Schwab was ranked the best of online brokers, earning a summary score of 20. Note that this score is unique—no other firm matches the rating. Further, Charles Schwab's score is a full 15 percent higher than the score of its nearest competitor, National Discount. Thus, in this survey, the best online broker is both unequaled and unrivaled, standing "head and shoulders" above the rest. Contrast the Schwab ranking with those of the survey's worst brokers. Two firms, Web Street Securities and Brown and Co., are *tied* for this position. The two firms garner *identical* summary scores (11.5). Further, the data suggest that "bad" quality was apparently more difficult to pinpoint than "good" or "average" quality. While each of the survey's top nine brokers displays unique ratings, each of the survey's bottom six brokers is tied with a competitor for its position. These numbers suggest that the precision surrounding the designation of the best (and sustained to a degree in evaluating the average) all but disappears when it comes to deciphering the worst.

A similar pattern emerged when *SmartMoney.com* reviewed the overall quality of "navigator" online brokers. (Unlike do-it-yourself brokers, navigator brokers cater to investors who prefer help with their portfolios.) *SmartMoney.com* collected data on six brokers: A. G. Edwards, Merrill Lynch, Morgan Stanley Dean Witter, Paine Webber, Prudential, and Salomon Smith Barney. Brokers were evaluated according to six criteria: commission and fee structures, services and products, available stock research, online services,

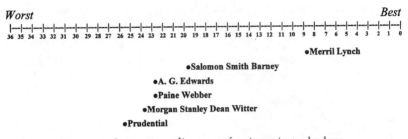

Figure 4.4. Summary quality scores for six navigator brokers.
Data derived from *SmartMoney*, http.smartmoney.com/brokers/
navigator/index.cfm?story=rankings (accessed April 11, 2001).

return on firm's mutual funds, and the firm's ability to stay out of trouble. *SmartMoney*'s summary scale of quality ranged from 6 to 36, with low scores indicating superior performance and high scores indicating inferior performance. Merrill Lynch garnered the title of best navigator broker, touting a summary score of 9.

Figure 4.4 shows that this score was both unique and distant from the pack. Indeed, Salomon Smith Barney, Merrill Lynch's nearest competitor, ranked a full 11 points higher. There is little, however, to distinguish the bottom four brokers on the list. Two of the brokers—Paine Webber and A. G. Edwards—tie with a score of 23; Morgan Stanley Dean Witter scored 24, only one point higher than its nearest competitor, and Prudential is merely two points higher, with a summary score of 26.

We can move to a completely different measurement arena—consumer product quality—and find, yet again, the decreased rigor so central to cloudy measures. *Consumer Reports*, a magazine devoted to measuring and ranking the quality of goods and services, helps illustrate the point.

Each month, the staff at *Consumer Reports* tests and evaluates dozens of products ranging from cameras to coffeemakers, shampoo to sheets, walking shoes to water filters. Table 4.2, for example, presents data on the magazine's assessment of budget hotel chains. Note that nine major hotel chains were evaluated, with quality ranks based on a hundred-point rating scale. As the table shows, the Sleep Inn chain was named the best budget establishment. It was the only chain to score 80 points and stood several points above its nearest competitor, Extended Stay America. Yet a somewhat different picture emerged at the bottom end of the quality scale. Two hotel chains, Days Inn and Travelodge, *shared* the title of worst, with each hotel earning only 63 points.

The same pattern emerged in the magazine's rating of five cellular carri-

Table 4.2. Quality ratings of budget hotels

Hotel Chain	Ratings
Sleep Inn	80
Extended Stay Inn	77
Microtel Inn/Suites	75
Red Roof Inn	70
Super 8 Motel	69
Motel 6	68
Econo Lodge	64
Days Inn	63
Travelodge	63

Data derived from *Consumer Reports* 2004b, 12–17.

Table 4.3. Quality ratings of cellular carriers

Carriers	Ratings
Verizon	71
Nextel	62
T-Mobile	59
Sprint	58
AT&T	58

Data derived from *Consumer Reports* 2004a, 12–20.

ers. The *Consumer Reports* measurement system rendered a clear best case but provided a less rigorous picture of the worst carrier. Table 4.3 shows the magazine's ratings of New York area carriers. Again, one and only one company, Verizon, was named the best cellular carrier, standing nine rating points higher than its nearest competitor, Nextel. In contrast, two companies, Sprint and AT&T, *tied* for the rank of worst, and these companies rate only a point lower than their nearest competitor, T-Mobile.

The decreased rigor that clouded the worst hotel chains and cellular carriers is hardly unique. I randomly selected four years of *Consumer Reports* issues published between the years of 1990 and 2000.[18] I then reviewed all of the quality tests conducted and printed in each issue—555 tests in all. In reviewing these tests, I found that the magazine's measurement strategy identified a single best product—one with a unique quality score that proved higher than its nearest competitor's—in 92 percent of its tests. But *Consumer Reports* had much more difficulty in identifying single worst products. Two- and three-ways ties for worst marked 31 percent of the tests. And while 69 percent of cases identified one unique worst case, runners-up in *almost all* of these tests displayed scores *nearly equal* to the last-place designates (that is, within one ranking point).

The *Consumer Reports* tests, like the other measurement tools reviewed in this section, suggest a clear pattern in the assessment of quality. These cloudy measures posit both quality highs and lows. Yet the rigor and energy applied to quality specification dramatically decreases as one considers anything less than the best. In this way, cloudy measures contribute to positive asymmetry, for while such measures mimic the assumptions of symmetry so central to the rhetoric of standardized measurement, they consistently fail to achieve that goal. The assessment measures reviewed here, and others like them, seem to muddle designations of the worst, with the worst often indistinguishable from poor-quality products in general.

∞

The rhetoric of measurement suggests that we take a symmetrical approach to quality. But the practice of measurement demonstrates that often the opposite is true. Asymmetrical visions of quality have clearly tainted an area that claims resistance to bias. When eclipsing enables best-case prototypes and oppositional measurement, when clouding decreases the rigor with which we specify low-end quality, then claims of objectivity in quality assessment must be viewed with a cautious eye.

The role of positive asymmetry in quality assessment suggests that those designing assessment tools may be initiating their task from the wrong conceptual vantage point. Rather than conceptualizing the *best* psychiatric care unit, budget hotel chain, student essay, or financial broker, measurement might more fruitfully begin by conceptualizing the acceptable or *average* entity. In essence, I am suggesting that one begin by constructing a meaning for the center of the normal curve. Starting at the middle and working one's way out may encourage measurement experts to consider each extreme of the normal curve with a more balanced eye. Resulting tools may then permit a broader, more inclusive picture of quality in all its facets.

CHAPTER FIVE

Being Labeled the Worst—
Real in Its Consequences?

"I did not have sex with that woman!" In our mind's eye, most of us can still see President Clinton's firm jaw, his angry eyes, and of course, that wagging finger. It was a politician's worst nightmare. The president had been caught in an unseemly and horribly unpresidential moment. Republicans vowed to drive Clinton from the White House. Democrats quietly began the shunning. The media gave us the minute-by-minute, promising to chronicle the dramatic fall of a giant. But before long, denials turned to apologies; impeachment fell short of conviction. And when all was said and done, nothing much happened. The Clinton presidency went on, his popularity returned, and ultimately the worst that could happen simply didn't.

Clinton's fate must have irked other public figures, because for many, the same "sin" proved far more devastating. Wilbur D. Mills, for example, eventually resigned his congressional seat when he was caught driving drunk with stripper Fanne Fox. Donna Rice turned Senator Gary Hart into "Gary Who?" And voters turned on Representative Gary Condit after his affair with Chandra Levy. For these men, things were indeed "all that bad." Their worst political nightmares became a fate from which they couldn't escape. Was it irony or bad luck that plagued Mills, Hart, and Condit? Perhaps. But more likely these men's stories, particularly when examined relative to Clinton's, indicate a broader pattern. Those labeled the "worst" routinely meet with highly variable ends. In some cases, the consequences of the label can be dire, leading to stigmatization, physical harm, or even destruction. Yet in other cases, the label of worst proves far less significant. Often the people, places, objects, and events marked as the worst are treated no differently than those identified as merely poor or average.

In the pages to follow, I argue that these varying fates are not haphazard or mysterious. Rather, the impact of the label "worst" varies in systematic ways. To understand these patterns, we will examine several cultural and social factors associated with the contexts in which labeling occurs: the intended durability of quality labels, the labeler's power vis-à-vis the target, and the normative reaction to criticism at work in the labeling context. Each of these elements has an impact on the power of the label in important ways, and understanding that impact can help us to predict whether the worst of people, places, objects, and events will be ravaged or redeemed.

The Intended Durability of the Label of Worst

The label of worst is, in many ways, akin to a medical diagnosis; it definitively identifies the condition of its target but, on its own, may fail to tell us the tenure of the disease. Is the label permanent, intended to signal its target's demise? Or is it temporary in nature, subject to alteration or removal? This issue—intended durability—is critical to the label's effect. For as we will see, when those labeled the worst have no opportunity to escape the designation, the consequences of the label can be far more serious than they are for those who have the ability to rectify or change their status.

To illustrate this phenomenon, let us compare those who occupy the lowest ranks of a rigid caste system and those on the bottom rung of an open class system. For example, India's traditional caste system was developed more than three thousand years ago and formally codified by Aryan priest-lawmakers in the Law of Manu (c. 200 B.C.–100 A.D.). The Law of Manu created five hereditary divisions that guide Hindu society to this day. The Brahmans, or priestly caste, formed the head and most valued part of the system. The Brahmans were followed by the Kshatriyas, or warrior caste. The Vaisyas, the farmer and merchant caste, were next in order; and the Sudras, laborers born to serve the members of the three higher castes, ranked fourth in the original system. Far below the Sudras, a group called the Harijans, or Untouchables, completed the system. While formally ranked, some say that the Untouchables were of no caste at all. They represented the worst of Indian society, far outside the social order, and were equipped to do only those tasks classified as polluting activities—taking life (human or animal), disposing of cattle, working with cattle hides, working with human bodily excretions, and the like.[1]

The religious doctrine that supported the Indian caste system doused any hope of status change. According to the Bhagavad Gita 18:41–40, the duties of caste members are "distributed according to the qualities born of their own nature. . . . No being on earth or again in heaven among gods is liberated from these qualities." The scripture also warns in verse 48 that those who abandon a caste assignment will find all their undertakings "enveloped by evil as fire by smoke." Thus, one's position in the Indian caste system is hereditary and immutable; all individuals must remain in the caste of their birth.[2] As one can imagine, this permanence carries serious social consequences. It restricts one's marriage partners and the occupations one may choose; it dictates one's associates and acceptable dietary habits; it defines the future of one's offspring. In essence, one's caste position completely controls the course of one's social experience and opportunity.

The caste system's rigidity was especially relevant for those labeled the worst in the system. Considered polluted, Untouchables were banned from Hindu temples. Higher caste members underwent elaborate purifying rituals when they encountered members of this lowest caste. If higher caste members made physical contact with an Untouchable, they were required to thoroughly cleanse their bodies. In some cases, they had to cleanse objects touched by the Untouchable and purify places in the home where the Untouchable had walked. Indeed, in parts of South India, even the sight of an Untouchable was considered sufficient to pollute a member of a higher caste. In 1949, the Indian government tried to soften the impact of the Untouchable label. They outlawed the use of the term, renaming Untouchables the "Scheduled Class." The government also declared discrimination against the Scheduled Class to be an illegal and punishable offense. But despite these measures, members of the caste continued to suffer. Shunned by others, they were "discriminated against, denied access to land, forced to work in degrading conditions and routinely abused at the hands of police and higher caste groups that enjoy the state's protection."[3]

According to current government estimates, approximately 17 percent of India's population belongs to the worst caste position. And among these, a significant number are "manual scavengers who clear feces from public and private latrines, dispose of dead animals, and clean up after funerals."[4] Thus, despite government dictates, the Scheduled Class remains below the "pollution line," their fate inescapable, their daily life unthinkable. As one man describes it:

> When we are working, they ask us not to come near them. At tea canteens, they have separate tea tumblers and they make us clean them ourselves and make us put the dishes away ourselves. We cannot enter temples. We cannot use upper-caste water taps. We have to go one kilometer away to get water. . . . When we ask for our rights from the government, the municipality officials threaten to fire us. So we don't say anything.[5]

Contrast the life of the Scheduled Class with the plight of those who occupy the worst position in an open class system—the poverty class.[6] To be sure, the consequences of class-system poverty are tangible and grave. In the United States, for example, poverty exerts significant effects on what sociologists refer to as one's "life chances," that is, the odds of obtaining desirable resources, positive experiences, and opportunities for a long and successful life. In this regard, one must note that infant mortality rates are twice as high among the poor than among the privileged. The poor also face greater risk of disease than do the privileged. And when the disadvantaged get sick, they are more likely than the privileged to die from their ailments, a pattern that holds true even for diseases that modern medicine can largely prevent (tuberculosis or influenza, for example) or render nonfatal (stomach ulcers, syphilis, and the like).

Poverty's link to mortality goes beyond issues of health and hygiene. Members of the poverty class face high levels of risk in other aspects of their lives as well. In the United States, being poor doubles one's chances of being murdered, raped, or assaulted. Similarly, the poor are more likely than members of other classes to die as a result of occupational hazards such as black lung and machine injuries. Among children, the poor are more likely than their affluent counterparts to drown, die in fires, or be killed in auto accidents. And during wars, it is the sons of the poor who are most likely to serve in the military and therefore most likely to be casualties. Note too that devastating life events befall the poor more often than any other class. In the United States, divorce rates are highest among the poor and steadily decrease as one moves up the socioeconomic ladder. Job loss and unemployment are also most common among the poor. And studies document that poverty-class membership negatively influences one's psychological stability. The poor are less likely than their more wealthy counterparts to report feelings of happiness, hope, and satisfaction.[7]

In the U.S. class system, the consequences of being labeled the worst are unmistakably negative. Yet the consequences are not certain, and most important, they are not insurmountable. American culture has always defined poverty as a flexible state, a status that—with enormous effort or great luck—can be overcome. We call it the "American Dream," and our culture is ripe with Horatio Alger tales—stories of impoverished individuals who achieve wealth and fame through hard work and perseverance. The rags-to-riches stories of figures such as Andrew Carnegie or John D. Rockefeller, the legendary rise of political icons such as Abraham Lincoln or Bill Clinton, the catapult to stardom of common folk such as Elvis Presley, Marilyn Monroe, or Oprah Winfrey, the collective tales of immigrants who worked their way from dire poverty to "the good life": these stories honor those who successfully throw off the yoke of poverty; they provide "proof" that the worst can be a temporary condition. In contrast to the hopeless fate imposed on India's Scheduled Class, the American Dream presents salvation from poverty as an ever-real possibility.

When the worst class location is defined as a temporary condition, people embrace and believe in positive potential. Public opinion polls, for example, show that 75 percent of Americans define themselves as significantly more upwardly mobile than their parents—even when they themselves are living in poverty. Further, the large majority of Americans (80 percent) describe the United States as a place exceedingly rich in economic opportunity.[8] These perceptions appear to increase with every generation. Indeed, roughly half of all contemporary Americans surveyed identify the current environment as more conducive to mobility than ever before.[9] This optimism corresponds, in part, with actual achievement levels, for in the United States, dire poverty is not a life sentence. Sociologist David Gilbert tells us that membership in the U.S. poverty class is likely to be short term. While long-term poverty is difficult to measure, the best studies show that less than 25 percent of the poorest Americans remain so for longer than six years.[10]

Durable versus nondurable labels: the varying impact found in the socioeconomic realm holds true in the world of morality as well. This pattern becomes clear when we look to the ways in which different religions confront the issue of sin. Most religions define sin as a serious offense against God, an act that represents the worst of human volition. Yet the consequences of sin can vary from religion to religion. When religious doctrine allows for the repentance of sinful acts—when it defines sin as a temporary rather than a permanent stain—the consequences of sin are far less serious than when contrition is denied.

Calvinism, for example, defines the stigma of sin in permanent terms. In Calvinism, the damned are forever lost, their fate unchangeable, their pain eternal. This destiny is summarized in the "Five Points," a central doctrine of the religion. Point one establishes human beings' "total depravity." In this regard, Calvin contended that Adam's sin left an indelible stain on humanity (original sin), which "extends to every part of human personality—thinking, emotions and will."[11] Because of it, "all men are sinners by nature, bound hand and foot to an evil inheritance they *cannot escape.*"[12] Should one doubt original sin's link to damnation, Calvin's notion of "unconditional election" assures the result. In this, the second of his Five Points, Calvin contends that God, solely of his own counsel, predestines some for eternal salvation. Human actions, in and of themselves, can do nothing to alter one's fate. Only God's election can save an individual from the torments of hell.[13] But Calvin notes that divine intervention is rare; it cannot be beckoned or predicted. Thus, most of us walk the earth as victims of Adam and Eve's transgression. Bearing original sin, most must accept the certainty of a fiery demise.[14]

Mormon theology also entertains the permanence of sin. While repentance and salvation are possible for many earthly offenses, Mormon doctrine teaches that some sins simply cannot be erased. In these cases, repentance holds no place in the process; permanent sins exact a damnation from which no one can escape. We see this doctrine in action when we look to the case of murder. Mormons consider it the worst of atrocities and treat it like no other offense. Brigham Young, for example, wrote that linking murder and repentance was "nonsense."[15] Mormon theologian Bruce R. McConkie takes a similar stance. For the murderer, he writes, "there is no forgiveness . . . a murderer can never gain salvation. . . . He cannot join the Church by baptism; he is outside the pale of redeeming grace."[16] The *Doctrines and Covenants* echo this sentiment: "He that kills shall not have forgiveness in this world, nor the world to come."[17] In the case of murder, Mormonism mirrors the teachings of Calvin. The worst of sins affords eternal stigmatization. And when the mark of a sin is immutable, retribution must be swift and immeasurably severe.

Contrast the position of Calvin and the Mormons with that of the Catholic Church. Because Catholicism recognizes the potential for active redemption, the consequences of sin are generally far less serious than those outlined in previous models. To be sure, sin is conceived as a heinous affront to God. The catechism tells us:

> Sin is an offense against reason, truth, and right conscience. . . . It wounds the nature of man and injures human solidarity. . . . The root of sin is in the heart of man, in his free will, according to the teaching of the Lord: "For out of the heart come evil thoughts, murder, adultery, fornication, theft, false witness, slander. These are what defile a man."

At the same time, hope abides in the church's discussions of sin. The catechism teaches: "In the heart also resides charity, the source of the good and pure works, which sin wounds." And thus, by tapping the portion of the heart in which charity and love abide, the sinner can effectively repent. "All mortal sins can be forgiven. With a conversion of heart through the Sacrament of Confession, the sinner can seek God's mercy and reinstate the state of grace that was previously obtained through the Sacrament of Baptism." Thus sin, whether predestined or an act of free will, is never inevitably damning. In Catholicism, the consequences of the worst human actions can be tempered by contrition and cleansing: "When the mortal sin is forgiven through the Sacrament of Penance, merit revives in proportion to the sincere and loving sorrow with which the sinner receives the Sacrament." Indeed, only by actively *rejecting* God's grace and mercy can one fail to achieve this reconciliation: "To be denied entry into the Kingdom of heaven, the sinner must . . . reject the grace of God and reject the mercy of God by refusing to confess his sins through the Sacrament of Reconciliation."[18]

In Catholicism, the reversibility of sin is central to scriptural teaching. Readings that reiterate that lesson are often featured during Mass and other regular services. Consider, for example, this excerpt from Luke 24:39–43. Jesus' forgiveness of the crucified thief is a staple of Lenten services:

> And one of the malefactors which were hanged railed on him saying, "If thou be Christ, save thyself and us." But the other answering, rebuked him saying, "Does not thou fear God, seeing thou art in the same condemnation? And we indeed justly; for we receive the due rewards of our deeds: but this man has done nothing amiss. And he said unto Jesus, Lord remember me when thou comest into thy kingdom." And Jesus said unto him, "Verily I say unto thee, Today thou shalt be with me in Paradise."

Repentance and salvation form the cornerstone of another popular Catholic reading, the story of the prostitute's stoning as told in John 8:4–11:

> "Master, this woman was taken in adultery, in the very act. Now Moses in the law commanded us, that such should be stoned; but what sayest thou?" . . . (Jesus said) "He that is without sin among you, let him first cast a stone at her." . . . When Jesus had lifted himself, and saw none but the woman, he said unto her, "Woman where are those thine accusers? Hath no man condemned thee?" She said, "No man, Lord." And Jesus said unto her, "Neither do I condemn thee; go and sin no more."

Forgiveness and the eradication of sin permeate the Catholic dogma. And in the face of surmountable sin, stigma is diminished and consequence far less severe.

Like Catholicism, Judaism allows for the reconciliation of the sinner. Sin, while wrong and damaging to the community, need not be a permanent mark. Judaism teaches that through repentance, prayer, fasting, and good works, the sinner can return to a direct relationship with God. Indeed, the Talmud raises repentance to the pinnacle of virtue: "Where repenters stand, even the very righteous cannot stand."[19]

Reconciliation proves quite rational in the context of Judaic doctrine. For at the core of Judaism lies the personal relationship between the people and the Lord. While sin may temporarily sever that bond, the health of the community demands that nothing preclude the potential for reconnection. Toward that end, the prophet Malachai instructs sinners of the Lord's mercy: "Return to Me and I shall return to you." Similarly, the prophet Ezekiel proclaims the way to redemption: "If the wicked turn from all his sins that he has committed, and keep all My statutes, and do that which is lawful and right, he shall surely live, he shall not die."[20] And in one of Judaism's most well-known stories—the return of Moses from Mount Sinai as told in Exodus, chapters 32 and 33—we learn that repentance can rectify even the worst of sins: questioning God's supremacy. Recall that Moses' visit to the mountaintop takes much longer than expected. In his absence, the Israelites grow weary and full of doubt. Their despair brings them to the altars of false idols, to the sins of gluttony, violence, and flesh. In the face of these indiscretions, God threatens the Israelites' destruction and vows to make a new covenant restricted to Moses and his direct descendants. Moses, recognizing that his followers have sinned, still pleads on their behalf. He offers the Lord sacrifice and atonement:

> And Moses returned unto the Lord, and said, Oh this people have sinned a great sin, and have made them gods of gold. Yet now, if thou wilt forgive their sin, and if not, blot me, I pray thee, out of thy book which thou has written.

While the Lord's wrath is strong, Moses' repentance eventually softens his anger. God reconciles the Jews to himself and reinstates his covenant:

> And the Lord said unto Moses, depart, and go up hence, thou and the people which thou has brought up out of the land of Egypt, unto the land which I sware unto Abraham, to Isaac, and to Jacob, saying, Unto thy seed will I give it: And I will send an angel before thee: I will drive out the Canaanite, the Amorite, and the Hittite, and the Perizzite, the Hivite and the Jebusite: Unto a land flowing with milk and honey.

This story, like so much of Jewish teaching, emphasizes the opportunity represented by sin. Through repentance comes reconciliation; through reconciliation comes renewal, making sin's consequences far less severe.

Permanence breeds severity when it comes to worst-case labels. The issue of honor provides further evidence of this trend. We know that in some cultures, particularly premodern cultures, losing one's honor is the worst that can happen. Dishonorable acts are durable and permanently stain an individual's reputation and value. And in the face of permanence, consequences for dishonorable conduct prove exceptionally severe. Consider the treatment of honor in feudal Japan. Japanese traditions taught that the loss of honor was an unspeakable fate. Once dishonored, one could never recover from the shame. Indeed, only with the ultimate sacrifice could the tainted restore honor to their offspring. In this regard, *seppuku* (perhaps better known to English-speakers as *hara-kiri*) provided the primary rejoinder to shame. This act, a highly ritualized suicide by disembowelment, originated among the samurai and warrior noblemen. "Honor for the samurai was dearer than life, and in many cases, self-destruction was regarded not simply as a right, but as the only right course."[21]

For centuries, *seppuku* became Japan's most frequent prescription for dishonor. Only in 1868 did the Japanese government formally outlaw the ritual. While such laws significantly diminished the prevalence of *seppuku*, the practice never fully disappeared. During World War II, for example, many Japanese soldiers committed *seppuku* as an alternative to capture.[22] Indeed, Tojo, the mastermind of the Japanese military, attempted to kill himself upon Japan's defeat in the war, although he chose shooting as opposed to the *hara-kiri* method.[23] Even in contemporary Japan, remnants of the *seppuku* tradition exist. "Although suicide is deplored in Japan today, it does not have the sinful overtones that are common in the west. People still kill themselves for failed businesses, involvement in love triangles, or even failing school examinations." When dishonor carries a permanent stain, death may be viewed as the lesser of two evils.[24]

In many Asian, Latin American, and Middle Eastern countries, the cultural stance toward honor mirrors that of feudal Japan. Family dishonor can represent the worst of all evils, and those responsible for shaming the unit are shown little mercy. In reporting on honor killings in Palestine, for example, journalist Susanne Ruggi confirms this view: "The family constitutes the fundamental building-block of Palestinian society. Family status is largely dependent upon its honor, much of which is determined by the respectability of its daughters, who can damage it *irreparably* by the perceived misuse of their sexuality."[25] Because dishonor carries permanent shame, it is punished in the extreme. Thus, a father or brother may "justifiably" murder the woman who sullied the family name, viewing their act as a duty to the family unit. In interviews with CNN reporter Walter Rodgers, several Middle Eastern men shared their perspective in this regard. Kamel Hader, for example, killed his unmarried sister when she came home pregnant. Hader vowed "he would do it again. 'If a woman does something wrong, you are supposed to kill her to regain family honor,' Hader said, 'Otherwise, we live in shame.'"[26]

In keeping with such beliefs, family murderers are rarely held accountable for their acts. Rather, the murders are viewed as fitting punishment for a heinous crime. Thus, Brazilian men have successfully invoked the "honor defense" for more than thirty years. In certain regions of Turkey, it has been used even longer. And in Jordan, the parliament itself has repeatedly refused to revoke "article 340 of the Penal Code, which provides for the lessening or elimination of penalties for men who commit honor murders."[27] Throughout Asia, Latin America, and the Middle East, the permanence of worst-case labels legitimates extreme responses, and adjudicators of punishment are lauded as protectors of order and virtue.

Power of the Labeler

The notion of power has long been central to discussions of social phenomena. Power's place in the analysis of the worst proves no exception. Whether one views power as inherent in structural relations (as argued by Karl Marx) or connected to rational choice (a position preferred by Max Weber), the result is ultimately the same. When the label "worst" is applied by a dominant person or group, its consequences are typically devastating in kind. But when the label is issued by a powerless or subordinate source, the impact of the label proves far less severe. This pattern is easy to understand, for a central advantage of power is the ability to exercise social control in the service of one's interests. Thus, in addition to defining a person or group as the worst of a setting or context, the powerful have the ability to enforce their view of the world. In so doing, they reify a social arrangement that destines the labeled to inescapable harm.

Consider the consequences of a powerful majority labeling a powerless minority the worst of humanity. History is replete with monstrous examples. The Ottoman Empire circa 1915: Following the deposition of Abdülhamid II, whose government had itself persecuted and massacred Armenian villages, the ruling Young Turk party defines the Armenian minority as the worst of infidels and traitors. The label inflicted by the regime leads to the violent death of over 1.5 million Armenians. Germany circa World War II: The Nazi war machine defines the Jewish minority as the worst specimens of human-ity. The declaration results in the torture and extermination of nearly 6 mil-lion Jews. Cambodia circa 1975: Those labeled the worst of political enemies by the powerful Pol Pot regime pay an excruciating price. In prisons such as Security Prison 21 and extermination camps such as Choeung Ek (the Killing Fields), over a million people are murdered in a campaign of terror. Rwanda circa 1994: The dominant Hutus define the Tutsi minority as an affront to humanity. The label enables a planned and systematic genocide in which over a million Tutsis are killed—nearly a third of those on the planet. In these sit-uations, and scores of others like them, the labels applied by the powerful completely subsume the oppressed. The powerful create a context in which their targets have little recourse or chance of escape.

The story ends quite differently when a community's less powerful apply the label of worst to their oppressors. Such attempts at "social control from below" generally fail to accomplish their goal.[28] Consider, for example, some initiatives waged by U.S. civil rights leaders of the 1950s and 1960s. Elijah Muhammad, Malcolm X, Stokely Carmichael, H. Rap Brown, or Eldridge Cleaver often labeled whites as black Americans' worst enemies. "The white man knows that his acts have been those of a devil!" preached Elijah Muham-mad. "For four hundred years, the white man has had his foot long knife in the black man's back," argued Malcolm X.[29] These leaders urged black Amer-icans to seek power—via violence if necessary—and to tirelessly fight the abuses of their white oppressors. But the power of blacks vis-à-vis whites diminished the impact of such rhetoric. The national media (of course, pre-dominantly white) reported the Black Power movement as a new and dan-gerous development in the cause of civil rights. Most whites condemned the movement's racially separatist message; they condemned black activists as instigators of national division and needless violence. Despite the fervency with which black activists promoted their arguments, their labels and accu-sations emanated from a position of subordination. Consequently, the labels applied by Black Power leaders failed to significantly affect those to whom they were applied.

The same can be said of the period's women's liberation movement. In the rhetoric of the day, some of the movement's leaders labeled men as the worst purveyors of female oppression. The term "male chauvinist pig" became a common denigration for men who failed to acknowledge women's equality, and activists encouraged their followers to shake off the yoke. In this regard, activist Beverly Jones argued, "it is really very clever the way male society creates for women this premarital hell so that some man can save her from it and control her ever after by the threat of throwing her back."[30] New York City feminists distributed flyers at the Marriage License Bureau that cast marriage in the language of oppression:

> Did you know that you are your husband's prisoner? You have to live with him wherever *he* pleases. If he decides to move someplace else, either you go with him or he can charge you with desertion, get a divorce, and according to law, you deserve nothing because *you're the guilty party*. And that's if *he* were the one who moved.[31]

And in the SCUM Manifesto (Society for the Cutting Up of Men), artist and activist Valerie Solanis proclaimed men's deplorable nature and called for the destruction of the male sex. "The male," she wrote, "because of his obsession to compensate for not being female combined with his inability to relate and to feel compassion, has made of the world a shitpile."[32] Radical feminists' attempts to denigrate male oppressors were frequent and intense. But their efforts to cast male practices as worst-case oppression failed in large measure. As social subordinates, feminists did not speak from the same ground as their opponents. The feminists' depictions of their dominant male counterparts were often censored and ridiculed, trivialized and dismissed by the very group the comments were intended to portray.

෯

On the global stage, where leaders and diplomats jockey for advantage, the label of the worst punctuates the rhetoric of exchange. Indeed, applying the label seems a "must do" when it comes to framing one's enemies of the moment. During World War II, Allied diplomats dubbed Adolf Hitler the personification of evil.[33] (At the time, Japan's Tojo ran a close second.) And since World War II, Cambodia's Pol Pot, China's Mao Zedong, Cuba's Fidel Castro, Iran's Ayatollah Ruhollah Khomeini, Iraq's Saddam Hussein, Libya's Moammar Gadhafi, Panama's Manuel Noriega, Saudi terrorist Osama bin Laden, and Serbia's Slobodan Milosevic have "all had their day in the Rogue's Gallery of American (and Western European) foreign policy."[34] In keeping with such labeling habits, the U.S. State Department has adopted the term "rogue states," reportedly applying it to nations identified as worst-case security threats. Cuba, Iran, Iraq, Libya, Nicaragua, North Korea, and Syria have all been members of this troublesome class, a group former secretary of state Madeleine Albright describes as "the greatest challenges of our time because . . . they are there with the sole purpose of destroying the system."[35]

The labeling efforts of the United States and its western European allies have been quite effective. "Evildoers" are routinely brought to task, and rogue states suffer embargo and attack. But when the labeling tables are reversed and relatively powerless nations initiate accusations, the consequences of the labels are far less severe. Consider, for example, that during the Reagan era, Castro accused the United States of attempting to "wipe socialism off the face of the earth," and he denounced Ronald Reagan as "an unscrupulous opportunist" who was as "irresponsible as Hitler and potentially more dangerous." Libya's Moammar Gadhafi made similar accusations, labeling Ronald Reagan as "Hitler No. 2."[36] The Serbian government entered the dialogue as well. In response to the U.S. labeling of Milosovic, the Serbian leader condemned President Clinton for creating a "mass grave" with bombs that "massacred" scores of innocent civilians. Mrs. Milosevic said of U.S. actions, "This is not very courageous. This is as if a man who is 40 years old beat up a boy who is 10 years old."[37] Saddam Hussein has also joined this chorus of voices. In 2004, for example, as the dictator was arraigned in an Iraqi court, he proclaimed his innocence, calling President George W. Bush "the real criminal."[38] In every case, the words were harsh, but consequences were few. In keeping with the patterns of labeling and power, these accusations had little impact beyond the accusers' most avid followers. When labels of the worst emanate from those less powerful, accusations rarely carry a significant punch.[39]

Among ethnicities, races, genders, and nations, where minorities and majorities battle, the impact of power on labeling consequences remains steady and predictable. We should not be surprised, then, to learn that this pattern is woven into formal law and thus consistently replicated in the definition and treatment of crime. Consider the crime of murder. In most legal arenas, murder is considered the worst offense one can commit. Yet the consequences of the label "murderer" differ with reference to the relative power of victim and accused. Suspicion of murder proves far more dangerous to those of lower socioeconomic status than it does to those who occupy more privileged positions. Indeed, historically, many societies attach especially severe penalties to crimes involving subordinate attacks on dominants. Sociologist Mary Pat Baumgartner tells us, for example, that English law elevated murder to the level of "petty treason" when the act was committed by servant against master or wife against husband.[40] The same can be said with reference to racial status and power. Racial minority and majority status have historically been associated with differential punishment. In the United States, for example, blacks who murder blacks receive harsher treatment than whites who murder blacks, and blacks who murder whites receive harsher treatment than whites who murder whites. Note too that homicide is most likely to result in capital punishment when a black perpetrator murders a white victim.[41]

Sociologist Donald Black tells us that "the vertical direction of behavior influences its texture."[42] Thus, when the powerful engage in heinous crimes such as murder, their acts are often recast as necessary or justifiable, their punishments consequently lenient or simply nonexistent. In this regard, Southern whites freely engaged in the lynching of blacks, and their powerful status ensured that "no one was arrested, much less prosecuted or punished, though killers were frequently well known and readily available."[43] In Renaissance Europe, poor and powerless vagrants were recast as dangerous werewolves; they were killed without contention by the community's powerful, all in the name of public protection.[44] In Brazil, wives were bludgeoned to death by their legally dominant husbands, crimes justified by a man's right to protect his honor and interests. While these events constituted murderous acts, their perpetrators were protected by their status. Murder was recast as a moralistic response for which victims had no recourse and perpetrators paid no price.

᳁

Label a thing as real and it is real in its consequences? W. I. Thomas's statement requires some qualification, for power does not only influence the consequences of the label worst. In many instances, power determines which definition of worst will reign in a community's mind. We see this pattern quite clearly in contemporary debates addressing gun violence and gun control in the United States. Proponents of gun control—including organizations such as the Center to Prevent Handgun Violence, the Coalition to Stop Gun Violence, the Million Mom March, and the Violence Policy Center—work to define the availability of guns as the worst of all evils. In this regard, the Web site of the Million Mom March strives to raise Americans' consciousness to the danger of guns:

- In 2000, 1,776 children and teenagers were murdered with guns, 1007 committed suicide with guns, and 193 died in unintentional shootings. A total of 3,042 young people were killed by firearms in the U.S., one every three hours.
- For every child killed by a gun, four are wounded.
- Firearms are the second leading cause of death (after motor vehicle accidents) for young people 19 and under in the U.S.

- The rate of firearm deaths of under 14-year-olds is nearly 12 times higher in the U.S. than in 25 other industrialized countries combined.
- The presence of a gun in the home triples the risk of homicide in the home and increases the risk of suicide fivefold.[45]

The Coalition to Stop Gun Violence makes a similar effort, noting the proliferation of guns and the dangers they present:

> America is a nation flooded with an overwhelming number of firearms. There are currently an estimated 192 million guns in private hands. Studies report that 25% of individuals and 35% of households own at least one gun. . . . Seventy-four percent of gun owners own more than one firearm. . . . Forty-two percent of individuals and 34% of households report owning 4 or more guns. . . . These small arsenals are very dangerous since, as one study noted, a firearm in the home is 43 times more likely to be used for suicide or murder than self-defense.[46]

The worst is lurking, but it can be avoided if we act now. Thus, the Violence Policy Center urges Web site visitors to rally their legislators. Only government regulation will stop the ticking time bomb of gun accessibility:

> Firearms are exempt from Federal health and safety requirements, unlike virtually all other products—from toys to jumbo jets. The Firearms Safety and Consumer Protection Act would subject the gun industry to the same safety standards as virtually all other products sold in America.[47]

Of course, opponents of gun control reject accessibility as the worst-case scenario of guns. Instead, pro-gun groups forward government regulation as the worst that could happen. The National Rifle Association (NRA), for example, equates gun control with a loss of personal freedom, and provides statistics, research articles, and commentary that substantiate the point. In an article entitled "The 'Million Mom' Posse," for example, David Lampo argues that gun violence is decreasing, a feat accomplished, he argues, without government control:

> They're still lying about kids and guns. That is not a good thing. It sets a bad example for "the kids." On their web site they still talk about honoring "the memory of the 10 children who die from gunfire every single day in America." This is simply not true. According to the National Center for Health Statistics, in 1998 there were 609 firearm-related fatalities

among children up to and including 14 years of age, and of these, 121 were accidental. The number of children accidentally killing other children with handguns could be counted on two hands. More kids drown in backyard pools or from accidents involving space heaters or bicycles than die in gun accidents. In fact, the number of gun accidents *are at record lows*, so one would think that Moms everywhere would be celebrating. But not *these* Moms. They're on a mission.[48]

For the NRA, regulation is a gun owner's worst-case scenario, and the association urges its membership to fight for citizens' rights. In an address to the NRA membership, James Jay Baker warned:

> The never-ending tendency of government to aggregate more power and control over our lives remains, as do thousands of bureaucrats who were the line workers of the Clinton/Gore gun control machine. We are just getting started on reversing eight years of sweeping attacks on our rights. . . . Don't look in the sky for our enemies—nor do we need to look past our borders. Our enemies are hiding in plain sight—deep within the bowels of every federal bureaucracy, and in the back rooms of offices occupied by anti-gun politicians.[49]

In an effort to avoid the worst-case scenario of control, the NRA designs scores of educational programs intended to protect the right to arms and normalize the role of the gun in everyday life.

The anti-gun and pro-gun lobbies forward opposite definitions of the worst. Each lobby presents a compelling set of claims; each argues their case with equal enthusiasm. But in the public sphere, the pro-gun lobby has won the definitional war. The notion of government regulation as the worst-case scenario enjoys clear prominence and effectiveness. Gallup polls document increased support for the NRA's position. While 70 percent of those polled in 1993 thought gun laws should be stricter, only 51 percent of those polled in 2003 held such a position. Note too that those supporting no change in gun laws increased from 24 percent to 33 percent during the same time period; and the number of people supporting less strict gun laws nearly quadrupled— from 4 percent to 15 percent. Even when gun violence is linked to children, the public is more likely to embrace the NRA position—namely, gun control will not solve the problems of gun-related deaths. For example, when asked, "In your opinion, what is the single most important thing that could be done to prevent another incidence of school shootings by students, like the recent ones in California," only 11 percent of respondents believed that better gun control laws would decrease levels of school violence.[50]

The NRA and its allies appear the victors in these definitional wars. But given the organization's power relative to the anti-gun lobby, we should not be surprised. While the anti-gun lobby is a newly organizing group, the NRA is considered by many to be the most powerful lobby in the United States. Indeed, in *Fortune* magazine's most recent "Power 25," a list that identifies lobbies with the greatest national influence, the NRA ranked number one.[51] Even the organization's most vocal opponents acknowledge the NRA's position. In a Dan Rather interview, conducted immediately prior to the 2001 inauguration, President Bill Clinton noted, "You've got to give it to [the NRA]. They've done a good job." The president credited the NRA with "the fact that the Democrats didn't win the house this time. And they hurt Al Gore."[52]

⁓

The powerful define the worst: that relationship peppers the public discourse. We saw it, for example, in the political debates surrounding one of the most controversial trade agreements of a generation, the 1993 North American Free Trade Agreement (NAFTA). Upon its proposal, NAFTA became the Clinton administration's most significant eco-political battle. And during the campaign for the treaty's passage, pro-NAFTA and anti-NAFTA forces fought to define the agreement's worst-case consequences. The former, led by President Clinton and his (unlikely) allies Senator Robert Dole, Representatives Newt Gingrich and Bob Michel, and former presidents Gerald Ford and George H. W. Bush, argued that NAFTA would better integrate the international trade arena, enabling the United States to exert more control in world markets. Pro-NAFTA forces were especially sure that NAFTA would open the Mexican market to American goods. Within five years, it was argued, free trade with Mexico alone would increase U.S. production and create close to a million new American jobs. For the pro-NAFTA forces, the treaty was a "no-brainer." Clinton argued that its passage would make the United States "the model of democratic capitalism and free trade for the rest of the world," and that NAFTA's defeat would preclude free international trade and permanently damage U.S. stature in the global economy.[53]

Of course, anti-NAFTA forces presented the treaty in a very different light, fighting to define the agreement as "the worst treaty of all time." For the anti-NAFTA group—again, a collection of strange bedfellows, including Ross Perot, Pat Buchanan, Jesse Jackson, Jerry Brown, Ralph Nader, and the

AFL-CIO—NAFTA was a disaster that "will send U.S. jobs hurtling into Mexico."[54] Indeed, Perot argued that the passage of NAFTA would put nearly 6 million American jobs "at risk" as businesses moved their operations south "to take advantage of Mexico's $2.25-an-hour wages." In Perot's memorable phrase, "You're going to hear the giant sucking sound of jobs pulled out of this country."[55]

Which trajectory truly represented the country's worst economic fate? The winning answer had much to do with the relative power of the combatants. Anti-NAFTA forces simply lacked the stature of their opponents. Perot and Buchanan were attacked as ultraconservatives who were out of touch with the Republican Party; Jackson, Nader, and Brown as ultraliberals out of touch with most Democrats.[56] "And with Union membership shrinking to barely 15% of the workforce, labor's clout in legislative policy-making proved increasingly weak."[57] The power of the pro-NAFTA contingency helped ensconce their definition of the worst. And despite the treaty's disappointments—most notably the hefty loss of apparel-related union jobs and a rush of speculative peso investments linked to Mexico's 1994 economic collapse—public opinion remained true to the pro-NAFTA definition of reality. In Gallup polls taken both during the NAFTA debate and after the agreement's successful passage in Congress, a majority of Americans supported the legislation, considering it a positive step for the U.S. economy.[58]

Normative Reaction to Criticism at Work in the Labeling Context

Power tells us something about the actors who label. Durability tells us something about the label itself. But what of the settings in which labeling occurs? Does the context surrounding quality evaluation impact a label's consequences? In this section, we will see that certain aspects of context matter greatly. The contextual norms that govern the use of criticism prove especially important in this regard. For when criticism is common and accepted within the evaluative context, the label of worst carries far less impact than it does in settings where criticism is unwelcome or taboo.

I use the term "caldron" to describe a setting in which criticism proves routine. Caldrons present us with a context in which competition is always bubbling; alliances are fluid; social bonds are constantly forming and reforming in accord with groups' and individuals' current interests and goals. In such settings, criticism functions as the currency of competitive exchange, and the label of worst is showered on opponents without hesitancy or concern. But in an environment where such a serious label proves common-place, prevalence can easily detract from the label's ultimate impact.

Consider the caldron of U.S. national politics, a setting defined by the struggle for power and control. As the battle for dominance ensues, alliances are forged then broken, groups configured then redesigned. In these political war zones, the label of worst flies freely between combatants, tossed like a grenade into opposing political camps. In the eyes of opponents, every ad-ministration's scandal becomes history's worst moment, be it Watergate, Iran-Contra, Monicagate, or Karl Rove's indiscretions. With each new ses-sion, a congressional group discovers a worst-case offender in its opponents' ranks: Barney Frank and his pages, Robert Packwood and his female staffers, the illicit affairs of Henry Hyde and Newt Gingrich, the corruption of Al D'Amato and Bob Toricelli, of Scooter Libby and Karl Rove. The list, of course, goes on and on.

When it comes to the real work of politics—namely, lawmaking—politi-cians are at the ready, defining their opponents' legislation as the worst propo-sition in the history of democracy. Democrats labeled Reagan's 1986 Tax Reform Act as the worst tax law on record; Republicans said the same of Clinton's 1993 legislation; and members from both sides of the aisle claimed that Bush's $1.3 trillion plan would stand as the undisputed worst-case tax law. "Don't ask, don't tell," universal health care, the privatization of Social Security, or Alaskan oil drilling—all of these proposals have been dubbed the worst by their authors' legislative opponents. Indeed, the worst is so com-mon to American politics that elections often become a time for voters to exclude the worst of two evils. In his coverage of the momentous 2000 presi-dential election, journalist Dan Balz captured the sentiment: "Much of Cam-paign 2000 will be run through a rear-view mirror, with the debate already being framed as a choice between the worst scandals of Clinton-Gore and the worst policies of Reagan-Bush-Gingrich."[59] And so it goes in American poli-tics, being the worst is hardly distinguishing. People and programs are likely to share the title with countless others. As a result, the label of worst be-comes normative, not unique, tempering the effect of an otherwise isolating mark.

Politics is a caldron, and it is one of many in a society's fields of action. The area of diet and nutrition provide another illustration. As experts jockey for marketing position, the label of worst emerges with startling frequency. Indeed, at one time or another, most of the foods in Americans' daily diet, as well as the strategies and settings in which they are consumed, have been touted as a worst-case example of bad health practices. Consider, for instance, the highly competitive field of dieting. In the 1980s and 1990s, nutritional gurus argued over the foundations of a healthy diet. The majority sang the praises of diets rich in carbohydrates. At the same time, they condemned high protein diets as one's worst nutritional course. In recent years, of course, the nutritional tables have turned. "Proteiners" have gained the edge in the national dieting discourse. Now experts forward high protein diets as the best approach to eating while labeling carbohydrates the villains of healthy cuisine.

Where to eat? Here too the caldron bubbles with worst-case scenarios. There is scarcely a newscast that does not spotlight "deadly" restaurants and supermarkets—locations that failed tests of cleanliness. According to some nutritionists and health inspectors, eating out—even in the most expensive and exclusive venues—can be a recipe for disaster.[60] So too can a simple trip to one's favorite supermarket or local grocery store. How about the amounts we eat—what is best and worst in this regard? Some experts warn that eating too little is the worst thing one can do, for it taxes the system and sends the body into a starvation response. But according to experts, supersizing your meals can tax the body as well. Thus, packing on the pounds represents another popular worst-case scenario.

It is simply hard to identify an eating strategy or setting that one group or another has not linked to disaster. And unfortunately, the same holds true when we examine the report card on specific foods. Fish, for example, was long forwarded as the best eating choice because of its rich concentration of Omega-3 fatty acids. But then came the discovery of high mercury levels, rendering fatty fish a long-term health risk. Chicken and eggs had their salmonella woes, pork its trichinosis, and eating beef could put one at risk for E. coli infection, mad cow disease, or dangerous elevations of saturated fat. The worst of foods—the pundits' lists go on and on. Wine may be good for your heart but bad for your liver, and a potential contributor to cancer. Fresh vegetables are good, unless farmers continue to treat them freely with pesticides. Chocolate, eggs, coffee, tea, margarine, oil, soy, and dairy: each of these foods has enjoyed its day as the worst thing one can eat.

Eat at your own risk. At times, that seems to be the message to food lovers. But does this caldron of worst-case labels carry any consequence? Polls suggest that in the area of nutrition, worst-case labels have little impact. Despite the stories of danger forwarded by various nutritional camps, recent surveys show that 85 percent of Americans say they are confident about the safety and cleanliness of the foods they buy at the grocery store; 77 percent feel equally confident in the safety of restaurant food, as well as the safety of the food supply from bioterrorism. Indeed, warnings about the worst of foods have become so numerous that, more and more, people are choosing to ignore them completely. Only 23 percent of Americans report paying "a lot of attention" to the labeling of food-related worst-case scenarios.[61]

◦◦∞◦◦

Caldrons have their converse. I use the term "fraternities" to denote contexts that are intolerant of criticism. In fraternities, criticism is generally smothered through the exercise of power; it is routinely stifled by demands of community loyalty. And in those rare moments when criticism is expressed, it is done in accord with the strictest guidelines. Thus, in fraternities, criticism typically flows from dominant to subordinate; it is expressed within a group but forbidden from traveling beyond the group's borders. These rules greatly influence the impact of the label "worst," for when criticism is so vehemently discouraged, the label becomes a dangerous anomaly—one capable of infecting more than those who carry the title. Given its seriousness, the label must be met with swift, forceful consequences. Only rapid and severe responses can limit the label's effect on the broader community.

The police provide a prototypical example of a fraternal context, with blind loyalty and intense cohesion fueling communal relations. Within the ranks of the police, criticism is strongly discouraged, which explains, in part, why police officers routinely despise internal affairs bureaus. If a police officer directs criticism toward an authority, he will likely be punished for insubordination. And if one officer criticizes another to those outside the community, she will likely be viewed as a traitor to the group. Note too that when "outsiders" direct criticism toward the police, it rarely results in group reflection or evaluation. In the face of attacks, police typically close ranks, creating "the blue wall of silence" so common to law enforcement.[62]

The routine aversion to criticism demonstrated by the police results in what some researchers call a special moral code. Sociologist Jay Livingston notes that "the police draw the lines in extremely different ways and at different points than do either the court system or the public." While an ordinary citizen may criticize a police officer's use of force as excessive, a fellow officer will "turn a blind eye," legitimating the need for brutality. Similarly, police corruption may be loudly criticized by civilians, but generally tolerated by the perpetrator's fellow officers.[63] Averting one's gaze, refusing to acknowledge and criticize a colleague's dishonesty, protects the broader community from a sullying mark.

Of course, there are times—even in police fraternities—when the worst becomes impossible to hide. In such instances, the label's consequences are unmistakably severe. Consider, for example, the highly publicized case of Stephanie C. Mohr, a police officer with a canine unit in Prince George's County, Washington, D.C. Mohr encountered two homeless men sleeping on the roof of a Tacoma Park printing company. The men were unarmed and showed no resistance to arrest. Yet seemingly without cause, Mohr (an officer with a record of questionable behavior) released her attack dogs on the men. The act was considered so heinous and the public outcry so vocal that prosecutors successfully broke the police fraternity's wall of silence. They convinced several of Mohr's fellow officers to testify against her in court.[64] As a result, Mohr was found guilty of aggravated assault and sentenced to ten years in jail—the maximum penalty. Similar penalties were handed down in one of the new millennium's most publicized police corruption trials—the brutal beating and sodomizing of New York City resident Abner Louima. Prosecutors were especially interested in officer Justin Volpe, the man identified as Louima's prime attacker. (According to court testimony, Volpe took Louima to a secluded men's room, wrestled him to the ground, and sodomized him with a toilet plunger.) Here as well, a crack in the blue wall of silence ensured that justice was served. Volpe's acts were so brutal, so impossible to hide, that the police fraternity cooperated in the assignment of blame. Several officers from the 70th Precinct testified against Volpe (as well as against three other officers who helped Volpe cover up his actions).[65] As a result, Volpe received an especially harsh sentence—thirty years in a maximum-security prison.

The police force provides a lucid illustration of a fraternal context. But similar settings exist across the social terrain. Consider, for example, what religious educator Donald Cozzens calls the "clerical fraternity," more commonly known as the Catholic priesthood.[66] The priesthood, like the police, displays an authoritarian style of leadership. Demands for obedience and loyalty leave little room for criticism. Thus, in clerical fraternities, the "good" priest does not question his pastor, bishop, or pope; the good priest does not expect (and indeed, may not tolerate) criticism from the laity he leads. Criticism offends the fraternity's emphasis on loyalty and cohesion, a stance to which oaths of fidelity bind every priest. Once ordained, the good priest proclaims his allegiance not simply to Jesus Christ, but to his colleagues and leaders—to the church itself.

Cozzens suggests that the church's demands for unquestioned obedience and loyalty lead to the emergence of a dark side in the community. In discouraging criticism, fraternal rules create a veil of secrecy. Such secrecy protects the group's "sinners" from public exposure and allows fraternal leadership to quietly sweep infractions under the rug. In recent years, such practices have been widely scrutinized in the news—particularly with reference to sexual indiscretions. Research and journalistic investigations suggest that priests violate their most sacred vow of celibacy with shocking frequency. Journalist David Firestone, for example, quotes studies that claim "only half of all American priests abstain from sex."[67] And John F. Cleary, general counsel for Church Mutual Insurance of Merill, Wisconsin, notes: "Today, the number of credible sexual abuse and misconduct cases is astounding."[68] Cleary's research suggests that these widespread sexual activities are often nonconsensual; other studies support that contention. In 2001, for example, both the *National Catholic Reporter* (a newspaper based in Kansas City, Missouri) and the *New York Times* published portions of a scathing report documenting priests' involvement in unwanted intimacy and rape. The O'Donahue report cites examples of sexual promiscuity and abuse occurring within twenty-three countries, including the United States, Ireland, Italy, Brazil, Colombia, India, and Africa:

> For six years, as Maura O'Donahue toured five continents raising awareness of HIV and AIDS, she heard stories from nuns, priests and doctors she was reluctant to accept: the sexual exploitation, including rape, of nuns by priests. . . . Dr. O'Donahue would write, in a report that reached the Vatican, of her "shock and disbelief at the magnitude of the problem. . . . Some priests are known to have relations with several women, and also to have children from more than one liaison," she reported. . . . In one country, angry parishioners with guns attacked the priest's home. . . . In some cases, would be nuns had to provide priests with sexual favours in order to acquire the recommendations necessary to work in the diocese.[69]

According to the *New York Times:*

> "Examples were also given of situations where priests were bringing sisters (and other young women) to Catholic health institutions for abortions," O'Donahue wrote in a follow up memo. "I gave one example of a priest who had brought a sister for an abortion. She died during the procedure, and the priest officiated at the requiem Mass.[70]

In keeping with the fraternity's aversion to criticism, the church has been less than diligent in acknowledging that such acts occur. While the church is quick to punish those who bring such stories to light, it has been much less inclined to punish the sexual offenders themselves. Indeed, the church's own reports reveal a consistent failure in this regard. The O'Donahue report, for example, notes that errant priests were often given nothing more than a mild reprimand.[71] Jason Berry of New Orleans, a freelance investigator of such cases, comments that

> the essential moral and pastoral positions of the church have been betrayed by local bishops who have resorted to strategies of concealment, sheltering priests and bunkering in behind defense attorneys. Sealed records and secret settlements allow the offenders to continue their patterns of abuse. . . . In many instances, attorneys bargain dollars for silence.[72]

Thus, despite the "ungodliness" of priestly sexual activity, the clerical leadership routinely looks the other way. Priests are transferred, lawsuits quietly settled, and the worst of sins need never be fully articulated or acknowledged.

But in the priesthood, as in police fraternities, there are times when the worst cannot be concealed. And when shocking behaviors become public, they are severely sanctioned. Consider the case of John J. Geoghan, a priest who, starting in the 1960s, reportedly molested more than fifty children. While the church often protects the child molesters in its ranks, Geoghan's crimes proved too plentiful to ignore. And when several of Geoghan's victims pressed criminal charges, the priest's story entered the public domain. In the face of widespread publicity, the church was forced to acknowledge that one of its members had committed the worst of sins. Once that label was applied, the consequences were unprecedented. Geoghan was defrocked—an extraordinary punishment authorized by the pope himself. He became the first priest to suffer such a punishment in the 125-year history of the Boston Catholic Diocese.[73] Similar consequences concluded the church's treatment of Bishop Joseph Keith Symons of Palm Springs, Florida. When a middle-aged man publicly accused the bishop of molesting him in his youth, Symons relented, confirming the charge as well as four other molestations. The public nature of the case made the worst of activities difficult to deny. And once he had been labeled, the church dealt Symons a swift and forceful punishment. The bishop tendered his resignation to Pope John Paul II, an act accepted without discussion or debate. The resignation was the first in the history of American Catholic bishops to be linked to sexual misconduct.[74]

⌒∞⌒

Being the worst—it may not always be as bad as it seems. Indeed, this chapter suggests that those laden with the title face widely varying consequences.

Why do we find such differences? The answer to that question rests, in part, in cultural and social dimensions of the labeling context. The label's intended durability, the power relations of the labeler and target, the norms of criticism that govern the labeler's domain—all of these factors have effects on the impact of worst-case titles. Our exploration of consequences shows, once again, that the assessment of quality is a highly social affair— one that, in the end, may be somewhat disconnected from the actual characteristics of the person, place, object, or event under evaluation.

CHAPTER SIX

Exceptions to the Rule

Throughout this book, I have argued that anticipating the worst is a rare and unusual phenomenon. This is because the cultural practices heretofore reviewed direct most groups and communities to images of the best. But while best-case vision is widespread, it is not universal. Exceptions to the rule of positive asymmetry can certainly be found. Indeed in some communities, one observes an inversion of quality-perception norms, with visions of the worst *consistently* dominating a community's attention.

As I researched the ways in which various groups address issues of quality, two communities seemed *especially* tied to such perceptual inversions: medical practitioners and computer information technicians. As we will see, medical practitioners and computer information technicians painstakingly specify the worst-case scenario as a matter of course. Indeed, the worst is so central to these groups' modus operandi that they present us with something more than a mere exception to the rule of positive asymmetry. Rather, medical practitioners and computer information technicians provide us with a systematic variation to that rule—the routine exercise of a phenomenon I call "negative asymmetry." Negative asymmetry stands in direct opposition to the ways of seeing heretofore discussed. As a perceptual mode, it foregrounds the worst, while rendering the best vague and inaccessible.

So striking is negative asymmetry among medical practitioners and computer information technicians that one must seize the groups as valuable analytic case studies.[1] As we explore the perceptual stance of these negative asymmetry "prototypes," we gain two important insights. First, we obtain a sense of daily action that is guided by visions of the worst. Second, we learn of certain striking similarities among communities that approach quality evaluation in this way. This chapter highlights such parallels and considers their role in negative asymmetry's development.

The Sites of Negative Asymmetry: Medical Practitioners

"Whatever houses I may visit, I will come for the benefit of the sick . . . keeping them from harm and injustice."[2] These words, of course, come from the Hippocratic oath, and in many ways, they capture the negative asymmetry that drives physicians' modus operandi. Sickness and physiological disorders are the raison d'être for the medical profession. And in order to protect patients from physical demise, doctors and other medical professionals (hereafter referred to as MPs), must diligently attend to the worst. Indeed, the good MP must, as a matter of course, vigilantly search for signs of the body's most dire fates.

Such vigilance is a hallmark of MPs' training, a point confirmed by the textbooks that initiate students to the field.[3] Consider, for example, Harrison's *Principles of Internal Medicine,* one of the most widely used texts in the United States. The very first chapter of the textbook, "The Practice of Medicine," sets the ground rules of medical performance: MPs are looking for trouble, nothing more. Their attentions must be focused on the signals of physiological danger. In this regard, students are taught that "the examination of a new patient must extend from head to toe *in an objective search for abnormalities.*" And once that search is complete, the physician must "*identify the crucial elements* in a complex history and physical examination and *extract the key laboratory results* from the crowded computer printouts of laboratory data in order to determine in a difficult case *whether to "treat" or "watch."*"[4] Treat or watch—are these really the doctor's only options? What if nothing unhealthy is found in a history or exam? Instructional texts rarely address the possibility of an innocuous conclusion. Indeed, most texts imply that a benign exam is highly unlikely.

We witness this stance in another of American medicine's most central medical texts, Pfenninger and Fowler's *Procedures for Primary Care Physicians.* This book contains 216 instructional categories, addressing treatment techniques for conditions ranging from acne to burns to cervical polyps to hernias. The following excerpt, for example, describes the exercise, or stress, test. Here the authors review the "how and why" of this now routine diagnostic procedure. Note that, initially, the discussion of the test seems informative, perhaps even upbeat:

> Twelve million Americans have known coronary heart disease (CAD). Unfortunately, over half of individuals with CAD first discover their diagnosis after a bad outcome, namely a myocardial infarction (MI) or sudden cardiac death. . . . Exercise testing is not only a safe and cost-effective

method for diagnosing coronary artery disease (CAD). . . . The sensitivity
of exercise testing exceeds 90% (perhaps 95%).

But in keeping with MPs' propensity for negative asymmetry, the worst-case
scenario soon works its way into the text. The authors assume, for example,
that most tests will prove problematic. Thus, they encourage MPs to perform
the exercise test as a means of decreasing "liability for the clinician from failure to diagnose." Assumptions of worst-case results also permeate the
authors' advice regarding post-test protocol. In essence, the authors instruct
their students to prepare patients for radical medical responses:

> With immediately available results . . . the patient can be immediately
> counseled from an outcomes or prognosis perspective. Such data will
> allow a patient to make a truly informed decision before undergoing a
> major procedure such as coronary artery bypass surgery. With personal-
> ized data, the patient can compare his or her known risks of surgery,
> thereby reserving surgery for those who choose to accept the risks.

In discussing the exercise test, the authors send students a clear message: disaster lurks in the patient's body. And with the worst so present, so likely to
emerge, the responsible doctor can only hope to prepare for it and stop it. So
grave is this responsibility that the authors advise medical students to routinely scan patients for the worst. The exercise test should be seriously considered even when clear symptoms of heart disease are absent from patient's
complaints:

> In addition to managing those with symptoms or known CAD, primary
> care clinicians can use exercise testing to screen certain asymptomatic
> individuals. Such screening may be especially helpful for diabetics,
> firemen, or older individuals about to embark on a vigorous exercise
> program.[5]

One might argue, of course, that books on diagnosis and clinical care are
naturally skewed to the consideration of problems. After all, most patients
consult MPs only when something is amiss. But even in texts of a different
sort—biology and physiology texts that are typically designed to explain the
body's standard functioning—discussions of malfunctions often eclipse those
of normal processes. Consider this excerpt from Arthur Guyton and John

Hall's very popular *Textbook of Medical Physiology.* Chapter 61, entitled "Cerebral Blood Flow," promises to explain the normal routines of blood flow, oxygen distribution, and cerebrospinal fluids in the brain. But by the time one completes the chapter's very first paragraph, it becomes clear that normal performance will be relegated to the background of the discussion. In its place, the worst of cerebral abnormalities will control the medical lesson:

> Thus far, we have discussed the function of the brain as if it were inde-
> pendent of its blood flow, its metabolism, and its fluids. However, this is
> far from true because abnormalities of any of these can profoundly affect
> brain function. For instance, total cessation of blood flow to the brain
> causes unconsciousness within 5 to 10 seconds. . . . abnormalities of the
> cerebrospinal fluid, either in its composition or in its fluid pressure, can
> have equally serious effects on brain function.[6]

The same can be said for the textbook's treatment of basic respiratory processes. At first glance, it appears as if the book devotes three chapters to normal respiratory operations and only one chapter to respiratory abnormalities. But upon closer scrutiny it becomes clear that discussions of normal
respiration are filled with considerations of respiratory malfunctions. Thus
"alveolar ventilation" (the rate at which new air reaches the elements of the
respiratory system) cannot be considered without a discussion of "dead
space" (a problematic area in the respiratory passages where gas exchange
does not occur). Similarly, pulmonary circulation (blood flow through the
lungs) cannot be fully explained without reference to elevated pulmonary
capillary pressure or pulmonary edema (increases in pressure that cause
harmful fluid retention in the lungs).

Guyton and Hall are not alone in adopting this negative approach. *Gray's
Anatomy,* a book many consider the bible of the human body, follows a similar tact. With every normal process, with every routine instruction, comes
a warning of multiple dysfunctions and potential disasters. Consider, for
example, the book's description of a routine chest exam. The instructions
make little mention of the healthy chest:

> The nipples in the male and the breasts in the female should be inspected.
> Accessory nipples are not infrequent and carcinoma of the breast, the
> most common carcinoma of females in the United Kingdom, may pro-
> duce visible abnormalities. Normal chest expansion is symmetrical. The
> subject should be observed breathing normally and taking deep breaths.

A stiff or shrunken lung, or pleural disease will impair expansion on that side. . . . The size of the chest should also be noted. It may, for example, be barrel shaped with increase in the anteroposterior diameter when the lungs are over inflated as in emphysema.

The same can be said of the manual's discussion of a routine mouth exam. MPs are instructed to seek abnormalities:

> With the mouth open, it is possible to examine all the teeth, to inspect and palpate the orifice of the parotid duct and to see the lymphoid tissue forming the palatine tonsils. The tongue may be examined for its general appearance and any abnormalities of movement which may reflect neuronal damage.[7]

These excerpts, and countless others like them, show that the lessons of basic biology mirror those of clinical practice. In training MPs, the focus on problems prevails. Good health is eclipsed or clouded in a student's perceptual field and illness is presented as the standard or norm.

The negative asymmetry that dominates early medical training is, of course, part of a broader phenomenon. In examining the knowledge base upon which training tools are built, one trend appears repeatedly. Worst-case scenarios form the core around which all medical knowledge is organized. We can look to one of medicine's most central informational tools for an illustration of this point, namely, diagnostic criteria. Diagnostic criteria represent mini–knowledge systems. And in these systems, a disease's worst manifestation forms the diagnostic reference point. Diagnostic criteria specify, in painstaking detail, gradations of infirmity. But such systems routinely eclipse the best-case outcome of an illness. Indeed, across diagnostic systems, recovery or good health—what one might reasonably define as the best of medical conditions—forms nothing more than a broad default class, a category defined by the *absence* of worst-case symptoms.

The dominance of the worst proves quite stark in the assessment of terminal illnesses. Most such diseases are evaluated and treated with reference to diagnostic stage models. Note that the development of a stage model always involves "backward" thinking. Models emerge from crystallized definitions of the worst case, or "end stage," of a disease. And only after fully defining the worst-case scenario are the preliminary stages of the illness demarcated and fine-tuned. Given this logic, we should not be surprised to learn that stage models never differentiate best-case and worst-case health. Rather, they are restricted to quality lows, distinguishing the serious from the critical from the hopeless. Consider, for example, the diagnostic criteria used in the treatment of breast cancer. MPs typically assess the disease using a detailed four-stage model:

> *Stage 0* (Noninvasive or In Situ Breast Cancer): Included in Stage 0 are both lobular carcinoma in situ and ductal carcinoma in situ.
>> *Lobular carcinoma in situ* (LCIS): Also called lobular neoplasia; sometimes classified as Stage 0 breast cancer. Abnormal cells grow within the lobules (milk-producing glands), but do not penetrate through the lobule walls. Most breast specialists do not consider LCIS a true breast cancer.
>> *Ductal carcinoma in situ* (DCIS): Cancer cells located within a duct; no invasion of surrounding fatty breast tissue.
> *Stage I:* Tumor measures smaller than 2 centimeters in diameter (three fourths of an inch or less). Does not appear to have spread beyond the breast.
> *Stage II:* Tumor measures larger than 2 centimeters in diameter and/or it has spread to lymph nodes under the arm on the same side as the breast cancer. Lymph nodes have not yet adhered to one another or to the surrounding tissues, a sign that the cancer has not yet advanced to stage III.
> *Stage III:* Stage III is divided into substages known as IIIA and IIIB.
>> *Stage IIIA:* Tumor or tumors either measure larger than 5 centimeters (over 2 inches) in diameter and/or have spread to lymph nodes that adhere to one another or surrounding tissue.
>> *Stage IIIB:* Breast cancers of any size that have spread to the skin, chest wall, or internal mammary lymph nodes (located beneath the breast and inside the chest).
> *Stage IV:* The cancer, regardless of its size, has spread (metastasized) to distant sites such as bones or lungs, or to lymph nodes not near the breast.[8]

While these criteria are quite elaborate, they mention nothing about the healthy breast. In this regard, the best-case scenario is peripheral to patient treatment. Rather, the criteria with which MPs assess and treat breast cancer emerge from the definition of stage 4 cancer. Once the worst manifestation of breast cancer is determined, lesser degrees are defined by "subtract-ing" stage 4 qualities.[9]

The diagnostic criteria for prostate cancer embody a similar logic. In the United States, the TNM system (developed by the American Joint Commit-tee on Cancer) represents the most commonly used diagnostic tool for this disease. The system assesses three dimensions of prostate cancer: the condi-tion of the tumor (T), nearby metastasis (N), and distant metastasis (M). Like the breast cancer model, the TNM system assumes the presence of serious disease. Within this framework, a healthy prostate proves irrelevant to the assessment process. Also like breast cancer, all stages of the TNM model are defined in relation to the end point of the disease:

T Stage

T1: *T1* refers to a tumor that is not felt during a digital rectal exam. But, cancer cells are found in a prostate biopsy or prostatectomy speci-men. T1 prostate cancers can be further subclassified as *T1a, T1b,* and *T1c.*

> *T1a and T1b:* These categories describe prostate cancers found inci-dentally (by "accident") during TURP (transurethral resection of the prostate) surgical procedures done to relieve symptoms of benign prostate enlargement. This operation is usually done because the enlarged prostate gland presses on the urethra and makes it difficult for a man to urinate. When prostate tissue is removed and checked under the microscope, cancer may be found, even though the doctor who removed the tissue did not expect cancer to be present. *T1a* indicates that less than 5% of the tissue removed is cancer and more than 95% is benign. If more than 5% is cancer, it is classified as *T1b.*

> *T1c:* *T1c* cancers are also found only by biopsy, but in these cases a core needle biopsy is done because the PSA blood test result suggested that a cancer might be present.

T2: *T2* means that a doctor can feel the prostate cancer by DRE and that the cancer is felt to remain within the prostate gland. This category is subclassified into *T2a* or *T2b.*

> *T2a:* This category means that the tumor involves only the right or left side of the prostate, but not both sides.

> *T2b:* This category means that both the left and right sides are involved.

T3: *T3* cancers have spread to the connective tissue next to the prostate and/or to the seminal vesicles (two small sacs next to the prostate that store semen), but do not involve any other organs. This group is divided into *T3a* and *T3b*.

T3a: In *T3a*, the cancer extends outside the prostate, but has not spread to the seminal vesicles.

T3b: With *T3b*, the cancer has spread to the seminal vesicles.

T4: *T4* means that the cancer has spread to tissues next to the prostate (other than the seminal vesicles), such as the bladder's external sphincter (muscles that help control urination), the rectum, and/or the wall of the pelvis.

N Stages

N0: *N0* means that the cancer has not spread to any lymph nodes.

N1: *N1* indicates spread to one or more regional lymph nodes in the pelvis.

M Stages

M0: *M0* means that the cancer has not metastasized beyond the regional nodes.

M1: *M1* means metastases are present in distant (outside of the pelvis) lymph nodes, in bones or other distant organs such as lungs, liver, or brain.[10]

In the TNM system, the road to the worst is defined in meticulous detail. But how is good health addressed in the TNM system? Recovery or remission carries no distinct specification. Rather, remission involves a period in which worst-case cues remain at bay. Thus, the healthy prostate is necessarily defined as one missing the signs of disease.

Diagnostic criteria are oblivious to the best case of heath; and in reviewing the medical knowledge base, one must note another important tendency. Articulation is inversely related to the seriousness of the disease. While the worst cases of health are meticulously specified, less serious diseases carry far less detail. And good health, supposedly the goal of medical treatment, is at best vaguely defined. Consider, for example, medical matters of the heart. The basic medical definition of heart failure, one of the worst human coronary conditions, is defined via a precise four-stage model:

Class I (Mild): No limitation of physical activity. Ordinary physical activity does not cause undue fatigue, palpitation, or dyspnea (shortness of breath).

Class II (Mild): Slight limitation of physical activity. Comfortable at rest, but ordinary physical activity results in fatigue, palpitation, and dyspnea (shortness of breath).

Class III (Moderate): Marked limitation of physical activity. Comfortable at rest, but less than ordinary activity causes fatigue, palpitation, and dyspnea (shortness of breath).

Class IV (Severe): Unable to carry out any physical activity without discomfort. Symptoms of cardiac insufficiency at rest. If any physical activity is undertaken, discomfort is increased.[11]

Further, most diagnostic manuals and medical dictionaries do not stop with the statement of stages; definitions of heart failure become much more elaborate.[12] For example, *The Merck Manual of Diagnosis and Therapy* devotes two pages to defining the problem, and an additional ten pages to elaborating that definition. *Mosby's Medical Nursing and Allied Health Dictionary* devotes eighty lines to the definition of heart failure, making it one of the longest entries in the text. Contrast such precision with that devoted to another heart disease: mitral valve prolapse. Mitral valve prolapse is a rather common heart malady. Indeed, estimates suggest that this problem is found in nearly 5 percent of the U.S. population. But the condition is much less serious than heart failure. Thus, in keeping with the medical community's tendency to highlight the worst, definitions of this minor disease are almost cursory in nature. According to *Mosby's,* "Mitral Valve Prolapse is a protrusion of one or both cusps of the mitral valve back into the left atrium during ventricular systole."[13] The criteria for diagnosis are equally minimal. As *The Merck Manual* states, "MVP is primarily diagnosed by auscultation (listening with a stethoscope). When a click and murmur are present, mitral regurgitation is usually mild to moderate."[14]

Diseases of the breast other than cancer provide a similar example. Contrast the detailed breast cancer specifications presented earlier with the definition of fibrocystic breast disease. Fibrocystic breast disease is a far more common and far less serious malady than cancer, and in keeping with medical convention, the condition is specified in comparatively simplistic terms. *The Merck Manual* tells us, for example, that "mastalgia, breast cysts, and nondescript lumpiness are common and often occur together; none of these conditions is abnormal. The combination is frequently described under the catchall term fibrocystic disease." Similarly, *Stedman's Medical Dictionary* simply states of the condition, "pertaining to or characterized by the presence of fibrocysts."[15]

Minor diseases are simply not well specified. And when one considers the quality highs of medicine—namely, good health—specificity all but disappears. Indeed, the medical field is nearly silent regarding definitions of best-case health. To illustrate this point, I consulted my sample of best-selling medical texts and diagnostic manuals, as well as a collection of medical Web sites.[16] Note that none of the books contained an entry for "good health," "normal health," or any similar term. The concept seemed beyond the purview of medical teaching. Approximately 15 percent of the Web sites I analyzed addressed the issue. But as one can see, these Web definitions of good health were, at best, broad and imprecise. Consider, for example, the definition provided by the Good Health Information Center:

> Waking up each and every morning and feeling vibrant and alive! Feeling the youthfulness and energy to accomplish all that's important in your life! To have the energy to conquer fears, stand up for more success in your life, and live every moment with maximum joy, wellness and living. To be a symbol of the beautiful gift of life.[17]

A similar definition was offered by the information and resources page on a Meniere's disease site:

> For most people, health and wellness is a physical AND mental state. It is the overall feeling of fitness: of having all your body systems performing the way they are meant to: without pain or discomfort: and a desire to conquer your own world! Just lots of energy and confidence![18]

To be sure, these Web sites enthusiastically pronounce the concept of good health. (One never finds exclamation marks in descriptions of terminal illnesses.) But the definitions clearly lack precision or detail. This vagary is not simply a product of such sites' "commercial" nature. Indeed, "technical" definitions of good health are equally enigmatic. For example, the Department of Health and Human Services defines good health as "the prevention or reduction of chronic disease." The World Health Organization is similarly brief. According to the WHO, good health is "a state of complete physical, mental and social well-being, and not merely the absence of disease or infirmity."[19]

It is worth noting that some holistic and homeopathic practitioners have attempted to balance the medical establishment's conceptualization of health. For example, Omraam Mikhaël Aïvanhov of Switzerland's Fraternité Blanche Universelle suggests that good health be redefined strictly in its own terms. He proposes the following treatment of the concept: "Health is the result of the work all the organs of our body carry out together and in harmony for the good of our whole being."[20] Doctor Manish Bhatia also comments on the need for a succinct definition of good health:

Health is a state of being free from disease. . . . [The definition] has a basic
fault in it—it tries to define a primary state through a secondary state.
Health is a primary state. It cannot be fully defined through a secondary
phenomenon, disease. And then there is a larger question. Does being
free from any disease which can be given a name make one healthy? I
think, no.[21]

Bhatia, of course, underscores the central flaw of negative asymmetry. The
approach ignores the unique integrity of quality highs. It treats good health
as a condition with only a relative existence, a condition that can be gauged
only with reference to the absence of the worst.

Given the centrality of negative asymmetry in medicine's knowledge base,
we should not be surprised to discover its prominence in MPs' routine clinical protocols. Imagine, for example, that on a visit to the doctor, a patient
complains of chest pain. In assessing the complaint, the doctor will execute
a standardized procedure. She will likely begin by obtaining a medical history. In executing this task, the doctor will *not* inquire about the presence of
healthy cues. She will *not* ask, for example, "Has your heart been beating
smoothly and steadily?" or "Have you remained energetic and pain free
when you exert yourself in exercise or strenuous activities?" Rather, the doctor will pose questions related to the worst-case scenarios of heart disease,
questions that alert the physician to signals of, for example, heart attack,
heart failure, cardiomyopathy, or unstable angina. A patient may be asked
about the presence of chest pain, palpitations or shortness of breath, about
feelings of light-headedness or fatigue. In every case, the doctor will remain
riveted to the worst-case perceptual porthole, with questions geared only to
negative physiological cues.

Negative asymmetry will characterize the doctor's physical exam as
well. When assessing the patient, for example, the physician will note the
patient's skin pallor. The doctor's search will not be geared to healthy skin
tones, but rather to signs of cyanosis (a bluish color that signals inadequate
circulation). The doctor will also check the size of the lower extremities. But
note that normal sized extremities are not on the doctor's mind. Rather, the
physician will look for swollen ankles or legs, as these characteristics signal
edema (the accumulation of fluid). Using a stethoscope, a doctor will assess
the patient's breath sounds, attending only to obstructive sounds that signal
fluid accumulation. She will listen to the opening and closing of the patient's
heart valves, searching for murmurs that indicate turbulent blood flow.

Throughout the exam, the doctor will attend to specific cues of calamity. And she will consider the patient healthy only when such worst-case signals fail to emerge.

Medical protocol carries physicians to the worst-case porthole of reality even during the most routine patient exams. Think back for a moment to your last annual physical. How did the visit unfold? You probably began by completing a patient history. That form immediately framed your visit in considerations of the worst. You noted, for example, previously diagnosed medical problems, alerting your doctor to the worst-case scenarios lurking in your physiology. You listed the diseases and ailments suffered by your parents, siblings, perhaps even your maternal and paternal grandparents, aunts or uncles. In so doing, you flagged for your doctor the worst-case scenarios proposed by your genes. Finally, you reported on your routine behaviors: smoking, drinking, taking drugs, both the frequencies and amounts; you reported being overweight, undernourished, overactive, under stress, spelling out all the worst-case scenarios you could be tempting with your actions.

When the forms were complete, and face-to-face interaction began, the worst continued to frame your encounter. Most likely your doctor or nurse inquired: "Are you having any physical complaints?" or "What seems to be the problem today?" One could confidently guess that no one inquired about the best features of your health. "What's working just right since the last time I saw you?" or "Do you feel marvelous?" Such questions are never posed, for medical protocol discourages your doctor from applauding your body's peaks and triumphs. Your doctor's job is to assess your problems, gauge their potential seriousness, and alleviate your suffering if possible.

When you and your doctor parted company, the worst continued to guide your experience. Billing for your visit was gauged with reference to a massive checklist of ailments. (Such ailments correspond to insurance codes that, in turn, dictate appropriate fees as negotiated by doctors and health insurance companies.) Thus, these forms continued to eclipse the role of good health in medical treatment. Indeed, most forms contain only one entry applicable to a healthy patient—a category typically labeled as "wellness care." Financially speaking, wellness may place you at a disadvantage. A majority of insurance companies either sharply limit or fail to cover services that denote the absence of disease. In eclipsing and clouding good health, medical billing, much like medical procedure, relegates the best-case diagnosis to the horizon of medical attention.

MPs' propensity toward negative asymmetry proves, perhaps, most blatant in the community's definitions of life and death. Consider, for example, that definitions of life—the best-case scenario of humanity—appeared in none of the medical textbooks, manuals, or reference books I analyzed. Medical dictionaries sometimes tackle the concept. But in such cases, the definitional elements are generally brief, vague, and often tautological. *Harper-Collins Illustrated Medical Dictionary* defines life as "the rate of quality manifested by active metabolism. Also called vitality." *Mosby's Medical, Nursing and Allied Health Dictionary* is similarly sparse and superficial: "[Life is] the energy that enables organisms to grow, reproduce, absorb and use nutrients, evolve, and in some organisms, achieve mobility, express consciousness, and demonstrate a voluntary use of the senses." *Stedman's Medical Dictionary*, currently the best-selling book of its kind, offers the most circular and thus least satisfying definition: "Vitality. The essential condition of being alive; the state of existence characterized by such functions as metabolism, growth, reproduction, adaptation, and response to stimuli." The entry then continues, although one can hardly say elaborates, by identifying life as "living organisms such as animals and plants." The definitions of life found on medical Web sites provide even less information. For example, Total Wellness, a health information site, states that the medical (and legal) definition of life is "a nerve impulse." A nerve impulse, nothing more; the site provides no further elaboration or specification.[22]

When one looks to medical definitions of death—humanity's worst-case scenario—a very different picture emerges. Indeed, MPs have worked for centuries to refine the concept, and with each attempt, the definition of death has grown more detailed and precise. The earliest definitions of death attended to elements detectable via the senses—that is, the absence of pulse or heartbeat, the absence of breathing, the absence of reflexes, dilated pupils, glassy corneas, and patchy skin pallor.[23] While these criteria were clear-cut, they left room for error. Indeed, mistakes in the pronouncement of death were sufficiently common that many individuals contracted for burial "safeguards" when making postmortem arrangements. Coffins, for example, were sometimes equipped with alarm systems. Such alarms allowed the "corpse" to pull a string in the coffin that, in turn, would ring a bell stationed above ground. The system was designed to alert the cemetery groundskeeper that an error had occurred.

In the 1960s and 1970s, advances in cardiac monitoring and resuscitation technology brought precision to definitions of death. By the 1970s, the pronouncement of death involved several highly technical criteria, including a flat line on the heartbeat monitor and the irreversibility of heart, respiratory, and reflex patterns. By the 1980s, MPS were able to track still finer gradations of death; they introduced the designation of "clinical death," a condition defined by the documented cessation of organ functioning. Later, the specification of death became even more explicit with the introduction of the category "brain death." Brain death involved irreparable neural damage resulting in the loss of functions such as perception, mentation, and motor response. The diagnosis involves painstaking assessments and measurements of, for example, specific levels of cerebral oxygen consumption, cerebral blood circulation (tested via a technique called angiography), as well as the presence of a "flat" electroencephalogram. As technologies continue to develop, the diagnosis of brain death is becoming even more detailed. For example, some MPs distinguish between total and partial loss of brain function, requiring that total loss occur before the label of brain death is applied.[24]

In each of these areas—professional training, the medical knowledge base, everyday practice, definitions of life and death—medical practitioners offer a clear example of a community driven by negative asymmetry. While most communities cannot be shifted from the best-case perceptual porthole, this group occupies the opposite vantage point. For MPs, it is the worst that remains centered in consciousness, with the best often eclipsed or clouded from active view. But as we shall see, MPs are not alone in this tendency.

The Sites of Negative Asymmetry: Computer Operators and Programmers

Theoretically speaking, computer operations involve three considerations: (1) the provision of smooth service, (2) the anticipation of mechanical error, and (3) the correction of mechanical error when it occurs. Note that these job criteria address both the best case (smooth operations) and the worst case (error) of computing. Yet computer operators, programmers, and systems analysts (hereafter referred to collectively as COPS) rarely maintain such a balanced perspective. In its enactment, computer work emphasizes system failure. As a consequence, the field focuses its technicians on the seemingly high likelihood of error. Indeed, according to computer experts, the modus operandi of COPS rests in the idea of "trouble." Philip Agre and Douglas Schuler capture the mindset:

> In order to apply their specialized expertise to real situations in the world, computer people need those situations to be packaged into discrete problems—problems that their particular techniques can expect to solve. *To*

be a computer person is to possess a certain repertoire of specialized
hammers and to be constantly looking out for nails to hit with them.[25]

Trouble: it lies at the center of the field's job definitions. We can see this
is in the Department of Labor's official description of computer operations:

> Computer equipment operators oversee the operation of computer hard-
> ware systems and equipment. They must make sure that expensive com-
> puters and related equipment are used as efficiently as possible. *This*
> *includes foreseeing problems before they occur and taking preventive*
> *measures as well as solving problems when they do occur.*[26]

The same is true for the Department of Labor's description of computer programming; programmers exist to solve problems:

> Computer programmers write, test, and maintain the detailed instruc-
> tions, called programs, that computers must follow to perform their func-
> tions. *They also conceive, design, and test logical structures for solving*
> *problems by computer.*[27]

And in concert with the specifications forwarded by the Department of
Labor, troubleshooting dominates the descriptions of employers' ideal job
candidates. Indeed, in searching a sample of online job postings, I found that
trouble—the ability to find it and fix it—ruled the employment terrain.[28] For
example, a job posting at Stony Brook University Hospital read, "Computer
operators monitor, operate and *provide first-level troubleshooting.*" Similarly, a job posting for a position at the University of Syracuse noted that the
best candidates were those who could "*determine the source or cause of system problems* and take appropriate corrective action." A Harley Davidson
listing described the candidate's major duties as "monitoring systems, *log-
ging errors, providing problem resolutions* and insuring that system performance is met," while the University of Utah advertised for someone who
could "provide computer support by *troubleshooting and correcting problems* with computer hardware or software applications." For the SVS Technology Group, the prime candidate would "analyze current operational procedures, *identify problems,* upgrade systems, and *correct errors.*" And EBIX
Inc. searched for someone who could "maintain *and troubleshoot* for the network and the company's PCs." A candidate's ability to recognize the worst
proved central to employers. Indeed, 80 percent of the ads I analyzed listed

troubleshooting among the top three job requirements, and 20 percent of the ads listed it as the *primary* requirement.[29]

As is true for MPs, training does much to position COPS at the worst-case perceptual porthole. Indeed, computer experts Agre and Schuler contend that only the "detailed study of trouble can lead to the (necessary) insights about design processes and their limitations."[30] A content analysis of the field's most popular instructional texts verifies Agre and Schuler's position.[31] Most training manuals avoid the discussion of smooth operations. Rather, they are organized around means of *restoring* operations once a problem has occurred. This approach, what expert Karen Ferris calls "fire fighting," routinely molds the section and chapter headings common to central COPS texts.[32]

Note, for example, the problems addressed in just the first twenty pages of one of the field's best-selling manuals, David Stone and Alfred Poor's *Troubleshooting Your PC:*

My computer crashes when I touch it.
My computer crashes after it has been working for a while.
My system started crashing after I installed some hardware or software.
My computer may be crashing because of power management problems.
My computer may be crashing due to insufficient resources.
My computer may be crashing due to power problems.
I don't have any good clues about what's making my computer crash.

Stone and Poor introduce trainees to trouble early in the process. And as lessons continue, the notion of trouble remains center stage. Indeed, worst-case scenarios dominate the book's subsequent chapters—chapters such as "Computer Noises," "Computer Slow or Losing Time," "Computer Startup: Blank Screen," "Computer Startup: Won't Boot," "Display: Blank after Bootup," "Display: Quality Flaws," and so on. David Karp sets a similar tone in his training manual *Windows XP Annoyances: Tips, Secrets and Solutions.* As the title suggests, Karp's book is designed to teach COPS-in-training ways to master the Windows operating system. But note that the author has little positive to say regarding the software's design. He rarely discusses what to expect when Windows is operating properly. Rather, Karp socializes his readers to one normative reality—with Windows, trouble is routine:

Do you get a sinking feeling every time you're about to install new software on the computer? Do you get tired of having to turn off all the bells and whistles integrated into new products just to make them usable? Does your day-to-day experience with Windows make you want to chuck the whole system out the window? *Have you calmly accepted the fact that your new operating system will most likely contain more bugs than improvements? Why fight it?*

Karp instructs his students to expect the worst, perhaps even to embrace it. For like other computer experts, Karp presents trouble as the vehicle that drives computer operations:

> If we lump together the crash-a-day tendency of Windows, the irritating little animations, the clutter on the desktop, the lack of decent documentation, and the fact that the performance rarely meets expectations . . . *we assume the burden of solving our own problems.* This is a valuable attitude to adopt; it motivates us to learn more about the operating system so that we can work more efficiently. And more importantly, it gives us the power to resolve the problems we encounter, so that we can get through the day with some degree of sanity.[33]

COPS-in-training learn that trouble comes in infinite shapes and forms. Debra Dinnocenzo, a veteran telecommuter and president of ALLearnatives, makes this point clear in her instructions to trainees. As an experienced operator and programmer, Dinnocenzo notes that the best of technicians will be "in the ready" and poised for the inevitable disasters:

> Consider what back-up you may need in order to continue being productive even when your equipment fails you (*because it will, you know!*). This is where *having a "Chicken Little" mindset is not a bad idea. Imagine that the sky is falling . . . or worse.* What if your computer crashes? . . . think ahead, consider your options, ask lots of What If questions, *be prepared for the worst.*[34]

Author Dan Gookin takes a similar position in *PCs for Dummies*, one of the best-selling instructional manuals in the world. From the very first page of his book, Gookin makes clear that computers are steeped in trouble. "Don't be fooled," writes Gookin, "computers aren't easy to use." Knowing this, Gookin painstakingly itemizes the multitude of disasters that await operators at literally every phase of computing. Were you aware, for example, that simply unpacking your computer could be a dangerous experience?

Be careful opening any box. The "grab and rip" approach can be dangerous, since those massive ugly staples used to close the box can fling off
and give you an unwanted body piercing. . . Same holds true with using a
box knife; use a small blade since you don't want to slice through or into
anything electronic—or fleshy, for that matter.

Similarly, Gookin makes powering a computer on or off sound like entering
a minefield:

- Never use an extension cord to meet your power needs. People trip
  over extension cords and unplug them routinely.
- Don't use any power splitters or those octopus-like things that turn
  one socket into three. Computers need grounded sockets, which must
  have three prongs in them.
- Don't lick the plug before you stick it into the wall.

Shouldn't powering up or powering down your computer be rather straightforward? According to Gookin, not necessarily: "Should turning your computer on or off be complicated? Of course not. But then again, a computer
isn't known for being the most logical of devices." And once your computer
is up and running, the potential for trouble should diminish, shouldn't it?
Not according to Gookin. Consequently, the author provides readers with
special chapters that instruct them on "when to scream for help," "how to
scream for help," and "how to bribe computer gurus when seeking help."
Each section provides COPS-in-training with a host of problems to savor
and anticipate, including "The page didn't come out of my laser printer!"
"Does my PC have a virus?" or "I can't see anything on my screen!" Trouble,
trouble, trouble—according to Gookin, it is the norm of computer work:

> Why is it that computers run amok? If cars had the same troubles, no one
> would drive. Heck, no one would walk, sit, or play anywhere near a road.
> As humans, we count on things to be reliable and consistent. Life is sup-
> posed to be that way. Heaven must be that way. Hell? It's probably wall-
> to-wall computers down there.[35]

One might think that trouble would be confined to the computer itself.
But author Stephen Bigelow encourages COPS-in-training to cast their worst-
case nets much wider. Trouble can emerge from a technician's work environment or from the customers that one supports. Thus in the very first pages

of his manual, Bigelow instructs his students on a varied number of worst-case fronts. All operators, for example, must think seriously about limiting their legal liability. "Unfortunately, we live in a litigious society," writes the author, "where seemingly innocent mistakes or oversights can have enormous consequences (especially for small businesses)." Bigelow urges operators to consult a lawyer to have a legally drafted work order prepared—one that absolves the operator of responsibility for catastrophes such as lost data, viral infection, or the loss of software applications. Bigelow also warns his students to consider the "deadly" aspects of computer operations. Technicians must practice static control, electricity control, guarding, and shielding, all safeguards designed to avoid both damage to the machine or the electrocution of the operator.[36]

The lessons of trouble so central to the training of COPS are reinforced by the workplace jargon that characterizes their professional exchanges. Such jargon rarely emphasizes constructive, stable images. Rather, symbols of disaster and catastrophe routinely lace professional talk. In such lingo, computer work emerges as a war against evil, a job that routinely forces COPS to look the worst case square in the eye. Excerpts from *The New Hacker's Dictionary* aptly illustrate this point.[37] The dictionary represents one of the field's most comprehensive sources of computer jargon, and its various entries underscore the very negative way in which professionals reference and discuss daily operating tasks.

Consider, for example, the issue of "interfacing." When software applications and computer operating systems fail to interface or communicate correctly, smooth computer operations can be interrupted. The problem is annoying, but generally very correctable. Yet despite operators' ability to deal with interfacing issues, the field's jargon casts the problem in doomsday imagery. *The New Hackers Dictionary* refers to poor interfacing as the "Blue Screen of Death":

> This term is closely related to the older Black Screen of Death but much more common (many non-hackers have picked it up). Due to the extreme fragility and bugginess of Microsoft Windows, misbehaving applications can readily crash the OS (and the OS sometimes crashes itself spontaneously). The Blue Screen of Death, sometimes decorated with hex error codes, is what you get when this happens. (Commonly abbreviated BSOD.)

Network disruption—the inability of linked machines to communicate with one another—represents another common operations problem. And while COPS routinely encounter and correct this situation, professional jargon frames the problem in the catastrophic language of a nuclear meltdown, namely, the "Chernobyl Packet":

A network packet that induces a broadcast storm and/or network meltdown, in memory of the April 1986 nuclear accident at Chernobyl in Ukraine. The typical scenario involves an IP Ethernet datagram that passes through a gateway with both source and destination Ether and IP address set as the respective broadcast addresses for the subnetworks being gated between.

Even routine activities such as quality-assurance tests—techniques designed to *prevent* service interruption or disaster—are referenced in the terms of catastrophe and ruin. Consider the term "earthquake":

The ultimate real-world shock test for computer hardware. Hackish sources at IBM deny the rumor that the Bay Area quake of 1989 was initiated by the company to test quality-assurance procedures at its California plants.

Perhaps the entry in *The New Hacker's Dictionary* for Murphy's law (among its longest definitions) best sums up the mindset of contemporary COPS:

The correct, original Murphy's Law reads: "If there are two or more ways to do something, and one of those ways can result in a catastrophe, then someone will do it." This is a principle of defensive design, cited here because it is usually given in mutant forms less descriptive of the challenges of design for users. For example, you don't make a two-pin plug symmetrical and then label it "THIS WAY UP"; if it matters which way it is plugged in, then you make the design asymmetrical (see also the anecdote under magic smoke).

Edward A. Murphy, Jr., was one of the engineers on the rocket-sled experiments that were done by the U.S. Air Force in 1949 to test human acceleration tolerances (USAF project MX981). One experiment involved a set of 16 accelerometers mounted to different parts of the subject's body. There were two ways each sensor could be glued to its mount, and somebody methodically installed all 16 the wrong way around. Murphy then made the original form of his pronouncement, which the test subject (Major John Paul Stapp) quoted at a news conference a few days later.

Within months "Murphy's Law" had spread to various technical cultures connected to aerospace engineering. Before too many years had gone by variants had passed into the popular imagination, changing as they went. Most of these are variants on "Anything that can go wrong, will"; this is correctly referred to as Finagle's Law. The memetic drift apparent in these mutants clearly demonstrates Murphy's Law acting on itself!

The negative asymmetry so common to COPS closely resembles the cognitive stance held by MPs. In reading the work of computer experts, we learn that this is no accident. Indeed, experts report that many of their professional training strategies are intentionally formulated with reference to traditional medical models and tenets. In *Troubleshooting Your PC*, for example, Stone and Poor teach students "six golden rules" of troubleshooting—rules that are also firmly anchored in existing medical knowledge.[38] Consider the first golden rule, "Do no harm":

> No doubt, you've heard the medical credo to first do no harm. What you may not have realized is that the same rule applies to computer problems. You've probably never thought about it this way, but when you try to diagnose a computer problem you're doing much the same thing as a doctor diagnosing a disease. The particulars are different, but the strategies are similar.

The second golden rule of the Stone and Poor paradigm—"Don't overlook the obvious"—draws from medical knowledge as well:

> Doctors have a relevant saying: *When you hear hoof beats, think horses not zebras.* It's a way of reminding medical students and new doctors that when a patient presents with a set of symptoms, the symptoms are most likely due to the most common causes of those symptoms, rather than some exotic disease they just read about in a medical journal.

And just as the physician's exam is driven by a search for the worst, so too are computer professionals' examinations of machinery. In assessing computers, COPS are taught to ask about what is wrong, not what is right; they are told to *start* from the worst-case scenario and work backward toward less serious possibilities. Consider, for example, the computer professional faced with a computer crash. Stone and Poor instruct COPS to approach the problem via a well-crafted series of diagnostic responses. In response step 1, COPS are told to explore the absolute worst-case scenario, namely, the computer is completely faulty and crashes every time it is touched. According to Stone and Poor, COPS must eliminate this catastrophic possibility before pursuing any other remedial action. If universal crashing proves an inappropriate diagnosis, COPS are instructed to explore a slightly less serious condition. Response step 2 focuses on the problem of intermittent crashing, that is, a computer crashes only when it has been on for a while. If intermittent crashes are eliminated by a diagnostic exam, COPS are free to move to response step 3. Step 3 assumes that a computer crashes only after new hardware installation, a fairly common problem with a clear cause and a straightforward solution. If step 3's assumption proves inappropriate to the client's problem, then COPS can move to response step 4, the simplest diagnosis of all. In step 4, COPS consider that crashing may simply be the product of an improper power management setting. From a client's perspective, an improper power management setting is a best-case scenario because the solution involves nothing more than a "point and click" prescription.

Conceptualize the worst and move backward from there. Jean Andrews takes a similar tact in her instruction manual, *Enhanced PC Troubleshooting Pocket Guide for Managing and Maintaining Your PC.* Having trouble with your modem? Andrews's first instruction focuses on complete system failure. She suggests that COPS check to see if the computer has ceased to operate entirely. If this worst-case scenario fails to emerge, then and only then are COPS encouraged to move to a second-line strategy, namely, the less devastating condition of improper software configuration. How about the simple solutions—trying a different dial-up number, for example, or checking for a dial tone on the phone line? It is fascinating to note that Andrews's diagnostic instructions define these straightforward possibilities as last resort efforts.[39] For those instructing COPS, assumptions of disaster are clearly the first line of action.

In charting the influence of medical protocol in the COPS approach to the computer, one additional point bears mention. Often, the field's routine tasks are framed in terms of serious physiological conditions. In computer work, medical metaphors abound, and one cannot help but wonder if the prevalence of such jargon helps to center the worst in experts' perceptual field. Consider, for example, that when COPS scan programs for unwanted or unintended properties, they do not look for irregularities; rather, they look for "bugs" or "viruses." When a computer freezes, COPS do not refer to service interruptions, but to "catatonic" episodes. And the potential for system failure in the early life of a computer is typically described by the medical term "infant mortality":

It is common lore among hackers (and in the electronics industry at large; this term is possibly techspeak by now) that the chances of sudden hardware failure drop off exponentially with a machine's time since first use (that is, until the relatively distant time at which enough mechanical wear in I/O devices and thermal-cycling stress in components has accumulated for the machine to start going senile). Up to half of all chip and wire failures happen within a new system's first few weeks; such failures are often referred to as "infant mortality" problems (or, occasionally, as "sudden infant death syndrome"). See bathtub curve, burn-in period.

Even constructive activities executed by COPS take on the jargon of serious medical disease. When COPS prepare amendments or additions to established computer programs, they routinely refer to these additions as "bags on the side," a clear reference to a colostomy bag:

> An extension to an established hack that is supposed to add some functionality to the original. Usually derogatory, implying that the original was being overextended and should have been thrown away, and the new product is ugly, inelegant, or bloated. Also v. phrase, "to hang a bag on the side [of]." "C++? That's just a bag on the side of C. . . ." "They want me to hang a bag on the side of the accounting system."

Finally, when upgrading a computer processor, a highly constructive action, COPS nevertheless refer to the procedure as a "lobotomy" on the system: "The act of removing the processor from a microcomputer in order to replace or upgrade it. Some very cheap clone systems are sold in 'lobotomized' form— everything but the brain."[40]

According to computer professionals, computers get "viruses," "warts," "core cancers," "terminal illnesses," and they "cough and die." Thus COPS, like MPs, are vigilant toward "disease" rather than good health. In light of this discussion, we should not be surprised to learn that COPS, like MPs, have trouble defining the positive. Physicians' vague definitions of "good health" correspond to computer experts' equally obscure pronouncements of "smooth operations." Indeed, among COPS, smooth operations are never discussed as an independent condition. Rather, they are the product of a troubleshooting "correction." In the Stone and Poor manual, for example, smooth operations are identified by "*minimizing the problems* you might otherwise have to troubleshoot." Similarly, Bigelow defines smooth operations as "the *return of a broken PC to operations* as quickly, efficiently, and cost effectively as possible." And for author Steve Bass, smooth operations are *the short spans of time that reside amid the repairs*. This collective inability to focus on smooth operations is a symptom of negative asymmetry. Like their counterparts in medicine, COPS remain riveted to the worst, with the best-case scenario eclipsed or clouded in their perceptual field.[41]

The Sources of Negative Asymmetry

Why are MPs and COPS so prone to negative asymmetry? The question is complicated, and a satisfactory answer to the query will stretch beyond this chapter. But I begin the analysis here by exploring the characteristics that these two communities hold in common. In identifying these elements, we gain some important clues regarding the broader social structures in which negative asymmetry is most likely to emerge.

To begin, it is important to note that both MPs and COPS are strongly "service oriented." MPs seek to cure and improve patients' quality of life. COPS seek to correct and improve practical capabilities. In this regard, one might say that, in their inception, both professions emphasized what social theorist Max Weber called "substantive rationality" (linking the achievement of goals to social values and ideals) as opposed to "formal rationality" (linking goal achievement to rules, regulations, and efficiency). This orientation results in an outward-looking focus, and an acknowledgment that each community's subsistence requires a balanced consideration of "self" and "other."

Service orientation is, of course, at the heart of the doctors' Hippocratic oath. Recall the statement's introductory words: "Whatever houses I may visit, I will come for the benefit of the sick . . . keeping them from harm and injustice." And for COPS, service has grown so central to the profession that it is now the first consideration of software design. Computer experts note that old design paradigms required users to conform to a corporation's unrelenting and uniform user profile. But now, the "law of personalization" guides software design. Indeed, new software encourages users to adapt the technology to their own special needs, whether instrumental needs served by certain word processors, spreadsheets, or type fonts or expressive needs served by special icons, wallpapers, and screen savers.[42]

MPs and COPS display other key similarities. Both communities, for example, exhibit what we might call "porous boundaries."[43] Porous boundaries allow people, information, and resources to flow in and out of the community with frequency and ease. In medicine, for instance, specialized medical knowledge is routinely exported. Expert manuals such as *The Merck Manual of Medical Information* or *Stedman's Medical Dictionary* are best-sellers not only among doctors, but among the public at large.[44] Web sites such as Medline or Web MD are some of the most frequently visited of Internet destinations, and these sites (along with more than ten thousand others) bring to patients medical information once restricted to physicians' eyes. In the present day, no successful talk radio station lacks a weekly, or in some cases daily, call-in medical program. Most local and national TV news broadcasts offer a medical news feature as well. Although few professional bodies can claim a growing nonprofessional audience for their discipline's flagship journals, in recent years, both *JAMA* (*Journal of the American Medical Association*) and the *New England Journal of Medicine* have become household words.

The medical community's export of knowledge is indeed remarkable. And that phenomenon is matched by the community's growing acceptance of nonmedical input. Increasingly sophisticated forms of medical technology (particularly in the realm of surgery) require that doctors and other MPs regularly interface with computer and engineering experts. Similarly, explicit links between physiology and factors such as mental health and nutrition find a growing connection between doctors and "health-oriented" specialists. Acupuncture, exercise, meditation, nutrition, and therapy are working their way into established medical regimes. Note too that both the Internet and the emergence of patient-physician computer networks have provided the patient with a more central role in the diagnostic and treatment process. And for better or worse, MPs' reliance on insurance companies have brought economic regulation and negotiation into the treatment of patients. "Business" is now paramount to the operation of most medical groups.[45]

A similar porousness characterizes the boundaries of the COPS community, as people and ideas regularly flow across the profession's borders. Like MPs, COPS freely export much of the field's most specialized knowledge. In this regard, many of the community's most technical training manuals are openly marketed to experts and amateurs alike. (And sales figures suggest that a broad base of nonprofessionals enthusiastically embrace these specialized books.) Highly technical software, software patches, and computer solutions are also often exported to nonexperts free of charge, even when such innovations emanate from profit-oriented companies. For COPS, the export of computer "product" is integral to success, for when it comes to programs and designs, knowledge is legitimated and expanded only through use.

The importation of resources and information proves equally important to the COPS community. Indeed, computer experts contend that a thoughtful consideration of their clientele is integral to effective computer work. Martine Devos and Michel Tilman elaborate on the issue: "Working in face-to-face projects where the end user is known, where the user has a face that is happy or upset, we are reminded every day that our task is to build software that delights the user, that there is more to software than firmness and function."[46] Computer experts Agre and Schuler make a similar point: "Computer professionals have another set of significant relationships—to the people who will use their systems. . . . Every system incorporates certain assumptions about the users and about the larger network of human activities within which the system will be used." According to Agre and Schuler, designers must embrace a shared commitment to learning through use— permitting groups of users to explore the system's possibilities, watching what they do, and interacting with them."[47]

Service orientation and porous boundaries—the similarities between medical professionals and computer experts extend even further. Consider, for example, the knowledge base that fuels each community's routine actions. Both groups are clearly dominated by formal knowledge (or what some call ideology) as opposed to tradition or common sense. What is the difference? Formal knowledge is a set of explicit beliefs about the way in which elements of the world work. These beliefs form a script for action that is highly articulated and self-consciously invoked. Further, formal knowledge is flexible, in that it is constantly contested and amended. In this way, it never appears natural, essential, or automatic, but rather is understood as a product of continual discovery. Contrast this definition to those of tradition and common sense. While tradition is composed of well-articulated beliefs, it is far from flexible. Rather, tradition presents itself as a fixed and essential part of the arenas in which it appears. Common sense is neither well articulated nor flexible. It consists of beliefs and assumptions that are rarely elaborated or explained, making it so automatic or "unselfconscious as to seem a natural, transparent part of the structure of the world."[48]

When we review medical practice or computer work, the dominance of formal knowledge is clear. In treating patients, for example, doctors never unconsciously "go through the motions." Rather, they follow a meticulously specified protocol, documenting and reviewing their choices at each performative stage. Doctors dictate their actions to nurses or assistants; they record their actions on patients' charts and records; they consult with staff regarding subsequent medical options and responses. In this way, medical practice involves deliberate articulation and review; it is firmly embedded in consciousness rather than habit. The same can be said of COPS. As we learned in reviewing the computer field's diagnostic and response protocols, the treatment of both hardware and software malfunctions is a deliberate process. In troubleshooting, COPS thoughtfully move through sequential procedures, documenting findings at each phase before proceeding to subsequent steps. It is also true that the knowledge base guiding both MPs and

COPS is flexible and subject to constant amendment and change. In keeping with the definition of formal knowledge, both MPs and COPS treat expert information as a "work in progress." Thus, the etiologies of diseases can and do change over time. Programs and programming styles undergo rapid transformation. Medicine and computer knowledge conform to models of science, undergoing careful observation, conscious review, thorough analysis, and constant amendment.

MPs and COPS display one final similarity. Members of both communities are quite autonomous. We can think of individuals from both professions as independent contractors of sorts, who despite their affiliation with organizations or broader communities, maintain considerable ability to monitor and control themselves. In the case of medicine, one of the primary goals of the American Medical Association (AMA) involves the protection of the physician as "an independent practitioner largely free of public control."[49] And in keeping with the belief for which it fights, the AMA lobbies on behalf of doctors without demanding their formal affiliation. (Indeed, less than half of all physicians belong to the AMA.) On the same note, successful medical practice requires that physicians affiliate with one or more hospitals. Knowing this, one might be tempted to conclude that hospital administrators exert strict control over physicians. Traditionally, however, doctors have faired quite well in this power struggle. Indeed, in most hospital settings, doctors maintain the ability to monitor and regulate themselves.[50] To be sure, contemporary physicians may be less autonomous than their counterparts of the mid-twentieth century, a period social scientist John McKinlay refers to as the "golden age" of doctoring.[51] Government regulation, managed care, and the emergence of health care corporations are greatly threatening the physicians' once unfettered authority.[52] But while MPs' autonomy may no longer be absolute, it remains considerable, with doctors exerting substantial decision-making power in the production of medical knowledge and the diagnosis and treatment of patients.

Like MPs, COPS are often affiliated with larger organizations. Indeed, less than 10 percent of COPS are self-employed.[53] Yet, within their varied work arenas, COPS enjoy a high degree of autonomy. Computer experts Agre and Schuler contend that such autonomy is rooted in the very nature of the work:

> Lacking a guild-like system of collective control over the market supply of technical skill, computer professionals must individually place continual "bets" on the direction that the industry is taking, choosing jobs, and undertaking training courses that will position them adequately in

the labor market of a few years hence. The size and complexity of the computer industry as autonomous and uncontrollable when viewed from any given individual's perspective—[this] is something to be predicted and accommodated rather than collectively chosen.[54]

The constant developmental flux of the computer industry likens the work of COPS to that of improvisational jazz musicians, of whom Tone Bratteteig and Erik Stolterman have this to say:

> The creativity of the jazz group is based on competence of the various players, on their ability and possibility to move within given structures, but also their ability to improvise by transcending given or traditional structures. They may come up with something neither the audience nor the [other] group members expected.[55]

Daniel Couger draws a similar conclusion from his national and international research on the structure of computer professional groups. According to Couger, COPS exhibit what he calls "low social need." Thus, "programmers and analysts don't need meetings . . . and show frustration at lengthy and frequent meetings. . . . Programmers and analysts are not anti-social . . . but they are intolerant of group activities that are not well organized and conducted efficiently."[56]

The "go it alone" mindset of computing work means that decision making usually occurs at the local level. Typically, the onsite professionals will decide how to handle and fix problems without referring to supervisors for advice or clearance. Indeed, COPS that occupy supervisory positions are more apt to coordinate, train, and coach than to issue orders.[57] Supervisors tend to adopt a hands-off stance, leaving COPS to "rely on their own convictions," motivate themselves, and execute independent decisions.[58] Keeping with the analogy of the improvisational jazz group, Bratteteig and Stolterman describe this supervisory style in terms of music making: "Orchestration does not mean rigorous leadership by an almighty conductor, but rather a dialogue between the conductor, responsible for the overall sound of the music, [and] the musicians, who have the skills and responsibility for their particular contribution to the overall sound."[59]

In support of their autonomy, note that COPS enthusiastically endorse the adoption of an official code of ethics. Many believe that such action will win public confidence and stave off government regulation.[60] As management expert David Vance argues, "Unless national and international professional associations are able to police their own members, society at large may seize the reins. For professional, political, philosophical, and economic reasons, it is preferable to institute measures of self-governance."[61]

⌒∞⌒

MPs and COPS hold four key factors in common: a service orientation, porous community boundaries, a formal knowledge base, and high levels of individual autonomy. Certainly, we can think of disciplines or professions that posses some of these same characteristics. But we can think of far fewer that embody all of them. This point is key, for I wish to suggest that this full configuration of elements creates a structure—a context of action—that favors negative versus positive asymmetry. Indeed, negative asymmetry may not be a product of any specific profession per se, but rather is a way of seeing that emerges in social fields defined by very particular combinations of social relationships, resources, and patterns of action.

While the work of this chapter suggests such a possibility, it provides an insufficient basis for a full exploration of the hypothesis. Thus, chapter 7 takes readers to several new contexts that provide quite appropriate testing grounds.

CHAPTER SEVEN

Emancipating Structures and Cognitive Styles

In chapter 6, we saw that communities that routinely invoke negative asymmetry display similar characteristics. Such communities maintain a service orientation; they display porous community boundaries. These communities are also fueled by a formal knowledge base and exhibit high levels of autonomy among community members. I have argued that these four characteristics are something more than a checklist of professional identity elements. Indeed, these characteristics, when occurring in combination, create a distinct type of social structure.[1] I dub this structural type an "emancipating structure," and I argue that such a structure can free groups and communities from the constraints of perceptual conventions. Thus, beyond MPs, beyond COPS, any group or community structured in this way can leave positive asymmetry behind. When freed to move from the best-case porthole, such groups come to anticipate quality conditions that those in other settings simply cannot see.[2]

To expound on the role of emancipating structures in the development of negative asymmetry, I present a comparison of four events. Each is a recent, high-profile case involving a worst-case scenario: the SARS outbreak of 2003, the Y2K threat of 2000, the FBI's handling of the "Phoenix memo" in 2001, and the NASA *Challenger* disaster of 1986. Readers will recall that two of these potential disasters—SARS and Y2K—were quite successfully disposed. But we know all too well that the other incidents ended in catastrophe. What explains the difference? We will see that those addressing SARS and Y2K brought negative asymmetry to the problem-solving site, and this cognitive style came to dominate competing views. But in the case of the Phoenix memo and the *Challenger* disaster, the opposite occurred. Those who practiced positive asymmetry overpowered group members who championed a worst-case image of the world.

How did negative asymmetry "break through" in the former cases? And what role did emancipating structures play in this regard? Using media coverage of these four events, the official protocols of the organizations involved, and previously published scholarly research, I explore what was seen and what was not, what was done and what failed to be done. And in analyzing the data, I find that the flexible nature of emancipating structures was key to the emergence of negative asymmetry, and thus to the recognition and avoidance of worst-case scenarios. In essence, emancipating structures "loosened" the hold of routine cultural practices, freeing groups and communities to pursue unanticipated problems and creative solutions. Such findings are important, for they introduce another dimension to the study of quality assessment. We have seen that cultural practices undoubtedly influence the cognitive categories by which we specify quality. But the pages to follow suggest that structure may be equally important to the process. As we will see, the structure of the settings in which quality assessment is embedded influences the ways in which cultural practices are invoked and applied.

My inquiry begins with a narrative describing the four events at hand, exploring what happened and when. Once these stories have been told, we will revisit each narrative with an analytic eye, carefully considering social structure's role in the progression of events.

Story 1: Negative Asymmetry in Medicine and the Successful Containment of SARS

In 2003, the world faced a potential health catastrophe when a new disease, identified as severe acute respiratory syndrome, or SARS, entered the public domain. According to the World Health Organization (WHO), SARS was "the first and readily transmissible disease to emerge in the 21st century." The disease was especially troublesome to the medical community because it showed "a clear capacity for spread along the routes of international travel."[3]

The story of SARS began in China's Guangdong Province. In the winter of 2002, 305 people, mostly health care workers, began to show signs of an atypical pneumonia. There would be five fatalities from this initial outbreak, but the disease had already begun to spread, not only beyond Guangdong, but beyond China's borders. During the first three months of the outbreak, an infected physician from Guangdong carried the disease to the ninth floor of a Hong Kong four-star hotel. While there, the physician contaminated more than a dozen hotel guests—guests who, in turn, transported the disease to their home countries. With these infections SARS became a global health threat:

Guests and visitors to the hotel's ninth floor seeded outbreaks of cases in the hospital systems of Hong Kong, Vietnam, and Singapore. Simultaneously, the disease began spreading around the world along international travel routes as guests at the hotel flew home to Toronto and elsewhere, and as other medical doctors who had treated the earliest cases in Vietnam and Singapore traveled internationally for medical and other reasons.[4]

By May of 2003, the WHO estimated that 8,098 people had contracted SARS. Of that number, 774 died, with most of those fatalities in Asian nations.

To be sure, 774 deaths represent a significant loss of life. Yet the death toll also signals an amazing success story. The virus responsible for SARS was known for frequent mutations, and upon its emergence medical professionals knew of no vaccine for its successful treatment. Further, the epidemiology of the disease was poorly understood, and its presenting symptoms were common and nonspecific. Most important, the disease's lengthy incubation period meant that SARS could be widely transmitted via international travel.[5] These three characteristics formed a deadly combination. Indeed, in contemporary medicine, *none* of the serious viruses under the scrutiny of medical experts—the AIDS, avian influenza, Ebola, West Nile, and Nipah viruses, for example—meets *all* of these criteria. How, then, did the world avert a public health disaster?

The SARS success story is closely linked to the world health community's truly rapid identification of the disease. Consider the chain of events. Official records show that in December of 2002, the WHO became aware of a problem in Guangdong. At the time, the problem seemed localized and under control. But on February 28, 2003, the story changed considerably. Epidemiologist Carlo Urbani examined a patient in Hanoi, Vietnam. The patient presented a severe case of atypical pneumonia with unknown etiology. "By 11 March, at least 20 hospital workers in Hanoi's private French Hospital, and 23 at a hospital in Hong Kong, were ill with a similar acute respiratory syndrome." Were there connections between Guangdong, Hanoi, and Hong Kong? On March 12, the WHO assessed the situation with teams of medical professionals in Hanoi, Hong Kong, and Beijing. Based on these briefings, the WHO issued a global alert identifying SARS. A research laboratory network was established and the disease was further scrutinized. And on April 17, *less than five months after the first reported outbreak of the disease,* researchers provided the world with "conclusive identification of the SARS causative agent: a new coronavirus unlike any other known human or animal virus in its family."[6]

What accounts for the rapid action of public health officials? According to both the WHO and the U.S. Central Intelligence Agency, the successful disposition of SARS began with a community "mindset." That mindset was based on the culture of negative asymmetry. At the time of the outbreak, medical, public health, and government professionals worldwide were increasingly focused on the potential for another global influenza pandemic. Outside experts assembled by the CIA were convinced of the reality of the threat: "Previous patterns of such events suggest that the next serious outbreak is long overdue. You've heard of the film, 'The Perfect Storm.' . . . The perfect microbial storm is yet to come; and it will come, have no doubt."[7] Further, the terrorist attacks of September 11, 2001, and the anthrax scares of later that year, had the world health community on the alert for outbreaks of bioterrorism:

> In the U.S., for example, the Department of Health and Human Services sought to further expedite quarantine procedures by reducing potential delays involved in adding new diseases to the list of quarantinable diseases. On June 12, 2002, President Bush signed into law the Public Health Security and Bioterrorism Preparedness and Response Act of 2002, which, among other things, eliminated the need to convene an advisory committee to amend the list of diseases.[8]

Thus, in the year of SARS, the world health community was poised at the worst-case vantage point, and vigilance to catastrophe was necessarily high. At the first sign of SARS, these groups *assumed* something unusual was afoot. As a consequence, they began to prepare for all negative possibilities.

Those battling SARS also took advantage of several routine public health practices and structured them in ways that created a targeted, proactive response. In the public health arena, for example, a standing emergency infrastructure allowed for rapid response to disaster—even when the disaster was unnamed. Thus, the earliest cases of atypical pneumonia as they occurred in Guangdong were quickly detected by two established operating systems: the WHO's Global Alert and Response Network and ProMed, a private health-reporting network.[9] These systems put Guangdong's problem on the medical radar. And by making this information available to doctors and hospitals throughout Asia, the medical community was able to connect the dots when similar outbreaks occurred. For example, when SARS appeared in Vietnam and Hong Kong, the WHO quickly applied travel advisories and warnings. When SARS moved to Beijing, the Chinese government was positioned to purchase emergency equipment without delay. Given the resilience of the virus and the fact that it could be spread from surface contact, items like surgical masks, gowns, latex gloves, and shoe covers proved critical to curtailing transmission.[10]

The emergency infrastructure also provided in-place protocols that those on the ground could tailor to the SARS outbreak. Most SARS protocols came to include four specific elements designed to curtail rampant transmission of the disease: the establishment of fever clinics, the use of quarantine, transit-site surveillance, and public information campaigns. We will explore each of these initiatives in turn.

Fever clinics were specially established hospital sites designed to isolate those suspected of the SARS infection. In some countries, these clinics were located in secondary or tertiary hospitals, which then became specialized SARS centers. In other cases, clinics were established in specially designated sections of primary care facilities. All persons assigned to a clinic received a physical exam, white blood cell count, and chest x-ray. Depending on these test results, one could be further detained.

A fever clinic typically consisted of two rooms, a treatment room and an anteroom. Both rooms maintained negative air pressure. Doors in such rooms were kept closed with the exception of the entry and exit of medical personnel. (Only one door at a time could be opened for such transit.) The fever clinic's staff were assigned to one station only in order to minimize exposure to the broader hospital population. And those assigned to the clinic followed strict medical guidelines. They wore gloves, disposable gowns, respiratory protection, and protective eyewear, all of which were carefully discarded in the anteroom. Infected patients could leave the clinic only for essential tests. In such cases, SARS protocol demanded that testing rooms be adjusted to a negative air pressure reading. Testing equipment was thoroughly disinfected once used on a suspected SARS patient, and lab specimens were carefully disposed of.[11]

A confirmed SARS diagnosis resulted in a patient's quarantine. "The purpose of quarantine was to reduce the incidence of new cases to [a figure] below the total rate of deaths plus patients who had recovered. As a result, the total number of infected individuals would peak, decline, and then reach zero."[12] During the outbreak, a variety of quarantine measures were used. Those with definitive diagnoses were isolated in fever clinics or acute care hospitals. They remained there until they became symptom free or succumbed to the disease. Contact cases—that is, inadequately protected individuals who came in close proximity to infected patients—were quarantined as well. Household and family members were the most likely suspects here. But the fact that so many Asian nations maintain national identification numbers meant that any SARS patient could be tracked and all of their contacts identified. In Singapore and Hong Kong, for example, identification numbers meant that all close contacts of known SARS patients were quarantined. "In Hong Kong, officials passed identity numbers to the Immigration Department to ensure that these individuals did not leave the territory."[13]

Contact cases were typically quarantined in their homes for a period of ten days. During that time, a public health official did periodic follow-ups. Quarantined persons were unable to leave the site of quarantine, except for rare circumstances like funerals, during which they were required to wear masks.[14] When exposure proved less certain, a milder form of quarantine was used, including "'snow days,' the closure of schools, child care facilities, or other buildings or locations at which large numbers of people usually gathered (for example, markets, public services, homeless shelters), and the cancellation or postponement of public events." But in countries hard hit by the SARS virus, quarantine measures could become extreme. China, for example, adopted measures such as "the cordoning off of certain neighborhoods and villages and restriction on travel, including the closing of public transit."[15]

As previously mentioned, SARS was readily transmissible, and travelers quickly spread the virus across the globe. Transit-site surveillance became critical to avoiding further contagion. Surveillance involved the careful tracking of people both leaving infected nations and entering a country from an infected nation. Singapore, for example, one of the countries most successful in curtailing the outbreak of SARS

> introduced [a] strict screening measure for all outbound passengers. Selected incoming passengers from areas with recent local transmission of SARS were also screened. Nineteen thermal infrared scanners were in place in the airport, on loan from the military. The machines were capable of detecting a fever within a .2°C degree range of accuracy.[16]

In China, fever checks were instituted at the Beijing airport, the city's major train stations, and at the seventy-one major roads that connected the city to other areas. "Infrared thermometers were used to screen passengers, followed by auxiliary thermometers on those found to be febrile on screening.[17] SARS airport screenings took place in Canada as well, with incoming and outgoing patients completing detailed information cards. And in keeping with transit-site surveillance efforts, the WHO issued detailed treatment guidelines to airlines for patients who became ill in flight.

The final facet of the SARS protocol called for rapid information dissemination, both between health care professionals and from professionals to the public. Among professionals, Internet, e-mail, and teleconferencing allowed doctors and health officials to share information on patient treatment and disease control measures.[18] Further, the WHO's Global Outbreak Alert and Response Network enabled professionals to track the evolving course of the outbreak and document response activities in real time. Medical and health officials also worked closely with local governments, which, in turn, quickly dispersed instructions to the public. The Beijing municipal government, for example, held frequent press conferences that provided information on outbreak status and preventive measures. The government also distributed educational pamphlets and compact discs, erected informational billboards, and arranged for community seminars. Beijing television ran daily two-hour specials educating the public on SARS, and the Beijing Center for Disease Prevention started a twenty-four-hour hotline.[19] Singapore also moved quickly to inform its population:

> All types of media were used, including a public television channel, the "SARS Channel," established to give current and comprehensive information on world infection trends and Singapore's situation. The Ministry of Health provided SARS information on its Web site, taking advantage of the fact that, as of December 2001, Singapore had 1.9 million Internet subscribers (out of 3.3 million population).[20]

Information dissemination encouraged the public to increase simple hygienic measures (such as frequent hand-washing), which drastically lessened the spread of this contact disease. Information also aided local governments in quarantine efforts. Indeed, many credit these educational initiatives with citizens' high rate of cooperation with quarantine. Information dissemination educated organizations with regard to airborne contact and droplet precautions that could contain transmission. Finally, information dissemination helped to keep health care workers—those facing the greatest risk of infection—on the job:

> Continued efforts by local health care workers in a high-risk environment were facilitated when the workers were reassured their families would be cared for and when the press portrayed them to the public as heroes. Conversely, when these measures were not taken, workers were much less willing to put in the long hours and expose themselves to SARS.[21]

The success of the protocol was linked to another important factor, namely, global cooperation. According to Jerome Hauer of the U.S. Department of Health and Human Services, "Rarely have the international and national health communities worked so well and so rapidly together in response to an emerging infectious disease."[22] It is worth noting that this striking level of cooperation occurred even in the face of great costs. Consider, for example, that when nations cooperated with the WHO travel restrictions, they suffered significant economic hardship. Both business travel and tourism dropped dramatically in most of these locations. Note too that governments' cooperative exchange of public health information often threatened government sovereignty. Free and open exchange forced many otherwise authoritarian regimes to admit vulnerability. To be sure, cooperation was difficult, but those involved feel it was critical to success. Indeed, the cooperative strategies used to combat SARS have initiated plans for fighting future infectious diseases. We know now, for example, that airline flight personnel underwent on-the-spot medical training to instruct them in recognizing possible SARS victims. The International Transport Association plans to standardize these procedures, bringing all carriers up to the same high level of disease recognition and prevention. Similarly, the improvements in worldwide laboratory coordination enacted in response to SARS have left the world community better poised for its next health emergency.[23]

Medical, public health, and government officials met SARS head on . . . and won. And as we will see, the emergency workers fighting Y2K adopted similar strategies and met with similar success.

Story 2: Negative Asymmetry and the Aversion of Y2K

SARS was just one of the potential catastrophes encountered during the past decade. Recall that as the year 2000 approached, so too did one of the largest technological disasters of the modern information age. Y2K referred to a series of critical computer malfunctions anticipated by the year 2000 date change. In essence, many computers were unable to recognize four digit years that began with the number 2. Thus, when the world transitioned from the year 1999 to 2000, certain computers would be unable to adjust and would operate as if the date were 1900.

Y2K was a programming problem born over fifty years ago. It resulted from programmers' efforts to conserve precious computer memory and thus speed up computers' processing time. In service of these goals, programmers decided to shorten a variety of COBAL, or command language instructions, including the treatment of digits used to signify dates. What did the changes mean? In early computing, a date such as December 31, 1999, was represented by eight digits: 12311999. In this string, the first two digits indicate the month, the next two signify the day, and the last four digits represent the year. Programmers decided to truncate the digits representing the year, reducing their number from four to two (Thus, the paired digits 1 and 9 were cut from the date.) In making this change, programmers also instructed computers to attribute any digits signifying a year to the 1900s. Thus, when your computer saw the paired digits 5 and 7, it would translate the date to 1957; when it saw 0 and 0 coupled, it would translate the date to 1900.

Recording dates with six rather than eight digits saved significant computer memory. And the strategy proved perfectly viable throughout the 1900s. But computer experts knew that truncating dates would establish an unsettled environment. They understood that the strategy represented a "short-term fix," and that in the decades to come, the problem would have to be revisited:

> Y2K . . . is not the only bug programmers have inadvertently put into programs. Most software that you use has bugs and it is known that it is impossible to produce bug free programs. (In fact, it reaches a point where trying to remove a bug introduces new ones.) Y2K was therefore another bug that the computer professionals were aware of and were actually fixing before it came to the limelight.[24]

In chapter 6 we learned that COPS are quite attuned to the worst-case scenario. Thus, we should not be surprised to learn that they understood the implications of Y2K. COPS saw the worst-case scenario and were poised to correct the problem before disaster ensued. Indeed in the 1960s, a time when computers were becoming more and more central to society's basic operations, COPS began to issue warnings and recommendations about Y2K. While the year 2000 seemed far in the future, experts hoped to correct the problem before it became too deeply entrenched. In 1960, for example, Greg Hallmuch of the U.S. Bureau of Standards alerted government officials to this escalating problem. Similarly, in 1967, Susan Jones, the assistant director of the U.S. Department of Transportation, urged Congress to address the situation.[25] In both cases, however, the government treated such warnings as overly alarming and unnecessarily disruptive to computers' growing popularity. Industry was no better. In 1983, while working for the "big three" U.S. automakers, computer programmer William Schoen flagged the Y2K problem both for his clients and for the captains of industry at large. Schoen designed the "Charmer Correction," a programming solution to the predicament. He created Charmer Enterprises, a consulting company through which he marketed his Y2K correction.[26] But despite his best efforts, Schoen made only two sales. He was forced to dissolve Charmer Enterprises in 1984, a year after its establishment.

For nearly forty years, experts' warnings on Y2K went virtually unheeded. And unless the problem was addressed, experts knew that, on January 1, 2000, many computers would roll their clocks back to 1900. One should not underestimate the problems a mistaken century can create. Computers could be frozen in a programming time warp, disrupting finance, business, health, and government. In this regard, scores of worst-case scenarios were bandied about by the experts. Y2K errors might interrupt the movement of global capital flows; they might impede government payroll and benefits checks. Such errors could upset the ability to track inventory, disrupting consumer markets; they could confuse defense warning systems, triggering mistaken responses and reactions. Power grids might fail, making transportation impossible and daily survival a hardship. As the time grew near, published warnings of Y2K read like an episode of the *Twilight Zone*:

It is an instant past midnight, January 1, 2000, and suddenly nothing works. Not ATMs, which have stopped dispensing cash; not credit cards, which are being rejected; not VCRs, which now really are impossible to program. The power in some cities isn't working, either; and that means no heat, lights, or coffee in the morning, not to mention no televisions, stereos, or phones, which even in places with power, aren't working either. Bank vaults and prison gates have swung open; so have valves on sewer lines. The 911 service isn't functioning, but fire trucks are on the prowl (though the blaze had better be no higher than the second floor, since their ladders won't lift). People in elevators are trapped, and those with electronic hotel or office keys can't get anywhere, either. Hospitals have shut down because their ventilators and x-ray machines won't work and, in my case, it's now impossible to bill the H.M.O.

Traffic is a mess, since no streetlights are working. Trains are running, but their control switches aren't, which is bad news for supermarkets, utilities, car dealers, and international trade, which can't move by ship either. Only the brave or foolhardy are getting on airplanes—but with so many countries degenerating into riots and revolution, it's wiser to stay home anyway. There are no newspapers to read or movies to go to or welfare checks to cash. Meantime, retirees are opening letters saying that their pensions have been canceled because they are minus 23-years-old. Many banks and small businesses have gone bust, and it will be weeks if ever before the mess that is the broker's statement is sorted out.

On the brighter side, no one can punch a time clock; on the darker, most of the big manufacturing plants have shut down because their lathes and robots aren't working. Pharmacies aren't filling prescriptions; the D.M.V. is not processing license renewals, and everybody's dashboard keeps flashing SERVICE ENGINE. Now, mortgage payments sent on time have been marked late, and everyone's phone bill is messed up because of all those calls that began in 1999 and ended in 1900. On the Internet where thousands of web sites are suggesting how to find God and when to move to the wilderness, the acronym for what's occurring is TEOTWAWKI: The End of the World As We Know It.[27]

COPS knew that avoiding this scenario would require significant re-sources—both in manpower and dollars. How did these experts garner the support of a reluctant audience in the fight against Y2K?

As in the case of SARS, COPS did not attempt to hide potential disaster from the public. Rather, broad information dissemination was key to suc-cessfully confronting the Y2K dilemma. At the forefront of this effort was computer technician and consultant Peter de Jager. In 1989, de Jager began a rigorous campaign designed to center the Y2K problem in the public's per-ceptual porthole. De Jager delivered more than eighty-five speeches a year. He published a book, *Managing 00: Surviving the Year 2000 Computer Crisis.* He produced videotape seminars on the subject and constructed a web site that, at its height of popularity, averaged 600,000 visits per month. By 1995, de Jager had become, as the *New York Times* put it, the "Paul Revere" of Y2K. In fact, "the American Stock Exchange named a listing of Y2K remediation companies after him. During its first year in operation, the value of the 'de Jager Year 2000 Index' jumped 100 percent—two and a half times more than the Dow." De Jager's efforts at spotlighting Y2K had paid off. In 1995, IBM, one of the most prominent names in computers, mounted a massive public relations campaign promoting a series of steps designed to help their customers make the year 2000 transition.[28]

Once public awareness of Y2K had been raised, COPS turned their atten-tions to building an emancipating structure—one in which a community of technical, political, and policy officials could coordinate and monitor pro-gramming solutions. In this regard, two agencies played a central role: the U.S. government and the United Nations. At the behest of computer pro-fessionals, the United States established the President's Y2K Council. The United Nations addressed Y2K through its Work Group on Informatics. In December of 1998, both bodies joined forces to organize an international meeting; the gathering included representatives from over 120 nations.[29] Participants legitimated the Y2K problem in no uncertain terms and acknowledged that the problem had to be tackled at the highest levels of government. They reached a consensus concerning regional cooperation. They also agreed to exchange information regarding solutions, new discoveries, and progress reports. National governments agreed to appoint Y2K coordinators. Public and private organizations appointed Y2K managers. Finally, the World Bank and the United Nations Development Program devoted over $300 million to fund the massive job ahead.

The 1998 meeting also established the International Y2K Cooperation Center (IYCC), a body designed to organize and coordinate problem-solving efforts. The IYCC, headquartered in Washington, D.C., formally opened its doors in March of 1999. Before long, three virtual branch offices opened in Seoul (addressing Y2K telecommunications issues in developing nations), London (addressing Y2K in the health sector), and Tokyo (addressing the Asian energy sector).[30] The IYCC executed six major tasks. First, it provided technicians worldwide with quality information on best practices and protocols. In this regard, the body established a Web site containing more than three thousand pages of relevant assistance, and every ten days, it sent update bulletins to over four hundred contact persons worldwide.[31] Second, the IYCC organized forty-five regional conferences and two global conferences designed to speed the repair process. Such meetings established dynamic regional and global networks, uniting professionals focused on the Y2K problems. Third, the IYCC created a flexible response network, a safety net should Y2K disruptions exceed any nation's capacity to act. Fourth, the IYCC organized news conferences, press releases, and interviews, using the media to channel rapidly changing information to the general public. Fifth, the IYCC provided outcome predictions as repairs and assessments ensued, enabling professionals to identify remaining weak spots in public and private systems. Finally, the IYCC created a window into the date-change event, allowing nations to both report and monitor computer operations as the date change occurred across the globe.[32] Much like the WHO and its impact on the treatment of SARS, the IYCC coordinated and hastened Y2K problem-solving activities around the world.

In the previous section, we learned that the world health community followed strict protocol in fighting the SARS virus. The world techno-political community did much the same in combating Y2K. The Y2K protocol generally involved five steps. First, technicians assessed the machines in their care—including large mainframe computers, networked PCs, and independently operating PCs—itemizing each machine's programs, utilities, subroutines, macros, and so on. They noted existing date fields; they also sorted, compared, calculated, and moved any operations involving dates. Finally, they examined external data feeds, coordinating date amendments with external source vendors when necessary. Step two of the protocol called for "baseline testing." Here, technicians confirmed that a computer was correctly handling all dates up to the year 2000. They also documented each machine's present capacity so that the computer could be returned to normal operations after Y2K corrections were made. In step three—remediation— technicians corrected all date-related functions. Remediation also allowed technicians to determine that (a) programs now recognized years from 2000 forward (unit testing); (b) data was correctly sorted and moved easily between various applications (string testing); (c) daily, weekly, and other time-related processes functioned correctly (systems testing); and (d) data bridges and other application integrations worked correctly (integration testing). When remediation was complete, step four—regression testing—occurred. Regression testing assured that Y2K-related updates did not alter the computer's normal operations or introduce new errors into the computer's applications. Finally, technicians performed Y2K compliance certification. This fifth step of the protocol officially documented a computer's ability to withstand the transition from 1999 to 2000.[33]

Computer technicians' Y2K know-how was critical to solving the technical aspects of the problem. But if Y2K solutions were to be successfully applied, cooperation with politicians and policy officials was equally essential. Thanks to the efforts of the IYCC and other like-minded bodies, the world witnessed unprecedented levels of cooperation—between national governments, as well as between the public and private sectors.[34] At the international level, for example, countries worked together, developing assessment plans that could flag both internally and externally generated risks:

> Honduras and Nicaragua, which depend under some circumstances and periods of the year on the energy power of their neighbors Costa Rica and Panama, needed to know if any of these countries were planning to cut off their connections with the grid or to increase their supply during the rollover period. Unprecedented action either way could have created power surges or outages. Through discussions, these countries developed energy sector contingency plans in unison and avoided any problems.[35]

Similarly, U.S. and Russian military forces joined together to ensure the safety of nuclear and other missile systems. The President's Council on Year 2000 Conversion Information Coordination Center (ICC) notes:

In a collaboration that would have been inconceivable before the Cold War ended a decade ago, American and Russian military personnel sat side by side inside an ad hoc Center for Y2K Strategic Stability, where they monitored data that would reflect any ballistic missile activity around the world.[36]

In every nation, computer technicians, government agencies, business leaders, business managers, and politicians built productive bridges. As the ICC explained, "It soon became evident that it would not do a government agency or corporation much good to solve its own problems without being equally concerned with whether a neighbor, on whom it depended for critical services or supplies, was unable to function because of Y2K failures."[37] Even those most skeptical of the Y2K threat—that is, the latecomers who did not fully recognize the problem until 1998—came to realize that cooperation made good financial sense. The willingness of the world techno-political community to share information resulted in a "leapfrog" effect. In this way, the cost and time needed to repair the problem decreased dramatically for these latecomer nations and sectors.

On Friday night, December 31, 1999, the world watched and waited. Country after country made the date transition, and few problems emerged. "The overwhelmingly successful cure of the Y2K bug—an effort that stretched over several years and cost perhaps $500 billion—ranks among the world's greatest techno-political mobilizations in peacetime."[38] Along with SARS, Y2K's defeat represents a landmark example of worst-case vision successfully applied. But not every potential disaster meets with such a positive resolution.

Story 3: Positive Asymmetry in the FBI and the "Phoenix Memo" Disaster

September 11, 2001: it is a day that has forever changed Americans' ideas of a worst-case scenario. For the first time, Americans were forced to acknowledge that their cities, their families and friends, were vulnerable to attack. They were forced to amend their active vocabulary to include words like al Qaeda, terror cells, and orange alerts. Prior to that catastrophic day, such visions were clouded and eclipsed, both among the general public and among those entrusted with the nation's safety. One tragic example of this failure to see involves an electronic communication now dubbed the "Phoenix memo."

William Kurtz, a supervisor in the FBI's Phoenix office, directed investigations of suspected Islamic terrorists for nearly ten years. And one group consistently occupied his attentions:

> Several bin Laden operatives had lived and traveled to the Phoenix area in the past, one of whom was Wadih El-Hage, a bin Laden lieutenant convicted for his role in the 1998 embassy bombings. He had lived in the Tucson area for several years in the 1990s. . . . El-Hage established an Osama bin Ladin support network in Arizona while he was living there and that network is still in place.[39]

In April of 2000, things in Arizona became unsettled. Terrorist chatter began to escalate, and Kenneth Williams, a member of Kurtz's team, was asked to spearhead surveillance efforts. Williams was to cast fresh eyes on the question, What is al Qaeda's presence in the United States? In probing the issue, agent Williams's eyes were opened to a series of alarming facts.

It started when Williams reviewed the notes of an intriguing interview with a Middle Eastern flight student living in the Phoenix area:

> This individual told the agent directly that he considered the U.S. government and military legitimate targets of Islam. In looking around the individual's apartment, the agent noticed a poster of bin Laden and another poster of a wounded Chechnyan mujaheddin fighter. He was also concerned by the fact that this individual was from a poor Middle Eastern country and had been studying a non-aviation related subject prior to his arrival in the United States. The agent also described for us another incident that increased his suspicion about Middle Eastern flight students in the Phoenix area. During a physical surveillance of the subject . . . the agent determined that he was using a vehicle registered to another individual. In 1999, the owner of the car and an associate of his were detained for trying to gain access to the cockpit of a commercial airliner on a domestic flight.[40]

As Williams continued to scour the case files assigned to his team, his concerns grew progressively stronger. In May of 2001, for example, Williams noted that a number of the FBI's active suspects apparently shared an "educational goal." Several had enrolled in courses designed to teach them how to fly airplanes. Williams also learned that "some of the men at the local Embry-Riddle Aeronautical University were asking a lot of questions about airport security."[41]

When Williams reported his findings to his supervisor, Kurtz met the information with some alarm. Having worked previously in the FBI's International Terrorism Unit (the Osama bin Laden Unit in particular), Kurtz was primed to the implications of Williams's report. Consequently, on July 10, 2001, Kurtz and his team prepared a detailed electronic memo. They forwarded the document to several key FBI units: one focusing exclusively on the threat posed by Osama bin Ladin; two offices located in the Counterterrorism Division at FBI headquarters in Washington, D.C. (the "Radical Fundamentalist Units"), and several special agents in the New York Field Office's International Terrorism Squad.[42]

The memo outlined the team's concerns regarding a coordinated terrorist effort. It specifically warned that Osama bin Laden might be using local flight schools as a means to infiltrate the U.S. civil aviation system. According to the memo, "Islamic extremists, studying everything from aviation security to flying, could be learning how to hijack or destroy aircraft and to evade airport security."[43] In light of these events, the Phoenix team recommended several actions designed to forestall a catastrophe:

- Headquarters should accumulate a list of civil aviation universities/ colleges around the country.
- FBI offices should establish liaisons with the schools.
- Headquarters should discuss the Phoenix theories with the intelligence community.
- Headquarters should consider seeking authority to obtain visa information on individuals seeking to attend flight school.[44]

The memo was extensive, full of details, facts, and productive ideas. And the memo carried one additional resource, namely, the impressive reputation of its authors. We now know that Williams, the FBI agent who brought the report's pieces together, had impeccable credentials. As former colleague Ron Myers described him, Williams was "a 'superstar,' a former SWAT sniper and family man who coaches Little League, and in 1995, helped track down Michael Fortier, Timothy McVeigh's former Army buddy. 'Anything he says you can take to the bank.'"[45]

But neither the memo nor its authors' credibility seemed to resonate with its recipients. In both Washington and New York, midlevel supervisors reviewed the information. But none of these operatives forwarded the warnings to the FBI's top managers. Indeed, until the memo resurfaced after the September 11 attacks, FBI senior officials were completely unaware of its existence:

New York personnel who reviewed the memo found it to be speculative and not particularly significant. . . . About a week after its receipt, head-quarters personnel determined that no further action was warranted on the Phoenix memo's recommendations. . . . No one apparently considered the significance of the Phoenix memo in light of what else confronted the FBI counterterrorist team during the summer of 2001: the unprecedented increase in terrorist threat reporting, the investigation and arrest of Zacarias Moussaoui in August 2001, and the possible presence of bin Ladin associates al-Mihdhar and al-Hazmi in the United States.[46]

What accounts for the FBI's failure with regard to the Phoenix memo? The answer is, of course, quite complicated and is still under scrutiny. But in comparing the way in which this event unfolded, one cannot help but note stark contrasts to the handling of the SARS and Y2K affairs.

In reviewing both SARS and Y2K, I spoke of participants' propensity for negative asymmetry. But no such mindset existed in the FBI organization, particularly among those in positions of high authority. Indeed, the FBI's top brass may have been engulfed in a broader field of blindness, reporting to authorities as oblivious to catastrophe as those they governed. At the White House, for example, top-level administrative officials were warned about the al Qaeda threat. But the group's potential for terror was apparently eclipsed by the more positive issues on the new administration's agenda:

When in 2001, [Sandy] Berger [Clinton's national security advisor] gave [Condoleezza] Rice her handover briefing, he covered the bin Laden threat in detail, and sources say, warned her: "You will be spending more time on this issue than on any other. Rice was alarmed by what she heard, and asked for a strategy review. But the effort was marginalized and scarcely mentioned in ensuing months as the administration committed itself to other priorities like National Missile Defense (NMD) and Iraq.

A similar indifference permeated the thinking of policymakers working at the Department of Defense. Top administrators placed the worst-case scenario of a terrorist attack on the far back burner. Indeed, Defense Secretary Donald Rumsfeld eventually abandoned a Predator drone that had been tracking bin Laden and monitoring his actions. He also "vetoed a request to divert $800 million from missile defense into counterterrorism." Even the new attorney general, John Ashcroft, had minimal time for terrorism. And as the FBI's direct authority, Ashcroft's policy preferences may have contributed most significantly to the bureau's faulty vision:

In the spring of 2001, the attorney general had an extraordinary confrontation with the then FBI Director Louis Freeh at the annual meeting of special agents in charge in Quantico, Va. The two talked before appearing, and Ashcroft laid out his priorities for Freeh . . ."basically violent crime and drugs," recalls one participant. Freeh replied bluntly that those were not his priorities, and began to talk about terror and counterterrorism. "Ashcroft didn't want to hear about it," says a former senior law enforcement official.[47]

Thus, while a small group of agents at the Phoenix FBI office recognized the potential for catastrophe, the FBI decision makers and related government agencies were situated at a more positive perceptual porthole. There were new initiatives to consider, new programs to launch, visions of a better America. That agenda eclipsed the worst-case scenario lurking on the horizon.[48]

Positive asymmetry exacted consequences on the FBI's routine operations. In studying SARS and Y2K, I noted that negative asymmetry was an integral part of the organizational network that helped participants effectively attack the problems at hand. Recall that the WHO established a global information network that provided physicians across the world with up-to-date facts on SARS outbreaks, treatments, and successes. In the case of Y2K, the IYCC and other agencies established an information network that guided those correcting faulty programs. But in the FBI, such coordination was sorely lacking. Indeed, investigations that followed the September 11 attacks make all too clear that serious problems regarding information sharing plagued the bureau. Despite the unsettled environment presented in the summer of 2001, FBI units operated in isolation. The Osama bin Ladin and the Radical Fundamentalist Units, for example, were not required to exchange information; and neither unit routinely shared data with the international terrorism analytic unit. Similarly, field offices rarely saw one another's reports. One can only wonder what might have happened had the Minnesota agents investigating French-Moroccan flight student Zacarias Moussaoui been privy to the findings forwarded in the Phoenix memo. The self-containment of FBI units may help us to understand why those at the FBI's upper echelons failed to connect the dots. With information floating in, disconnected and irregular, against the backdrop of positive asymmetry, it proved difficult for top administrators to see the big picture.[49]

The FBI's problems with information exchange were compounded by an outdated, and sometimes faulty, technological infrastructure. These flaws in the electronic communication system had unintended adverse effects. In the

case of the Phoenix memo, for example, a number of its addressees failed to
see the memo until after the attacks. Why?

> The FBI's electronic system is not designed to ensure that all addressees
> on a communication actually receive it. Instead, the electronic version of
> the communication is sent to the unit and then forwarded electronically
> only to the individual to whom the lead is assigned. Furthermore, the sys-
> tem is capable of recognizing units only if they are precisely designated in
> the leads sections; otherwise a unit would not receive the communica-
> tion. In the case of an inaccurate address, the communication would be
> sent into either the Counterterrorism Division's main electronic folder or
> to the International Terrorism Operation Section's folder where it would
> sit until the secretaries checked their folders and forwarded it on to the
> appropriate unit for handling. . . . The Joint Inquiry Staff has been in-
> formed [that] the FBI recently determined that there are 68,000 outstand-
> ing and unassigned leads assigned to the counterterrorism division dating
> back to 1995.[50]

The troublesome flaws in the FBI's routines of information exchange were
further exacerbated by poor communications *between* intelligence agencies.
Traditionally, a competitive undercurrent taints relations between the FBI,
the CIA, and the INS. And such competition hindered the healthy flow of
investigative findings. Consider, for example, that the FBI failed to notify the
Immigration Naturalization Service, the State Department, or the CIA regarding the identity of the suspects flagged in the Phoenix memo. As a result,
several of the hijackers left the country and then reentered without detection. Similarly, we now know that the CIA had information on the Phoenix
memo suspects. But like the FBI, the agency made no efforts to circulate the
data. Indeed, the CIA, the FBI, and the INS were monitoring the same individuals. Yet each agency remained unaware of the others' findings, and unwilling to share data of their own.[51]

When we compare the handling of SARS and Y2K with that of the
Phoenix memo, another critical difference emerges. Recall that the general
public was fully informed of both the magnitude and the efforts necessary to
curtail both SARS and Y2K. Indeed, citizens played an important role in
averting widespread disaster. But in the case of the Phoenix memo and the
catastrophe to which it alluded, the public was kept completely in the dark.
Of course, when it comes to intelligence matters and issues of national security, complete disclosure may be impossible. But is complete secrecy truly
necessary or desirable? Consider that prior to the September 11 attacks, not

to mention the color-coded risk scale initiated by the Department of Homeland Security, the public had little or no idea regarding conditions of heightened national threat. Yet experiences such as SARS, Y2K, and many others suggest that public involvement may provide important resources. Had the FBI allowed the public into its informational "loop"—even in the most minimal of ways—it may have stimulated increased public vigilance toward potential suspects, greater public preparedness should disaster strike, and a more abiding sense of public trust in government.[52]

In handling the Phoenix memo, the FBI seemed to lack all of the factors that led the world's health and techno-political communities to success. And as we will see, a very similar set of circumstances plagued the managers at NASA when they proved unable to anticipate the *Challenger* disaster.

Story 4: Positive Asymmetry in NASA and the *Challenger* Disaster

Dateline January 28, 1986: At the Kennedy Space Center in Cape Canaveral, Florida, NASA's space shuttle *Challenger* prepared to take to the skies. The mission had suffered several postponements, and the crew was anxious to begin their adventure. Millions watched as Commander Richard Scobee and six other crew members—Gregory Jarvis, Christa McAuliffe, Ronald McNair, Ellison Onizuka, Judith Resnik, and Michael Smith—enthusiastically boarded their craft. The day was filled with excitement; the launch had generated a special enthusiasm. Christa McAuliffe, a teacher from New Hampshire, was the shuttle's first citizen passenger, and she was initiating NASA's new, high-profile "Teacher in Space" mission. During the coming days, the world looked forward to "sitting in" as Christa taught elementary school from space.

At 11:38 A.M., it all began. *Challenger* left the ground against the backdrop of a glorious blue sky. But the crew's flight in space lasted only seventy-three seconds. To the horror of scientists and family members watching from the ground, to the horror of millions watching on television, the space shuttle *Challenger* exploded right before our eyes. The nation was stunned. What could possibly explain the tragedy? The question would be asked again and again in government reports, in journalistic accounts, and in scholarly research. And in reviewing the analyses on the disaster, we find another startling example of positive asymmetry and its ability to mask the potential for disaster.

The immediate cause of the *Challenger* disaster was technical in nature. According to the presidential commission that investigated the event, "The loss of the Space Shuttle *Challenger* was caused by a failure in the joint between the two lower segments of the right Solid Rocket Motor." Failure occurred because the pressure of ignition destroyed the seals—what we have now come to know as O-rings—that prevented "hot gases from leaking through the joint during the propellant burn of the rocket motor." The resiliency of the Shuttle's O-rings was directly related to temperature. Thus, the unusually cold temperatures on the day of the launch most likely accounted for the O-rings' inadequate performance.[53]

While technological failure proved the direct cause of *Challenger*'s demise, the shuttle's fate was the product of a much more complicated story. The story begins with the design engineers who were working on the shuttle's hardware. Investigations of the *Challenger* disaster show that several engineers at both NASA and Morton Thiokol (the seals' manufacturer) recognized the potential for O-ring malfunction.[54] In 1982, "the space agency found that pressure exerted by hot gases in the rocket could cause the joints to rotate slightly, making one of the synthetic rubber seals ineffective."[55] The issue was discussed only among the agency and its contractors. There was a remedy, and engineers were working on the problem. In 1982, they designed what was called a "capture feature" that would lock the problematic seals firmly in place. The capture feature was "quietly applied to new booster designs in 1982 and 1985." Records show that in July 1985, NASA ordered seventy-two new steel booster casings that included the new capture features. "When the *Challenger* exploded, these casings were in production."[56]

Knowing the casings were in production, should the engineers have advised NASA management to postpone the launch? In July of 1985, NASA analyst Richard Cook argued that he warned managers "a catastrophe might result if erosion ate through the seals." So too did a seals expert at Thiokol, Roger Boisjoly. And the night before launch, "Thiokol engineers also warned that cold weather might reduce the effectiveness of the seals."[57] Indeed, Allan McDonald, Morton Thiokol's representative at the Kennedy Space Center in Florida said, "If I were launch director, I'd cancel the launch."[58] How did these engineers' warnings translate to the green light for launch? The specialists working directly with the O-rings recognized the potential for disaster. Why were other engineers, and in particular, those in management—the ultimate decision makers—unable to see the risk?

In *The Challenger Launch Decision*, sociologist Diane Vaughan provides the richest, most ambitious and well-respected account of the decision making that surrounded the *Challenger* disaster. And in so doing, she identifies the intricate ways in which positive asymmetry came to eclipse the worst-case vision of the few. Vaughan turns first to the culture that guided NASA's engineering work groups. She contends that the work group culture was the product of a faulty decision-making sequence that, when repeated without consequence, became a trusted scientific paradigm—one that powerfully nudged the groups to the best-case perceptual porthole. The problematic culture of the work groups, a culture that was entrenched well before the *Challenger* disaster, rested in the idea of redundancy. What does this mean? When NASA technicians and engineers became aware of the O-ring problem, they chose to solve the problem not by redesigning the O-ring, but by developing a secondary or redundant joint. Why redundancy over replacement? Vaughan links the problem to a context of uncertainty:

> Technological uncertainty created a situation where having problems and anomalies on the shuttle was itself a taken for granted aspect of NASA culture. The shuttle technology was of unprecedented design, so technical deviations from performance predictions were expected. Also, the forces of the environment on the vehicle in flight were unpredictable, so anomalies on returning space flights were frequent on every part of every mission and therefore routine and normal.[59]

In the face of uncertainty, every redesign is likely to carry its own problems. Thus, the idea of backup systems seems the more logical route. While some engineers contended that catastrophic events would destroy both a primary and secondary seal, most technicians and engineers simply could not envision a situation of sufficient magnitude to cause such a failure.[60] And when a number of launches produced successful tests rather than joint failure, technicians and engineers became confident in the redundancy strategy. In the culture of redundancy, danger, ever present, is routinely recast as normal, with the assumption that scientific correction will prevail.

According to Vaughan, the work group culture of redundancy was encouraged and strengthened by NASA's broader culture of production. NASA was characterized by a can-do attitude, a stance established during the Apollo missions.[61] But by the 1980s, economic scarcity and political and bureaucratic accountability had worked their way into the organization, making cost and scheduling equally important to the organization's focus. Merging a can-do philosophy with a can't-do budget led to what Vaughan calls a bureaupathology—a condition in which production goals were hopelessly out of synch with system capabilities. Pathologies must be resolved. And in the end, the people at NASA emphasized "procedural regularity and schedule [to] the detriment of safety."[62] The decision beckoned trouble, but the positive culture of production precluded NASA's bureaucrats from seeing the disasters lurking in their choices.

Finally, positive asymmetry was both a cause and a product of what Vaughan calls a "structural secrecy." At NASA, it became quite routine to reduce the details of reports as they made their way up the management hierarchy. Indeed, divisions outside the work group did not see it as their task to produce data and tests based on the work groups' product. Rather, the work of technicians and engineers was reviewed and supported as it moved up the hierarchy. "Dependent on the work group for information and its interpretation, [the upper ranks] became enculturated. They reviewed the engineering analysis and agreed."[63]

There were some who recognized the threats attending NASA's propensity toward positive asymmetry. In March of 1986, for example, John W. Young, a veteran astronaut at NASA, issued two internal memoranda to George W. S. Abbey, head of NASA crew operations. Young had no doubt that the current course was to NASA's detriment:

> There is only one driving reason that such a potentially dangerous system would ever be allowed to fly—launch pressure. . . . Shuttles [are launched] with less than certain full reliability and full redundancy of the systems, including the flight crews, that we operate. . . . We are under continuing pressure to launch without full-up avionics, from computers to sensors. [64]

The president's commission reached a similar conclusion in reviewing the disaster:

> In 1985, NASA published a projection calling for an annual rate of 24 flights by 1990. Long before the *Challenger* accident, however, it was becoming obvious that even the modified goal of two flights a month was overambitious. . . . The capabilities of the system were stretched to the limit to support the flight rate in winter 1985/1986.[65]

Positive asymmetry created management pressures and overambitious goals. But research reveals other critical problems as well. For example, many contend that poor internal communication played a role in the *Challenger* accident. Much like the FBI, NASA comprised several self-contained units. The Lyndon B. Johnson and John F. Kennedy Space Centers, the George C. Marshall Space Flight Center, and the National Space Technology Laboratories were four distinct operating units—both regionally and bureaucratically. There was little or no overlap in each center's personnel, and information exchange between the centers was typically stilted rather than smooth. Arnold Aldrich, operational chief of the shuttle program (housed at the Johnson Space Center), concretized the problems inherent in such a system. Aldrich told the presidential commission that he had simply never heard of the problems with the O-rings because it was being studied at the Marshall Center rather than at his "home base."[66]

This same isolationist mentality plagued NASA's vertical communications. Indeed, testimony showed that some of NASA's middle managers took warnings of O-ring malfunction seriously. But they never shared those concerns with those above them in the chain of command.[67] In the end, it was these middle managers who took the fall for the *Challenger*'s demise. Reports of both presidential and congressional commissions concluded that middle managers violated safety protocols when they failed to forward pertinent warnings about the launch to top-level NASA officials.

∞

SARS, Y2K, the Phoenix memo, and the *Challenger* disaster: these cases illustrate two important lessons. First, potential disasters can be met with very different cultural responses. In the case of SARS and Y2K, those involved saw the problem through a worst-case perceptual porthole, allowing negative asymmetry to guide their actions. But in the case of the Phoenix memo and the *Challenger* disaster, positive asymmetry won the day. The second lesson of the analysis is elaborated in the pages to follow. For as we will see, certain structural configurations may help to free groups and communities from the cultural practices that impede visions of the worst.

Culture, Structure, and Cognitive Deviance

In reviewing the handling of both the Phoenix memo and the *Challenger* disaster, we learned that members of the FBI and NASA championed positive asymmetry. Unfortunately, this tendency to focus on the best embroiled each community in monumental disaster. Unable to anticipate the worst, both communities proved unable to avoid it. Contrast this experience with the response of the communities that dealt so successfully with SARS and Y2K. Negative asymmetry, an atypical way of seeing, guided these groups as they assessed and acted on the issues at hand. This point is crucial. For negative asymmetry—in essence, a type of "cognitive deviance"—saved these communities from living the worst-case scenario.

If cognitive deviance can truly save a community from the worst, one question naturally emerges. Why does cognitive deviance take root in certain communities and not others? As we have seen, culture alone cannot satisfactorily answer this question. For while cultural practices function to sustain, even exaggerate, a particular way of seeing, these practices do not create those perspectives. To explore the issue of origins, I contend that we must consider the role of structure; we must look to social structure and the ways in which it interacts with culture and cognition.

Why structure? Previous work in cultural sociology suggests that certain elements of cognition (symbolization, beliefs, schematic formation and disruption, memory, and so forth) are strongly linked to the structure of the social settings in which thinking occurs.[68] This is not to say that the social structure *determines* cognition. Rather, it means that certain ways of thinking, certain ways of articulating and institutionalizing ideas, are *facilitated* by some structural factors and discouraged by others. Several examples from the sociological literature help to illustrate the point. Consider the area of symbolization. Research shows certain structural configurations—that is, political arrangements or levels of group cohesion—can influence the strategies by which communities symbolize their thoughts and experiences. Within certain configurations (for example, those formed by authoritarian arrangements or high group cohesion), groups and communities tend to express their thoughts—aurally, visually, or verbally—using a symbolic "shorthand." Under other conditions (democratic arrangements or low social cohesion, for example), groups and communities favor a dense and fully articulated style of symbolic expression.[69] In the area of cognitive beliefs, structure proves equally important. Sociologists have demonstrated that the structure of power in a community can influence the "tightness" and consensus that characterize the community's belief systems.[70] Power structures can also influence the construction of collective memory, with subjects and events favored by the powerful being better remembered and more reliably stored than subjects considered controversial or taboo.[71] Finally, structure has been linked to the mental logics that influence attitude development. Some situations are associated with attitudes informed by the identification of common ground; others encourage attitudes that grow from a focus on contradictions; and still other structures are linked to attitudes developed from attention to both similarity and contrast.[72]

When we look specifically to cognitive deviance, the links between structure and cognition prove especially strong. The literature shows, for example, that certain structural factors (say, a peripheral location in a structural network) or certain structural arrangements (say, low network integration) are strongly associated with innovative or deviant thinking and the initial diffusion of nonnormative ideas.[73] Studies also show that those embedded in structures characterized by social instability and moral heterogeneity are more apt to "think outside the box" and break with established cultural conventions.[74] And structural factors such as social strain and information overload have been linked to schematic disruption.[75] Those located in socially volatile arenas display a greater tendency to stray from routinized cultural and cognitive connections and to establish new ones.[76]

This body of research suggests strong links between structure and cognition. And given this association, it seems reasonable to expect that structure plays a role in the cognitive process of quality evaluation as well. What is the nature of that role? I argue that certain structural characteristics may emancipate groups and communities from the conventions of positive asymmetry, thus allowing them to give the worst-case scenarios a presence in perception. Of course, the issue is complicated, and I only begin to address the problem here. Yet the four case studies reviewed in this chapter provide a starting point for analysis. In the next section, I examine several stark differences in the structure of negative and positive asymmetry settings. And I show the way these differences combine to form two distinct settings of action.

The Structure of Negative-Asymmetry Sites

The sites of negative asymmetry visited in this chapter display a common structural configuration. Decision making and subsequent action occurred in the context of what we might call a structural web.[77] Figure 7.1 highlights the characteristics of this distinct and ultimately emancipating arrangement.

Structural webs contain a "center of operations"—a core to which all of the web's other elements are directly and indirectly linked. In the case of SARS, the WHO functioned as the center of operations. The IYCC occupied this position in the Y2K affair. In a structural web, the center of operations forwards a service orientation and is designed to fulfill one critical task: it coordinates both the web's resources and its information. This task may involve fundraising, resource distribution, data collection and analysis, program design, or innovative research. But in the face of a problem, the center of operations spearheads the drive toward resolution.

A web's center of operations typically subdivides itself, forming "regional

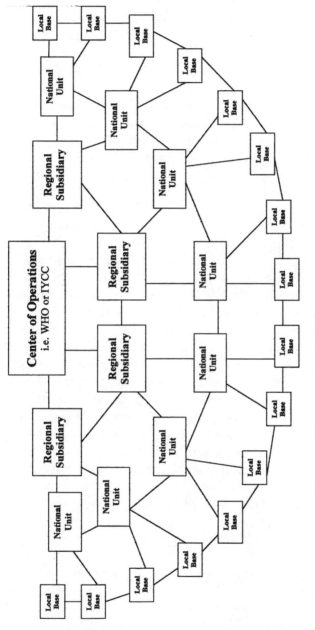

Figure 7.1. The structural web configuration of negative-asymmetry sites

subsidiaries." These subsidiaries enhance the core's practical reach by providing it with a "meso," or midlevel, presence. How does the center determine the number and location of subsidiaries? Again, service orientation proves key. After perusing the scope of a given problem, central operations creates specialized support systems that will expedite the broadest flow of goods, information, and services. In the case of SARS, for example, the WHO's central office collected local and national reports on incidents of viral outbreak. The WHO then used this information to construct elaborate models on global infection trends. With these trends in hand, the WHO developed subsidiaries or regional offices that could put the information on the ground and provide a magnified, more intensive view of especially hard-hit areas (such as China, Taiwan, and Canada). A similar pattern emerged in the Y2K affair. Local bases and national divisions reported their levels of Y2K preparedness to the IYCC. Once it had synthesized this information, the IYCC created regional subsidiaries that could best cater to the varied needs of fully modernized versus technologically challenged areas of the globe.

In the face of global emergency, national governments are critical to the enactment of any problem-solving strategy. Thus, in a structural web, regional subsidiaries routinely develop direct links with national divisions. These connections prove reciprocal and mutually beneficial. For the subsidiaries, ties to national governments enable the continuous collection of data, which better targets resource distribution and facilitates timely action. For national units, the contact maximizes nations' problem-solving arsenals. It also provides nations with an enhanced perspective of their plight. Via their contact with central and subsidiary units, nations gain the ability to evaluate their circumstances relative to the global stage. This view generally crystallizes the scope of a nation's problem, fine-tunes problem-solving efforts to the specific circumstance, and ultimately expedites recovery time. In the case of SARS, for example, nations that evaluated internal outbreaks vis-à-vis the global community initiated the correct medical protocol more rapidly and hence limited their physical and economic exposure. (China's tardiness in this regard may have stemmed, in part, from its status as the site of origin, and thus its lack of relative perspective.) The story was much the same in the Y2K incident. Nations that understood the relative status of their technological infrastructure reached Y2K resolution most quickly. The IYCC facilitated professional dialogue among early comers, accelerating these "pioneer" nations' ability to resolve the problem quickly. The IYCC also provided governments of less developed nations with the ability to "piggyback" on the gains made by early resolvers.

Local bases form the final and most fundamental unit of a structural web. These bases are the source of all primary information. Local bases are the sites in which hypotheses and assumptions are tested, the battlegrounds upon which wars are won or lost. In the case of SARS, the government agencies, hospitals and clinics in Guangdong, Toronto, and other global cities—units that counted and reported each case of infection, provided treatment, and enforced quarantine—these entities represented the local bases involved in detection and treatment. In the case of Y2K, it was the universities, the corporations, the state and local agencies, and the computer technician consultant firms that became the local bases in which hands-on resolution occurred.

The center of operations, regional subsidiaries, national divisions, and local bases: these are the components of a structural web. But how exactly do these elements interface and interact? The nature of a structural web is defined, in part, by the characteristics of its center, that is, by its strategies of action, particularly with reference to the exercise of power. In a structural web, the center of operations primarily functions to coordinate, serve, and advise rather than to control. To be sure, the core may possess certain unique powers, but those powers are limited in scope. In the case of SARS, for example, the actions of "WHO central" were true to the organization's general mission statement, namely, "To publish and disseminate scientifically rigorous public health information of international significance that enables policy makers, researchers, and practitioners to be more effective and improves health, particularly among disadvantaged populations."[78] Thus the WHO tracked the spread of the disease and alerted both national and local communities to increased risk; it readied and distributed treatment protocols, consulted with local communities on setbacks and anomalies, and provided worldwide access to global progress reports. These tasks represented cooperative, service-oriented action rather than authoritative control. Indeed, the WHO's only act of uncontested power involved the imposition of travel restrictions. But even here, the organization enacted restrictions in consultation with national units and local bases. Travel warnings were flexible, temporary, and molded with reference to the specific needs of an area.

The center of operations for the Y2K affair adopted a similar stance. Like the WHO, the IYCC refrained from wielding independent power. The organization took service as its mission, "helping regions and countries work together," and "providing a clearing house where they can share their knowledge and learn from others."[79] Thus, the organization garnered and distributed resources, both financial and informational; it provided online help and consultation; it monitored progress and helped latecomers to piggyback on the success of early resolvers. Further, the IYCC's help was not contingent or conditional, and those late to seek it were not in any way sanctioned. Rather, every effort was made to bring national divisions and local bases "on board" before the critical transition date.

The limited powers of the center of operations permits significant autonomy among the web's other elements. In essence, each unit of the web enjoys some flexibility of action. In the case of SARS, the WHO advised local bases on treatment protocols, but each local base had the freedom to alter that protocol in accord with its own special needs. Recall, for instance, that some localities established fever clinics in their hospitals, while others devoted entire hospitals to infected patients. Similarly, some localities established quarantine centers while others allowed infected patients to be quarantined at home. The web elements involved in the Y2K affair displayed significant autonomy as well. Once the IYCC had mapped out the problem, its scope, and possible solutions, local bases and national divisions exercised significant freedom of choice. Some organizations chose to replace the lion's share of their equipment; others chose to execute programming patches and corrections. Some organizations hired outside consultants to do the work; others helped users enact corrections on their own. And independent computer technicians were free to reprogram in their preferred styles, provided they tested and readied systems, and evaluated success before and after the new millennium. In these structural webs, strategies of action were quite varied. Local autonomy allowed different paths to a common end.

The characteristics described thus far could hardly be possible if structural webs were not themselves porous institutions. Sociologist Robert Wuthnow identifies porous institutions as "permeable" or "loosely confederated" entities with "social boundaries that permit people, goods, information, and other resources to flow across them with relative ease."[80] The institutions involved in fighting both SARS and Y2K fit this description quite clearly. In the case of SARS, recall that successful resolution required medical practitioners to interact regularly with public health authorities. Public health authorities, in turn, regularly engaged with both community leaders and residents. The flexible boundaries between these various local bases made it possible to coordinate resolution efforts, facilitating speedy, inclusive treatment and effective quarantine plans. The porousness of international boundaries necessarily increased as well, enabling governments to exchange medical personnel and information quickly. In this regard, nations that rapidly brought SARS under control often shared their methods and their personnel with nations at the onset of an outbreak. Similarly, nations exchanged tissue and blood samples in the interest of rapid analysis. Indeed, postepidemic reports suggest that such exchange hastened researchers' ability to identify definitively the coronavirus that triggered the epidemic.[81]

Porousness characterized the institutions at work on Y2K as well. At the local level, boundaries between experts and users were necessarily permeable. In some cases, experts required access to otherwise private technological systems. In other instances, experts were required to interact with users and teach them to install precautions on their own. And often, information and programs designed to ward off Y2K had to be exchanged quickly by the various computer systems at work within or across local bases. National governments, corporations, and other organizations maintained similar flexibility. The scope of the Y2K threat required computer technicians to move with ease between companies and organizations within a single sector (for example, the medical sector and the banking sector); technicians had to move freely between the public and private sectors as well. Further, computer technicians had to coordinate corrections in both the interorganizational and international spheres, for just one failure—say, a banking system that malfunctioned, a power grid that failed—could cause a ripple effect within the larger structural web. Finally, personnel and information had to flow freely between various national divisions and the center of operations. If progress was to be tracked effectively and deadlines met, the center of operations required access to the latest information, thus allowing it to match the resources of ready nations with those that lagged behind.

Porous boundaries encourage easy movement. This, in turn, affects the communication patterns that characterize structural webs. Thus, structural webs display what we might call multidirectional communication patterns. This means that information in the web moves both vertically and laterally, and that it flows through the web reciprocally rather than unidirectionally. This style of exchange endows structural webs with a certain transparency, keeping problem-solving efforts public, traceable, and for the most part, void of secrecy.[82] Multidirectional communication was quite evident in the treatment of the SARS dilemma. Recall the various channels of information exchange. In their efforts to contain outbreaks and hasten recoveries, local bases such as hospitals, public health agencies, and local governments compared notes—openly and frequently—on the practical aspects of clinic setup, treatment tactics, and methods of quarantine. Similarly, the WHO's various regional subsidiaries regularly communicated with regard to the international movement of the disease. In this way, regions in the thick of an outbreak could share information with those whose problems had just begun.

Note too that communication in the SARS structural web was not confined within rank. Information traveled from center to periphery and vice versa. Thus, local bases were encouraged to report the latest infection rate to their national health agencies, which in turn passed the information to regional and central locations. Local bases were also encouraged to contact the WHO directly regarding unanticipated changes in infection trends and amendments to treatment protocols. Similarly, the WHO's center of operations constantly dispersed information through the web. In the case of official policy (travel advisories or restrictions, for example) information might move through a vertical communication chain (center to regional to national to local). But the WHO's global information network also communicated directly with subsidiaries when necessary.

The same communication patterns emerged with reference to Y2K. Information flowed between the elements within a rank as well as from core to periphery. Within local bases, for example, departments and divisions often exchanged notes on effective resolution techniques. (In my own university, for example, one department's success against Y2K often expedited another department's or division's progress.) Communication proceeded across local bases, with government agencies aiding utilities or businesses helping one another. And communication between local bases and national, regional, and operations centers was constant. Once local bases resolved the Y2K problem, they reported their progress to national monitoring commissions. At the same time, the IYCC was in contact as needed, sending information through the web and entertaining questions directed its way.[83]

Porous boundaries, and the multidirectional communication channels they encourage, are important to the essence of a structural web. But structural webs are also defined by the type of information in which they trade. The information that binds the elements of the web is typically formal knowledge. Recall that in chapter 6, I defined formal knowledge as a set of explicit beliefs about the way in which elements of the world work. These beliefs form a script for action that is highly articulated and self-consciously invoked. But while explicit and consciously stated, formal knowledge is also constantly contested and amended, the product of continual discovery. In this way, formal knowledge is uniquely compatible with the milieu of a structural web, for unlike traditional knowledge and common sense, the dynamism of formal knowledge corresponds to the flexibility of the web.

Where would the fight against SARS have led without a flexible, well-articulated foundation? The ability to consider all possible sources and mutations of the virus, the capacity to amend hypotheses with information garnered in new outbreaks—such a stance was critical to the ultimate (and rapid) discovery of the disease's unique etiology. The same can be said for the Y2K bug. Those working on Y2K understood that knowledge grows and changes with reference to the empirical world. That stance both gave birth to the Y2K problem and led to its antidote. In dealing with Y2K, nothing was absolute or final. Rather, solutions led to problems that led to additional solutions, and so on. Recognizing the potential for change and diversion freed members of the SARS and Y2K webs to consider unconventional solutions and avenues of action.

Figure 7.1 illustrates the workings of the structural web. The figure adapts the model to reflect the cases analyzed here. But this structural arrangement could easily exist in other contexts as well. One could imagine, for example, self-contained organizations configured as structural webs. Central operations might correspond to a home office, subsidiaries to regional centers, nations to distribution centers in specific countries or states, local bases to field offices. What is critical is that such an organization's elements share the characteristics of the web, including the service orientation of its center, the autonomy of its elements, the nature of its institutional boundaries, its mode of communication, and its use of formal knowledge.

The Structure of Positive-Asymmetry Sites

When we look to the structure of sites in which positive asymmetry prevailed, we find a very different configuration. The sites of positive asymmetry displayed what historian Alfred Chandler called the "M-form," for its multidivisional arrangement of elements."[84] Figure 7.2 illustrates this arrangement.

M-forms contain a "control peak," a unit that dominates a chain of command. In the case of the Phoenix memo, the FBI's central offices fulfilled this role. NASA's upper-level management occupied the slot in the *Challenger* incident. A control peak fulfills two primary functions. First, it controls the hierarchy's resources and information, making all decisions on the ways in which they are acquired and dispersed. Second, it controls all final decisions and policy initiatives made within the structure.

In an M-form, the control peak typically establishes regional subsidiaries. Like the subsidiaries of the structural web, these units give the control peak a presence on the ground. But in an M-form, the location of the subsidiaries is based on coverage rather than need. The control peak uses its subsidiaries to disperse its reach evenly and ensure uniform control. In the

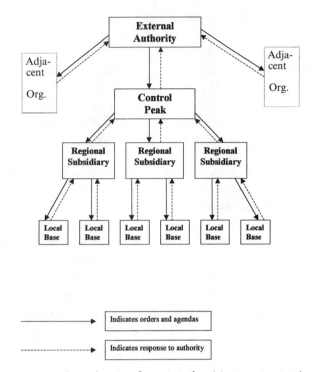

Figure 7.2. The M-form configuration of positive-asymmetry sites

FBI, for example, regional offices are located in every state of the nation. At NASA, subsidiaries translate to departments, with departments established for every substantive area of the NASA mission.[85]

Local bases form the third major component of the M-form. Such bases are the foot soldiers of the structure. They enact the policy developed by the control peak and they collect information upon which new policy is built or old policy revised. In the case of the FBI, offices in Phoenix and Minnesota represent local bases. In the case of NASA, the engineering work groups fit the description.

Unlike structural webs, M-forms may be highly subject to an external authority. This authority may have designed or initiated the hierarchy; it may fund its operations. As a consequence, the M-form's successes and failures, its continued existence, is subject to the external authority's review. In the case of the FBI, the White House and the Office of the Attorney General function in this regard. For NASA, the U.S. Congress represents the most important external authority. It is also important to note that M-forms exist in a broader organizational field, where they are surrounded by other hierarchies with structures identical to their own. Yet as figure 7.2 indicates, most M-forms fail to generate meaningful connections with external authorities. While each M-form may be beholden or logically linked to the same external authority, each operates according to its own specialized rules and procedures. The insular nature of M-form structures helps to explain why the FBI failed to exchange vital information with the CIA, the INS, the FAA, or the NSA. It explains as well why Morton Thiokol, a corporation key to the *Challenger*'s success, remained both bureaucratically and functionally separate from NASA when final safety decisions were made.

As was true for structural webs, the nature of the M-form is defined, in part, by the characteristics of the structure's core—in this case, the control peak. In M-forms, authority is driven by much more than service. Beyond coordinating and advising, control peaks direct and control the actions of the elements they govern. In so doing, authoritative bodies preclude all but a very limited local autonomy. Recall, for example, the circumstances facing the FBI's Phoenix operatives. While those working in this local base had strong and reasoned suspicions regarding regionally based terrorist cells, Phoenix agents had no power to authorize a wider investigation. Authorization for such an operation—one that might confirm or deny the Phoenix agents' fears—rested solely in the hands of the FBI's central office. In this M-form structure, power flowed downward and major action by local elements was tightly controlled. The same can be said of NASA's control peak. Local units, such as the engineering work groups, executed insulated tasks. In the case of the *Challenger*, these groups assessed data relevant to O-ring performance; the groups calculated risks that might emerge from O-ring failure. But the work groups' determinations were, in no way, absolute or final. Rather, the calculations rendered by working engineers became part of a broader information packet reviewed by decision makers at the top of the hierarchy.

Earlier, I noted that structural webs are porous institutions. But the boundaries of the elements comprised by M-form structures are typically rigid and impermeable. Personnel function largely within the confines of their particular divisions. Information is guarded and moves only through authorized chains of command. This arrangement discourages comparisons and consultations between the hierarchy's elements, which, in turn, can seriously impede cooperative action. Recall, for example, that in the case of the Phoenix memo, offices in both Phoenix and Minnesota were working on related theories of terrorist infiltration. But the insular nature of these local bases precluded information exchange, thus denying both offices the chance to connect the dots of their investigations. (Imagine how different perception could have been if the Minnesota and Phoenix offices enjoyed unfettered information flow.) Impenetrable boundaries also impeded communication between local bases and the control peak. The structure of the FBI hierarchy strictly channeled information exchange. Thus, once information left a local base like Phoenix, follow-up was nonexistent; local involvement stopped until or unless the control peak requested further action. The impenetrable boundary around the M-form itself further curtailed worst-case vision. Had the FBI and related agencies such as the CIA, the NSA, Congress, or the White House cooperated rather than engaging in competition or isolated execution, the danger signaled by the Phoenix memo may have resonated with other ongoing investigations, bringing danger to the foreground of attention in one or more of these M-form structures.

The same can be said for the boundaries within NASA. Engineering workgroups were often geographically and organizationally separated from managerial sectors, and their links to the control peak were distant and indirect. Further, the boundaries between local bases were thickened by competition. The Marshall Space Flight Center, for example, perceived itself in competition with other local bases such as the Kennedy Center, the Johnson Center, or Cape Canaveral. Similarly, engineers at Thiokol competed with engineers at the Marshall Center. Such solid boundaries, and the adversarial environment they sustained, discouraged a fruitful exchange of information between local elements. Solid boundaries tainted vertical exchange as well. Engineers, for example, operated quite separately from the NASA managers. Indeed, Vaughan suggests that these two groups occupied different structural niches. Engineering decisions originated with engineers; managerial recommendations originated with managers; and final decisions were the product of a distinct internal authority:

> Many mechanisms were built into the process so that people outside the work group could (and did) challenge the [engineering] group's risk assessment. Nonetheless, limiting informational dependencies remained that restricted challenges. The ability of others to intervene, altering the work group's paradigmatic worldview, was inhibited by systematic censorship of information; its patterned reduction due to official organizational practices, specialization, and the tendency of top decision makers to rely on signals when unable to discriminate in decision-making situations.[86]

Just as porous boundaries can enhance communication channels, impenetrable boundaries can limit them. And in keeping with the insularity of the M-form's elements, communication occurs through rigidly unidirectional and specialized channels. Assignments are passed downward with little opportunity for discussion or debate. Finished products are passed upward with no expectation of dialogue. And channels for lateral exchange may be nonexistent, as such interaction is deemed largely unimportant to problem-solving tasks. Consequently, information is routinely compressed and summarized as it is passed through the chain of command. By the time a message reaches the control peak, it presents a forest with no mention of the trees. Consider the impact this method of communication had on the Phoenix memo incident. The Phoenix memo simply traveled the chain of command, targeting the three appropriate branches of the bureau's control peak. Those in the Phoenix office never really knew if FBI central had shown interest in their recommendations—nor did they expect to find out. Indeed, based on normal operating procedures, there was little reason to believe that the control peak would provide the Phoenix office with a direct response. In the control peak, there was no effort made to follow up with the memo's authors, and there was no mechanism by which the three memo recipients might compare notes or discuss the memo's merits. Reciprocal communication simply proves foreign to M-forms such as the FBI. Similar limits on communication were in place at NASA as well. Information was streamlined; communication was predominantly vertical and almost always unidirectional. As Vaughan describes it:

> The division of labor between subunits, hierarchy, and geographic dispersion segregate knowledge about tasks and goals. Distance—both physical and social—interferes with the efforts of those at the top to "know" the behavior of others in the organization and vice versa.[87]

In discussing the structure of positive-asymmetry sites, one final point is worth noting. While structural webs favor the fuel of formal knowledge, M-forms are more likely to be fueled by traditional knowledge. Recall that in chapter 6, I defined traditional knowledge as a system of well-articulated but inflexible beliefs, beliefs that present themselves as fixed and essential parts of the arenas in which they appear. In relying on traditional knowledge, the participants in M-forms can become hopelessly tied to operational rituals and rules. Their decisions are steeped in a system's historical experience rather than the unique characteristics of any single event. Trapped in the frame of traditional knowledge, the FBI's control peak failed to see the unusual nature of the Phoenix memo. When faced with the memo's novel claims, it reinterpreted these signals of danger in terms of the bureau's past experience. Thus, FBI central focused on isolated hijackings or attacks on foreign embassies. But never did the intricate worst-case scenario of September 11 appear as a viable possibility.[88] Similarly, when NASA engineers warned of danger in the *Challenger* launch, NASA managers redefined those warnings as acceptable risk. When assessed in the rich fabric of the organization's traditional knowledge, all risk seemed routine.[89]

The Social Foundations of Cognition

The key players in both SARS and Y2K were members of communities that championed negative asymmetry—communities for which cognitive deviance was "normal." The opposite proved true for those involved in the Phoenix memo incident and the *Challenger* disaster. Members of the FBI and NASA were cognitive conformists, seeing events through the normative lens of positive asymmetry. Are these cognitive stances and the cultures that support them, in and of themselves, enough to explain the very different outcomes observed in these four cases? In this chapter, I suggest that we must consider something more. I argue that certain structures—specifically what I call emancipating structures—play a pivotal role in nurturing the cognitive deviance needed to anticipate and avoid disaster.

The four cases reviewed here provide insufficient data to substantiate this claim fully. Yet these cases are so strongly patterned that they beg future analysis. Toward that end, I propose a set of formal research propositions—propositions that would enable us to examine systematically the specific links between social structure and cognitive deviance.

Proposition 1: Structures that emphasize service over competition are most likely to enable cognitive deviance. Service requires extension and alliance—often between very different groups and communities. Competition, in contrast, beckons guardedness and isolation. The service orientation may encourage openness to and tolerance for varied and potentially unusual paths in the problem-solving process.

Proposition 2: Structures containing porous versus impenetrable boundaries are most likely to enable cognitive deviance. The sites of negative asymmetry suggest that porous boundaries keep social systems well integrated. Such boundaries facilitate high levels of informational exchange, encourage rich, multidirectional paths of communication, and thus stimulate the kind of cognitive intersections that can encourage new ways of seeing.

Proposition 3: Structures that favor autonomy over strict centralized control are most likely to enable cognitive deviance. While integration maximizes cognitive intersections, it does not ensure the freedom to develop them or act on them. Systems that give operators in various locations the freedom to assess and react provide a forum in which cognitive deviance can thrive and take root.

Proposition 4: Structures that favor formal knowledge over traditional knowledge or common sense are most likely to enable cognitive deviance. Traditional knowledge invites the repetition of established patterns. In contrast, formal knowledge requires the continuous thinking and rethinking of issues. In this way, formal knowledge increases the potential for new visions and deviation from cognitive norms.

Proposition 5: Service orientation, porous boundaries (and the multiplex communication channels they spur), knowledge type, and levels of autonomy are intricately connected and must "move together" if cognitive deviance is to ensue. It is the co-presence of these elements that forms emancipating structures. Without this configuration of characteristics, cognitive deviance may be difficult to achieve.

These propositions, of course, do not exhaustively address the complicated role of structure in thought. Yet they provide a point of departure for a new and well-targeted research agenda. In probing the interplay between structure and thought, we can learn much regarding the factors that facilitate and impede certain workings of the mind.

⁓

In previous chapters, we explored the process of quality evaluation, paying special attention to the connections between culture and cognition. Here, social structure entered our inquiry, as we probed the role variable structures play in perceptions of best and worst. The role of structure is intricate, and in this chapter, we have only begun to scratch the surface of discovery. Yet we leave with several fruitful propositions to explore in future research.

In broadening this inquiry to include considerations of structure, we have seen that culture and structure play distinctive roles in the process of thought. Structure appears to influence a community's cognitive variety, with some structures encouraging variations on cognitive rules. Culture, in contrast, governs the entrenchment of cognitive styles, as practices conventionalize particular perceptual patterns. Thus, in the realm of thought, culture and structure are not causally connected. The role of each sphere, while complementary, is also independent. Each proves important to our way of seeing, making visions of quality the product of an intricate sociocultural system.

Learning the role of culture and structure in the evaluation of best and worst represents a mere first step in the fight against worst-case scenarios. But how generalizable are the lessons we have learned? Can we apply them in ways that enhance our ability to anticipate the worst? And is such a goal advisable? These are the questions probed in the final chapter of this book.

CHAPTER EIGHT

Can Symmetrical Vision Be Achieved?

A merican novelist and short story writer Alice Hegan Rice once declared, "It ain't no use putting up your umbrella till it rains."[1] Rice's view mirrors that of most of the groups and communities we have visited in *Never Saw It Coming*. For most of us, there appears little ability to see the worst, little reason to acknowledge it until it happens. We have seen that such blindness appears especially acute within American culture. Yet the practice extends well beyond the American experience. In a host of examples, across contexts and throughout history, I have shown that positive asymmetry, as a way of seeing the world, proves the road more traveled, the medicine most often prescribed.

And yet there are times, so many times, when we regret our inability to imagine the worst. And during such times, we bemoan our biased perceptual tendencies. If only you had thought to perform more faithful breast self-exams, stopped smoking twenty years ago, agreed to call a cab after drinks with friends. If only you had seen the signals that your partner was unhappy, given more thought to financing your old age, considered the potential for violence in the tormented, lonely child at your school. If only the FBI's top brass had seen the Phoenix memo, the FBI and CIA had communicated more directly, NASA's managers had heeded their engineers' warnings. If only— probably two of the most frequently uttered words in the American lexicon.

Is there a way to avoid the "if only's" that seem to travel with positive asymmetry? Can anything we have learned in *Never Saw It Coming* help us pinpoint the moment at which to "open our umbrellas," a moment that does not dampen the spirit and yet mitigates regret? The answer to these questions grows from this book's chief lessons.

What Have We Learned?

The initial chapters of this book took readers on a whirlwind tour. We visited the everyday worlds of couples and families, the minds of teenagers and senior citizens alike; we studied those at work, at play, and on the road; we examined small groups, organizations, and cultures at large. In all of these places, among all of these groups, we learned that one particular way of seeing dominates the scene. Positive asymmetry—the tendency to see the best and background the worst—proves an overwhelming perceptual pattern.

Why is positive asymmetry such a dominant way of seeing? In chapter 1, I suggested that a general sense of asymmetry is rooted in the workings of the brain. Cognitive scientists' notion of graded membership tells us that the brain has a strong tendency to foreground in consciousness the best-case specimen of a category. In so doing, the brain distances all else—especially worst-case specimens—from active consideration. But graded membership is only part of the story. Culture, I have argued, harnesses the brain's propensity toward asymmetry and encodes that process into a much more targeted and specialized experiential bias. Groups and communities attend to and prioritize people, places, objects, and events. And overwhelmingly, most groups and communities define the best of these categories as highly relevant, highly important, and worthy of intense focus. The source of these priorities and rankings varies from group to group—dictated, for example, by community survival, shared values and goals, power structures. But one fact is key. As relevance structures become institutionalized, visions of quality are routinely transformed. Asymmetry becomes positive asymmetry, and the emphasis on the best case of *any* specimen becomes an emphasis on specimens that triumph only best-case scenarios. So strong is this emphasis that groups and communities develop specialized cultural practices to enforce it. Eclipsing, clouding, and recasting strategies help communities maintain truncated considerations of quality. And as these cultural practices become entrenched in communities, biased and unbalanced definitions of quality come to feel "natural."

Cultural practices prove immensely powerful in riveting groups and communities to a best-case perceptual porthole, even in arenas committed to unbiased, objective evaluations. And cultural practices, in combination with certain social factors, can influence the consequences of being labeled the worst. We learned that elements such as the durability of quality labels, the labeler's power vis-à-vis the target, and the normative reaction to criticism at work in the labeling context affect the power of the label in important ways.

Understanding this impact is critical, for it can help us to predict whether the worst of people, places, objects, and events will be ravaged or redeemed.

But while positive asymmetry is a widespread phenomenon, it is not a universal one. In chapter 6, I presented two specific communities—medical practitioners (MPs) and computer operators, programmers, and system analysts (COPS)—that are prototypical exceptions to the rule. In examining MPs and COPS, we learned that both groups routinely exercise positive asymmetry in reverse, a phenomenon to which I referred as negative asymmetry. I suggested several possibilities that might contribute to this anomaly. Both communities, for example, are service oriented. Their focus necessarily extends beyond the community itself, as each community's subsistence requires a balanced consideration of "self" versus "other." Both MPs and COPS exhibit porous community boundaries, allowing people, information, and resources to flow in and out of the community with frequency and ease. Both groups are clearly dominated by "formal knowledge," explicit beliefs that form a highly articulated and self-consciously invoked script for action. Finally, members of both communities are quite autonomous, and despite their affiliation with organizations or broader communities, maintain considerable ability to monitor and control themselves.

I suggested that the characteristics displayed by MPs and COPS are something more than a checklist of professional identity elements. Rather, I contended, these elements in combination constitute an emancipating structure. An emancipating structure is a context of action that supersedes any particular profession and frees those within it to deviate from cognitive norms. Any group or community configured in this way may come to favor negative asymmetry.

To explore the links between structure, culture, and cognition further, I took readers to four specific sites: the first outbreak of SARS, the fight to contain the Y2K millennium bug, the FBI Phoenix memo and its connection to the September 11 terrorist attacks, and the NASA *Challenger* disaster. In the first two settings, action emerged in a particular type of emancipating structure, one I called a structural web. Readers learned that the workings of the web encouraged those involved to deviate from the cultural and cognitive conventions that typically govern the assessment of quality. But the settings in which the Phoenix memo and *Challenger* disasters occurred displayed very different identifying characteristics. Specifically, both settings displayed a rigid M-form structure. And the rigidity of the structure in which thought and action took place helped support the cognitive normalcy of positive asymmetry.

Where Do We Go from Here?

What do these findings tell us about quality perception? Do they provide any insight that might help groups and communities better anticipate the worst?

The first important lesson rests in recognizing the connections between neural mechanics and cultural practices. As we have seen, both cognitive assessment and cultural evaluation rely on some form of asymmetry. In the brain, graded membership foregrounds best-case examples of a concept, while simultaneously backgrounding worst-case examples. In cultural experience, practices such as eclipsing, clouding, and recasting background not only a category's worst-case examples, but worst-case categories themselves. To be sure, the cultural phase of evaluation must be viewed as a variation—perhaps even a distortion—of graded membership, for in the cultural realm, asymmetry is always biased toward positive qualities. Yet cultural assessment necessarily *resembles* cognitive assessment, as both processes rely on the establishment of disequilibrium.

The similarities between cognition and culture do not stop there. Consider that in the brain, neurons connect with other neurons to perform graded membership. In so doing, they create paths or "traces" in the brain that, with repetition, becomes strong and ingrained, eventually overpowering other potential processing chains.[2] A similar process occurs in cultural enactment. When cultural practices are repeated and embraced by the members of groups and communities, they become entrenched, institutionalized, and often capable of hindering other ways of seeing. In essence, practices construct and maintain cultural traces or routines that direct the way in which groups and communities evaluate quality.

The similarities between cognitive and cultural processes are important to note. For in attempting to change the cultural practices that distance the worst from view, we must be fully cognizant that we are fighting patterns that feel "natural" to most individuals. When cultural practices resemble the workings of the mind, they come to feel "right," automatic, or indigenous even though they are constructed. In this way, those attempting to change cultural evaluative practices, as well as those who experience such change, may feel as if they are contradicting human nature.

⚬⚬⚬

But even if groups and communities acknowledge the constructed nature of evaluative practices and categories, these practices and categories can prove difficult to change. Indeed, sociological research suggests that cultural change often requires innovation—the discovery of new ideas or phenomena that promise improvement of older ways. Would the institutionalization of negative asymmetry provide such innovation? Would it improve quality assessment as we know it?

The question cannot be answered with a simple yes or no. For while positive asymmetry can often leave us vulnerable to disaster, many contend that this porthole on the world and the optimism that it supports fuel not only a community's survival, but its energy and growth. Imagine, for example, the changes to U.S. history had our population been unable to regain optimism and hope after the plague of 1900, the Great Depression, or the September 11 terrorist attacks. Consider the fate of the American labor force if workers became obsessed with the probabilities of injury during their morning showers, their commutes to work, or their hours on the job. Could families survive if their members could not re-embrace life after the death of a spouse or a child? Could any one of us thrive if we did not regularly shirk the fears of being a victim of disease or crime? Clearly, optimism is critical not only to our emotional stability, but to the stability and flourishing of the groups and communities to which each of us belongs.[3]

To be sure, there will be some value in switching our perspective. Seeing the worst may indeed help us discover a tumor in its early stages or stave off a health pandemic. It may help us avert a technological shutdown or a "deadly" computer virus. It may better protect us from mechanical failure or enemy attacks. But we must remain mindful that negative asymmetry will carry some costs as well. As a rule, negative asymmetry requires that those who practice it remain uncertain and pessimistic. Groups and communities guided by worst-case vision are necessarily waiting for the ax to fall, anticipating impending doom. Communities that subscribe to negative asymmetry must therefore remain fixed at the "defensive line"; they must remain blind to the potential and hope embodied in the "Hail Mary pass."

If negative asymmetry offers no definitive improvement over its positive counterpart, can cultural change occur? Or are we doomed to accept the stance of positive asymmetry, continuing to be blindsided by incidents of the worst? Perhaps there is another alternative.

Toward Cognitive Symmetry

The innovation sufficiently strong to spur cultural change may rest in the establishment of "symmetrical vision." A symmetrical vision of quality would provide an equal presence for best and worst. And the simultaneous perception of both best and worst would afford groups and communities the

luxury of optimism tempered with caution. Symmetrical vision: the prescription seems easy, almost obvious. But achieving symmetrical vision may
be a challenging task. It will require reorienting most groups' and communities' ways of seeing, and demand the establishment of new cultural practices.
Toward that end, I suggest three specific steps that could initiate movement
toward the symmetrical vision goal.

Step 1: Acknowledgment

As I have implied, groups and communities must consciously and explicitly
acknowledge that in most settings and circumstances ways of seeing favor
best-case assumptions. This consciousness-raising is key to ultimate change,
for the conventions of positive asymmetry are so well entrenched, so longstanding, that they must be directly addressed and fully recognized if change
is to occur.

Acknowledgment may seem like an obvious prescription. Yet those who
have successfully instituted the type of large-scale cultural change I am advocating identify the step as crucial to their task. Mothers Against Drunk Driving (MADD), for example, recognized this fact in their highly successful
fight against drinking and driving. At its inception in 1980, the organization
adopted a lofty goal: "20% × 2000," meaning a 20 percent reduction in drunk-
driving fatalities by the year 2000. The leaders of MADD understood that
reaching this goal would require important cultural changes—changes in the
ways Americans thought about alcohol and the road, changes in Americans'
leisure practices. In service of this valiant fight, acknowledgment proved a
central strategy. The group worked hard to educate Americans, raising their
consciousness to the devastation caused by drunk drivers. The organization's
leaders contend that the quest for acknowledgment paid off. MADD was so
successful in changing cultural norms of alcohol use that the organization
reached its goal of "20% × 2000" in 1997, three years ahead of schedule.

Acknowledgement—those struggling to decrease U.S. vulnerability to
terrorism are advocating this step as well. Stephen Flynn, author of *America
the Vulnerable,* contends that the "joyride" is over and the United States
must finally face "the hard problems of our vulnerability here at home." According to Flynn, we simply "need to come clean with how vulnerable we
are."[4] It is worth noting that members of the 9/11 Commission came to a similar conclusion. In their report to the nation, chairman Tom Kean and his colleagues advised the Bush administration to acknowledge quickly that "we are
not safe." According to Kean, the government's eyes must be fully opened
before it can fix the holes in America's national security.[5]

The aftermath of hurricane Katrina brought similar pleas to light. We know, for example, that three years prior to Katrina, the New Orleans *Times-Picayune* published a Pulitzer Prize–winning series of articles on New Orleans's vulnerability. The pieces warned that the city's levees would be inadequate to shield New Orleans from the water surge that a category 4 or 5 storm would likely generate. The writers at the *Times-Picayune* were not alone in their fears. In October of 2001, the *Scientific American* published a report that reached similar conclusions. But despite the warnings of experts, administrative and congressional officials failed to acknowledge the reality of such a scenario. As a result, funding for projects designed to enhance the New Orleans levees never fully materialized. Had the problems been acknowledged and the levees been strengthened, many experts contend that Katrina would have been far less devastating to the city.[6]

Step 2: Develop New Evaluative Practices

I have noted that the cultural practices currently steering quality evaluation are, in many ways, variations on the brain's graded-membership function. But the brain utilizes other functions in assessing and evaluating external stimuli, and we would do well to translate some of those functions to the cultural domain.

The cultural assessment of quality is based on unidimensional continua. Such a strategy purports that the best and worst of people, places, objects, and events are simply opposite faces of the same coin. To be sure, this strategy can be quite useful for certain evaluative tasks. If, for example, one is measuring the degree of color concentration in a fabric, a wall, or a painting or gauging the density of a stone or a forest, if one is assessing a diamond's degree of brilliance or the intensity of a rock band's sound, if one is evaluating the elasticity of a human muscle or the seriousness of a criminal's actions—in all such cases, unidimensional continua are quite appropriate, for one is interested in the relative presence of a single element. But when measuring quality in its broadest sense, unidimensional continua may be insufficient. Best and worst may often be distinct elements rather than opposite ends of a unified conceptual dimension.[7]

To illustrate my point, let us revisit the students I discussed in the very first chapter of this book. When I asked my students to name the best thing that could happen to them, recall that one person wrote, "The best thing that could happen to me is that Tom and I finish school and get married." Another wrote, "To get all A's this semester." Still another said, "I would win three hundred million dollars instantly." And one student reported, "I would become an NBA franchise player within the next three years." Recall too that the students recounted the worst thing that could happen to them. These "worsts" were never polar opposites of the bests. Best and worst were in no way a continuum of experience. Answers like "maybe, death?" "getting sick," or simply "failure" had their own integrity. That fact alerts us to an important consideration in the evaluation of quality. In experience, the worst may not be the opposite of the best—the two may represent two distinct categories. And, if we continue to restrict quality assessment to unidimensional continua, we will lose the opportunity to explore the broadest meaning of quality.

I propose that in the evaluation of quality we add a new tool to our conceptual arsenal. I advocate the adoption of a "separate-but-equal" strategy— one that would allow us to consider a variety of quality dimensions simultaneously.

As figure 8.1 illustrates, separating best and worst produces a denser categorization system than that afforded by unidimensional considerations of quality. When we approach best and worst as separate but equally important, we are forced to consider each dimension of quality independently.[8] This, in turn, demands a greater degree of conscious discrimination, as best and worst cannot be defined simply by adding or subtracting elements of one from the other. As distinct categories, best and worst must display unique characteristics, and the relationship between the categories must be discovered rather than assumed. In this way, a separate-but-equal strategy creates the potential for quality copresence—an increased likelihood that both the best and worst of people, places, objects, and events will remain part of the dialogue, elaborated to the maximum, and thus ever visible in a community's perceptual field. Every setting will contain multiple frames of reference, creating a system in which a community or its subgroups can engage in a process of cognitive checks and balances.[9]

Several examples help to illustrate my point. Suppose, for instance, that pharmaceutical researchers at Hoffman-La Roche had applied a separate-but-equal strategy when evaluating the now problematic drug Accutane. Accutane treats severe cystic acne that proves unresponsive to other common treatments. The drug works by (1) reducing the production of a skin lubricant called sebum, (2) shrinking the skin glands that produce sebum, and (3) inhibiting the hardening of skin cells. What did pharmacologists see as the best- and worst-case results of Accutane treatment? Using a unidimensional quality continuum to address the issue, researchers defined the best-case scenario of Accutane as a fifteen-to-twenty-week course of treatment that

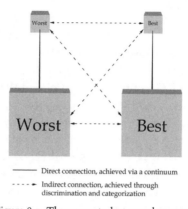

Figure 8.1. The separate-but-equal strategy

ultimately results in the complete disappearance of acne-related cysts. Pre-dictably, they defined the worst-case scenario of the drug as total ineffec-tiveness. We now know that Accutane's worst-case scenario is something much worse than cystic skin. Indeed, the drug has been linked to severe depression, psychosis, and suicidal tendencies.[10] Researchers simply did not see the drug's potentially destructive effects. For them, the worst that Accu-tane could do was to fail in accomplishing the best. Invoking a separate-but-equal strategy in the quality assessment of Accutane might have led re-searchers to very different conclusions.[11]

Best and worst, separate but equal. One can cite other examples in which such a strategy might have helped evaluators anticipate the worst-case sce-nario. Consider, for instance, the development of asbestos and other insula-tion materials. In creating these products, manufacturers defined best and worst using a unidimensional quality continuum. The best insulations were those that achieved specific design goals—goals involving heat retention and noise deflection. The worst insulations had no distinct characteristics; they were simply the substances that failed to meet the manufacturer's preestab-lished design goals. In the marketing of housing insulation, no one antici-pated that the worst-case scenario would involve something much more severe, let alone deadly. No one considered, for example, that asbestos might be toxic, or that insulation foam, because of its appropriateness for nesting, would attract destructive rodents to the houses in which it was used. Had a separate-but-equal strategy been invoked, had manufacturers considered quality lows without tying them to quality highs, manufacturers might have increased the potential to envision worst cases that were independent of best-case outcomes.

The same conclusions apply to the development of technologies such as automobile seat belts and airbags. In testing these new technologies, manufacturers defined the best case with reference to the product's ability to restrain and cushion auto occupants during impact. The worst case was not viewed as an independent condition, but rather, as the product's failure to meet the highest safety goals. No one considered the possibility that seat belts or air bags might function in a way that actually decreased their protective power. No one dreamed that some seat belts would lock so rigidly that they would break the bones of auto passengers, or that air bags would inflate in ways so powerful that they could smother passengers to death. Defining quality via a unidimensional continuum precluded such foresight.

One wonders, How might the Bush administration's plans for the invasion of Iraq have changed with the adoption of a separate-but-equal strategy? In the Bush plan, invading Iraq and deposing Saddam Hussein was the best-case outcome of U.S. action. Failure was defined as "a smoking gun—that could come in the form of a mushroom cloud."[12] But thinking in terms of such unidimensional continua—win or lose, conquer or be conquered—may have diverted the administration from equally disastrous potentials, including the costs of faulty intelligence, the loss of international support, and a postwar environment of increased hatred and instability. Could a separate-but-equal approach to the best and worst components of the invasion of Iraq have led to different conclusions? We will never know for sure, but we can reasonably assume that such an approach would have increased the factors considered by those making decisions about war.

Step 3: Consider the Structural Settings in which Cognitive and Cultural Change Is Best Implemented

Adding a separate-but-equal strategy to a group's or community's arsenal of evaluative practices demands that such groups do two things. First, they must stray from established cognitive strategies and the cultural practices that support them. Second, they must adopt and institutionalize more variable—indeed deviant—ways of seeing. I have argued that certain structural configurations appear better suited to this task. In chapter 7, I suggested that emancipating structures provide the necessary flexibility to support cognitive deviance. Thus, in order to establish symmetrical vision as a viable cognitive alternative, we would do well to initiate the strategy in such emancipated settings. (The structural web represents one such setting. Future research must determine if other emancipating structures exist.) If emancipating structures fail to exist where needed, we may consider reconfiguring rigid decision-making contexts in ways that loosen the grip of cognitive norms.

This point requires further elaboration. To be sure, we cannot realistically reconfigure every group or community, every decision-making context, in ways that are amenable to symmetrical vision. Yet we may do well to reexamine the structure of critical decision-making settings, especially those involving collective safety. Would the family prove a safer place if considerations of risk were embedded in an emancipating rather than a rigid structure? Could one say the same about school systems' abilities to avert violent disasters? And what of organizations such as the FBI, the CIA, or NASA? Would a less rigidly hierarchical structure permit the cognitive and cultural freedom needed to envision the worst?

Perhaps it is impossible to affect massive change systematically in traditional and historically private institutions such as the family. In these contexts, one can only suggest ways of reconfiguring the unit's authority structure or the nature of its boundaries. In this regard, one might educate families regarding the new cognitive styles such structural changes would allow, and encourage the adoption of new evaluative practices and strategies. But there may be a more concrete solution for organizations such as the FBI and NASA. In such formal organizations, it may be possible to alter hierarchical structures in novel yet minimally disruptive ways. For example, one could imagine a setting in which emancipating substructures could be embedded in the control centers of M-form hierarchies. These substructures would provide a haven for a "troubleshooting community" committed to anticipating worst-case scenarios and reporting them directly to organizational elites.[13] But in such a setup, precautions must be taken to give these divisions a prominent role at the decision-making table.[14] Only then, can decision makers enter "dialectic deliberations." We can think of dialectic deliberations as a form of reasoning that allows the contradictions and distinctions of any topic to be considered fully and carefully. Such deliberations produce a synthesis, a more complete conceptual field. Thus, while the cognitive tradition of an organization may favor positive asymmetry, dialectic deliberations between elites and troubleshooting divisions could force a community to consider potential disasters with equal vigor. This, in turn, encourages community members to "reweight" their conceptions of best and worst, ultimately creating a more balanced consideration of quality. Both the social psychological and organizational literature provide examples of communities who successfully execute dialectic deliberations and thus enhance their groups' growth, safety, and overall stability.[15] Such findings encourage us to explore this approach with reference to anticipating the worst.

⚬∞⚬

Acknowledgment, new evaluative strategies, amendments to structure—could these three steps help to make the worst a more prominent sight in our perceptual portholes? To be sure, it is an empirical question that beckons further research. Yet our efforts will be well spent, for the answers we generate could carry enormous social benefits.

But while we may successfully broaden our perceptions of danger, we must recognize that we may never fully eradicate the potential for tragedy. As sociologist Charles Perrow taught us many years ago, some systems may be too complex to anticipate the interaction of every element and force. In short, the complete avoidance of catastrophe may be an impossible task.[16]

But a less-than-perfect trajectory cannot deter us. Our newfound knowledge of the interactions between culture, cognition, and the structures in which those interactions occur suggests that most groups and communities can do significantly better in fighting calamity and catastrophe than current efforts allow. Given the stakes—given a better chance to recognize the worst and diminish its occurrence—we would truly be remiss if we simply failed to try.

NOTES

1. Trump 1987, 34.

2. I polled four different undergraduate classes, questioning a total of 397 students over the course of a year. The response rate was 97 percent. Of course, this was a convenience sample, and it thus is in no way representative of the general population. I offer these responses merely for illustrative purposes.

3. Note that 68 percent of my respondents offered similarly targeted descriptions of the best thing that could happen to them. Only 32 percent of respondents produced general or vague answers to my query, answers such as "love," "to be happy," or "health."

4. Clayman's reports are based on work by Atkinson (1984, 374–75) and by Heritage and Greatbatch (1986, 111n).

5. Clayman 1993, 126, 116.

6. Durkheim 1951, 248. In confirmation of Durkheim's contentions, M. Joseph Sirgy (1998) shows that materialists experience greater dissatisfaction with their standard of living and with life in general than do nonmaterialists. Sirgy contends that this unsettlement stems from materialists' tendency to set remote, nonspecific, and often unreachable goals. Materialists are, as Durkheim proposed, walking toward infinity.

7. Durkheim 1951, 249.

8. Some organizational sociologists suggest that economic considerations motivate this strategy. Striving for best practices, as opposed to considering a balanced continuum of quality, allows organizations to constantly raise the bar; it allows organization leaders to continually establish new goals, redefine the meaning of success, and further measure performance. See Applebaum and Batt 1994; Klein 1994; Lawler et al. 1996; or Manley 2000.

9. Begley 2001, 58. Also note that, according to the 9/11 Commission, "the FAA's security branch generated 105 so-called daily summaries between April 1 and September 10, 2001. . . . Fifty-two of those summaries mentioned bin Laden or al Qaeda,

and five discussed hijacking 'as a capability al Qaeda was training for or possessed'" (Hirschkorn 2005).

10. *Sixty Minutes* (CBS network) reported the details of these investigations on its September 17, 2001, broadcast. For elaborations and important follow-ups, see, for example, reports by Hirsh and Isikoff 2002), Isikoff and Klaidman (2002), the 9/11 Commission (Kean et al. 2004), Orr (2003), Risen and Johnston (2002), Stout (2002), and Tyler (2002). In testimony given to the 9/11 Commission, former FAA associate administrator of civil aviation security Cathal Flynn reported, "Nine of the 19 hijackers responsible for the 9/11 terrorist attacks were flagged that morning by a computerized airline passenger screening system as being a potential threat to U.S. aircraft. . . . However, because the system was meant to alert officials to threats from explosives in checked baggage, not the passengers themselves, none of the nine flagged as potential threats were physically inspected or questioned before boarding the plane" (Meeks 2004).

11. Solomon 2001.

12. Indeed, the government's own self-study confirms this. See, for example, Kean et al. 2004. Also see Johnston 2003 and Orr 2003.

13. Chambliss (1996), Clarke (1999), Collins (2001), Diamond (1992), Heimer (1992), Tierney, Lindell, and Perry (2001), and Weick (1995) offer some interesting examples of this phenomenon. And, of course, government responses to Hurricane Katrina provided a vivid reminder of the phenomenon.

14. Both Perrow (1999) and Vaughan (1996, 2002) provide excellent discussions of this phenomenon. Vaughan also spoke quite openly on this matter, both to the press and in testimony before NASA following the 2003 *Columbia* disaster. See Schwartz and Wald 2003a for some of her comments.

15. The failure to anticipate the terrorist attacks on September 11 was not unique. The attack on Pearl Harbor and the presence of German U-boats off the New Jersey coast, the 1993 bombing of the World Trade Center, and the 2000 attack on the USS *Cole*—these events and many more were sights unseen. Such blindness has been well noted as well both by those who investigated and those who experienced the tragic school shootings in places such as Littleton, Colorado; Springfield, Oregon; Fayetteville, Tennessee; Edinboro, Pennsylvania; Jonesboro, Arkansas; Paducah, Kentucky; and Pearl, Mississippi.

16. On misguided optimism for marital success, see, for example, studies by Greenblat and Cottle (1980), Swidler (2001), and Vaughan (1986, 2002). The unwillingness to address potential failure is reflected in comments made by Erik Weihenmayer, the first blind man to scale Mount Everest. Like many such risk takers, Weihenmayer refused to visualize the worst. See reports by Chang (2001) and Swift (2001).

17. I use the term "shared frame of reference" in the spirit of sociologists such as Alfred Schutz, Peter Berger, and Erving Goffman, all of whom problematized the social basis of thought and the ways in which societal members engage in intersubjective understanding.

18. I define a normal action as one that exhibits certain regularities and meets the common expectations of the group or community in which it occurs.

19. Cognitive scientists typically refer to the apprehension and centering of data as "sensation and attention"; they refer to the sorting and organizing of data as "discrimination and classification." See my review of literature in these areas (Cerulo 2002a, 15–17, 57–60).

20. In addition to concepts, note that cognitive scientists study higher-order constructs, mega-concepts such as frames, formats, and schemata.

21. Eleanor Rosch (1973) offered the first empirical support for this phenomenon.

22. For a good review of these debates, see my edited volume *Culture in Mind* (Cerulo 2002a, 114–18), as well as work by Hampton (1997), Medin and Goldstone (1994, 77–83), and Reisberg (2001, 271–99).

23. Cognitive scientists' "ideal prototype" should not be confused with Weber's concept of the "ideal type." The cognitive term denotes perfection within a category; it is the best-case example and can indeed exist in reality. Weber's term, in contrast, presents an exaggeration of characteristics; the ideal type is used to illuminate the social world.

24. Of course, for purposes of illustration, I am simplifying the process. In fact, graded membership entails complex calculations, which cognitive scientists continue to study. At this time, for example, there is some debate in the literature as to whether the brain compares observations and prototypes via an additive operation (referred to as the "modal model") or an averaging process (referred to as the "average model"). For more details, see Solso 2005.

25. Reisberg 2001, 276.

26. For a very readable discussion of cognitive scientists' approach to thought, see my review essays (Cerulo 2002a). Gardner (1987) provides a lively history of the field. Similarly, Pribram reflects on the essence of cognitive science in his article "The Cognitive Revolution and Mind/Brain Issues" (1986). And for a good review of critical differences between cognitive science and its intellectual predecessor, behaviorism, consult Baars's analysis (1986). Two additional works provide readers with a sense of the field's current controversies and future trajectories. Baumgartner and Payr have edited a wonderfully engaging set of interviews (1996), allowing cognitive scientists to provide candid commentary on some of the field's most central issues. Cognitive scientists' perspectives on the future can be found in Solso and Massaro's 1995 study.

27. Culture cannot be disregarded in any study of thought, for it powerfully directs the information that enters the neural stream. While one's culture does not determine how the brain operates, it certainly plays a pivotal role in determining what the brain thinks about. Put in another way, one might say that the neural process of conceptualization is likely universal to the human species, but the products of that process are not. For more detailed excursions on this point, see works by Cerulo (2002a, 2004), DiMaggio (1997), and Zerubavel (1997).

28. Berger and Luckmann 1967, 41–46. In reviewing this definition, one cannot

help but note its compatibility with sociologist Ann Swidler's conception of culture as a "tool kit." Swidler defines culture as "diverse, often conflicting symbols, rituals, stories, and guides to action . . . from which actors select differing pieces for constructing lines of action" (1986, 277). Of course, Swidler's perspective on culture differs from Berger and Luckmann's in important ways. In particular, Swidler emphasizes the agency of actors in ways that Berger and Luckmann do not address. Swidler's emphasis on culture's diversity also is more explicit than Berger and Luckmann's.

29. Bourdieu 1977, 72. While the enactment of culture may become second nature, the process is not in any way instinctual or essential. Internalizing culture does not negate actors' ability to choose between cultural strategies. Thus habitus allows for the exercise of agency. Swidler helps us to understand how habitus and agency can coexist: "People may have in readiness cultural capacities they rarely employ; and all people know more culture than they use" (1986, 277).

30. Bourdieu generally equated social location with class. However, I would argue that the notion of habitus might be more fruitfully applied if one considers social location in its broader dimensions—that is, as a mapping of one's status that represents the product of one's age, class, ethnicity, gender, marital status, occupation, religion, special interests, and so forth.

31. The term "thought communities" is derived from Ludwig Fleck (1979). Eviatar Zerubavel suggests that all of us are members of multiple thought communities, and thus, inhabit "several different social worlds. . . . We each have a rather wide 'cognitive repertoire' and often think somewhat differently in different social contexts" (1997, 17).

32. See Merleau-Ponty 1962. This is not to say that every member of a thought community will experience reality in the same way. It simply means that each member's view of reality originates from a common location and will be interpreted using the same array of possible tools.

33. Berger and Luckmann 1967, 45.

34. It is important to clarify that I am not making claims for a universalistic phenomenon. I am, however, probing a notably common phenomenon that emerges in a wide variety of social contexts and historical circumstances.

35. I borrow this term from sociologist Eviatar Zerubavel (1997. 33). Zerubavel defines an optical tradition as a learned way of seeing influenced by each community's particular cultural lens.

36. In many ways, my argument is compatible with sociologists Roger Friedland and Robert Alford's notion of "logics" (1991). Like them I suggest that cultural practices interact with cognitive structures, thus generating routine behaviors.

37. Douglas S. Massey (2002) and Theodore Kemper (1987) rightfully encourage sociologists to confront the biological basis of emotions. On the activation of emotions before rational operations, see LaDoux 1996.

38. Kemper 1987, 276.

39. See, for example, Hochschild 1983 and Thoits 1990.

40. In forwarding this position, I break to some degree with David R. Heise's affect control theory (1979), as Heise equates culture and meaning with affect.

41. At the individual level, there is some evidence to suggest that one's emotional mood can sometimes influence the perception of new stimuli (Bower 1991; Clore, Schwartz, and Conway 1993; Mayer and Hanson 1995), or the ability to remember past experiences (Eich 1995; Schachter and Kihlstrom 1989). This phenomenon is much less common at the collective level.

42. For a good review of research in the sociology of emotions, see works by Barbalet (2002), Lively and Heise (2004), and Thoits (1989).

43. The majority of my examples will be drawn from contemporary U.S. culture. Yet I make a concerted effort to include cross-cultural and historical data as well, suggesting that this phenomenon goes beyond our particular culture and moment. Of course, further empirical study will be required to determine the international prevalence of positive asymmetry.

CHAPTER TWO

1. *The 9/11 Commission Report* cites several other terrorist attacks on the United States that occurred during this period. See Kean et al. 2004, 2.

2. Quoted from Smith 2002b. The FAA's "mistake" is especially interesting to note. From January through September 2001, the agency issued at least fifteen memos warning of the potential for airline hijackings inside the United States. In each of these memos, Osama bin Laden was named as the prime suspect. In essence, the FAA failed to heed its own advice. See Hirsch and Isikoff 2002, 31.

3. *New York Times* 2002. For follow-ups to this story, see reports by Isikoff and Klaidman (2002), Johnston (2003), the 9/11 Commission (Kean et al. 2004), Lichtblau (2005), and Scheer (2005).

4. Quoted from Schiliro 2001.

5. Hirsch and Isikoff 2002, 30.

6. Hirsch and Isikoff (2002, 30), Johnston (2003), and Oreskes (2004) reported similar mistakes.

7. Smith 2002a (emphasis added).

8. Friedman 2002 (emphasis added).

9. Viorst 2002 (emphasis added).

10. Kean et al. 2004, 9, 339–48.

11. Citations from *The Dinner Party* are to the text published by Samuel French (Simon 2002).

12. Greenblat and Cottle 1980, 34.

13. Greenblat and Cottle 1980, 69–72.

14. Greenblat and Cottle 1980, 67 (emphasis added).

15. Greenblat and Cottle 1980, 222. In some cases, Greenblat and Cottle's subjects were directly confronted by those wishing to focus them on worst-case scenarios, for

example, lawyers who urged the making of wills or prenuptial agreements, salesmen promoting life insurance. Yet even when some outside force directed couples' attention to the worst, they refused to dwell on it, refused to bring such potentials into focus. One male subject commented: "Now I won't be married for another two-and-a-half months—but they're already talking to me about how much money I would leave my wife to live alone. We haven't even been living together yet! . . . It's the most preposterous damn thing I have ever encountered in my life." On the brink of the happiest transition of his life, this subject, like others in the study, simply does not want to balance his thinking to include the worst of future events.

16. Swidler 2001, 125 (emphasis added).

17. Swidler 2001, 123, 124.

18. Vaughan 1986, 63, 68, 74 (emphasis added).

19. Vaughan 1986, 62, 71–72 (emphasis added).

20. These figures are taken from the General Social Survey. This question on marital happiness was last posed in 1998: "Taking things all together, how would you describe your marriage? Would you say that your marriage is very happy, pretty happy, or not too happy?" Findings from a CBS news poll were even more striking. There, 80 percent of married Americans say that they are happy in their marriages and 93 percent say they would marry their spouses all over again (see CBS 2001).

21. Whitehead, Defoe, and Popenoe (1999) provide information on teens' expectations of marriage; Kemp, Wilson, and Lincicome (2001) offer similar findings. For the results of a recent Harris poll on Americans' attitudes toward prenuptial agreements, see "A Study about Prenuptial Agreements," http://www.lawyers.com/legal_topics/legalresources/content/show_contentphp?&articleid=1002260 (accessed June 22, 2004). Even when marriages go hopelessly wrong, when they are plagued by violence and abuse, both victims and perpetrators typically fail to see the worst possible outcome of their actions. Batterers blur the severity of their abuse, pretending that they have not put their partners in harm's way (see, for example, Dugan, Umberson, and Anderson 1998; Hattery 2001; Heckert and Gondolf 2000; Langhinrichsen-Rohling and Vivian 1994; McLaughlin, Leonard, and Senchak 1992; Szinovacz and Egley 1995). In the same way, victims background their trauma and the potential for serious injury; they distance such ideas from their clear, sharp visions of the happy relationship (see, for example, Andrews and Brewin 1990; Fry and Barker 2001; Ferraro and Johnson 1983; Hattery 2001; Heckert and Gondolf 2000). When it comes to domestic violence, positive asymmetry may ultimately serve to normalize the violence. In such situations, sociologist Stanley Cohen writes, "we find not literal denial, but cultural interpretations and neutralizations which encourage a dulled, passive acceptance of violence" (2001, 52).

22. Strahley 2002, 1.

23. Farkas, Johnson, and Duffett 2002. The survey was preceded by discussions with twelve focus groups conducted in various sites around the country.

24. See, for example, research by Mazumder (2001) and by McMurrer, Condon, and Sawhill (1997), and on related work Lears (2003) or Leland (2004).

25. See the online version of the General Social Survey, http://www.icpsr.umich .edu:8080/GSS/nd1998/merged/cdblk/kidssol.htm (accessed May 16, 2005).

26. I analyzed six manuals in all, selected in June of 2003. Using Amazon.com, I located the top three best-selling parenting manuals (Eisenberg, Murkoff, and Hathaway 1996a; Sears and Sears 2003; and Shelov and Hannemann 1998). I randomly selected two additional manuals from the top thirty best-sellers (Eisenberg, Murkoff, and Hathaway 1996b; Ezzo and Bucknam 2001). Finally, I analyzed arguably the most famous of child-rearing manuals, *Dr. Spock's Baby and Child Care* (Spock and Parker 1998).

27. Eisenberg, Murkoff, and Hathaway 1996a, 1996b.

28. Spock and Parker 1998, 22–23 (emphasis added).

29. Sears and Sears 2003, 53–54.

30. Eisenberg, Murkoff, and Hathaway 1996a, 318.

31. Ezzo and Bucknam 2001, 141–42, (emphasis added).

32. Shelov and Hannemann 1998, 243.

33. Shelov and Hannemann 1998, 671; Eisenberg, Murkoff, and Hathaway 1996a, 489; Sears and Sears 2003, 638.

34. I "Googled" the terms "parent and advice and child and problem." Google returned 515,000 sites. I randomly chose 515 sites (0.1 percent of the initial search) from the first 2,000 listings. Among those 515 sites, approximately 129 (25 percent) were designed for parents whose children have physical, mental, or emotional disabilities. I content analyzed these 129 sites. The stance that emerges in manuals and Web sites has been documented in the observational research of Carol Heimer (1992). In her study of neonatal intensive care units, Heimer finds that "no one tells bad news unless they have to" (p. 179). This reluctance to be the bearer of bad tidings is supported both by cultural practices (discussed in the chapter 3 of this book) and by organizational concerns for legal liability.

35. Brownlow 2001 (emphasis added).

36. This special was broadcast on WCBS, New York, April 25, 2003. The program was produced by Paramount Pictures in Hollywood, California.

37. In some cases, therapists and other professionals have attempted to change the positive asymmetry that dominates the family context. Online sites devoted to parents with problem children provide some perspective on efforts to realign parental focus. For example, on its home page, POTADA, a parental support group for parents of drug or alcohol abusers, cites as its main goal "breaking down the walls of parental denial of chemical abuse by a child." The group offers strategies that will help parents see and confront the problem. See POTADA, http://trfn.clpgh.org/potada/wip.html (accessed April 30, 2003). Similarly, NarcKnowledge, an organization devoted to helping parents fight drug abuse, cites parental myopia as one of the "most important reasons for the failure of teen drug treatment." See NarcKnowledge, http://www .narcknowledge.com/fail.html (accessed April 30, 2003). Like POTADA, NarcKnowledge strives to develop parents' sustained focus on the worst-case scenario. The strategy of such professionals is amazingly consistent: first, foreground the blurry worst case; then relocate parents to a porthole that will keep the worst in focus.

38. Despite some modest declines, the United States still maintains a high teen pregnancy rate. Indeed, we rank among only five countries with teenage pregnancy rates of seventy or more per thousand: Belarus, Bulgaria, Romania, the Russian Federation, and the United States. See Alan Guttmacher Institute 2002.

39. Kaiser Family Foundation 2003.

40. American Academy of Pediatrics, "Adolescent Health," http://www.aap.org/ advocacy/washing/chiah.htm (accessed June 23, 2003).

41. Further, recent estimates suggest that fifteen-to twenty-year-olds account for 48 percent of sexually transmitted diseases. See Health Line Clinical Laboratories 2005 or Marullo 2004.

42. Statistics on teenage STDs are from Alan Guttmacher Institute 2002 and Kaiser Family Foundation 2003; on HIV infection rates among teens, see comments by the American Academy of Pediatrics quoted in "Safe Sex Is *Your* Responsibility" on the Web site of the Stop Aids Project, http://www.10percent.org/safe_sex.html (accessed August 15, 2002). See Marullo 2004 or Raghubir and Menon 1998 for discussion of teens' false sense of invulnerability to HIV-infection.

43. Kaiser Family Foundation 2002b. This sense that sexual worst-case scenarios "could never happen to me" is widely reported in the literature. See, for example, work by Chapin (2001), Marullo (2004), Mishra and Serzner (1994), and Out and Lafreniere (2001).

44. Resource sites include RECAPP (Resource Center for Adolescent Pregnancy Prevention) and "What You Need To Know About," which provide summaries and source materials on all forms of teen sexual activity. Interactive sites include "Sex Talk," a place where teens can pose questions and be answered by a "peer-like" medical professional. Foundations and policy groups include the Alan Guttmacher Institute, the Kaiser Family Foundation, and Planned Parenthood.

45. Darroch, Landry, and Singh 2000. Note that 51 percent of school systems that agree to sex education programs require that abstinence be taught as the *preferred* option.

46. Kaiser Family Foundation 2002a.

47. Childbirth figures for U.S. women are from the National Center for Health Statistics (2000). Childbirth mortality figures are from U.S. Bureau of the Census (2004, page 78, table 100); for figures on a variety of birth complications, see U.S. Bureau of the Census 2002, page 69, table 87. Pregnancies that result from in vitro fertilization carry a greater risk for the developing fetus. According to the National Center for Policy Analysis (2002), the number of birth defects increases to 9 percent for infants born after in vitro fertilization.

48. I analyzed seven manuals in all, selected in June 2003. Using Amazon.com, I chose the top three best-selling pregnancy manuals (Douglas 2002; Iovine 1995; Simkin, Whalley, and Keppler 2001). I randomly selected three additional manuals from the top thirty best-sellers (Curtis and Schuler 2000; Murkoff, Eisenberg, and Hathaway 2002; Sears and Sears 1994). Finally, I analyzed the *Merck Manual of Medical Information* (Berkow 2000), the best-selling medical manual on the market. For

Web sites, I "Googled" the terms "pregnancy and childbirth and health." Google returned 278,000 sites. I randomly chose and analyzed 278 sites (0.1 percent of the total) from the first 2,000 listings.

49. Douglas 2002, 223, 262 (emphasis added).

50. Curtis and Schuler 2000, 19.

51. Murkoff, Eisenberg, and Hathaway 2002, 221.

52. Amniocentesis presents women with one of the most difficult decisions of their pregnancy—should I or shouldn't I place my baby at risk? Yet most manuals devote only one to three pages to the topic, less than one-half percent of a given book's pages.

53. American Academy of Physicians, http://familydoctor.org/handouts/144html (accessed June 2003).

54. Murkoff, Eisenberg, and Hathaway 2002, 53.

55. Iovine 1995, 86.

56. Risk statistics are from the *Merck Manual of Medical Information* (Berkow 2000).

57. Kestin van den Hoonaard 2001, 15.

58. Kestin van den Hoonaard 2001, 27–28.

59. Lopata 1996, 74; Carr et al. 2001. Of course, my discussion centers on widows. The literature on widowers is extremely limited.

60. In chapter 1, I noted that positive asymmetry is common, but not universal. The exceptions to the best-case outlook will be discussed at length in chapters 6 and 7. But in this chapter, I periodically discuss the ways in which factors such as age, gender, region, social class, and the like, influence the concentration of positive asymmetry within or across groups. Such findings underscore the cultural basis of the phenomenon. Here it is interesting to note that positive asymmetry toward widowhood is most common among those in higher social locations. On this skewing of positive asymmetry at one end of the social scale, as well as the general underestimation of numbers of widows, see the study by Baily (1998, 174, 181); Lesnoff-Caravaglia (1984, 138) also discusses this inability to anticipate widowhood.

61. U.S. Administration on Aging 2002; National Center for Health Statistics 2002.

62. The Health Insurance Association of America reports that only 6 percent of Americans have invested in long-term health care insurance. See the report "Americans Uninformed about Long-Term Care," http://www.nbc4columbus.com/health/1125475/detail.html (accessed June 23, 2004).

63. AARP 2003, 20, 3.

64. Alliance for Aging Research 2001. A recent Gallup poll echoes these findings (Arora 2004b).

65. For some interesting commentary on this phenomenon, see, for example, articles by Dinnen (2001) and Dover (2002).

66. Rosenbaum and Rosenbaum 2002.

67. Ariès 1974 and Elias 1985.

68. Darwin 1994.

69. Statistics tell us that heart disease and cancer are the most likely causes of death among Americans. See figures collated by the U.S. Bureau of the Census (2004, page 79, table 102).

70. American Association for Cancer Research 2002.

71. For more on this topic, see Cerulo and Ruane 1997, 2004.

72. Media Watch 1996.

73. Death comes alive on the Internet as well. Today one can visit Web sites like Death Become You at blulips.com to purchase death memorabilia (a coffin paperweight or a statue of the Grim Reaper on a Harley), CDs, or films.

74. *MacNeil/Lehrer Newshour*, show number 4204, aired on WNET in New York on November 12, 1991.

75. Greeley and Hout 1999. More recent surveys suggest a slightly higher percentage. See Cerulo and Ruane 2004.

76. Figures collated by the U.S. Bureau of the Census (2004, page 371, table 569; page 416, table 631).

77. The Harvard Center for Risk Analysis, http://www.hcra.harvard.edu (accessed July 3, 2003). Some believe official statistics underestimate workplace accidents. For example, injured workers often are afraid to file workers compensation reports. In such cases, a significant number of workplace injuries fall through the cracks (Oregon Consumer and Business Services 2001). When disease is incurred on the job, there may be a substantial delay between acquiring the disease and showing symptoms of it. As a result, disease victims can remain invisible in statistical estimates (Reiman 2004).

78. This point seems especially stark with reference to 9/11 survivors. In reading interviews with this group published on the *New York Times* Web site, it is important to note that none of them saw the WTC as a likely target of attack. This despite the fact that most survivors remembered the 1993 attacks, and some actually worked in the towers at the time. See "Accounts from the North Tower," http://www.nytimes.com/NTOWER.html, and "Accounts from the South Tower," http://www.nytimes.com/STOWER.html (both accessed July 12, 2002).

79. On the failure of American workers to obtain disability insurance, see Curry 2001. For accounts and analysis of the conditions and attitudes leading to work-related hazards, see studies by the American Academy of Orthopaedic Surgeons (2001), Auerbach (1999), Baron (1993), Pesticide Education Program (2001), Schottman, Baker, and Crawford (1999), and Woodford and colleagues (1996). It is worth noting that positive asymmetry in the workplace varies across communities. For example, groups such as teenagers and immigrants (especially Hispanic immigrants) typically are exposed to dangerous work and yet tend to be poorly trained. The lack of safety discussions and training for members of these groups makes the worst-case scenario especially remote. It is no wonder, then, that teens and Hispanic immigrants suffer higher rates of workplace injury than the population at large. The National Institute for Occupational Safety and Health (NIOSH) estimates that 200,000 teens under the age of eighteen are injured each year. And according to NIOSH (2003), Hispanic immigrant workers make

up a higher percentage of occupational deaths than any ethnic or racial group in America (Maier 2001).

80. Robinson 2003.

81. *The World Almanac and Book of Facts* (2003).

82. Centers for Disease Control 2002; Brain Injury Resource Center, http://www.headinjury.com/sports.htm (accessed April 12, 2003).

83. On bike injuries, see statistics reported by the Centers for Disease Control (2002) and the Virginia PTA (2003). In commenting on riding's potential dangers, one enthusiast captured the trend: "I don't think any of us ignore risk. *But we minimize it*" (Huddleston 2003, 8). On scuba risks see discussion by Hunt (2003) and Viders (1991). One of Hunt's recreational scuba divers crystallized the sentiment: "I never let it enter my mind that I would be permanently crippled or dead" (Hunt 2003). Finally, cases of sun-induced skin cancer have tripled in the past fifteen years. See reports by the Gallup Organization (2004d), in *Pediatrics* (2002), and the *Week*'s "Briefing" of June 13, 2003 (http://www.the weekmagazine.com/briefing.asp?/a_id=412 [accessed July 3, 2003]).

84. Gambaccini 1998; May 2003.

85. Tennis Masters Series 2002; Ainsworth 2001.

86. Hamill 1996.

87. Gram-Hansen 2003.

88. Positive asymmetry in sports is not peculiar to Americans. In Australia, for example, the government reports that 60 percent of injured sportspeople, seemingly blind to the very real risk of injury, carry no health insurance. See Williams 2001.

89. Jones 2004; National Gambling Impact Study Commission 1999; Will 1999 (dollar amounts refer to legal wages).

90. Gonzalez and Wu 1999. Also see studies by Chapple and Nofziger (2000), Jarvik and Kulbach (1983), and Knox and Inkster (1968).

91. See, for example, the work of Adams (2000) and Rachlin, Siegel, and Cross (1994).

92. On the "cashing in" mentality, see, for example, studies by Delfabbro and Winefield (2000), Golin (2001), Ladouceur (1994), and Marignoni-Hutin (1994). On gamblers' false sense of control, see the work of Davis, Sundahl, and Lesbo (2000), in addition to the cited Delfabbro and Marignoni-Hutin studies.

93. See work by Eckel and Grossman (2002), Jones (2004), and Weber, Blais, and Betz (2002) on gender differences in gambling behavior, and by Cheng (1993) and Papineau (2001) on gambling as a pathology of hope.

94. Quoted from the Gamblers' Anonymous Web site, http://www.gamblers anonymous.org/qna.html (accessed July 1, 2003). Many years ago, I was in Atlantic City, observing a game of "craps." (Those familiar with craps know that this intricate game provides multiple ways to wager.) On that day, the players at the table took an immediate dislike to one particular person who repeatedly bet on a box entitled the "don't-come" bar. With each such bet, those at the table issued a loud "boo." After a

few such outbursts, I asked a floor manager to explain the crowd's discontentment. "He's betting on the worst-case scenario," I was told. "A 'don't-come' bet means that the better wins when the shooter fails—when the shooter rolls craps!" This experience illustrated for me the powerful stigma applied to gamblers who defy the best-case scenario. It is simply unacceptable to bet on the worst, that is, to bet on loss. Of course, John Poindexter of the U.S. Department of Defense learned that lesson the hard way. Recall the outrage directed toward Poindexter when he proposed a new futures market based on the prediction of terrorist attacks. In essence, investors would wager on the probability of terror within a predefined period of time. Should an attack occur, successful predictors would receive a return on their money. It is hard to imagine, however, the real winners and losers in such wagering. For more on the Poindexter affair, see Norris 2003.

95. U.S. Surgeon General's Office 2000; the CDC issued similar statistics in 2002 (see Moniz 2002).

96. Critser 2003, 5.

97. Critser 2003; Fontaine et al. 2003; Freedman et al. 2002, Hedley et al. 2004; U.S. Surgeon General's Office 2000. Further, recent polls suggest that many Americans have effectively distanced themselves from the worst-case realities of their weight. For example, while 30 percent of Americans fit the medical definition of obese, only 8 percent describe themselves as such. See Blizzard 2005.

98. Statistics reported by the U.S. Bureau of the Census (2004, page 603, table 962) and in *The World Almanac and Book of Facts* (2003, 79).

99. U.S. Bureau of the Census (2002, page 677, table 1068).

100. Fatalities reported by the AFMC Public Affairs Link (2002) and the U.S. Bureau of the Census (2004, page 79, table 102). Put in another way, over 21 million drivers (about 11 percent of all licensed drivers) were involved in auto accidents last year, and approximately 42,000 deaths resulted from such accidents.

101. National Sleep Foundation 2000, 2005.

102. Many believe this figure may be higher than one-third. This is because part-time users often report themselves as full-time users (AFMC Public Affairs Link 2002).

103. O'Donnell 2003; Slovic (2000, 73-79) provides a more detailed discussion of the perception of risk.

104. All statistics are from the Substance Abuse and Mental Heath Services Administration (2001).

105. The Volkswagon survey also revealed that many teens and young adults simply feel that seatbelts are "uncool." The survey is summarized on the Road and Travel Web site, http://www.roadandtravel.com/safetyandsecurity/vwteenseatbelts.htm (accessed November 11, 2003).

106. Statistics from the Substance Abuse and Mental Heath Services Administration (2001).

107. Buxton 2002; also see MADD 2005.

108. Statistics reported by the AFMC Public Affairs Link (2002), the American Prosecutors Research Institute (2002), the Substance Abuse and Mental Heath Ser-

vices Administration (2001); O'Donnell (2003), and the U.S. Department of Transportation (2001, 2002a, 2002b).

109. Janis 1971, 1989. For follow-ups to Janis's work, see, for example, studies by Esser and Lindoerfer (1989), McCauley (1989), Moorhead, Ference, and Neck (1991), and Tetlock and others (1992).

110. Stoner 1961.

111. See studies by Lykken (1997), Veysey and Messner (1999), and Whyte (1993), for example. It is worth noting that some researchers believe that risky shift is more likely to occur among Americans than among other nationalities. This is because American culture is defined as a risk-oriented culture. See Hong's analysis (1978) or that of Morgan and Aram (1975).

112. Gilovich, Savitsky, and Medvec 1998; Latane and Darley 1968; Takooshian and Bodinger 1982.

113. Some organizational theorists, as well as many, many journalists, suggest that small-group dynamics can help us understanding large-scale, organizational behavior. Some contend, for example, that groupthink led to the *Challenger* and *Columbia* disasters at NASA. Others suggest that groupthink could explain the faulty decision-making that plagues the postwar occupation of Iraq. And some wonder if the risky shift phenomenon might help us better understand the brazen actions of Enron executives. To be sure, group dynamics may certainly play a role in worst-case scenarios such as these. But at the organizational level, positive asymmetry is likely spurred by more intricate factors.

114. Feldman and March 1981, 174.

115. Shrader-Frechette 1993; Clarke 1993, 1999; Freudenberg and Youn 1993; Davis 1989.

116. Perrow 1999, 4-5 (emphasis added).

117. DiMaggio and Powell 1991, 11.

118. Vaughan's comments have been widely quoted. See, for example, Feldstein 2003 and Lozano 2003.

119. All quotes taken from Vaughan 1996, xii, xiv.

120. Friedland and Alford 1991, 248.

121. We will see in subsequent chapters that groups and communities in many other cultures and historical periods exhibit positive asymmetry as well.

122. Synonyms taken from Laird and Agnes 1999.

123. I am reminded here of "Debby Downer," a recurring character on the NBC show *Saturday Night Live*. Downer speculates uncontrollably on the worst-case scenario of *any* topic introduced in conversation. In so doing, she routinely clears the room at whatever dinner party, business meeting, or sporting event she may have been invited to.

124. Weinstein 1989. Polls executed by Gallup, Harris, and Time consistently illustrate this phenomenon of optimism in U.S. culture. By way of example, see reports by Harper (2004), Regan (2004), and Ross and Newby-Clark (1998).

125. Reich 2001.

126. CNN/Money 2002. The TechnoMetrica Institute of Policy and Politics produced similar results through June 2002 (TIPP 2002).

127. Bartlett 2000; Arora 2004a; Newport 2005. And note that Gallup polls uncovered similar positive asymmetry among the British during the especially trying economic times of 2004 and 2005 (see Catterall 2005). Of course, while many consider such biased visions of the economy a productive aspect of American culture, others view it as a serious drawback. In the 1920s, for example, positive asymmetry led Americans down a dangerous economic path. Robert D. Lamb notes that "many in the 1920s felt the prosperity would never end. That prosperity was fueled by new technology—primarily the automobile—and by new methods of industrial production that made the technology easier to produce in mass quantities and at lower costs. . . . This combination of efficient production, increased consumer spending, and a wide availability of credit led to a period of growth that made a handful of people extraordinarily wealthy. . . . And while just 13% of the population held 90% of the nation's wealth, rags-to-riches stories abounded" (Lamb 1999, 1).

Lamb contends that, seemingly blind to the worst-case scenario, Americans devoured goods and stock, often with money they did not have. Positioned at the best-case porthole, they were simply unable to recognize signals of impending doom.

128. Poll results reported by the National Science Foundation (1999) and Langer (1999).

129. Jones 2005.

130. Rosin 2002. Note that in March 2002, six months after the attack, a USA Today/CNN/Gallup poll showed that only 35 percent of Americans reported being either very afraid or somewhat afraid of terrorists. And such positive asymmetry remained relatively constant through this writing, with roughly 80 percent of Americans reporting confidence in the U.S. government's ability to protect the nation from attack, and only about 8 percent reporting that they feel another terrorist attack is likely. See Gallup Organization 2004b and Carroll 2005.

131. This phrase became the calling card of internationally renowned motivational speaker Zig Zigler. And, of course, there is a long history of this approach among self-help motivators such as Norman Vincent Peale, who championed positive thinking, and Robert Schuller, who coined the phrase "possibility thinking."

132. Chopra 1993, 44, 30.

133. McGraw 2001.

134. Winfrey 2001, 232

135. Slovic 2000, 105–9. Glassner (1999) makes a similar argument in describing what he calls the "culture of fear." According to Glassner, we may be unable to recognize the ultimate worst-case scenarios, but there are countless topics and events that we are convinced to fear. Research on the perception of risk constitutes a massive literature. However, for two valuable reviews of research in the field, see studies by Slovic (2000) and Tierney, Lindell, and Perry (2001).

136. This idea must be credited in part to my colleague Janet Ruane, as it emerged from her approach to teaching type 1 and 2 errors in her sociological methods courses.

137. Exceptions to the rule of positive asymmetry will be more systematically examined in chapters 6 and 7

138. American Psychiatric Association 2000.

139. Other drugs used to treat this disorder include Celexa, Prozac, and Zoloft.

140. This commercial was aired throughout the 2002 and 2003 broadcast television season.

141. Festinger, Riecken, and Schachter, 1956, 1.

142. For a more recent excursion into the world of doomsday soothsayers, see Alex Heard's *Apocalypse Pretty Soon* (1999). Heard toured a number of contemporary apocalyptist communities. Through Heard, one can meet, for example, Annie Kirkwood, leader of Earth Changes. This group believes that "Mother Nature is tired of mankind's blighting presence, so she's planning to kill most of us off in the next few years by 'willing' a rise in natural disasters, strife, and disease" (106). Heard insists that he tries "as much as possible as an outsider . . . to understand things from the believers' perspective," trying "not to be overly harsh" in his judgments (chap. 1). Yet as Heard comments on the groups under study, he cannot hide his assumptions of each group's "marginal" status. Of Kirkwood and her Earth Changers he writes, "Earth Changers tend to have very healthy egos and a large measure of narcissistic delusion" (118).

143. Indeed, it is not unusual to see anger directed toward those who fixate on worst-case scenarios. Sociologists of emotions tell us that anger is often invoked as a tool to refocus such individuals—a tool that leads individuals from negative to positive affective states. See work by Lively and Heise (2004) and Thoits (1996) by way of example.

144. Henry 1997, 4. Readers may recall that in order to hasten their arrival in heaven, all thirty-nine members of the cult engaged in a mass suicide.

145. Klebnikov 1997.

146. Hedges et al. 1997, 26-27.

147. Weber 1999, 3.

148. Bell retired from full-time hosting in 2002. He now appears on weekend nights, with George Noory manning the Monday through Friday slots.

149. Cuprisin 2002.

150. Layne 1998.

151. *Daily Hog* 2000.

152. Baker 1997. Some may recall the 2004 motion picture release *The Day after Tomorrow*. The movie was based, in part, on Art Bell's writings. In keeping with the tendency to dismiss apocalyptists like Bell, the film was panned by critics and considered a box office flop.

153. A recent Harris poll shows that about 60 percent of Americans do not trust the media. Research suggests that the media's propensity to sensationalize plays a large role in the distrust. See Shaw 2003; Taylor 2005; Winseman 2004, and Zoglin 1996.

154. For example, see Altheide 2002a, 2002b; Gerbner et al. 2002; and Glassner 1999. Indeed, many studies show that unusually high exposure to the media can distance one from the best-case perceptual porthole. Among others, Bryant and Zillman

(2002), Diefenbach and West (2001), and Gerbner and colleagues (2002) provide recent findings on this issue.

155. Associated Press 2000; Frommer 2002; Meltz 2003; Steger 2000.

156. Carlson 2002; also see Winseman 2004.

157. For more on the issue, see Burggraf 2000 and Zuckerman 1994.

158. Note that this manual also gave rise to *The Worst-case Scenario Survival Game.*

159. Blais 2000.

CHAPTER THREE

1. Swidler 2001, 191. Swidler, of course, is expanding on ideas forwarded earlier by Foucault (1965, 1978) and Bourdieu (1977, 1990b) among others.

2. For a masterful discussion of denial as a sociocognitive phenomenon, see recent work by Zerubavel (2002, 2006).

3. According to Greek mythology, Cronus is destined to be overthrown by one of his children, just as he himself had overthrown his own father. In an attempt to pre-empt this fated challenge to his power, he swallows each of his children upon their birth. Rhea saves her son Zeus from his siblings' fate by giving Cronus a stone wrapped in the infant god's swaddling clothes.

4. Sophocles 1973, 697.

5. Maas 1999.

6. I call this the worst of all sins because throughout the Bible, particularly in the Old Testament, the recognition of God's supremacy is demanded above all else. Harsh punishments befall those who fail to render their fealty to God. We see this in the punishment of the Israelites, when Moses finds them worshipping false gods, or in God's testing of Abraham, as he challenges the patriarch to sacrifice his only son. We see it in the destruction of the Tower of Babel, and in the first of the Ten Commandments: "I am the Lord thy God; thou shalt have no other gods before me" (Exodus 20:1–2).

7. Note that theologians equate the serpent with the angel Lucifer. Many cite Lucifer's transfiguration as a serpent, and his subsequent temptation of Eve, as the events that signaled Lucifer's open defiance of God and his declaration of war on his creator.

8. Reilly 1999.

9. The Qur'an, 59:2, 4; Al-Ahzab 33:66–68, as quoted On the Al Islam Web site, http://www.islam.org.uk/ie.ilm/purification/0054_page3.htm (accessed on February 8, 2002); Surah An Nisa, chap. 34, as quoted on Authentic Islamic Literature site, http://www.quraan.com/Pickthall/Surah4.asp (accessed February 8, 2002).

10. Grimm and Grimm 1994.

11. Andersen 1992.

12. Shepard 1995.

13. Both Greek and Hebrew law forbade the execution of criminals.

14. Of course, banishment is not the only practice applied to those that groups or communities define as the worst. But it is a far more common strategy than mass mur-

der or genocide. Even in infamous cases such as Hitler's final solution, the Turks' and Kurds' 1915 attack on the Armenians, the ethnic cleansing of Bosnia in the 1990s, or, during the same period, the Rwandan military's treatment of Tutsis and moderate Hutus, those banished far outnumber those who are killed—sometimes as much as ten to one.

15. Ward 2001. Among Native Americans, modern banishment is much more humane than the practices of ancient cultures or other modern societies. For example, banished individuals can receive professional counseling if their offense is connected to alcoholism, drug use, or mental illness.

16. As described in the Napoleon entry on Stargaze, http://www.skygaze.com/content/mystreries/Napoleon.shtml (accessed August 27, 2003).

17. "Israeli Troops Storm Arafat Compound," *Online Newshour* report, March 29, 2002, http://www.pbs.org/newshour/updates/compound_3-29-02.html (accessed November 8, 2004).

18. ABC News 2003; *USA Today* 2003.

19. CBS News 2003.

20. These examples merely scratch the surface of banishment's role in political history. Consider, for example, just a few of the prominent figures banished by their successors in an effort to eclipse their influence within a community: Aristides "the Just" of ancient Athens, Romans Cicero and Marcus Furius Camillus, Popes Alexander III and Pius IX, Charles II and James II of England, William II of the Netherlands, Louis XVII of France, Hungarian statesman Count Gyula Andrássy, South American leaders and revolutionaries José Gervasio Artigas, Simón Bolívar, Bernardo O'Higgins, José Antonio Páez, and Fructuoso Rivera, and of course, Karl Marx. The practice of banishment continued in the twentieth century, with the fate imposed on familiar figures such as Isabel Allende, Jean-Bertrand Aristide, Fulgencio Batista, Banazir Bhutto, Charles de Gaulle, Faruk I of Egypt, George II of Greece, Ferdinand Marcos, Juan Domingo Perón, African leader Oliver Tambo, Leon Trotsky, and German statesman Walter Ulbricht.

21. Cerulo 1995b.

22. Bowler 1996.

23. Greene 1999.

24. Quoted from the "Shameful Book Banning in Rockford, Illinois," http://www.ultranet.com/~kyp/rockbann.html (accessed March 22, 2002). "Empty Shelves," an anticensorship movement based at the University of Maryland, Baltimore County, contends that book banners see themselves as protectors of readers, particularly young readers. They take as their mission the complete eclipsing of evil, and the construction of a space that promotes only the best. Thus, book banners expunge from the sight of young readers all descriptions of undesirable human qualities, condemning books for "showing the devil as a friendly force," "promoting an ungodly lifestyle," or detailing violent or sexual acts (Bowler 1996). By eliminating the worst people, places, objects, and events from a community's cultural menu, readers are left to concentrate on loftier ideals.

25. The full Senate report, "Comic Books and Juvenile Delinquency," can be accessed at http://www.geocities.com/Athens/8580/kefauver.html.

26. For more details, see "List of Words Banished from the Queen's English," http://www.lssu.edu/banished (accessed June 3, 2005).

27. Rothman 1971, 138.

28. Rothman 1971, 240.

29. Staples 1997, 21; see also Rothman 1971, 1980.

30. Lombardi 2000.

31. Smith 2000.

32. Lewis 1967, 15; see also Staples 1991, 1997.

33. Sutherland and Cressey (1974, chap. 22) offer more on this subject.

34. Of course, Michel Foucault (1979) has much to say on the birth of the prison, linking the isolation of prison life and the total control of prisoners to the rise of capitalism and the centralized state.

35. In medieval and colonial times, executions were considered purification rituals that restored a community's equilibrium. Consequently, executions were highly public affairs, and most communities insisted that their members witness the event.

36. Ryan 1992.

37. Bessler 1997, 99–100.

38. Allen 2001, 2.

39. In recent years, certain media figures (as well as a small group of social activists and scholars) have lobbied for a return to public execution. But to date, the courts have remained recalcitrant. The case of Timothy McVeigh, perpetrator of the Oklahoma City bombing, underscored the courts' adamancy on this point. At the time of the bombing (pre-9/11), McVeigh was identified as "a public figure connected to the worst act of terrorism on American soil." Knowing this, McVeigh challenged both the prisons and the courts to change their practice of secluding the worst. "Hold a true public execution—allow a public broadcast," he declared in a letter to the *Daily Oklahoman*. In essence, McVeigh hoped to centralize his cause in the public's perceptual porthole. But, the Federal Bureau of Prisons refused McVeigh's request, citing a longstanding federal rule that "no photographic or other visual or audio recording of an execution shall be permitted" (Jurkowitz 2001). The courts vigorously upheld the position of the Federal Bureau of Prisons, greatly strengthening positive asymmetry. By sustaining physical seclusion, the courts precluded any possibility of magnifying evil within the public domain.

40. Parsons and Fox (1952) offer classic observations on this matter. Teno and her colleagues (2004) provide more current evidence, and Cerulo and Ruane (1997, 2004) offer a broad review of the pertinent literature.

41. Diamond 1992, 233–34.

42. See, by way of example, Deuteronomy 13:16 and 17:17 or Leviticus 10:2.

43. Broyde 1994, 6; also see Elon 1974, esp. 529.

44. Quotations from Broyde 1994, 11, 6. Modern rabbinical courts still make use of shunning. But the practice proves far less severe and far less effective in the contem-

porary era. Broyde (1994, 6) notes that in modern societies, a shunned individual can simply leave her or his community and join another, thus escaping ostracism and shame.

45. Quotes are from the Jehovah's Witness media page, http://www.jw-media.org/ beliefs/beliefsfaq.htm (accessed January 6, 2004). Note that several Internet discussion groups for "disfellowshipped" individuals suggest that the reversibility of shunning is less flexible than suggested by the church leadership.

46. See Amish FAQ, http://www.800padutch.com/atafaq.shtml#shun (accessed January 6, 2004).

47. *Los Angeles Times* 1998.

48. Snow and Anderson 1993,198–99.

49. The Christian Chat site, http://www.col.com/con/liberty.html (accessed January 7, 2004).

50. The chat group operates on the astronomy Web site Clear Dark Sky, http://cleardarksky.com/others/bigdob/posting_policy.html (accessed January 7, 2004).

51. The Embracing Mystery board runs on the discussion site Ezboard, http://pub130ezboard.com/fembracingmysteryfrom10.showMessage?topicID=29.topic (accessed January 7, 2004).

52. See Evans 2001 for a wonderful case study of shunning in Internet chat rooms. And note that because shunning is so central to online communities, several computer technology companies have perfected software designed to facilitate the practice. At the Microsoft Exchange Web site, for example, chat group organizers are taught how to use Windows software to effect a ban on shunned group members' contributions. Similarly, Cisco Systems has developed software that allows business users to shun "enemy" communicants and prevent them from invading or attacking an office or corporation network.

53. See Berger and Luckmann 1967, 112–16. Note that "nihilation" is similar to what Erving Goffman calls "civil inattention, "the ability for "one person to treat others as if they were not there at all, as objects not worthy of a glance" (1963a, 83).

54. Rosenhan 1973, 255–56 (emphasis added). Of course, sociologist Erving Goffman (1961) discusses similar phenomenon.

55. Derber 2000, 71 (emphasis added).

56. Pickersgill 1979, 8.

57. It is unclear if doctors of philosophy are included under this heading. One can only hope.

58. All quotes taken from Hontheim 1999a.

59. All quotes taken from Hontheim 1999b (emphasis added). The different characterizations of heaven and hell are also found in *Catechism of the Catholic Church* (2000). Though not as stark among Protestant sects, such differences also emerge in *Belonging to God: A First Catechism* (1998), a central publication of the Presbyterian Church of the United States of America.

60. Sotirios 2000.

61. Paul refers to these revelations in 1 Corinthians 2:9 and 2 Corinthians 12:4.

62. Historians refer to this artist as the Master of the Saint Lucy Legend because his most famous work is a 1480 altarpiece depicting episodes from the life of that saint.

63. As quoted from the brief guide to the piece on the Web site of the National Gallery of Art, http://www.nga.gov/cgi-bin/pinfo?Object=41322+0+none, (accessed March 14, 2001.).

64. The Fine Arts Museums of San Francisco holds the anonymous German biblical illustration of heaven, "Sinners in Hell," and Pinelli's "Canto VII." One can access these images at the museum's Web site, http://www.famsf.org (accessed January 21, 2004).

65. I also visited the Web sites for the Louvre, the Prado Museum, and the Royal Academy of Arts. However, at this writing, these sites did not permit online searching of their collections.

66. I randomly selected eleven of the paintings reviewed for this study (10 percent of the total number). An independent coder, blind to the hypothesis of the study, recoded those paintings for level of detail. Intercoder reliability was 86 percent.

67. DeStefano 2003; Shriver 1999; Albuom 2003; Sebold 2002; Rylant 1995, 1997. I did find one modern treatise on hell. Author Mary K. Baxter contends that Jesus Christ appeared to her and provided her with detailed revelations of both heaven and hell. She published each vision under a separate title (Baxter 1993, 1998).

68. The term "dismissal" is used when a commissioned officer receives a dishonorable discharge. The consequences of the two types of discharge are identical. Also note that the military considers the honorable, the general, and the other than honorable discharges as administrative (routine) discharges while the bad conduct and dishonorable discharges are classified as punitive discharges.

69. I spoke informally with twenty-five air force, army, and naval discharge officers spread across three states. (All requested complete anonymity.) The purpose of these conversations was (a) to determine the official symbolic representation of honorable and dishonorable discharges and (b) to determine openness with which these two avenues are discussed within military ranks.

70. D. Robinson 1999; *Money* 2000.

71. Savage 1999; Louis 1999.

72. *Los Angeles Times* 2001; Fuerbringer 2001; *Barton's* 2000 (emphasis added).

73. Byron 2000 (emphasis added).

74. Shiller (2005) writes extensively about this phenomenon.

75. King (2003) makes a similar point.

76. In addition to these worldwide competitions, several national and local competitions exist as well. For example, the Golden Spider Award honors the best Irish Web site; Australian Internet Awards honors the best Australian site; the Sacramento Web Awards honors the best Sacramento business Web site.

77. Mr. Showbiz 2000. The Razzie award is a statuette, a gold spray-painted raspberry resting on a mangled Super 8 film reel. For more info, visit the Razzies Web site, http://www.razzies.com.

78. Entries included the ten worst excuses not to spay your pet, the ten worst cor-

porations of 2000, the ten worst mistakes career changers make, the ten worst cars of the millennium, the ten worst earthquakes, the ten worst date movies, and the ten worst grammatical errors in college writing.

79. I conducted this study in 2003. These data archives are located on Gallup's Web site (http://www.gallup.com) and on the Roper Center's Web page (http://roperweb .ropercenter.uconn.edu).

80. Mclynn 1998; Kearns 1976, 326.

81. Bar-Illan 1991.

82. A collection of the minister's quotes has been assembled at a tongue-in-cheek Web site created in his honor, http://www.welovetheiraqiinformationminister.com (accessed September 16, 2003).

83. Quotes taken from CNN's Web site, http://www.cnn.com/2003/WORLD/ meast/04/08/sprj.irq.sahaf.profile.reut (accessed September 16, 2003).

84. Ferriman and McGhie 1991.

85. See the story of the search on the magazine's Web page, http://www.time .com/time/time100/poc.century.html (accessed May 11, 2000).

86. Background information on the editors' decision-making process was derived from a CBS News television special entitled *Time 100: Person of the Century*, broadcast on December 27, 1999.

87. Fine 2002, 232.

88. Dowd 2003.

89. The work of cognitive linguist George Lakoff supports this point.

90. See Boorstin 1965.

91. Cantor 2001, 202–11.

92. Quoted in Zimmerman 1971.

93. Elkind 1997, 17.

94. Weil 1995, 316.

95. Robbins and Lang 1995, 20, 37.

96. Siegel 1998, 127–29.

97. Strum is quoted on the inspirational Web site Heartwarmers, http://www .heartwarmers4u.com/members/?jimfulks (accessed September 24, 2003).

98. Kushner 1981, 27.

99. Kushner 1981, 64, 71, 139 (emphasis added).

100. Taylor 1995, 140–41.

101. Quoted from Zukav's appearance on the *Oprah Winfrey Show*, aired on WABC TV New York, March 26, 2001.

102. Frankl 1992, 116.

CHAPTER FOUR

1. Best 2001, 27.

2. Salsburg (2001) offers a very readable discussion of the history of modern statistics.

3. For the mathematically minded, this equation is $y = [100\%/\text{sqrt}\,(2\,\Pi)] \times (e^{-x2/2})$, where $e = 2.71828\ldots$

4. Babbie 2001, 132.

5. See Ruane's (2004) discussion of unipolar measurement.

6. See "Resources for Skaters," by Wick Smith, on the Web site of the White Rose Figure Skating Club, http//:www.wrfsc.org/Scoring.htm (accessed October 31, 2003). At this writing, the skating scoring system is being revamped.

7. See "Quick Guide for Judging 1 Meter Dive," by John Santos, on the Web site of the Northern Westchester Swimming Conference, http://nwsc.usswim.net/Forms .htm (accessed October 31, 2003).

8. See "The Judging Process," on the Miss America Pageant Web site, http://www .missamerica.org/pageant/judging.html (accessed April 2, 2001).

9. Some of this information comes from interviews done with a nonrepresentative sample of quality-control agents at several food production companies, including Arm and Hammer, Aunt Jemimah, Best Foods, College Inn, Heinz, Hormel, Progresso Foods, and Pillsbury. Many of these companies also provided me with printed materials detailing their quality-control techniques.

10. Of course, many manufacturers set tolerance levels in controlling quality. Some may, for example, set a standard of a particular content percentage, being satisfied with 0.5 percent plus or minus that standard.

11. A number of quality-control agents told me that rejected products are available to employees for use by them and their families. "These products are perfectly good," one officer told me. "Their rejection by the company simply means that the products did not meet the best-case prototype, but they are hardly inferior or harmful."

12. The description of this survey, as well as the survey results, were derived from the National Mental Health Association Web site, http://www.nmha.org/shcr/ bestprac/key.cfm (accessed May 12, 2000).

13. Note that all forty-five "worst care" criteria were simply reversals of those items appearing on the "best care" list.

14. Popham 1997, 72.

15. All rubric examples are taken from an article on rubric design by Simkins (1999, 26–27). Note that Simkins's article provides rubrics thought to be superior in design. This suggests that the problems inherent in oppositional thinking are rarely considered by assessment experts.

16. Quoted from "Criteria: The Webby Awards," http://www.webbyawards.com/ judging/criteria.html (accessed April 18, 2001). The evaluation criteria of the World Best Web Site Awards exhibit similar flaws. The organization's assessment scheme contains five evaluative categories: functionality, design, content, originality, and professionalism and effectiveness. In turn, these five categories house a hundred specific criteria of excellence. Judges evaluate Web site entries with reference to these dimensions; those receiving the highest scores constitute the best sites, while those receiving the lowest scores represent the worst. Thus, like all of the examples provided heretofore, the identity of the worst exists only in relation to the best. The best Web

site provides "uniqueness and rarity of offerings," while the worst provides common and pedestrian offerings. The best Web site provides "leading-edge activities," while the worst site provides passé activities. Again, there is nothing distinctive about being the worst. When oppositional thinking is in play, the integrity of the category is eclipsed; poor quality can only be conceptualized after excellence is determined. Evaluation criteria derived from the official World Best Awards site, http://www.worldbestwebsites.com/criteria.htm [accessed February 26, 2001].

17. Data taken from the online business journal *Money.com*, http://www.money.com/money/broker (accessed May 9, 2000). Data refers to 1999 performance. Note that *Money.com* did eventually identify a single worst broker. But in order to do so, the writers had to weight the various measurement dimensions in complicated ways, thus forcing the data into a normal distribution.

18. The sample consists of all issues published in 1994, 1995, 1999, and 2000.

Chapter Five

1. For more on the Hindu caste system, see Bhattacharya 1995 or Ross 1998.

2. Change can occur only through reincarnation, at which time individuals can be reborn into a caste higher than that which they occupied in a prior life.

3. Human Rights Watch 1998, 1.

4. Human Rights Watch 1998, 1.

5. Quote offered by a Dalit, a scavenger from the Ahmedabad district in Gujarat (Human Rights Watch 1998, 1).

6. In the United States, the poverty class consists of those whose annual income is below that which the government deems necessary to support certain basic needs.

7. For more on economic inequality in the United States, see Ruane and Cerulo 2004, chap. 11.

8. Even when responses are confined only to those who self-identify as being in the lowest of economic positions, over 50 percent identify the American system as replete with opportunity and the potential for mobility. See Gallup Organization 2001d.

9. Gallup Organization 2001e, 2001b, 2005.

10. Gilbert 2003, 249–53.

11. Text quoted from "The Five Points of Calvinism," http://www.reformed.org/calvinism/calvinism.html (accessed May 10, 2001).

12. Burns 1973, 417–18 (emphasis added).

13. Of course, individuals could not be indifferent to their conduct on earth. Righteous conduct was strenuously encouraged. Indeed, Calvin suggested that one's conduct was an indirect indicator of one's election status. Thus, good works could provide proof of one's election to salvation, while evidence of sin could indicate one's eventual damnation.

14. For more on Calvinism, consult Calvin (1995), Steele and Thomas (1989), or Van Til, Mouw, and Van Til (2001).

15. Teachings of the Presidents of the Church (p. 62), as quoted by McCann (2001).

16. McConkie as quoted by McCann (2001).

17. Doctrines and Covenants 132:27, as quoted by McCann (2001). For more on these issues, and on Mormonism in general, see work by Givens (2003).

18. All quotes taken from *The Catechism of the Catholic Church* (2000), sections 1849–53.

19. I am grateful to my colleague Chaim Waxman for familiarizing me with this scripture.

20. Malachai 3:7; Ezekiel 18:21.

21. Quoted from "Seppuku—Ritual Suicide," http://victorian.fortunecity.com/duchamp/410/seppuku.html (accessed June 6, 2001).

22. According to historians, the Japanese aversion to dishonor may explain the military's atrocious treatment of World War II prisoners of war. In the eyes of the Japanese, prisoners were failed, shamed men undeserving of respect. Thus, while the death rate for prisoners captured on the European front was one in twenty, the death rate for those captured in Japan was one in four.

23. Tojo misfired his gun, causing injury rather than death. As a result, he was forced to stand trial before an international court where he was sentenced to death by hanging. Tojo's inability to effectively reclaim his honor by committing suicide was viewed by many Japanese as the ultimate act of failure. These details are from *Tojo's War*, a PBS documentary broadcast on WNET, New York, June 4, 2001.

24. For more on *seppuku*, see Howarth and Leaman 2001.

25. Ruggi 1988, 1 (emphasis added).

26. Rodgers 1995, 2.

27. Cancel 2001, 1. See also Ralph 2000 and Turgut 1998.

28. Mary Pat Baumgartner (1984) originated this term.

29. Quotes from Malcolm X's autobiography (1964, 257, 270).

30. Jones 1970, 50.

31. Quoted in Morgan 1970, 601.

32. Solanis 1970, 578.

33. Indeed, the name Hitler is now synonymous with the worst. Thus, when President George W. Bush wished to vilify Saddam Hussein, he proclaimed him "Hitler revisited" (*Baltimore Sun* 1999). Similarly, both Prime Minister Tony Blair and President Bill Clinton dubbed Slobodan Milosevic "the Hitler of the 1990s." And Missouri Republican Christopher S. Bond found Milosevic so threatening that he advocated lifting the U.S. ban on assassinations. Said Bond, "One bullet at Hitler at the right time might have saved millions" (Wise 1999).

34. Dionne 1991.

35. Quoted in Litwak 2000a.

36. Reuters 1984, 1986; Associated Press 1986.

37. Eddy 1999; *Guardian* 1999.

38. Hendawi 2004.

39. Indeed, Baumgartner (1984) suggests that to maximize effect, the powerless must apply the label of worst in alliance with a more powerful group or community.

40. Baumgartner 1984, 306.

41. For more on this relationship, see Black 1989.

42. Black 1998, 151.

43. Black 1998, 39.

44. Oates 1989.

45. Quoted from the Million Mom March Web site, http://millionmommarch .com/chapters/national/learn_more/gun_facts (accessed March 11, 2004).

46. Quoted from the Coalition to Stop Gun Violence Web site, http://www.csgv .org/content/resources/resc_facts_gunowner.html (accessed June 1, 2001).

47. Quoted from the Violence Policy Center's Web site, http://www.vpc.org/ fact_sht/torkenfs.htm (accessed March 11, 2004).

48. Lampo 2001.

49. Quoted on the NRA-ILA Web site, http://www.nraila.org/News/Read/ Speeches.aspx?ID=21 (accessed March 11, 2004).

50. Gallup Organization 2004c, 2001c.

51. Jeffrey H. Birnbaum, a senior staff writer at *Fortune* magazine and head of its Washington bureau, compiled this list. Birnbaum based his rankings on a survey of approximately 2,900 individuals, including all members of Congress, senior congressional and White House staff members and aides, and professional lobbyists.

52. Quoted from a CBS *60 Mintues* interview, broadcast on January 16, 2001. Clinton made similar observations in a Charlie Rose interview, broadcast on PBS, June 30, 2004.

53. Debenport 1993; Lambro 1993.

54. Buchanan 1993.

55. Grady 1993.

56. Many also dismissed the efforts of Representative Richard Gephardt of Missouri, arguing that his opposition to Clinton was simply a positioning strategy for the 1996 presidential election.

57. Lambro 1993.

58. Mohan 1998; Kuttner 1997; Gallup Organization 2001a.

59. Balz 2000.

60. CBS News in New York has instituted a regular feature entitled "Eat at Your Own Risk." The feature alerts viewers to the dirtiest restaurants, stores, vending stands, processing plants, and so forth, in the tri-state area.

61. Gallup Organization 2003b.

62. Black (1980) and Hunt and Manning (1991) offer classic examples of these behaviors.

63. Livingston 1996, 422.

64. Castenada (2001) and Manning (2001) provide further details.

65. See, for example, a series of articles on the crime that appeared in *Newsday* (1999, 2000a, 2000b), as well as an article on the sentencing by Bryan Robinson (1999).

66. Cozzens 2002, 116.

67. Firestone 1990. Journalist Laurie Goodstein (2003) reports similar data in sum-

marizing a *New York Times* poll measuring the prevalence of sexual abuse. Not surprisingly, these studies have been widely criticized by Catholic Church leaders.

68. Quoted in Chandler 1990. The company insures approximately 46,000 churches with regard to sexual liability.

69. Harvey 2001. Dr. Maura O'Donahue is a physician and a member of the Medical Missionaries of Mary. She prepared her report in conjunction with her role as AIDS coordinator for the Catholic Fund for Overseas Development.

70. *New York Times* 2001.

71. *New York Times* 2001. On the church's unwillingness even to acknowledge abuse, see, for example, reports by Cozzens (2000) and Winters (2002). In regard to the punishment of whistleblowers, note that O'Donahue was quietly sanctioned by the Vatican. Similarly, Father Donald Cozzens, who writes prolifically on this problem, was stripped of his role as seminary rector in Cleveland. And Father Charles Curran, a scholar who repeatedly called for revision of Catholic sexual doctrine, lost his tenured professorship at Catholic University. Jenkins (1998) provides evidence from the church's own records of the failures to deal with the problem.

72. *St. Louis Dispatch* 1990.

73. Ribadeneira 1998.

74. Associated Press 1998; Goodstein 2002.

CHAPTER SIX

1. To be sure, other such communities exist. Meterologists, for example, routinely model the worst-case scenarios of weather systems, along with their probability of occurrence. Similarly, certain adjudicators—especially those dealing with sex offenders—consider the worst possible outcomes of a nonconviction and use these arguments in the penalty phases of trials. But negative asymmetry is so central to the day-to-day operations of medical professionals and computer operators that these cases stand as ideal case studies ripe for analysis.

2. Edelstein 1943. Currently, the Hippocratic oath is somewhat controversial. Many modern physicians feel that its directives have lost their meaning. For an interesting discussion of this issue, see Survivor MD, the Web site designed to accompany the NOVA special of the same name, http://www.pbs.org/wgbh/nova/doctors (accessed December 2, 2003). In addition to discussion and debate, the site contains both the original and an updated version of the Hippocratic oath.

3. I analyzed six textbooks. Using Amazon.com, I selected the top two best-selling medical training textbooks. I randomly selected an additional four books from the top thirty best-sellers. My sample consisted of the following texts: Bannister et al. 1999; Braunwald et al. 2001; Guyton and Hall 2000; Beers and Berkow 1999; Pfenninger and Fowler 2003; and Tierney, McPhee, and Papadakis 2004.

4. Braunwald et al. 2001, 2, 1 (emphasis added).

5. Fowler and Altman 2003, 685.

6. Guyton and Hall 2000, 709.

7. Bannister et al. 1999, 1681, 1913.

8. National Comprehensive Cancer Network 1999. Also see guidelines described by Greene and colleagues (2002), *The Merck Manual* (Beers and Berkow 1999), and Tierney, McPhee, and Papadakis (2004)

9. For more on this approach, consult the Web site of the American Society of Clinical Oncology (http://www.asco.org) or Greene et al. 2002.

10. American Cancer Society 2001. For more technical descriptions with more detailed category breakdowns, see Greene et al. 2002.

11. Heart Failure Society of America, http://www.abouthf.org/edu9.html (accessed August 8, 2001).

12. I analyzed six dictionaries. Using the Barnes and Noble Web site, I selected the top three best-selling dictionaries: *Stedman's Medical Dictionary* (2000), *Taber's Cyclopedic Medical Dictionary* (Venes and Thomas 2001), and *Dorland's Illustrated Medical Dictionary* (2003). I randomly selected three additional dictionaries from Barnes and Noble's list of the top hundred best-sellers: *Harper Collins Illustrated Medical Dictionary* (2001), *The Merck Manual* (Beers and Berkow 1999), and *Mosby's Medical, Nursing, and Allied Health Dictionary* (2002).

13. *Mosby's* 2002, 1110.

14. *The Merck Manual* (Beers and Berkow 1999, 1754). *The Merck Manual* devotes ten times the space to heart failure as it does to mitral valve prolapse. In *Mosby's*, the ratio is 16:1. Indeed, in my sample of medical dictionaries, the ratio of coverage for heart failure verses mitral valve prolapse ranged from 10:1 to 20:1.

15. Descriptions are from *The Merck Manual* (Beers and Berkow 1999, 1973) and *Stedman's Medical Dictionary* (2000, 669).

16. I "Googled" the terms "good health" and "definition." Google returned 83,200 sites. I randomly chose and content analyzed 85 sites (0.1 percent of the initial search) from the first 2,000 listings.

17. Good Health Checklist for Ultimate Wellness, http://www.drkogaard.com/goodhealth.html (accessed August 15, 2001).

18. "What is Health and Wellness?" http://www.menieres-disease.ca/health_wellness.htm (accessed December 9, 2003).

19. Beato 2003, 60393; Hassel and Hafner 2002.

20. Aïvanhov 1999.

21. Bhatia 2002.

22. The definitions are from the *HarperCollins Medical Dictionary* (2001, 335), *Mosby's* (2002, 1004), and *Stedman's* (2000, 996). See also Total Wellness, http://www.totalwellness.com/services.php?opage=1 (accessed December 3, 2003).

23. Heartbeat and pulse were gauged by human touch. A physician would lower his ear to the chest of the patient or feel the patient's wrist with his fingers. Electronic heartbeat monitors were not widely available until the 1960s. A physician typically used a mirror to detect the absence of breathing. One would place a mirror at the lips of the patient. If the mirror failed to cloud, one would assume that breathing had ceased. See P. M. Black 1977; H. C. Black 1999; Cerulo and Ruane 1997; Gervais 1986,

1–17, 45–74; Häring 1973, 131–36; Harvard Medical School 1968; Hillman 1972, 88; Veatch 1975 and 1988, 38–39; Walker 1974; Walton 1979, 6–7 and chap. 2; and Winter 1969, 12–13.

24. In the five medical dictionaries I analyzed, the entries on death contained subcategories and cross-references that itemized various gradations of death. Definitions of life contained no such specifics.

25. Agre and Schuler 1997, 11 (emphasis added).

26. "Computer Equipment Operators," *Occupational Outlook Handbook*, http://www.bls.gov/oco/ocos128.htm (accessed October 4, 2001; emphasis added).

27. "Computer Equipment Operators," *Occupational Outlook Handbook*, http://www.bls.gov/oco/ocos110.htm (accessed April 16, 2004; emphasis added). Note that the U.S. Department of Labor includes systems analysts under the computer programmer heading.

28. I "Googled" the terms "computer operator" and "computer programmer" and "systems analyst" and "job description." Google returned 19,980 descriptions. I randomly chose 200 sites (0.1 percent of the initial search) from the first 1,000 listings and content analyzed them.

29. For the specific ads cited above (emphasis added), see "Data Center Operations," http://info.techserv.sunysb.edu/datacenterops.html (accessed August 2001); "Computer Operator," http://seo.syr.edu/jobdesc.htm (accessed December 15, 2003); "Job Title: Computer Operator, Sr—2nd Shift" (accessed August 2001), http://job14 .cbdr.com/Scripts/cgihndlr.ed . . . =L/JB=8692/S1=771210/R=771210/TECT=1/PT=2 (accessed October 4, 2001); "Computer Operator," http://www.hr.utah.edu/comp/ jobdescriptions/viewjd.php?id=714 (accessed December 15, 2003); "Computer Programmer," http://www.systechnologygroup.com/jobbank/jb_sd_intro.php (accessed April 16, 2004); "Programmer-Systems Analyst," http://www.ebic-inc.com/pages/ employ/employ_prog-sys_analyst.htm (accessed April 16, 2004).

30. Agre and Schuler 1997, 12.

31. I analyzed seven texts. Using Amazon, I selected the top two best-selling training textbooks. I randomly selected an additional five books from the top thirty bestsellers. My sample consisted of manuals by Andrews (2001), Bass (2004), Bigelow (2000), Gookin (1996, 2002), Karp (2003), and Stone and Poor (2001).

32. Ferris 2000. "Fire fighting" means that operators address only the failing parts of a system.

33. Karp 2003, 1, 3 (emphasis added).

34. Reprinted from Dinnocenzo's book *101 Tips for Telecommuters*, http://www .bkpub.com/tipoftheweek/story13.html (accessed August 2001; emphasis added).

35. Gookin 1996, 319. For the previous citations from this manual, see pages 7, 21, 31, and 55.

36. See Bigelow 2000, 3–7.

37. *The New Hacker's Dictionary*, edited by Eric S. Raymond (1996), has long been considered the definitive source of hacker jargon and slang. The definitions reported

here are from the updated online version of the dictionary, http://www.tuxedo.org/
~esr/jargon.html#A%20 Terms (accessed October 11, 2001).

38. Stone and Poor 2001, xvi.

39. Andrews 2001, 70.

40. All definitions in this section come from *The New Hacker's Dictionary*,
http://www.tuxedo.org/~esr/jargon.html#A%20Terms (accessed October 11, 2001).

41. Stone and Poor 2001, xix; Bigelow 2000, 2; Bass 2004.

42. Zimmerman 1999, 4–5.

43. This concept builds on Robert Wuthnow's (1998, 59) notion of "porous institutions."

44. For the complete citation of this *Merck Manual*, see Berkow 2000.

45. Cockerham (2004) elaborates on such porous boundaries.

46. Devos and Tilman 2001, 8.

47. Agre and Schuler 1997, 9 13.

48. Swidler 2001, 96. I draw the definitions of formal knowledge, tradition, and
common sense from Swidler (1984, 2001).

49. Cockerham 2004, 212.

50. In this regard, note that professional courtesy often appears more important than
professional accountability. Studies show that physicians frequently downplay or overlook the mistakes of their peers in an effort to maintain independence and minimize
community conflict. Cockerham (2004, 232–35) gives a good review of this literature.

51. McKinlay 1999.

52. Hafferty and Light 1995; Light 2000; Ritzer and Walczak 1988.

53. See U.S Department of Labor, Bureau of Labor Statistics, *Occupational Outlook Handbook,* http://stats.bls.gov/oco/ocos110.htm (accessed October 24, 2001).

54. Agre and Schuler 1997, 7.

55. Bratteteig and Stolterman 1997, 290.

56. Quoted in McNurlin and Sprague 1996, chap. 18.

57. McNurlin and Sprague 1996, chap. 18; Sims and Manz 1982.

58. Baddoo and Hall 2003.

59. Bratteteig and Stolterman 1997, 290.

60. "Why Have Professional Codes of Conduct," http://www.cs.utexas.edu/users/
ethics/professionalism/why_ethics.html (accessed October 24, 2001).

61. Vance 2001.

Chapter Seven

1. By social structure, I refer to a specific configuration of statuses, resources,
power, and mechanisms of control within which social action occurs.

2. I do not wish to imply a causal relationship between structure and cognition.
The interaction between the social, the cultural, and the cognitive is clearly far more
complex.

3. World Health Organization 2003a, 1.

4. World Health Organization 2003a, 1; also see Gardner 2003.

5. The WHO estimates that the SARS incubation period is ten days.

6. All quotes taken from World Health Organization 2003a, 3.

7. U.S. Central Intelligence Agency 2003, 1.

8. Misrahi et al. 2004, 3; also see U.S. Department of State 2003.

9. The WHO established its networked information source in 2000.

10. Pang et al. 2003, 3218.

11. See Johns Hopkins 2003.

12. Rothstein et al. 2003, 25.

13. World Health Organization 2003b.

14. Pang et al. 2003, 5.

15. Rothstein et al. 2003, 24.

16. World Health Organization 2003b.

17. Pang et al. 2003, 3221.

18. U.S. Central Intelligence Agency 2003, 5.

19. Pang et al. 2003, 3221.

20. Quah and Hin-Peng 2004.

21. U.S. Central Intelligence Agency 2003, 7.

22. U.S. Department of State 2003, 1; also see Hughes 2003.

23. U.S. Central Intelligence Agency 2003, 5; Hughes 2003.

24. Gatune 2000, 2.

25. Maniona and Evan 2000, 370.

26. Maniona and Evan 2000, 370.

27. Anson 1999, 1–2.

28. Anson 1999, 14–15.

29. Eventually, 197 nations participated in the Y2K effort.

30. International Y2K Cooperation Center 2000a, 8.

31. This information was provided by a subsector of the IYCC, the Y2K Expert Service, known as YES.

32. U.S. Department of State 2000.

33. For details, see de Jager and Bergeon 1997, 128; Jones 1998, chap. 6; and Rochester Institute of Technology 1998.

34. International Y2K Cooperation Center 2000a, 2000b; Jones 1998; Quarantelli 2001a; and Tagarinski 2000.

35. International Y2K Cooperation Center 2000a, 11.

36. Quoted from an ICC press release for March 1, 2000, http://www.y2k.gov (accessed June 2, 2000).

37. Quoted from an ICC press release for January 3, 2000, http://www.y2k.gov (accessed June 2, 2000).

38. Von Drehle 2000, 1.

39. Hill 2002, 4; the members of the 9/11 Commission (Kean et al. 2004, 272) cite this report as the most thorough source on the incident.

40. Hill 2002, 4.

41. Hirsch and Isikoff 2002, 28.

42. Hill 2002, 2. Note that John O'Neill, the top counterterrorism agent in the FBI's New York office, was among those who received a copy of the memo. Ironically, "Mr. O'Neill [had] retired from the FBI in late August. He had just begun a job as the security chief of the World Trade Center when he was killed in the attacks" (Johnston and Van Natta 2002, 1).

43. Hill 2002, 4.

44. Hill 2002, 5.

45. Hirsch and Isikoff 2002, 28–29.

46. Hill 2002, 2.

47. Hirsch and Isikoff 2002, 30. Of course, Hirsch and Isikoff do report that "a Justice Department spokesperson hotly disputed this, saying that in May Ashcroft told a Senate Committee terrorism was his 'highest priority'" (30). But it is worth noting that the allocations requested by Ashcroft in his first prepared budget do not support the notion that terrorism was of primary concern.

The U.S. intelligence community may have been more attuned to the worst-case scenario than the White House and its cabinet. But according to the findings of the House and Senate Intelligence Committee's Joint Inquiry on the matter, the top brass were convinced than attacks from bin Laden would target U.S. interests overseas. Consequently, the potential for a domestic incident was eclipsed as inconsistent with reasonable expectations. See the "Abridged Findings and Conclusions of the Joint Inquiry Report," http//:www.thememoryhole.org/911/joint-report/conclusion/css/conclusions_4html (accessed January 27, 2004).

48. The 9/11 Commission (Kean et al. 2004, 272) argued that attention to the Phoenix memo's concerns might have helped FBI directors to connect the dots when, a month later, Minnesota operatives alerted them to Zacarias Moussaoui's activities.

49. For more details, see Kean et al. 2004.

50. Hill 2002, 9; see also Kean et al. 2004. One cannot overstate the archaic condition of the FBI's communication system. Prior to the September 11 attacks, many FBI agents were using "386" and "486" computers. Many also lacked Internet access or e-mail addresses, and the capacities of the agency's search engines were inferior to programs available to the general public. Reporters Chitra Ragavan and colleagues note that "after the attacks, FBI headquarters staff had to send photographs of the 19 hijackers to the 56 field offices by FedEx because they lacked scanners" (2003, 20).

51. See Hill 2002, 11; also "Abridged Findings and Conclusions of the Joint Inquiry Report, page 15," http//:www.thememoryhole.org/911/joint-report/conclusion/css/conclusions_4html (accessed January 27, 2004).

52. The FBI's propensity toward a "secret" fight on terrorism is, in no way, conspiratorial. Risk management experts tell us that such policies emerge from longstanding concerns with public panic. Sociologist Kathleen Tierney, one of the field's premiere disaster researchers, notes that most public officials and disaster managers fervently believe that emergency warnings will induce chaos. Tierney notes, however,

that such "chaos theories" are not supported by facts. Decades of study reveal that people rarely panic or lose control when faced with adversity or catastrophe. In fact, at a personal level, such events often elicit great bravery, and at a social level, they often strengthen communal bonds. See Tierney, Lindell, and Perry 2001, 87; see also Erikson 1995; Feinberg and Johnson 2001; Fischer 1998; Halbert 2002; Johnson 1987; Quarantelli 2001b.

53. Presidential Commission on the Space Shuttle *Challenger* Accident 1986, chap. 4, p. 1).

54. U.S. Congress 1986, 7.

55. Boffey 1986.

56. Broad 1986.

57. Boffey 1986.

58. Quoted in McDonald 1986.

59. Vaughan 2002, 39.

60. Sagan (1993, 40) makes a similar point, also noting that "when redundancy makes the system appear more safe, operators often take advantage of such improvements to move to higher and more dangerous production levels."

61. This attitude finds its parallel in the self-assurance expressed by the traditonal saying "The FBI always gets its man."

62. Vaughan 2002, 40.

63. Vaughan 1996, 398.

64. Quoted in Reinhold 1986.

65. Presidential Commission on the Space Shuttle *Challenger* Accident 1986, chap. 7, p. 1.

66. Sanger 1986.

67. Reinhold 1986.

68. Cerulo (1997, 2002a, 2004), DiMaggio (1997), and Mohr (1998) all offer good reviews of the literature.

69. See, for example, Bergesen 1979, 1984; Bernstein 1975; and Cerulo 1984, 1989, 1993, 1995b.

70. Martin 2002.

71. See, for example, Cerulo 1995b; Fine 2002; and Schwartz 1987, 1997.

72. Billing 1996, 263–86.

73. See, for example, Cerulo 1984; Burt 1987; Coleman, Katz, and Menzel 1966; Kuhn 1970; Rogers 1972.

74. Cerulo 1998.

75. Cerulo 1988, 1995a.

76. Cerulo 1984, 1995b, 1998.

77. The structural web bears some resemblance to what organizational sociologist W. Richard Scott calls a "matrix structure" (see Scott 2003, 242–44).

78. Quoted from the World Heath Organization Web site, http://www.who.int/bulletin/en/ (accessed March 4, 2004).

79. "USIA's Platt Remarks on Confronting Y2K," http://www.usembassy.iy/file9906/alia/99062814.htm (accessed March 4, 2004).

80. Wuthnow 1998, 5–6, 59.

81. Note that the WHO often facilitated such exchanges.

82. Indeed, when elements of a web fail to communicate openly, they are admonished by the other components of the system. China suffered such a fate in the early days of the SARS disaster. The CIA's Office of Transnational Issues reports that the world health community gave China "low marks" for attempting to hide early outbreaks of the disease. Similarly, Taiwan was admonished for its reluctance to report a second wave of outbreaks in May 2003 (U.S. Central Intelligence Agency 2003, 7–8).

83. An organizational theorist, considering the elements of porousness, multidirectional communication, and high levels of autonomy, might describe the structural web as "loosely coupled."

84. Chandler 1962; also see Miles and Snow 1994.

85. Vaughan (1996) offers a detailed structural flow chart of both NASA and its subsidiaries in appendix B of her book.

86. Vaughan 1996, 397.

87. Vaughan 1996, 250.

88. Hill 2002; Kean et al. 2004.

89. Vaughan 2002, 38–39.

CHAPTER EIGHT

1. Quoted in Edwards 1963, 744.

2. See work reviewed in Cerulo 2002a, Gardner 1987, Reisberg 2001, and Solso 1998.

3. Psychologist Martin Seligman makes this point quite forcefully, arguing for the development of a "positive psychology" (see, for example, Seligman 2003; Seligman and Csikszentmihalyi 2000).

4. Quoted from an interview on *Meet the Press*, broadcast on the NBC network on July 18, 2004. The transcript of the interview is available on the NBC Web site, http://msnbc.msn.com/id/5458209 (accessed July 26, 2004).

5. See Associated Press 2004; also Flynn 2004 and Kean et al. 2004. Recently, Clarke 2005 echoed these sentiments.

6. See McQuaid and Schleifstein 2002; Lavine 2005; and Fischetti 2001.

7. Psychologist John Cacioppo documents this point quite convincingly (see, for example, Cacioppo, Gardner, and Bernston 1997 and Larsen, McGraw, and Cacioppo 2001). Elsewhere, I have shown that imposing unidimensional conceptual continua in the analysis of social phenomena can lead to flawed perceptions of social processes and events (Cerulo 2002b).

8. Of course, *within* any single category—best or worst—unidimensional continua could prove a completely viable analytic tool.

9. Social scientist Michael Billing (1996, 253–86) would describe the separate-but-equal strategy as a two-sided model of social thought. Such situations can be viewed as fully articulated argumentative contexts that allow individuals to identify with opposing realities.

10. Dr. Joseph Mercola has amassed a broad collection of FDA and congressional proceedings on this matter. Consult his Web site, http://www.mercola.com (accessed July 19, 2004). See also Representative Bart Stupak's statement on Accutane on the Parker & Waichman Web page dedicated to problems with the drug, http://www .accutane-side-effects.com/page2.php (accessed July 19, 2004). Note that Stupak's son B.J. committed suicide while taking the drug.

11. Similar arguments could be made with reference to drugs such as Vioxx, Viagra, and many of the SSRI inhibitors.

12. Quoted from remarks by the president delivered at the Cincinnati Museum on October 7, 2002. See the White House press release, http://www.whitehouse.gov/ news/releases/2002/10 . . . print/20021007-8.html (accessed July 19, 2004).

13. Indeed, the 9/11 Commission suggested something of the kind in their idea for a National Counterterrorism Center (Kean et al. 2004, 23). However, the weblike characteristics I have discussed here—control versus service oriented, the autonomy of members, the porousness of boundaries, and so forth—were not part of this vision, and thus are not part of the system that is currently in place.

14. After all, NASA allowed its engineers to envision worst-case scenarios, but the conclusions drawn by such work groups carried little weight among decision-making elites.

15. See Ruane and Cerulo 2004, chap, 2, for a review of this literature; also see Billing 1996.

16. See Perrow 1999.

REFERENCES

AARP. 2003. "These Four Walls: Americans 45+ Talk about Home and Community." Report by Matthew Greenwald and Associates for AARP. http://research.aarp.org/ (accessed October 29, 2003).

ABC News. 2003. "French Negotiating Exile for Saddam." ABC News report on Rediff India Abroad, March 22. http://www.rediff.com/us/2003/mar/22french.htm (accessed August 27, 2003).

Adams, Cecil. 2001. "Do Americans Get Less Vacation than People in Other Developed Countries?" *Straight Dope.* http://www.straightdope.com/columns/010302/html (accessed July 8, 2003).

Adams, Douglas. 2000. "The Games People Play (and Why They Play Them): The 'Meaning' of Lottery Participation." *Humanity and Society* 24, no. 1:19–33.

AFMC Public Affairs Link. 2002. "Seat Belts Could Save 60% of People Killed." http://www.afmc.wpafb.af.mil/HQ-AFMC/PA/news/archive/2001/jun/Kirtland_Seatbelts.htm (accessed June 27, 2003).

Agre, Philip F., and Douglas Schuler. 1997. Introduction to *Reinventing Technology, Rediscovering Community: Critical Explorations of Computing as a Social Practice,* ed. P. F. Agre and D. Schuler, 1–19. New York: Ablex.

Ainsworth, Gareth. 2001. "On the Mend." The official Gareth Ainsworth Web site, October 26. http://www.garethainsworth.com/theword/26/10/2001.html (accessed July 1, 2003).

Aïvanhov, Omraam Mikhaël. 1999. "Definition of Health: Harmony." Fraternité Blanche Universelle. http://www.videlinata.ch/w_sante03_gb.html (accessed December 9, 2003).

Alan Guttmacher Institute. 1998. "Trends in Contraceptive Use in the U.S." *Family Planning Perspectives* 30 (January/February): 1.

———. 1999. "Facts in Brief: Teen Sex and Pregnancy." http://www.agi-usa.org/pubs/fd_teen_sex.html (accessed June 23, 2003).

———. 2002. "Teenagers Sexual and Reproductive Health: Developed Countries." http://www.agi-usa.org/pubs/fd_teen_sex.html (accessed June 23, 2003).

Allen, Francis A. 2001. Review of *Death in the Dark: Midnight Executions in America*, by John D. Bessler, and *Death at Midnight: The Confession of an Executioner*, by Donald A. Cabana. *Law and History Review* 19, no. 1. http://www.historycooperative.org/journals/lhr/19.1/br_19.html (accessed April 5, 2002).

Alliance for Aging Research. 2001. "Great Expectations: Americans Views on Aging." National Survey on Aging. http://www.agingresearch.org/survey/pollsummary1.htm (accessed July 8, 2002).

Alter, Karen J. 2002. "Is 'Groupthink' Driving Us to War?" *Boston Globe*, September 16, A15.

Altheide, David L. 2002a. *Creating Fear: News and the Construction of Crisis.* New York: Aldine de Gruyter.

———. 2002b. "Tracking Discourse." In *Culture in Mind: Toward a Sociology of Culture and Cognition*, ed. K. A. Cerulo, 172–85. New York: Routledge.

American Academy of Orthopaedic Surgeons. 2001. "Climb It Safe Program Urges Public to Use Ladders Properly." http://www.aaos.org/wordhtml/press/sciwrit/climb.htm (accessed July 8, 2003).

American Association for Cancer Research. 2002. "Americans Attitudes toward Cancer Research." http://www.aacr.org/1000/1100/1120bj.html (accessed July 5, 2002).

American Cancer Society. 1998. "Cancer Facts and Figures." Revised June 11. http://www.cancer.org/bottomcancinfo.html.

———. 2001. "Prostate Cancer Stages." http://www.cancer.org/nccn_acs/Prostate/body_04.htm (accessed May 2, 2001).

American Heart Association. 1998a. "Biostatistical Fact Sheets." http://www.amheart.org/Heart_and_Stroke_A_Z.Guide/biowo.html (accessed January 25, 1999).

———. 1998b. "Heart and Stroke Statistical Update." http://www.amheart.org/ (accessed January 25, 1999).

American Prosecutors Research Institute. 2002. "Child On Board." *Between the Lines* 11, no. 1. http://www.ndaa.org/publications/newsletters/between_lines_volume_11_number_1_2002.html (accessed August 15, 2002).

American Psychiatric Association. 2000. *Diagnostic and Statistical Manual of Mental Disorders*. 4th ed. Washington, D.C.: American Psychiatric Association.

Anderegg, David. 2003. *Worried All the Time: Overparenting in an Age of Anxiety and How to Stop It*. New York: Simon and Schuster.

Andersen, Hans Christian. 1992. "The Ugly Duckling." In *A Treasury of Children's Literature*, ed. A. Eisen, 260–69. Boston: Houghton Mifflin.

Andrews, Bernice, and Chris R. Brewin. 1990. "Attributions of Blame for Marital Violence: A Study of Antecedents and Consequences." *Journal of Marriage and the Family* 52, no. 3:757–67.

Andrews, Jean. 2001. *Enhanced PC Troubleshooting Pocket Guide for Managing and Maintaining Your PC*. Boston: Course Technology/Thomson Learning.

Anson, Robert Sam. 1999. "The Y2K Nightmare." *Vanity Fair*, January.

Applebaum, Eileen, and Rosemary Batt. 1994. *The New American Workplace: Transforming Work Systems in the United States.* Ithaca, N.Y.: ILR Press.

Ariès, Philippe. 1974. *Western Attitudes toward Death from the Middle Ages to the Present.* Baltimore: John Hopkins University Press.

Arora, Raksha. 2004a. "Optimism Fizzles on Stock Market Prospects." Gallup Organization. http://www.gallup.com/poll/content/default.aspx?ci=11833 (accessed June 1, 2004).

———. 2004b. "Retirement Dreams vs. Retirement Realities." Gallup Organization. http://www.gallup.com/poll/content/default.aspx?ci=14140 (accessed November 23, 2004).

Associated Press. 1986. "Khadafy Calls Reagan a Hitler No. 2." *San Diego Union-Tribune*, January 16.

———. 1998. "A Roman Catholic Bishop in Florida Resigns, Admitting He Molested 5 Boys." *New York Times*, June 3, A12.

———. 2000. "Connecticut Woman Sues Video Game Maker After Son's Death." December 28. Reprinted on the Freedom Forum Web site, http://www.freedomforum.org/templates/document.asp.documentID=4110.

———. 2004. "Intelligence Changes Must Come Quickly, Panel Says." July 23. Reprinted on the Positive Universe Web site, http://www.positiveuniverse.com/2000/July/ (accessed July 28, 2002).

Atkinson, J. Maxwell. 1984. "Public Speaking and Audience Responses: Some Techniques for Inviting Applause." In *Structures of Social Action*, ed. J. M. Atkinson and J. Heritage, 370–409. Cambridge: Cambridge University Press.

Auerbach, Paul S. 1999. *Medicine for the Outdoors.* New York: Lyons Press.

Baars, Bernard J. 1986. *The Cognitive Revolution in Psychology.* New York: Guillford Press.

Babbie, Earl. 2001. *The Practice of Social Research.* 9th ed. Belmont, Calif.: Wadsworth/Thomson Learning.

Baddoo, Nathan, and Tracy Hall. 2003. "Motivators of Software Process Improvement: An Analysis of Practitioners' Views." *Journal of Systems and Software* 66, no. 1:23–33.

Baily, Joan Gaskill. 1998. "The Anticipation of a Life Event: Married Midlife Women's Approach to Widowhood." Ph.D. diss., Rutgers University.

Baker, Robert A. 1997. "Art Bell's Quickening Is Sickening." Web site of the Committee for the Scientific Investigation of Claims of the Paranormal. http://www.csicop/sb9712/baker.html (accessed July 29, 2003).

Ballard, David T., Doran Williams, Anne L. Horton, and Barry L. Johnson. 1990. "Offender Identification and Current Use of Community Resources." In *The Incest Perpetrator: A Family Member No One Wants to Treat*, ed. A. L. Horton and B. L. Johnson, 150–63. Thousand Oaks, Calif.: Sage.

Baltimore Sun. 1999. "When Will We Learn Our Lesson about Ornery Dictators?" Editorial. February 2, 9A.

Balz, Dan. 2000. "Stage Is Set for a Nasty Gore-Bush Showdown." *Washington Post,*
    March 12, A1.
Bannister, Lawrence H., Martin M. Berry, Patricia Collins, Mary Dyson, Julian E.
    Dussek, and Mark W. J. Ferguson. 1999. *Gray's Anatomy: The Anatomical Basis
    of Medicine and Surgery.* 38th ed. Edinburgh: Churchill Livingstone.
Banzhaf, John. 1995. "Why Smokers Are Ignoring the Massive Cigarette Recall."
    Action on Smoking and Health. http://www.ash.org/pr/recall2.htm (accessed
    July 22, 2002).
Barbalet, Jack, ed. 2002. *Emotions and Sociology.* Malden, Mass.: Blackwell.
Bar-Illan, David. 1991. "Fantasies." *Jerusalem Post,* March 29, 10.
Baron, S. Anthony. 1993. "Violence in the Workplace." U.S. Department of Health
    and Human Services. http://www.hhs.gov/ (accessed July 7, 2003).
Bartlett, Bruce. 2000. "AARP Poll Shows American Optimism." National Center
    for Policy Analysis. http://www.ncpa.org/pd/social/pd052400a.html (accessed
    June 24, 2001).
Barton's. 2000. "Bear Getting Hungry." September 25. http://www.inet.co.th/
    cyberclub/barton/ (accessed June 24, 2001).
Bass, Steve. 2004. *PC Annoyances.* Beijing: O'Reilly.
Bateson, Gregory. 1972. "A Theory of Play and Fantasy." In *Steps to an Ecology of
    the Mind,* 177–93. New York: Ballantine. (Originally published 1955.)
Baumgartner, Mary Pat. 1984. "Social Control from Below." In *Toward a General
    Theory of Social Control,* vol. 1, *Fundamentals,* ed. D. Black, 303–45. Orlando:
    Academic Press.
Baumgartner, Peter, and Sabine Payr, eds. 1996. *Speaking Minds: Interviews with
    20 Eminent Cognitive Scientists.* Princeton: Princeton University Press.
Baxter, Mary Kay. 1993. *Divine Revelation of Hell.* Springdale, Pa.: Whitaker House.
——. 1998. *Divine Revelation of Heaven.* Springdale, Pa.: Whitaker House.
Beato, Cristina V. 2003. "Partners Invited to Participate in Steps to a Healthier US."
    Federal Register 68, no. 204 (October 22): 60393–94. Washington, DC: Depart-
    ment of Health and Human Services, Office of the Secretary.
Beers, Mark H., and Robert Berkow, eds. 1999. *The Merck Manual of Diagnosis and
    Therapy.* 17th ed. Whitehouse Station, N.J.: Merck Research Laboratories.
Begley, Sharon. 2001. "Will We Ever Be Safe Again?" *Newsweek,* September 24, 58.
Berger, Peter L., and Thomas Luckmann. 1967. *The Social Construction of Reality.*
    Garden City, N.Y.: Anchor Books.
Bergesen, Albert. 1979. "Spiritual, Jazz, Blues, and Folk Music." In *The Religious
    Dimension,* ed. R. Wuthnow, 333–50. New York: Academic Press.
——. 1984. The Semantic Equation: A Theory of the Social Origins of Art Styles."
    In *Sociological Theory,* R. Collins, 222–37. San Francisco: Jossey Bass.
Berkow, Robert, ed. 2000. *The Merck Manual of Medical Information, Home Edi-
    tion.* New York: Pocket Books.
Bernstein, Basil. 1975. *Class, Codes, and Control.* 3 vols. London: Routledge and
    Kegan Paul.

Bernstein, William M. 1984. "Denial and Self-Defense." *Psychoanalysis and Contemporary Thought* 7, no. 3:423–57.

Bessler, John D. 1997. *Death in the Dark: Midnight Executions in America.* Boston: Northeastern University Press.

Best, Joel. 2001. *Damned Lies and Statistics: Untangling Numbers from the Media, Politicians, and Activists.* Berkeley and Los Angeles: University of California Press.

Bhatia, Manish. 2002. "What Is Health? How Do You Define It?" Hpathy. http://www.hpathy.com/papersnew/concept_of_health_and_mental_health.asp (accessed December 9, 2003).

Bhattacharya, Jogendra N. 1995. *Hindu Castes and Sects: An Exposition of the Origin of the Hindu Caste System.* Ottawa: Laurier Books.

Biagojevic, Marina. 1989. "The Attitudes of Young People Towards Marriage: From the Change of Substance to the Change of Form." *Marriage and Family Review* 14, nos. 1–2:217–38.

Bigelow, Stephen J. 2000. *The Technician's Troubleshooting Pocket Reference.* 2nd ed. New York: McGraw Hill.

Billing, Michael. 1996. *Arguing and Thinking: A Rhetorical Approach to Social Psychology.* Cambridge: Cambridge University Press.

Black, Donald. 1980. *Manners and Customs of the Police.* New York: Academic Press.

———. 1989. *Sociological Justice.* New York: Oxford University Press.

———. 1998. *The Social Structure of Right and Wrong.* Rev. ed. San Diego: Academic Press. (Originally published 1993.)

Black, Henry Campbell. 1999. *Black's Law Dictionary.* 7th ed. Ed. B. A. Garner. St. Paul, Minn.: West Group.

Black, P. M. 1977. "Three Definitions of Death." *Monist* 60, no. 1:136–46.

Blais, Jacqueline. 2000. "Motto: Be Prepared. Be Very Prepared." *USA Today,* March 30.

Blizzard, Rick. 2005. "Obesity Epidemic: Are Americans in Denial?" Gallup Organization. http://www.gallup.com/poll/content/default.aspx?ci=16453 (accessed May 24, 2005).

Blume, E. Sue. 1998. *Secret Survivors: Uncovering Incest and Its Aftereffects in Women.* New York: Ballantine.

Boffey, Philip M. 1986. "Failure of Joint Accepted by NASA as Disaster Cause." *New York Times,* March 21, sec. 1, p. 1.

Boorstin, Daniel J. 1965. *The Americans: The National Experience.* New York: Vintage.

Bourdieu, Pierre. 1977. *Outline of a Theory of Practice.* Cambridge: Cambridge University Press.

———. 1990a. *In Other Words: Essays Towards a Reflexive Sociology.* Stanford: Stanford University Press.

———. 1990b. *The Logic of Practice.* Stanford: Stanford University Press.

Bower, G. H. 1991. "Mood Congruity of Social Judgements." In *Emotion and Social Judgements*, ed. J. P. Forgas, 31–55. Oxford: Pergamon Press.

Bowler, Michael. 1996. "Censorship Takes Center Stage." *Baltimore Sun*, January 28, C2.

Bratteteig, Tone, and Erik Stolterman. 1997. "Design in Groups—and All That Jazz." In *Computers and Design in Context*, ed. M. Kyng and L. Mathiassen, 289–316. Cambridge: MIT Press.

Braunwald, Eugene, Anthony S. Fauci, Dennis L. Kasper, Stephen L. Hauser, Dan L. Longo, and J. Larry Jameson. 2001. *Harrison's Principles of Internal Medicine*. 15th ed. New York: McGraw Hill.

British Dyslexics. 2003. "Dealing With Dyslexia." http://www.dyslexia.uk.com/ page36.html (accessed April 30, 2003).

Broad, William J. 1986. "Silence about Shuttle Flaw Attributed to Pitfalls of Pride." *New York Times*, September 30.

Broyde, Michael J. 1994. "Forming Religious Communities and Respecting Dissenter's Rights: A Jewish Tradition Model for a Modern Society." Paper presented at the Conference for Religious Human Rights in the World Today: Legal and Religious Perspectives, Emory University, Atlanta, Georgia. Available from the online journal *Jewish Law*, http://www.jlaw.com/Articles/excom.html (accessed January 6, 2004).

Brody, Jane E. 2002. "Risks and Realities: In a World of Hazards, Worries Are Often Misplaced." *New York Times*, August 20, B5.

Brownlow, Maureen. 2001. "Chronic Illness in Adolescence: Crisis or Challenge?" Lupus Canada. http://www.lupuscanada.org/en/archive/ chronicillnessin_adolescence.html (accessed April 30, 2003). (Originally published in *Lupus Canada Bulletin* 3, no. 1 [1993]: 17–21.)

Bryant, Jennings, and Dolf Zillmann. 2002. *Media Effects: Advances in Theory and Research*. 2nd ed. Mahwah, N.J.: Lawrence Erlbaum.

Buchanan, Patrick J. 1993. "Gergenizing the GOP: Clinton's 'Republican' Advisor is Shepherding GOP Support for one of the Worst Treaties of All Time." *Pittsburgh Post Gazette*, September 13, B3.

Burggraf, Susan Agnes. 2000. "Affective Responses to Horror Films." *Dissertation Abstracts International*, section B, *The Sciences and Engineering* 61, no. 4-B (October): 2269.

Burns, Edward McNall. 1973. *Western Civilizations*. 8th ed. New York: W. W. Norton.

Burt, Ronald. 1987. "Social Contagion and Innovation: Cohesion versus Structural Equivalence." *American Journal of Sociology* 92, no. 6:1287–1335.

Buxton, Dietra. 2002. "Drunk Driving: Teens Ignore Statistics, Continue Hazardous Behavior." My High School Journalism, an American Society of Newspaper Editors Web hosting site. http://my.highschooljournalism.org/nc/manteo/mhs/ article.cfm?eid=66&aid=279 (accessed July 22, 2002).

Byron, Chris. 2000. "Has the Market Finally Hit Bottom?" Report by CNBC and the *Wall Street Journal*, December 22. http://www.msnbc.com/news/ 507052.asp?cp1=1 (accessed May 26, 2002).

Cacioppo, John T., Wendi L. Gardner, Gary G. Bernston. 1997. "Beyond Bipolar Conceptualizations and Measures: The Case of Attitudes and Evaluative Space." *Personality and Social Psychology Review* 1, no. 1:3–25.

Calvin, John. 1995. *Institutes of the Christian Religion.* 2 vols. Trans. H. Beveridge. Grand Rapids, Mich.: William B. Eerdmans.

Cancel, Celia Marie. 2001. "Honor Killings as Violations of Women's Human Rights." Report from the Women's Issues page at About.com. http://www .women3rdworld.about.com/library/weekly/aa050801.htm?once=true& (accessed July 27, 2001).

Cantor, Norman F. 2001. *In the Wake of the Plague: The Black Death and the World It Made.* New York: Free Press.

Carlson, Darren K. 2002. "The Blame Game: Youth and Media Violence." In *Education and Youth.* Princeton: Gallup Organization.

Carr, Deborah, James S. House, Camille Wortman, Randolph Nesse, and Ronald C. Kessler. 2001. "Psychological Adjustment to Sudden and Anticipated Spousal Loss among Older Widowed Persons." *Journal of Gerontology: Social Sciences* 56B, no. 4:S237–48

Carroll, Joseph. 2005. "American Public Opinion about Terrorism." Gallup Organization. http://gallup.com/poll/content/default.aspx?ci=10009&pw=4/ (accessed April 19, 2005).

Castenada, Ruben. 2001. "Officers' Acts 'Shameful,' Prosecutor Says: 'Blue Wall of Silence' Punctured in Canine Case, Jury Told in Closing Argument." *Washington Post*, March 13, Metro section, B3.

Catechism of the Catholic Church. 2000. Saint Charles Borromeo Catholic Church Web site. http://www.scborromeo.org/ccc/p123a12.htm (accessed May 5, 2001).

Catterall, Albert. 2005. "Economic Woes Fail to Shake Britons' Optimism." Gallup Organization. http://www.gallup.com/poll/content/default.aspx?ci=16450 (accessed May 24, 2005).

CBS News. 2001. "Love and Marriage." February 25. http://cbsnews.com/stories/ 2001/02/25/opinion/main274410.shtml (accessed July 17, 2002).

———. 2003. "Saddam Interview Airs in Iraq." February 21. http://www.cbsnews .com/stories/2003/02/21/iraq/main541427.shtml (accessed August 27, 2003).

Centers for Disease Control (CDC). 2002. "Preventing Injuries in Sports, Recreation, and Exercise." http://www.cdc.gov/ncipc/pub-res/research_agenda/ 05_sports.htm (accessed July 1, 2003).

Cerulo, Karen A. 1984. "Social Disruption and Its Effects on Music: An Empirical Analysis." *Social Forces* 62, no. 4:885–904.

———. 1988. "What's Wrong with This Picture?" *Communication Research* 15, no. 1:93–101.

———. 1989. "Socio-Political Control and the Structure of National Symbols: An Empirical Analysis of National Anthems." *Social Forces* 68, no. 1:76–99.

———. 1993. "Symbols and the World-System: National Anthems and Flags." *Sociological Forum* 8, no. 2:243–72.

———. 1995a. "Designs on the White House: TV Ads, Message Structure, and Election Outcome." *Research in Political Sociology* 7:63–88.

———. 1995b. *Identity Designs: The Sites and Sounds of a Nation.* Arnold and Caroline Rose Book Series of the ASA. New Brunswick: Rutgers University Press.

———. 1997. "Identity Construction." *Annual Review of Sociology* 23:385–409.

———. 1998. *Deciphering Violence: The Cognitive Structure of Right and Wrong.* New York: Routledge.

———, ed. 2002a. *Culture in Mind: Toward a Sociology of Culture and Cognition.* New York: Routledge.

———. 2002b. "Individualism . . . Pro Tem: Reconsidering U.S. Social Relations." In *Culture in Mind: Toward a Sociology of Culture and Cognition,* ed. K. A. Cerulo, 135–71. New York: Routledge.

———. 2004. "Cognitive Sociology." In *Handbook of Social Theory,* ed. G. Ritzer, 107–11. Thousand Oaks, Calif.: Sage.

Cerulo, Karen A., and Janet M. Ruane. 1997. "Death Comes Alive: Technology and the Re-conception of Death. *Science as Culture* 6, no. 3:444–66.

———. 2004. "Who Is a Social Actor?" Paper presented at the Annual Meetings of the Eastern Sociological Society, New York, February.

Chambliss, Daniel F. 1996. *Beyond Caring.* Chicago: University of Chicago Press.

Chandler, Alfred D. Jr. 1962. *Strategy and Structure: Chapters in the History of the American Industrial Enterprise.* Cambridge: MIT Press.

Chandler, Russell. 1990. "Sex Abuse Cases Rock the American Clergy." *Los Angeles Times,* August 3, A1.

Chang, Andrew. 2001. "The Feeling at the Top." ABC News. http://abcnews.go.com/sections/world/Daily/News/everest010413.html (accessed October 4, 2001).

Chapin, John. 2001. "It Won't Happen to Me: The Role of Optimistic Bias in African American Teens' Risky Sexual Practices." *Howard Journal of Communications* 12, no. 1:49–59.

Chapple, Constance, and Stacey Nofziger. 2000. "Bingo: Hints of Deviance in the Accounts of Sociability and Profit of Bingo Players." *Deviant Behavior* 21, no. 6:489–517.

Cheng, Sinkwan. 1993. "From Fortuna to the Christian God: Gambling and the Calvinist Ethic." *American Journal of Semiotics* 10, nos. 3–4:81–108.

Chopra, Deepak. 1993. *Creating Affluence: The A-to-Z Steps to a Richer Life.* San Rafael, Calif.: Amber-Allen Publishing.

Claeys, Gregory, and Lyman Tower Sargent, eds. 1999. *The Utopia Reader.* New York: New York University Press.

Clarke, Lee. 1993. "The Disqualification Heuristic: When Do Organizations Mis-perceive Risk?" *Research in Social Problems and Public Policy* 5:289–312.

———. 1999. *Mission Improbable: Using Fantasy Documents to Tame Disaster.* Chicago: University of Chicago Press.

———. 2005. *Worst Cases: Terror and Catastrophe in the Popular Imagination.* Chicago: University of Chicago Press.

Clayman, Steven. 1993. "Booing: The Anatomy of a Disaffiliative Response." *American Sociological Review* 58, no. 1:110–30.

Clore, Gerald L., Norbert Schwartz, and Michael Conway. 1993. "Affective Causes and Consequences of Social Information Processing." In *Handbook of Social Cognition,* 2nd ed., ed. R. S. Wyer and T. K. Srull. Hillsdale, N.J.: Lawrence Erlbaum.

CNN/Money. 2002. "Consumer Optimism Surges." http://money.cnn.com/2002/03/20/news/economy/abc_money (accessed November 11, 2005).

Cockerham, William C. 2004. *Medical Sociology.* 9th ed. Upper Saddle River, N.J.: Prentice Hall.

Cohen, Stanley. 2001. *States of Denial: Knowing about Atrocities and Suffering.* Cambridge: Polity Press.

Coleman, James, Elihu Katz, and Herbert Menzel. 1966. *Medical Innovation.* New York: Bobbs-Merrill.

Collins, Jim. 2001. *Good to Great.* New York: Harper Business/Harper Collins.

Conrad, Peter. 1975. "The Discovery of Hyperkinesis: Notes on the Medicalization of Deviant Behavior." *Social Problems* 23, no. 1:12–21.

Consumer Reports. 2004a. "Cell Phones: New Rules, New Choices." *Consumer Reports* 69, no. 2:12–20.

———. 2004b. "Hotels: 50 Chains, 10 Ways to Save." *Consumer Reports* 69, no. 7:12–17.

Cooley, Charles Horton. 1962. *Social Organization: A Larger Study of the Mind.* New York: Schoken. (Originally published 1909.)

Cozzens, Donald. 2000. *The Changing Face of the Priesthood.* Collegeville, Minn.: Liturgical Press.

———. 2002. *Sacred Silence: Denial and Crisis in the Church.* Collegeville, Minn.: Liturgical Press.

Critser, Greg. 2003. *Fat Land: How Americans Became the Fattest People in the World.* Boston: Houghton Mifflin.

Cuprisin, Tim. 2002. "Art Bell Bids Farewell to His Creepy Show for the Third Time." *Milwaukee Journal Sentinel,* October 24. http://www.jsonline.com/enter/tvradio/oct02/90404.asp?/ (accessed July 28, 2003).

Currie, Elliott. 1992. *Reckoning: Drugs, the Cities, and the American Future.* New York: Hill and Wang.

Curtis, Glade B., and Judith Schuler. 2000. *Your Pregnancy Week by Week.* Cambridge, Mass.: Perseus Publishing.

Curtis, Helena. 1976. *Biology.* 2nd ed. New York: Worth Publishers.

Curry, Pat. 2001. "Protect your Finances with Disability Insurance." Bank Rate. http://www.bankrate.com/brm/news/insur/20011010a.asp?/prodtype=insir (accessed July 7, 2003).

Daily Hog. 2000. "Newfound Object Orbiting Earth Is Art Bell's Head." http://dailyhog.com/newmoon.htm (accessed July 28, 2003).

Darroch, Jacqueline E., David J. Landry, and Susheela Singh. 2000. "Changing Emphasis in Sexuality Education in U.S. Public Secondary Schools, 1988–1999." *Family Planning Perspectives* 32, no. 5:204.

Darwin, Michael. 1994. "Perspectives on Death and Dying Today." In *Standby: Care of the End-Stage Cryopreservation.* BPI Tech Brief no. 11. Cryo net/Life Extension Society. http//:keithlynch.net/cryonet/29/35.html (accessed July 8, 2002).

Davidson, Debra J., Tim Williamson, and John Parkins. 2003. "Climate Change and Risk Perception in Forest Based Communities." *Canadian Journal of Forest Research* 33, no. 11:2252–61.

Davis, Deborah, Ian Sundahl, and Michael Lesbo. 2000. "Illusionary Personal Control as a Determinant of Bet Size and type in Casino Craps Games." *Journal of Applied Social Psychology* 30, no. 6:1224–42.

Davis, Michael. 1989. "Explaining Wrongdoing." *Journal of Social Philosophy* 20, no. 1:74–90.

Debenport, Ellen. 1993. "One of These Guys Is Wrong on NAFTA." *St. Petersburg Times,* November 10, A1.

De Jager, Peter, and Richard Bergeon. 1997. *Managing 00: Surviving the Year 2000 Computing Crisis.* New York: Wiley.

Delfabbro, Paul H., and Anthony H. Winefield. 2000. "Predictors of Irrational Thinking in Regular Slot Machine Gamblers." *Journal of Psychology* 134, no. 2:117–28.

DeLillo, Don. 1998. "The Outer Limits: A Lone Voice in the Desert Lures 10 Million Listeners." *Washington Post,* September 29, C1.

Derber, Charles. 2000. *The Pursuit of Attention: Power and Ego in Everyday Life.* New York: Oxford University Press. (Originally published 1979.)

Devos, Martine, and Michel Tilman. 2001. "Incremental Development of a Repository-Based Framework Supporting Organizational Inquiry and Learning." CiteSeer Scientific Literature Digital Library. http://citeseer.ist.psu.edu/305338.html (accessed April 28, 2004).

Diamond, Timothy. 1992. *Making Gray Gold.* Chicago: University of Chicago Press.

Diefenbach, Donald L., and Mark D. West. 2001. "Violent Crime and Poisson Regression: A Measure and Method for Cultivation Analysis." *Journal of Broadcasting and Electronic Media* 45, no. 3:432–45.

DiMaggio, Paul J. 1997. "Culture and Cognition: An Interdisciplinary Review." *Annual Review of Sociology* 23:263–87.

DiMaggio, Paul J., and Walter W. Powell. 1991. Introduction to *The New Institutionalism in Organizational Analysis,* ed. W. W. Powell and P. J. DiMaggio, 1–38. Chicago: University of Chicago Press.

Dinnen, S. P. 2001. "Put Together the Pieces for an Estate Plan." *Des Moines Register,* December 31, Business section, 5.

Dionne, E. J. Jr. 1991. "Bush Casts Saddam as the Villain in a Fiercely Personal Test of Wills." *Washington Post,* February 23, A17.

Dong, Faye M. 2001. "The Nutritional Value of Shellfish." Washington Sea Grant Program, University of Washington. http://www.wsg.washington.edu/ (accessed December 9, 2003).

Dorland's Illustrated Medical Dictionary. 2003. 30th ed. New York: Elsevier Science.

Douglas, Ann. 2002. *The Mother of All Pregnancy Books.* New York: Hungry Minds. (Originally published 2000.)

Dover, Benjamin. 2002. "Getting Your Estate Together—and—Insuring Your Big Events." Official Benjamin Dover information site. http://www.bendover.com/ gnpquestion.asp?faq=5$fldAuto=219 (accessed July 8, 2002).

Dowd, Maureen. 2003. "Unbearable Lightness of Memory." *New York Times,* November 20.

Dugan, Sarah, Debra Umberson, and Kristin L. Anderson. 1998. "The Batterer's View of the Self and Others in Domestic Violence." Paper presented at the Annual Meetings of the American Sociological Association, San Francisco, August.

Durkheim, Emile. 1933. *The Division of Labor in Society.* New York: Free Press.

———. 1951. *Suicide: A Study in Sociology.* Trans. J. A. Spaulding and G. Simpson. New York: Free Press. (Originally published 1897.)

———. 1995. *The Elementary Forms of Religious Life.* New York: Free Press. (Originally published 1912.)

Easterbrook, Gregg. 1987. "Big, Dumb Rockets." *Newsweek,* August 17, 46–60.

Eckel, Catherine C., and Phillip J. Grossman. 2002. "Sex Differences and Statistical Stereotyping in Attitudes toward Financial Risk." *Evolution and Human Behavior* 23, no. 4:281–95.

Eddy, Melissa. 1999. "Milosevic Says U.S. Is against Kosovo Serbs." *Buffalo News,* August 27, 3A.

Edelstein, Ludwig. 1943. *The Hippocratic Oath: Text, Translation, and Interpretation.* Baltimore: Johns Hopkins University Press.

Edwards, Tryon. 1963. *The New Dictionary of Thoughts.* New York: Standard.

Eich, E. 1995. "Searching for Mood Dependent Memory." *Psychological Science* 6, no. 67–75.

Eisenberg, Arlene, Heidi E. Murkhoff, and Sandee E Hathaway. 1996a. *What To Expect the First Year.* New York: Workman Publishing.

———. 1996b. *What to Expect: The Toddler Years.* New York: Workman Publishing.

Elias, Norbert. 1985. *The Loneliness of Dying.* Trans. E. Jephcott. London: Blackwell.

Elkind, Arthur. 1997. *Migraines: Everything You Need to Know about Their Cause and Cure.* New York: Avon.

Elon, Menachem. 1974. *Principles of Jewish Law.* Jerusalem.

Epinions 2001. "What Evil Lurks behind Your Neighbors Blinds?" http://www .epinions.com/content_1621598340 (accessed April 30, 2003).

Erikson, Kai. 1995. *A New Species of Trouble: Explorations in Disaster, Trauma, and Community.* New York: W. W. Norton.

Esser, J. K., and J. S. Lindoefer. 1989. "Groupthink and the Space Shuttle Challenger Accident: Toward a Quantitative Case Analysis" *Journal of Behavioral Decision Making* 2:167–77.

Ezzo, Gary, and Robert Bucknam. 2001. *On Becoming Baby Wise.* Simi Valley, Calif.: Parent-Wise Solutions.

Farkas, Steven, Jean Johnson, and Ann Duffett. 2002. *A Lot Easier Said Than Done.* Washington, D.C.: Public Agenda.

Federman, Joel, ed. 1998. *National Television Violence Study: Executive Study.* University of California Center for Communication and Social Policy. http://www.ccsp.ucsb.edu/ntvs.htm (accessed July 25, 2003).

Feinberg, William E., and Norris R. Johnson. 2001. "The Ties that Bind: A Macro-Level Approach to Panic." *International Journal of Mass Emergencies and Disasters* 19, no. 3:269–95.

Feldman, Martha S., and James G. March. 1981. "Information in Organizations as Signal and Symbol." *Administrative Science Quarterly* 26, no. 2:171–86.

Feldstein, Dan. 2003. "NASA May Have Grown Blind to Warnings." *Houston Chronicle,* April 15, A1.

Ferraro, Kathleen J., and John M. Johnson. 1983. "How Women Experience Battering: The Process of Victimization." *Social Problems* 39, no. 3:325–35.

Ferriman, Annabel, and John McGhie. 1991. "NHS Cover-Up on War Gas Victims." *Observer,* January 13, 22.

Ferris, Karen. 2000. "Answering the ITIL Skeptics." KMF Advance Web site. http://kmfadvance.server101.com/publication_itil_sceptics.htm/ (accessed November 14, 2005).

Festinger, Leon, Harry Riecken, and Stanley Schachter. 1956. *When Prophecy Fails.* New York: Harper and Row.

Fine, Gary Allan. 2002. "Thinking about Evil: Adolf Hitler and the Dilemma of the Social Construction of Reputation." In *Culture in Mind: Toward a Sociology of Culture and Cognition,* ed. K. A. Cerulo, 227–37. New York: Routledge.

Firestone, David. 1990. "Bishop Defends Priests' Virtue." *Newsday,* November 16, 4.

Fischer, H. W. III. 1998. *Responses to Disaster: Fact versus Fiction and Its Perpetuation: The Sociology of Disaster.* New York: University Press of America.

Fischetti, Mark. 2001. "Drowning New Orleans." *Scientific American,* October 1.

Fleck, Ludwig. 1979. *Genesis and Development of a Scientific Fact.* Chicago: University of Chicago Press. (Originally published 1935.)

Flynn, Stephen. 2004. *America the Vulnerable: How Our Government Is Failing to Protect Us from Terrorism.* New York: Harper Collins.

Fontaine, Kevin R., David T. Redden, Chenxi Wang, Andrew O. Westfall, and David B. Allison. 2003. "Years of Life Lost due to Obesity." *JAMA* 289:187–93.

Foucault, Michel. 1965. *Madness and Civilization: A History of Insanity in the Age of Reason.* Trans. R. Howard. New York: Random House.

———. 1978. *The History of Sexuality.* Vol. 1. Trans. R. Hurley. New York: Pantheon.

———. 1979. *Discipline and Punish: The Birth of a Prison.* Trans. A. Sheridan. New York: Vintage Books.

Fowler, Grant C., and Michael Altman. 2003. "Exercise (Stress) Testing." In *Procedures for Primary Care,* 2nd ed., ed. J. L. Pfenninger and G. C. Fowler, 685–713. Philadelphia: Mosby.

Frankl, Victor. 1992. *Man's Search for Meaning.* Boston: Beacon Press. (Originally published 1959.)

Freedman, David S., Laura Kettel Khan, Mark K. Serdula, Deborah A. Galuska, and William H. Dietz. 2002. "Trends and Correlates of Class 3 Obesity in the United States from 1990 through 2000." *JAMA* 288:1758–61.

Freudenberg, William R., and Ted I. K. Youn. 1993. "A New Perspective on Problems and Policy." *Research in Social Problems and Public Policy* 5:1–19.

Friedland, Roger, and Robert R. Alford. 1991. "Bringing Society Back In: Symbols, Practices, and Institutional Contradictions." In *The New Institutionalism in Organizational Analysis,* ed. W. W. Powell and P. J. DiMaggio, 232–63. Chicago: University of Chicago Press.

Friedman, Thomas. 2002. "A Failure to Imagine." Week in Review. *New York Times,* May 19, 15.

Frommer, Frederic J. 2002. "Group Cites Video-Game Makers for Violence against Women." Associated Press report on the WTNH Web site, December 19. http://www.wtnh.com/global/story.asp?S=1055987 (accessed November 12, 2005).

Fry, Prem S., and Lisa A. Barker. 2001. "Female Survivors of Violence and Abuse: Their Regrets of Action and Inaction in Coping." *Journal of Interpersonal Violence* 16, no. 4:320–42.

Fuerbringer, Jonathan. 2001. "Markets Plunge in Wide Sell-Off: NASDAQ Falls 6%." *New York Times,* March 13.

Gallup Organization. 2001a. "Americans Favor China Trade Agreement, but Agree that Workers Could be Hurt; Support Is about the Same for NAFTA." http://www.gallup.com/poll/releases/pr991130.asp (accessed June 5, 2001).

———. 2001b. "Americans Most Satisfied with Living Conditions in Country, Opportunities to Get Ahead." http://www.gallup.com/poll/socialaudit/should_be_done.asp (accessed May 9, 2001).

———. 2001c. "Children and Guns." http://www.gallup.com/poll/indicators/indchild_violence.asp (accessed May 11, 2001).

———. 2001d. "Social Audit: Have and Have Nots." http://www.gallup.com/poll/socialaudit/have_havenots.asp (accessed May 9, 2001).

———. 2001e. "Social Audit: Perceptions of Opportunity in the United States." http://www.gallup.com/poll/socialaudit/opportunity_perception.asp (accessed May 9, 2001).

———. 2003a. "Is America Divided Into Haves and Have Nots?" http://www.gallup.com/content/default.aspx?ci=8275&pg=1 (accessed March 29, 2004).

———. 2003b. "Nutrition and Food." http://www.gallup.com/content/default.aspx?ci-0424 (accessed March 29, 2004).

———. 2004a. "Americans Maintain Love-Hate Relationship with TV, Movies." http://www.gallup.com/content/default.asp?ci=12961 (accessed September 11, 2004).

———. 2004b. "American Public Opinion about Terrorism." http://www.gallup.com/poll/focus/sr030520.asp (accessed April 27, 2004).

———. 2004c. "Guns." http://www.gallup.com/content/default.asp?ci=1645 (accessed March 11, 2004).

———. 2004d. "Most Teens Soak up the Sun Unprotected." http://www.gallup.com/content/default.asp?ci=12931 (accessed September 11, 2004).

———. 2005. "Update: Americans' Satisfaction with Aspects of Life in U.S." http://www.gallup.com/poll/content/?ci=14611&pg=1 (accessed June 20, 2005).

Gambaccini, Peter. 1998. "A Brief Chat with Melody Fairchild." Interview in *Runner's World.* http://www.runnersworld.com/events/footlock/intflmf1/html (accessed July 1, 2003).

Gardner, Amanda. 2003. "Journal Looks at Taming SARS." *Detroit Free Press*, December 30. http://www.freep.com/news/health/sars30_20031230.htm (accessed January 13, 2004).

Gardner, Harold. 1987. *The Mind's New Science: A History of the Cognitive Revolution.* New York: Basic Books.

Garfinkel, Harold. 1967. "Studies of the Routine Grounds of Everyday Activities." In *Studies in Ethnomethodology*, 35–75. Oxford: Polity Press. (Originally published 1964.)

Gatune, Julius. 2000. "Y2K Myths, Facts and Lessons." First Reinsurance Brokers. http://www.firstre.com/features/index.php3 (accessed January 16, 2004).

Geller, Max, Mary Devlin, Terrence Flynn, and Judith Kaliski. 1985. "Confrontation of Denial in a Father's Incest Group." *International Journal of Group Psychotherapy* 35, no. 4:545–67.

Gerbner, George, Larry Gross, Michael Morgan, Nancy Signorielli, James J. Shanahan. 2002. "Growing Up with Television: Cultivation Processes." In *Media Effects: Advances in Theory and Research*, 2nd ed., ed. J. Bryant and D. Zillmann, 43–67. Mahwah, N.J.: Lawrence Erlbaum.

Gervais, Karen G. 1986. *Redefining Death.* New Haven: Yale University Press.

Giddens, Anthony. 1984. *The Constitution of Society.* Berkeley and Los Angeles: University of California Press.

Gilbert, Dennis. 2003. *The American Class Structure in an Age of Growing Inequality.* Belmont, Calif.: Wadsworth/Thomson Learning.

Gilovich, Thomas, Kenneth Savitsky, and Victoria H. Medvec. 1998. "The Illusion of Transparency: Biased Assessments of Others' Ability to Read One's Emotions." *Journal of Personality and Social Psychology* 75:332–46.

Givens, Terryl L. 2003. *By the Hand of Mormon: American Scriptures That Launched a New World Religion.* New York: Oxford University Press.

Glassner, Barry. 1999. *The Culture of Fear: Why Americans Are Afraid of the Wrong Things.* New York: Basic Books.

Goffman, Erving. 1959. *The Presentation of Self in Everyday Life.* Garden City, N.Y.: Doubleday Anchor.

———. 1961. *Asylums: Essays on the Social Situation of Mental Patients and Other Inmates.* Garden City, N.Y.: Anchor Books.

———. 1963a. *Behavior in Public Places: Notes on the Social Organization of Gatherings.* New York: Free Press.

———. 1963b. *Stigma: Notes on the Management of Spoiled Identity.* Englewood Cliffs, N.J.: Prentice Hall.

———. 1974. *Frame Analysis: An Essay on the Organization of Experience.* New York: Harper Colophon.

Golin, Keith J. 2001. "The Role of Gambling, Risk-taking, and Cognitive Bias in Computer Trading." *Dissertation Abstract International*, section B, *Science and Engineering* 61, no. 11-B:6134.

Gonzalez, Richard, and George Wu. 1999. "On the Shape of the Probability Weighting Function." *Cognitive Psychology* 38, no. 1:129–66.

Goodstein, Lauie. 2003. "Trail of Pain in Church Crisis Leads to Nearly Every Diocese." *New York Times*, January 12, A1.

Gookin, Dan. 1996. *PCs for Dummies.* 4th ed. Foster City, Calif.: IDG Books.

———. 2002. *Troubleshooting Your PC for Dummies.* New York: Wiley.

Gordon, Kathryn. 2002. "Incest and Sept. 11." *Salon*, January 23. http://www.salon.com/mwt/feature/2002/01/23/whirlpool (accessed July 22, 2002).

Grady, Sandy. 1993. "NAFTA Duel Begins: It's Clinton vs. Perot." Viewpoints. *Buffalo News*, September 21, 3.

Gram-Hansen, Lasse. 2003. "An Interview with Alison Hine." Race Sim Central. http://www.racesimcentral.com/articles/interviews/alison/alison5.shtml (accessed July 1, 2003).

Greeley, Andrew M., and Michael Hout. 1999. "Americans' Increasing Belief in Life after Death: Religious Competition and Acculturation." *American Sociological Review* 64, no. 6:813–35.

Greene, Frederick L., David L. Page, Irvin D. Fleming, April Fritz, Charles M. Balch, Daniel G. Haller, and Monica Morrow. 2002. *AJCC Cancer Staging Manual.* 6th ed. New York: Springer Verlag.

Greene, Susan. 1999. "Age of Censorship Denounced: Panel Cites Columbine's Impact." *Denver Post*, November 21, B-02.

Greenbaum, Charles W., Chedva Erlich, and Yosef H. Toubiana. 1993. "Settler Children and the Gulf War." In *The Psychological Effects of War and Violence on Children*, ed. L. A. Leavitt and N. A. Fox, 109–30. Hillsdale, N.J.: Lawrence Erlbaum.

Greenblat, Cathy Stein, and Thomas J. Cottle. 1980. *Getting Married.* New York: McGraw Hill.

Grimm, Jacob, and Grimm, Wilhelm. 1994. *Grimms' Fairy Tales.* London: Penguin. (Originally published 1823.)

Guardian. 1999. "Mrs. Milosevic Says Cleansing Is a Myth." May 4, 4.

Guyton, Arthur C., and John E. Hall. 2000. *Textbook of Medical Physiology.* 10th ed. Philadelphia: W. B. Saunders.

Hafferty, Frederick W., and Donald W. Light. 1995. "Professional Dynamics and the Changing Nature of Medical Work." *Journal of Health and Social Behavior* 27, extra issue: 132–53

Halbert, Debora J. 2002. "Citizenship, Pluralism, and Modern Public Space." *Innovation* 15, no. 1:33–42.

Hamill, Pete. 1996. "Blood on Their Hands: The Corrupt and Brutal World of Professional Boxing." *Esquire,* June 1, 94.

Hampton, J. A. 1997. "Psychological Representations of Concepts." In *Cognitive Models of Memory,* ed. M. A. Conway and S. E. Gathercole. London: UCL Press.

Häring, Bernhard. 1973. *Medical Ethics.* Notre Dame: Fides Press.

HarperCollins Illustrated Medical Dictionary. 2001. 4th ed. Ed. I. G. Fox, J. Melloni, G. Eisner, and J. Melloni. New York: HarperCollins.

Harper, Jennifer. 2004. "Glass Half Full for Most Americans." *Washington Times.* http://www.washtimes.com/national/20040602-010026-1935r.htm (accessed March 16, 2005).

Harris, Mike. 2001. "Earnhardt's death Changes NASCAR Forever." Associated Press report on *SouthCoastToday.com,* December 30. http://www.s-t.com/daily/12-01/12-30-01/c04spo81.htm/ (accessed November 12 2005).

Harvard Medical School. 1968. "A Definition of Irreversible Coma: Report of the Ad Hoc Committee of the Harvard Medical School to Examine the Definition of Brain Death." *JAMA* 205:33740.

Harvey, Bob. 2001. "Violation and Betrayal: It Was a Test of Faith." *Ottawa Citizen Saturday Observer,* March 31, B2.

Hassel, Craig, and Chris Hafner. 2002. "On Health and Well-Being: Can We Learn from Ancient Perspectives?" *Food, Science and Nutrition,* March. http://www.fsci.umn.edu/nutrinet/2002%20Nutrinet/Mar/March.html (accessed December 9, 2003).

Hattery, Angela J. 2001. "Families on Crisis: Men and Women's Perceptions of Violence in Partner Relationships." Paper presented at the Annual Meetings of the Southern Sociological Society.

Haywood, Thomas W., and Linda S. Grossman. 1994. "Denial of Deviant Sexual Arousal and Psychopathology in Child Molesters." *Behavior Therapy* 25, no. 2:327–40.

Health Line Clinical Laboratories. 2005. "Sexually Transmitted Diseases Continue to Increase in Youth according to Recent Report." http://www.yubanet.com/artman/publish/printer_19804.shtml (accessed May 17, 2005).

Heard, Alex. 1999. *Apocalypse Pretty Soon.* New York: W. W. Norton.

Heckert, D. Alex, and Edward W. Gondolf. 2000. "Assessing Assault Self-Reports by

Batterer Program Participants and Their Partners." *Journal of Family Violence* 15, no. 2:181–97.

Hedges, Stephen J., Betsy Streisand, Mike Tharp, William F. Allman, Julian E. Barnes, Josh Chetwynd, Richard Folkers, Susannah Fox, Thom Geier, Brendan I. Koerner, Mary Lord, Douglas Pasternak, Eric Ransdell, Joshua Rich, Joshua Wolf Shenk, and John Simons. 1997. "www.masssuicide.com." *U.S. News and World Report*, April 7, 26–31.

Hedley, Allison A., Cynthia L. Ogden, Clifford L. Johnson, Margaret D. Carroll, Lester R. Curtin, and Katherine M. Flegal. 2004. "Prevalence of Overweight and Obesity among U.S. Children, Adolescents, and Adults, 1999–2002." *JAMA* 291:2847–50.

Heimer, Carol A. 1992. "Your Baby's Just Fine, Just Fine: Certification Procedures, Meetings, and the Supply of Information in Neonatal Intensive Care Units." In *Organizations, Uncertainties, and Risk*, ed. J. F. Short Jr. and L. Clarke, 161–88. Boulder: Westview.

Heise, David R. 1979. *Understanding Events, Affect, and the Construction of Social Action*. Cambridge: Cambridge University Press.

Hendawi, Hamza. 2004. "A Defiant Saddam Hussein Appears at Hearing, Says Bush 'Is the Real Criminal.'" Associated Press, International News report, *SFGate .com*, July 1. http://www.sfgate.com/cgi-bin/article.cgi?f=/news/archive/2004/07/01/international249EDT0568.DTL/ (accessed November 5, 2005).

Henry, William. 1997. *The Keepers of Heaven's Gate: The Millennial Madness*. Anchorage: Earthpulse Press.

Heritage, John, and David Greatbatch. 1986. "Generating Applause: A Study of Rhetoric and Response at Political Party Conferences." *American Journal of Sociology* 92:110–57.

Herman, Sonya. 1977. "Women, Divorce and Suicide." *Journal of Divorce* 1, no. 2:10717.

Hill, Eleanor. 2002. "The FBI's Handling of the Phoenix Electronic Communication and Investigation of Zacarias Moussaoui prior to September 11, 2001." Report to the Joint Committee of the U.S. Congress, September 24, 2002. *Frontline*, Readings and Links. http://www.pbs.org/wgbh/pages/frontline/shows/knew/etc/links.html (accessed February 6, 2004).

Hillman, H. 1972. "Death and Dying." *Resuscitation* 1:85–90.

Hirsh, Michael, and Michael Isikoff. 2002. "What Went Wrong?" *Newsweek*, May 27, 28–34.

Hirschkorn, Phil. 2005. "9/11 panel: FAA had Early al Qaeda Warnings." CNN report, February 11. http://edition.cnn.com/2005/US/02/11/911.memo (accessed February 25, 2005).

Hochschild, Arlie. 1983. *The Managed Heart: The Commercialization of Human Feeling*. Berkeley and Los Angeles: University of California Press.

Hong, Lawrence K. 1978. "Risky Shift and Cautious Shift: Some Direct Evidence on the Culture-Value Theory." *Social Psychology* 41, no. 4:342–46.

Hontheim, Joseph. 1999a. "Heaven." In *The Catholic Encyclopedia*, vol. 7. http://
    www.newadvent.org/cathen/07170a.htm (accessed January 16, 2001).
———. 1999b. "Hell." In *The Catholic Encyclopedia*, vol. 7. http://www.newadvent
    .org/cathen/07207a.htm (accessed January 16, 2001).
Howarth, Glennys, and Oliver Leaman, eds. 2001. *Encyclopedia of Death and
    Dying*. London: Routledge.
Hubbard, Grace B. 1989. "Mothers' Perceptions of Incest: Sustained Disruption and
    Turmoil." *Archives of Pediatric Nursing* 3, no. 1:34–40.
Huddleston, Phillip. 2003. "Why Do We Ride?" *DFW Rallycats Newsletter* 7, no.
    8:8–9.
Hughes, James M. 2003. "Valuable Lessons Learned from SARS." *JAMA* 290:3251–53.
Human Rights Watch. 1998. "Broken People." http://www.hrw.org/reports/1999/
    india/India994-02.htm (accessed May 8, 2001).
Hunt, Jennifer C. 2003. "Straightening Out the Bends." Cisatlantic. http://www
    .cisatlantic.com/trimix/AQUAcoprs/Bent/Hunt2.htm (accessed July 1, 2003).
Hunt, Jennifer C., and Peter K. Manning, 1991. "The Social Context of Police Lying."
    Symbolic Interaction 14, no. 1:51–70.
Hunter, James D., and Charles Bowman. 1996. *The State of Disunion: 1996 Survey of
    American Political Culture*. The Post-Modernity Project, University of Virginia
    and the Gallup Organization. http://religionanddemocracy.lib.virginia.edu/
    programs/survey.html.
Husserl, Edmund. 1950. *Ideen*. Vol. 1, *Allgemein Einfuhrung in die reine Pharnu-
    menologie*. The Hague: Nijhoff.
Iovine, Vivki. 1995. *The Girlfriend's Guide to Pregnancy, or Everything Your Doctor
    Won't Tell You*. New York: Pocket Books.
International Y2K Cooperation Center. 2000a. February 2000 Report. http://www
    .iyk2cc.org (accessed March 16, 2000).
———. 2000b. Executive Report. http://usembassy-australia.state.gov/hyper/
    2000/0217/epf41f.htm (accessed January 14, 2004).
Isikoff, Michael, and Daniel Klaidman. 2002. "The Hijackers We Let Escape." *News-
    week*, June 10, 20–28.
Jaeger, Carlo C., Ortwin Renn, Eugene A. Rosa, and Thomas. Webler. 2001. *Risk,
    Uncertainty, and Rational Action*. London: Earthscan.
Janis, Irving L. 1971. "Groupthink." *Psychology Today*, November, 43–46.
———. 1989. *Crucial Decisions: Leadership in Policymaking and Crises Manage-
    ment*. New York: Free Press.
Jarvik, Lissy F., and Marika Kulbach. 1983. "Atypical Miner: Prototype of the
    Pathological Gambler?" *Comprehensive Psychiatry* 24, no. 3:213–17.
Jenkins, Philip. 1998. "Creating a Culture of Clergy Deviance." In *Wolves within
    the Fold: Religious Leadership and Abuses of Power*, ed. A. Shupe, 118–32.
    New Brunswick: Rutgers University Press.
Johns Hopkins. 2003. "Inpatient Isolation and Cleaning Protocol for Patients
    Who Have or Are Suspected of Having Severe Acute Respiratory Syndrome

(SARS)." http://www.hopkins-heic.org/pdf/SARS_isolation.pdf (accessed January 9, 2004).

Johnson, Norris R. 1987. "Panic and the Breakdown of Social Order: Popular Myth, Social Theory, Empirical Evidence." *Sociological Focus* 20, no. 2:171–83.

Johnston, David. 2003. "Word for Word/Revisiting 9/11: The Warnings Were There, but Who Was Listening?" *New York Times,* July 27, sec. 4, p. 7.

Johnston, David, and Don Van Natta Jr. 2002. "Traces of Terror: The FBI Memo; Ashcroft Learned of Agebt's Alert Just after 9/11." *New York Times,* May 21, A1.

Jones, Beverly. 1970. "The Dynamics of Marriage and Motherhood" *Sisterhood Is Powerful: An Anthology of Writings from the Women's Liberation Movement,* ed. R. Morgan, 49–66. New York: Vintage. (Originally published 1967.)

Jones, Capers. 1998. *The Year 2000 Software Problem: Quantifying the Costs and Assessing the Problems.* Reading, Mass.: Addison-Wesley.

Jones, Jeffrey M. 2004. "Gambling a Common Activity for Americans." Gallup Organization. http://www.gallup.com/content/?ci=11098 (accessed March 29, 2004).

———. 2005. "Bush Ratings Show Decline." Gallup Organization. http://www.gallup.com/poll/content/?ci=16474&pg=1 (accessed May 24, 2005).

Jurkowitz, Mark. 2001. "The Media: McVeigh Request Spurs Debate Over 'Live Deaths' on Television." *Boston Globe,* February 23, D1.

Kahr, Brett. 1992. "The Sexual Molestation of Children: Historical Perspectives." *Journal of Psychohistory* 19, no. 2:191–214.

Kaiser Family Foundation. 2002a. "Communication: A Series of National Surveys of Teens about Sex." http://www.kff.org/content/archive/1373/datingrep.html (accessed June 23, 2003).

———. 2002b. "Drugs and Sex: Teens Talk Back." Session at the "Dangerous Liasons Conference," February 7, New York, New York. Transcripts available from the Kaiser Family Foundation Web site, http://www.kff.org/content/archive/1373/datingrep.html (accessed June 23, 2003).

———. 2003. "National Survey of Teens: Teens Talk about Dating, Intimacy, and Their Sexual Experiences." http://www.kff.org/youthhivstds/1373/datingsur_3.cfm (accessed November 12, 2005).

Kaplan, Meg. S., Judith V. Becker, and Jerry Cunningham-Rathner. 1988. "Characteristics of Parents of Adolescent Incest Perpetrators: Preliminary Findings." *Journal of Family Violence* 3, no. 3:183–91.

Karp, David A. 2003. *Windows XP Annoyances: Tips, Secrets and Solutions.* Sebastopol, Calif.: O'Reilly and Associates.

Kean, Thomas H., Lee H. Hamilton, Richard Ben-Veniste, Bob Kerrey, Fred F. Fielding, John F. Lehman, Jamie S. Gorelick, Timothy J. Roemer, Slade Gorton, and James R. Thompson. 2004. *The 9/11 Commission Report: Final Report of the National Commission on Terror Attacks upon the United States.* Washington, D.C.: U.S. Government Printing Office.

Kearns, Doris. 1976. *Lyndon Johnson and the American Dream.* New York: Signet.

Kemp, Jeff, Dawn Wilson, and Mindy Lincicome. 2001. *Teen Relationships Study:*

TeenTalk on Parents, Marriage, and Sex. Washington: Families Northwest. http://www.familiesnorthwest.org/pdf/reports/2001teen.pdf (accessed May 16, 2005).

Kemper, Theodore D. 1987. "How Many Emotions Are There? Wedding the Social and Automatic Components." *American Journal of Sociology* 887:336–61.

Kestin van den Hoonaard, Deborah. 2001. *The Widowed Self: The Older Woman's Journey through Widowhood.* Waterloo, Ontario: Wilfred Laurier University Press.

King, Jessica. 2003. "Americans Tend to Know Little." *Northern Star.* http://www .star.niu.edu/forum/articles/012803-americans.asp (accessed September 18, 2003).

Klebnikov, Peter. 1997. "Time of Troubles." *Newsweek,* April 7, 48.

Klein, Janice. 1994. "The Paradox of Quality Management." In *The Post-Bureaucratic Organization: New Perspectives on Organizational Change,* ed. C. Heckscher and A. Donnellon. Thousand Oaks, Calif.: Sage.

Knox, Robert E., and James A. Inkster. 1968. "Postdecision Dissonance at Post Time." *Journal of Personality and Social Psychology* 8, no. 4:319–23.

Kuhn, Thomas. 1970. *The Structure of Scientific Revolutions.* Chicago: University of Chicago Press.

Kushner, Harold S. 1981. *When Bad Things Happen to Good People.* New York: Avon.

Kuttner, Robert. 1997. "Why Clinton's 'Fast Track' Loss is a Win." *Washington Post,* November 16, C1.

Ladouceur, Robert. 1994. "The Psychology of Gambling: Fundamental and Clinical Aspects." *Society and Leisure* 17, no. 1:213–31.

LaDoux, Joseph. 1996. *The Emotional Brain: The Mysterious Underpinnings of Emotional Life.* New York: Simon and Schuster.

Laird, Charlton, and Michael Agnes, eds. 1999. *Roget's A–Z Thesaurus.* New York: Macmillan

Lamb, Robert D. 1999. "The Depression: A Look Back." *USA Today,* November 4, C1.

Lambro, Donald. 1993. "There Were Plenty of Winners, Losers in Bitterly Contested NAFTA Battle." *Atlanta Constitution,* November 22, A11.

Lampo, David. 2001. "The 'Million Mom' Posse." *National Review,* May 11. http:// www.national review.com/comment/comment-lampo051101.shtml (accessed June 1, 2001).

Langer, Gary. 1999. "Public Shows Little Y2K Fear." ABC News. http://www .abcnews.go.com/sections/politics/Daily/News/poll991220.html (accessed July 5, 2002).

Langhinrichsen-Rohling, Jennifer, and Dina Vivian. 1994. "The Correlates of Spouses' Incongruent Reports of Marital Aggression." *Journal of Family Violence* 9:265–83.

Larsen, Jeff T., A. Peter McGraw, John T. Cacioppo. 2001. "Can People Feel Happy and Sad at the Same Time." *Journal of Personal and Social Psychology* 81, no. 4:684–96.

Latane, Bibb, and John Darley. 1968. "Group Inhibition of Bystander Intervention in Emergencies." *Journal of Personality and Social Psychology* 10:215–21.

Lavine, Mark. 2005. "Warnings of Disaster Were Ignored, Funding Was Slashed." *Gulf Times*, September 3. http://www.gulf-times.com/site/topics/article.asp ?cu_no=2&item_no=51205&version=1&template_id43&parent_id=19 (accessed November 9 2005).

Lawler, Edward E. III, Susan A. Mohrman, and Gerald E. Ledford Jr. 1996. *Creating High Performance Organizations: Practices and Results of Employee Involvement and Total Quality Management in Fortune 1000 Companies*. San Francisco: Jossey-Bass.

Layne, Ken. 1998. "Art Bell's Terrible Secret." http://www.tabloid.net/layne/53/ (accessed July 28, 2003).

Lears, Jackson. 2003. *Something for Nothing: Luck in America*. New York: Viking.

Leland, John. 2004. "Why America Sees the Silver Lining." Week in Review. *New York Times*, June 13, 1.

Lesnoff-Caravaglia, Gari. 1984. "Widowhood: The Last Stage in Wifedom." *The World of the Older Woman*, ed. G. Lesnoff-Caravaglia, 137–43. New York: Human Sciences Press.

Lewis, Orlando. 1967. *The Development of American Prisons and Prison Customs, 1776–1845*. Albany: Prison Association of New York. (Originally published 1922.)

Lichtblau, Eric. 2005. "9/11 Report Cites Many Warnings about Hijackings" *New York Times*, February 10, A4.

Light, Donald W. 2000. "The Medical Profession and Organizational Change: From Professional Dominance to Countervailing Power." *The Handbook of Medical Sociology*, 5th ed., ed. C. Bird, P. Conrad, and A. Fremont, 201–16. Upper Saddle River, N.J.: Prentice Hall.

Litwak, Robert S. 2000a. "A Look At . . . Rogue States." *Washington Post*, February 20, B3.

———. 2000b. *Rogue States and U.S. Foreign Policy*. Baltimore: Johns Hopkins University Press.

Lively, Kathryn J., and David R. Heise. 2004. "Sociological Realms of Emotional Experience." *American Journal of Sociology* 109, no. 5:1109–36.

Livingston, Jay. 1996. *Crime and Criminology*. Upper Saddle River, N.J.: Prentice Hall.

Lombardi, Frank. 2000. "Rudy Won't Let City Go to Pot Smokers." *New York Daily News*, November 15, 28.

Lopata, Helena Znaniecka. 1996. *Current Widowhood: Myths and Realities*. Thousand Oaks, Calif.: Sage.

Los Angeles Times. 1998. "Police Shadowing Casino Slaying Figure." September 20. Metro Desk, 38.

———. 2001. "NASDAQ Dives to 3rd Worst Monthly Loss: Some Analysts Say Bottom Still To Come." March 1, Business section, C4.

Louis, Arthur M. 1999. "Up, Up and Away." *Business*, December 7, D1.

Lozano, Juan A. 2003. "Echoes of Challenger Explosion in Columbia Accident, Says Sociologist." *Newsday*, April 24.

Lykken, D. T. 1997. "The American Crime Factory." *Psychological Inquiry* 8:261–70.

Maas, A. J. 1999. "Lucifer." In *The Catholic Encyclopedia*, vol. 9. http://www
.newadvent.org/cathen/09410a.htm (accessed February 8, 2002).

MacDonald, Tara K., and Ross, Michael. 1999. "Assessing the Accuracy of Predictions about Dating Relationships: How and Why Do Lovers' Predictions Differ
from Those Made by Observers?" *Personality and Social Psychology Bulletin* 25,
no. 11:1417–29.

MADD. 2005. "New Survey: Teens Report Pressure to Engage in High-Risk Behaviors on Prom and Graduation Nights, Impacting Driving Safety." http://www
.madd.org/news/0,1056,9731,00.html (accessed May 18, 2005).

Maier, Thomas. 2001. "A Group in Danger: Hispanic Immigrants Face Greatest
Workplace Risk." *Newsday.* http://www.newsday.com/news/ny-work-hisp725
.story (accessed July 8, 2003).

Malcolm X. 1964. *The Autobiography of Malcolm X.* With the assistance of Alex
Haley. New York: Grove Press.

Maniona, Mark, and William M. Evan. 2000. "The Y2K Problem and Professional
Responsibility: A Retrospective Analysis." *Technology and Society* 22, no.
3:361–87.

Manley, Joan E. 2000. "Negotiating Quality: Total Quality Management and the
Complexities of Transforming Professional Organizations." *Sociological Forum*
15, no. 3:457–84.

Mannheim, Karl. 1936. *Ideology and Utopia.* New York: Harcourt Brace Jovanovich.

Manning, Stephen. 2001. "Prosecutors in K-9 Biting Case Say They Broke the 'Blue
Wall of Silence.'" Associated Press Wire Service report, *Maryland Daily Record,*
March 13. http://www.mddailyrecord.com/pub/l_212law/localnews/29080-1
.html (accessed November 11, 2005).

March, James G., and Herbert A. Simon. 1958. *Organizations.* New York: Wiley.

Marignoni-Hutin, Jean-Pierre G. 1994. "The Gambling Adventure." *Society and
Leisure* 17, no. 1:125–42.

Martin, John. 2002. "Power, Authority, and the Constraint of Belief Systems." *American Journal of Sociology* 107, no. 4:861–904.

Marullo, Shannon. 2004. "Teens: Pregnancy, STDS, Problems among Peers." Gallup
Organization. http://www.gallup.com/content/default.aspx?ci=11494 (accessed
April 27, 2004).

Massey, Douglas S. 2002. "A Brief History of Human Society: The Origin and Role
of Emotion in Social Life." *American Sociological Review* 67, no. 1:1–29.

May, Sean. 2003. "On His Ankle." Interview on the official University of North
Carolina Athletics Web site. http://www.tarheelblue.ocsn.com/sports/m-baskbl/
recaps/032603.aab.html (accessed July 1, 2003).

Mayer, John D., and Ellen Hanson. 1995. "Mood-Congruent Judgment over Time."
Personality and Social Psychology Bulletin 21:237–44.

Mazumder, Bhashkar. 2001. *Earnings Mobility in the U.S.: A New Look at Intergenerational Inequality.* Chicago: Federal Reserve Bank of Chicago.

McCann, Vincent. 2001. "Mormonism and the Sin of Murder: Is Murder Unforgivable?" Spotlight Ministries Web site. http://spotlightministries.org.uk/murder.htm (accessed November 12, 2005).

McCauley, Clark. 1989. "The Nature of Social Influence in Groupthink: Compliance and Internalization." *Journal of Personality and Social Psychology* 57:250–60.

McDonald, Allan. 1986. "Currents: Current Profile." *U.S. News and World Report,* March 10, 10.

McGarity, Thomas O., and Sidney Shapiro. 1993. *Workers at Risk: The Failed Promises of the Occupational Safety and Health Administration.* Westport, Conn.: Praeger Publishers.

McGraw, Phillip C. 2001. *Self Matters: Creating Your Life from the Inside Out.* New York: Simon and Schuster.

McKinlay, John. 1999. "The End of the Golden Age of Doctoring." *New England Research Institute's Newsletter* 1 (summer): 3.

McLaughlin, Iris G., Kenneth E. Leonard, and Marilyn Senchak. 1992. "Prevalence and Distribution of Premarital Aggression among Couples Applying for a Marriage License." *Journal of Family Violence* 7:309–19.

Mclynn, Frank. 1998. "The Ancient Historians Are Hopelessly Unreliable When It Comes to Numbers." *Herald* (Glasgow), May 30, 15.

McMurrer, Daniel P., Mark Condon, and Isabel V. Sawhill. 1997. "Intergenerational Mobility in the United States." Report by the Urban Institute. http:///www .urban.org/urlprint.cfm?ID=6177 (accessed May 5, 2003).

McNurlin and Sprague. 1996. *Information Systems Management in Practice.* Upper Saddle River, N.J.: Prentice Hall.

McQuaid, John, and Mark Schleifstein. 2002. "Evolving Danger." *Times-Picayune,* June 23 J12.

Medin, Douglas L., and Robert L. Goldstone. 1994. "Concepts." In *The Blackwell Dictionary of Cognitive Psychology,* ed. M. W. Eysenck. Cambridge, Mass.: Blackwell.

Media Awareness Network. 1997. "National Television Violence Study: Year Three." http://www.media-awareness.ca/english/resources/research_documents/reports/violence/na.htm (accessed July 25, 2003).

Media Watch. 1996. "Vatican 'Blesses' Contact with the Dead." Report posted at Australian Skeptics. http://www.skeptics.com.au/features/weird/media/mw-bless.htm (accessed February 16, 1999).

Meeks, Brock N. 2004. "9/11 Panel's Report Critical of FAA." MSNBC report, January 27. http://www.msnbc.msn.com/id/4062733 (accessed February 25, 2005).

Meltz, Barbara F. 2003. "Child-Caring: Legislation Would Target Violence in Video Games." *The Boston Globe* (May 22) H1.

Merleau-Ponty, Maurice. 1962. *Phenomenology of Perception.* Trans. C. Smith. London: Routledge and Kegan Paul.

Meyer, John W., John Boli, George M. Thomas, and Francisco O. Ramirez. 1997. "World Society and the Nation State." *American Journal of Sociology* 103, no. 1:144–81.

Miles, Raymond E., and Charles C. Snow. 1994. *Fit, Failure, and the Hall of Fame: How Companies Succeed or Fail.* New York: Free Press.

Mishra, Shiraz I., and Seth A. Serzner. 1994. "It Won't Happen to Me: Perceived Risk and Concern about Contracting AIDS." *Health Values* 18, no. 6:3–13.

Misrahi, James J., Joseph A. Foster, Frederic E. Shaw, and Martin S. Cetron. 2004. "HHS/CDC Legal Response to SARS Outbreak." *Emergency Infectious Disease* 10, no. 2:1–6. http://www.cdc.gov/incidod/EID/Vol10no2/03-0721.htm (accessed January 10, 2004).

Mohan, Geoffrey. 1998. "NAFTA's Impact: 5 Years Later Many Debate the Pact's Effectiveness." *Newsday,* December 29, A4.

Mohr, John W. 1998. "Measuring Meaning Structures." *Annual Review of Sociology* 24:345–70.

Money. 2000. "Stock Pros Share Picks for Prosperous New Year." January 3, 3B.

Moniz, Paul. 2002. "Overweight Americans: More Now Than Ever." CBS News report, January 31. http://www.cbsnews.com/stories/2002/01/31/health/main326811.shtml (accessed May 18, 2005).

Moorhead, Gregory, Richard Ference, and Christopher P. Neck. 1991. "Group Decision Fiascos Continue: Space Shuttle Challenger and a Revised Groupthink Framework." *Human Relations* 39:399–410.

Morgan, Robin, ed. 1970. *Sisterhood Is Powerful An Anthology of Writings from the Women's Liberation Movement.* New York: Vintage. (Originally published 1967.)

Morgan, Cyril P., and John D. Aram. 1975. "The Preponderance of Arguments in the Risky Shift Phenomenon."" *Journal of Experimental Social Psychology* 11:25–34.

Mosby's Medical, Nursing, and Allied Health Dictionary. 2002. 6th ed. St. Louis: Mosby.

Mr. Showbiz. 2000. "Razzies Name Hollywood's Worst." http://abcnews.go.com/enetrtainment/DailyNews/razzies000327.html (accessed February 28, 2001).

Mumford, Lewis. 1941. *The Story of Utopias.* New York: Peter Smith. (Originally published 1922.)

Murkoff, Heidi, Arlene Eisenberg, and Sandee Hathaway. 2002. *What To Expect When You're Expecting.* New York: Workman Publishing.

National Center for Health Statistics. 2000. *Health, United States, 2000.* With Adolescent Health Chartbook. Hyattsville, Md.: U.S. Department of Health and Human Services.

———. 2002. "Data Warehouse on Trends in Health and Aging." http://www.cdc.gov/nchs/agingact.htm (accessed July 9, 2003).

National Center for Policy Analysis. 2002. "Daily Policy Digest: Health Issues/Policy Issues." *Dallas Morning News,* October 28. http://www.dallasnews.com/shared content/dallas/healthscience/stories/102802dnlivlivfrisk.c448.html (accessed June 18, 2003).

National Comprehensive Cancer Network. 1999. "Breast Cancer Stages." http://www.nccn.org/patient_guidelines/breast_cancer/breast/Page3.htm (accessed May 2, 2001).

National Gambling Impact Study Commission. 1999. http://www.ngisc.org/ (accessed July 1, 2003).

National Institute for Occupational Safety and Health (NIOSH). 2003. "Massachusetts Report Calls for Improved Occupational Safety for Young Workers." Health and Human Development News report, January 2003. http://hhd.org/hhdnews/hhdstories/fs_01_2003.asp (accessed July 7, 2003).

National Science Foundation. 1999. "Updated Poll Finds Americans' Fear of Possible "Y2K" Problems Falls as Awareness Level Rises." http://www.nsf.gov/od/pa/events/fow/y2k/pr_sp992.htm (access July 5, 2002).

National Sleep Foundation. 2000. "Nearly One in Five Drivers Dozed Off at the Wheel Last Year." http://www.sleepfoundation.org/pressarchives/drowsy.html (accessed August 15, 2002).

———. 2005. "Facts and Stats." http://www.sleepfoundation.org/hottopics/index.php?secid=10&id=226 (accessed May 18, 2005).

Newport, Frank. 2005. "Consumer Views on Economy Show Little Change as September Ends." Gallup Organization. http://poll.gallup.com/content/default.aspx?ci=18919 (accessed November 2, 2005).

New York Times. 2001. "Catholic Church Reports Alleged Cases of Sexual Abuse of Nuns by Priests." March 21, A7.

———. 2002. "9 Hijackers Scrutinized." March 3, A1.

Newsday. 1999. "When Cops Go Bad." Viewpoints. June 10, A52.

———. 2000a. "City Power: Give Cops and Civilians a New Hearing." Viewpoints. February 22, A39.

———. 2000b. "Verdict Shows Good Cops Mustn't Cover for Bad Ones." Viewpoints. March 9, A46.

Norris, Floyd. 2003. "Betting on Terror: What Markets Can Reveal." Week in Review. New York Times, August 3, 5.

Oates, Caroline. 1989. "Metamorphosis and Lycanthropy in Franche-Comté, 1521–1643." Zone 3: Fragments for a History of the Human Body, ed. I. M. Feher, with R. Naddaff and N. Tazi, 304–63. New York: Urzone.

O'Donnell, Jayne. 2003. "U.S. Pushes for Wider Seatbelt Use." USA Today, May 19. http://www.usatoday.com/money/autos/2003-05-19-belts_x.htm (accessed on June 23, 2003).

Olick, Jeffrey K., and Joyce Robbins. 1998. "Social Memory Studies: From 'Collective Memory' to the Historical Sociology of Mnemonic Practices." Annual Review of Sociology 24:105–40.

Oregon Consumer and Business Services. 2001. "Research Alert." http://www.cbs.state.or.us/external/imd/rasums/wcresults/wcresults.html (accessed August 29, 2002).

Oreskes, Michael. 2004. "Where Does the Buck Stop? Not Here." Week in Review. New York Times, March 28, 1.

Orr, J. Scott. 2003. "Report Says Miscues Let 9/11 Happen." Star Ledger (Newark), July 25, A1.

Out, Jennifer W., and K. D. Lafreniere. 2001. "Baby Think It Over®: Using Role Play to Prevent Pregnancy." *Adolescence* 36, no. 143:571–82.

Page, Susan. 1990. "Bush: Hussein Is a Hitler." *Newsday,* October 16, 4.

Pang, Xinghuo, Zonghan Zhu, Fujie Xu, JiYong Guo, Xiaohong Gong, Donglei Liu, Zejun Liu, and Daniel P. Chin. 2003. "Evaluation of Control Measures Implemented in the Severe Acute Respiratory Syndrome Outbreak in Beijing, 2003." *JAMA* 290:3215–21.

Papineau, Elisabeth. 2001. "Pathological Gambling in the Chinese Community: An Anthropological Viewpoint." *Society and Leisure* 24, no. 2:557–82.

Parker, Kathleen. 2000. "Bag Lady: Clean Sweeps Offer No Shelter for Homeless." *Orlando Sentinel,* October 30, 11A.

Parsons, Talcott, and Renee Fox. 1952. "Illness, Therapy, and the Modern Urban American Family." *Journal of Social Issues* 8:31–44.

Pechmann, Cornelia. 2002. "Changing Adolescent Smoking Prevalence: Impact of Advertising Interventions." In *Changing Adolescent Smoking Prevalence.* Smoking and Tobacco Control Monograph 14. Division of Cancer Control and Population Sciences, National Cancer Institute, National Institutes of Health. http://dccps.nci.nih.gov/dccps/tcrb/monographs/14/14_10.pdf (accessed November 12, 2005).

Pediatrics. 2002. "Teens Ignore Skin Cancer Risk." *Pediatrics* 109:1009–14.

Perrow, Charles. 1999. *Normal Accidents: Living with High Risk Technology.* Princeton: Princeton University Press. (Originally published 1984.)

Pesticide Education Program. 2001. "PEP-Talk, November 2001." Ohio State University. http://www.osu.edu/pep-talk/pepv5i9.htm (accessed July 7, 2003).

Pfenninger, John L., and Grant C. Fowler, eds. 2003. *Procedures for Primary Care.* 2nd ed. Philadelphia: Mosby.

Pickersgill, Howard. 1979. *The Impressionists.* Secaucus, N.J.: Chartwell Books.

Pike, Kenneth. 1967. *Language in Relation to a Unified Theory of the Structure of Human Behavior.* The Hague: Mouton.

Piven, Joshua, and David Borgenicht. 1999. *The Worst-Case Scenario Survival Handbook.* San Francisco: Chronicle Books.

Popham, W. James. 1997. What's Wrong—and What's Right—with Rubrics." *Educational Leadership* 55, no. 2:72–80.

Presbyterian Church of the United States of America. 1998. *Belonging to God: A First Catechism.* http://www.pcusa.org.theologyandworship/confession/firstcatechism.htm (accessed November 12, 2005).

Presidential Commission on the Space Shuttle *Challenger* Accident. 1986. *Summary Report.* http://science.ksc.nasa.gov/shuttle/missi . . . 51-1/docs/rogers-commission/ (accessed February 18, 2004).

Pribram, Karl H. 1986. "The Cognitive Revolution and Mind/Brain Issues." *American Psychologist* 41:507–20.

Quah, Stella R., and Lee Hin-Peng. 2004. "Crisis Prevention and Management during SARS Outbreak, Singapore." *Emerging Infectious Diseases* 10 (February): 2.

Available from the Web site of the Centers for Disease Control, http://www.cdc
.gov/ncidod/eid/vol10no2/03-0418.htm (accessed November 12, 2005).

Quarantelli, Enrico L. 2001a. "Another Selective Look at Future Social Crises: Some
Aspects of Which We Can Already See in the Present." *Journal of Contingencies
and Crises Management* 9, no. 4:233–37.

———. 2001b. "Sociology of Panic." In the *International Encyclopedia of the Social
Sciences.* Oxford: Pergamon Press.

Rachlin, Howard, Eric Siegel, and David Cross. 1994. "Lotteries and the Time Horizon." *Psychological Science* 5, no. 6:390–93.

Ragavan, Chitra, Christopher H. Schmitt, Sheila Thalhimer, and Monica Ekman.
2003. "Mueller's Mandate." *U.S. News and World Report* 134, no. 18:18–22.

Raghubir, Priya, and Geeta Menon. 1998. "AIDS and Me, Never the Twain Shall
Meet: The Effects of Information Accessibility on Judgments of Risk and Advertising Effectiveness." *Journal of Consumer Research* 25, no. 1:52–63.

Ralph, Regan E. 2000. "Jordanian Parliament Supports Impunity For Honor
Killings." Human Rights Watch report, January 27. http://www.hrw.org/press/
2000/01/jordo127.htm (accessed November 12, 2005).

Regan, Tara. 2004. "Happiness." *Public Affairs Market Research—Time* poll. http://
srbi.com/timepoll_arc11.html (accessed May 16, 2005).

Reich, Robert B. 2001. "American Optimism and Consumer Confidence." *American
Prospect,* September 18. http://www.prospect.org/webfeatures/2001/09/
reich-r-09-18.html (accessed February 8, 2002).

Reilly, Thomas A. K. 1999. "Moses." In *The Catholic Encyclopedia,* vol. 9.
http://www.newadvent.org/cathen/10596a.htm (accessed February 8, 2002).

Reiman, Jeffrey. 2004. *The Rich Get Rich and the Poor Get Prison: Ideology, Class,
and Criminal Justice.* 7th ed. Boston: Allyn and Bacon.

Reinhold, Robert. 1986. "Astronaut's Chief Says NASA Risked Life for Schedule:
'Awesome' List of Flaws." *New York Times,* March 9, A1.

Reisberg, Daniel. 2001. *Cognition: Exploring the Science of the Mind.* 2nd ed. New
York: W. W. Norton.

Reuters. 1984. "Castro Says U.S. Seeks to Erase Communism." *New York Times,*
October 30, A5.

———. 1986. "Reagan More Dangerous Than Adolf Hitler Castro Says." *Toronto
Star News,* April 20, A15.

Ribadeneira, Diego. 1998. "Cardinal Announces Defrocking of Priest: Retired Cleric
Faces Molestation Charges." *Boston Globe,* June 7, Metro/Region section, A1.

Risen, James, and David Johnston. 2002. "Not Much Has Changed in a System That
Failed." *New York Times,* September 8, sec. 4, p. 1.

Ritzer, George, and David Walczak. 1988. "Rationalization and the Deprofessional-
ization of Physicians." *Social Forces* 67, no. 1:1–22.

Robbins, Lawrence, and Susan S. Lang. 1995. *Headache Help.* Boston: Houghton
Mifflin.

Robinson, Bryan. 1999. "Volpe Receives 30-Year Sentence for Sodomy in Louima

Brutality Case." Archived *Court TV* report, December 13. http://www.courttv
.com/archive/national/louima/121399_volpe_sentence_ctv.html (accessed
November 12,2005).

Robinson, David. 1999. "Bull Market Has Plenty of Room to Run, Salomon Strategist Predicts." *Business,* November 3, 1C.

Robinson, Joe. 2003. *Work to Live: The Guide to Getting a Life.* New York: Perigee.

Rochester Institute of Technology. 1998. "Method for Achieving Y2K Compliance."
http://www.rit.edu/y2k/methodology.html (accessed January 13, 2004).

Rodgers, Walter. 1995. "Honor Killings: A Brutal Tribal Custom." CNN World
News report, December 7. http://www2.cnn.com/WORLD/9512/honor_killings/
(accessed May 9, 2001).

Rogers, Everett. 1972. *The Diffusion of Innovation.* New York: Free Press.

Rosch, Eleanor. 1973. "On the Internal Structure of Perceptual and Semantic Categories." *Cognitive Development and the Acquisition of Language,* ed. T. E.
Moore, 111–44. New York: Academic Press.

Rosenbaum, Ernest H., and Isadore R. Rosenbaum. 2002. "Life and Death Instructions." Cancer Supportive Care Programs. http://www.cancersupportivecare
.com/end.html (accessed November 12, 2005).

Rosenhan, David L. 1973. "Being Sane in Insane Places." *Science* 179:250–58.

Rosin, Hanna. 2002. "9-11 Changed Everything, for a Little While." *Washington
Post,* March 19, Style section, C1.

Ross, Kelly L. 1998. "The Caste System and Stages of Life in Hinduism." *Proceedings of the Friesian School.* http://www.friesian.com/caste.htm (accessed
November 12, 2005).

Ross, Michael, and Ian R. Newby-Clark. 1998. "Construing the Past and Future."
Social Cognition 16, no. 1:133–50.

Rothman, David. 1971. *The Discovery of the Asylum: Social Order and Disorder in
the New Republic.* Boston: Little Brown.

———. 1980. *Conscience and Convenience: The Asylum and Its Alternatives in
Progressive America.* Boston: Little Brown.

Rothstein, Mark A., M. Gabriela Alcade, Nanette R. Elster, Mary A. Majumder,
Larry I. Palmer, T. Howard Stone, and Richard E. Hoffman. 2003. "Quarantine
and Isolation: Lessons Learned from SARS." Institute for Bioethics, Health Policy and Law, University of Louisville School of Medicine. http://www.louisville
.edu/medschool/ibhpl/publications/SARS%20REPORT.pdf (accessed January 21,
2004).

Ruane, Janet M. 2004. *Essentials of Research Methods.* Boston: Blackwell.

Ruane, Janet M., and Karen A. Cerulo. 2004. *Second Thoughts: Seeing Conventional
Wisdom through the Sociological Eye.* 3rd ed. Thousand Oaks, Calif.: Pine
Forge/Sage.

Ruggi, Suzanne. 1998. "Honor Killings in Palestine." Middle East Research and
Information Project. http://www.merip.org/mer/mer206/ruggi.htm (accessed
November 12, 2005).

Rushton, Cynda Hylton. 2000. "Pediatric Palliative Care: Coming of Age." *Innovations in End-of-Life Care* 2, no. 2:16–20. Report archived at the Education and Development Center, http://www2.edc.org/lastacts/archives/archivesMarch00/editorial.asp (accessed April 30, 2003).

Ryan, Perry T. 1992. *The Last Public Execution in America.* Full text posted at Geocities, http://www.geocities.com/lastpublichang/ (accessed July 28, 2004).

Sagan, Scott D. 1993. *The Limits of Safety: Organizations, Accidents, and Nuclear Weapons.* Princeton: Princeton University Press.

St. Louis Dispatch. 1990. "Sexual Misconduct Called Church 'Watergate.'" *Everyday,* August 11, 6D.

Salsburg, David. 2001. *The Lady Tasting Tea: How Statistics Revolutionized Science in the Twentieth Century.* New York: W. H. Freeman.

Salter, Anna C. 2003a. *Predators: Pedophiles, Rapists, and Other Sex Offenders — Who They Are, How They Operate, and How We Can Protect Ourselves and Our Children.* New York: Basic Books.

———. 2003b. "Protecting Your Kids and Yourself from Sexual Predators." MSNBC News. http://www.msnbs.com/news/907781.asp?cp1=1 (accessed May 8, 2003).

Sanger, David E. 1986. "Record Shows NASA Aide Told of Doubt on Seals." *New York Times,* August 7, A23.

Savage, Terry. 1999. "Stock Market Brings Out Predictions from Bull, Bear." *Chicago Sun Times,* August 8, Financial section, 53.

Schachter, Daniel L., and John F. Kihlstrom. 1989. "Functional Amnesia." *Handbook of Neuropsychology,* ed. F. Boller and J. Grafman, 3:209–30. New York: Elsevier.

Schaer, Roland, Gregory Claeys, and Lyman Tower Sargent, eds. 2000. *Utopia: The Search for the Ideal Society in the Western World.* New York: Oxford University Press.

Scheer, Robert. 2005. "What We Don't Know About 9/11 Hurts Us." *Los Angeles Times,* February 15, B15.

Schiliro, Lewis D. 2001. Interview on *Frontline,* November 14. http://www.pbs.org/wgbh/pages/frontline/shows/network/should/schiliro.html (accessed January 21, 2002).

Schmitt, Barton D. 1991. *Your Child's Health.* New York: Bantam.

Schottman, Robert W., David F. Baker, and Fred M. Crawford. 1999. "Electrical Safety for Center Pivot Irrigation Systems." G1695. Missouri-Columbia: University of Missouri.

Schramm, Tim. 2000. "The Holidays are a Time of Celebration at Work and at Home . . . and a Cause of Concern on the Nation's Highways." Driving survey by Progressive Insurance. http://www.progressive.com/newsroom/srvy_holiday00.asp (accessed August 15, 2002).

Schuller, Robert H. 1969. *Self-Love: The Dynamic Force of Success.* Old Tappan, N.J.: Spire Books.

Schutz, Alfred. 1964. "Making Music Together: A Study in Social Relationships." *Social Research* 18:76–97.

———. 1967. *The Phenomenology of the Social World.* Evanston, Ill.: Northwestern University Press. (Originally published 1932).

———. 1973. "On Multiple Realities." In *Collected Papers,* vol. 1, *The Problem of Social Reality.* The Hague: Martinus Nijhoff. (Originally published 1945.)

Schwartz, Barry. 1987. *George Washington: The Making of an American Symbol.* Chicago: University of Chicago Press.

———. 1997. "Collective Memory and History: How Abraham Lincoln Became a Symbol Of Racial Equality." *Sociological Quarterly* 38, no. 3:469–96.

Schwartz, John, and Matthew L. Wald. 2003a. "Echoes of *Challenger:* Shuttle Panel Considers Longstanding Flaws in NASA's System." *New York Times,* April 13, A27.

———. 2003b. "Groupthink Is 30 Years Old and Still Going Strong." *New York Times,* March 9, sec. 4, p. 5.

Schwartz, Pepper. 1999. "Quality of Life in the Coming Decades." *Society* 36, no. 2:55–59.

Scott, W. Richard. 2003. *Organizations: Rational, Natural, and Open Systems.* 5th ed. Upper Saddle River, N.J.: Prentice Hall.

Sears, William, and Martha Sears. 1994. *The Birth Book.* Boston: Little Brown.

———. 2003. *The Baby Book.* Boston: Little Brown.

Seligman, Martin E. P. 2003. "Positive Psychology: Fundamental Assumptions." *Psychologist* 16, no. 3:126–27.

Seligman, Martin E. P., and Mihaly Csikszentmihalyi. 2000. "Positive Psychology: An Introduction." *American Psychologist* 55, no. 1:5–14.

Sepkowitz, Kent. A. 2002. "The Antidote Is Still Whispered." Week in Review. *New York Times,* July 7, 5.

Shapiro, Sidney. 1999. "Occupational Safety and Health Regulations." *Encyclopedia of Law and Economics.* http://encyclo.findlaw.com/5540book.pdf (accessed July 7, 2003).

Shaw, David. 2003. "The More Pernicious Bias is Less Substance, More Fluff." *Los Angeles Times,* January 19, sec. 5, p. 37.

Shelov, Steven P., and Robert E. Hannemann. 1998. *The Complete and Authoritative Guide: Caring for Your Young Child, Birth to Age 5.* New York: Bantam.

Shepard, Aaron. 1995. *The Enchanted Stork.* New York: Clarion.

Shiller, Robert J. 2005. *Irrational Exuberance.* 2nd ed. Princeton: Princeton University Press.

Shrader-Frechette, Kristin. 1993. "Risk Methodology and Institutional Bias." *Research in Social Problems and Public Policy* 5, no. 207–23.

Siegel, Bernie S. 1998. *Prescriptions for Living.* New York: Harper Collins.

Silon, Betty. 1993. "Dissociation: A Symptom of Incest." *Individual Psychology: Journal of Adlerian Theory, Research and Practice* 48, no. 2:155–64.

Simkin, Penny, Janet Whalley, and Ann Keppler. 2001. *Pregnancy, Childbirth, and the Newborn: The Complete Guide.* New York: Simon and Schuster.

Simkins, Michael. 1999. "Designing Great Rubrics." *Technology and Learning* 20, no. 1:23–31.

Simon, Neil. 2002. *The Dinner Party.* New York: Samuel French.

Simpson, Jeffrey A., Bruce Campbell, and Ellen Berscheid. 1986. "The Association between Romantic Love and Marriage: Kephart (1967) Twice Revisited." *Personality and Social Psychology Bulletin* 12 (September): 363–372.

Sims, Henry P. Jr., and Charles C. Manz. 1982. "Conversations within Self-Managed Work Groups." *National Productivity Review,* summer, 261–69.

Sirgy, M. Joseph. 1998. "Materialism and Quality of Life." *Social Indicators Research* 43, no. 3:227–60.

Slovic, Paul. 2000. *The Perception of Risk.* London: Earthscan.

Smith, Brad. 2000. "Crackdowns Spread: New York on 'Meanest Streets' List." *Tampa Tribune,* October 29, Nation/World section, 6.

Smith, Hedrick. 2002a. "Reporter's Notebook." From "Inside the Terror Network," a *Frontline* report, January 17. http://www.pbs.org/wgbh/pages/frontline/shows/network/etc/notebook.html (accessed January 21, 2002).

———. 2002b. "Should We Have Spotted the Conspiracy?" From "Inside the Terror Network," a *Frontline* report, January 17. http://www.pbs.org/wgbh/pages/frontline/shows/network/should/shouldwe.html (accessed January 21, 2002).

Snow, David, and Leon Anderson. 1993. *Down on Their Luck: A Study of Homeless Street People.* Berkeley and Los Angeles: University of California Press.

Solanis, Valerie. 1970. "Excerpts from the SCUM (Society for the Cutting Up of Men) Manifesto." In *Sisterhood Is Powerful: An Anthology of Writings from the Women's Liberation Movement,* ed. R. Morgan, 577–83. New York: Vintage. (Originally published 1967.)

Solomon, John. 2001. "CIA Cited Growing Risk of Attack." Associated Press report, October 4. Yahoo News. http://dailynews.yahoo.com/h/ap/20011004/us/attacks_investigation.html (accessed October 4, 2001).

Solso, Robert L. 1998. *Cognitive Psychology.* 5th ed. Boston: Allyn and Bacon.

———. 2005. *Cognitive Psychology.* 7th ed. Boston: Allyn and Bacon.

Solso, Robert L., and Dominick W. Massaro, eds. 1995. *The Science of the Mind: 2001 and Beyond.* New York: Oxford.

Sophocles. 1973. *Oedipus Rex.* Trans. D. Fitts and R. Fitzgerald. In *Literature,* ed. J. B. Hogins, 645–91. Chicago: Science Research Associates. (Originally published 1949.)

Sotirios. 2000. "Eternal Life and Eternal Hell." *Orthodox Catechism,* published by the Greek Orthodox Metropolis of Toronto. http://www.gocanada.org/Catechism/catech.htm (accessed November 12, 2005).

Spock, Benjamin, and Steven J. Parker. 1998. *Dr. Spock's Baby and Child Care.* 7th ed. New York: Pocket Books.

Staples, William G. 1991. *Castles of Our Conscience: Social Control and the American State, 1800–1985.* New Brunswick: Rutgers University Press.

———. 1997. *The Culture of Surveillance: Discipline and Social Control in the United States.* New York: St. Martin's Press.

Stedman's Medical Dictionary. 2000. 27th ed. Baltimore: Lippincott Williams and Wilkins.

Steele, David N., and Curtis C. Thomas. 1989. *The Five Points of Calvinism: Defined, Defended, and Documented.* Nashua, N.H.: P&R Press.

Steger, Sabrina. 2000. Testimony before the U.S. Senate Commerce Committee, March 21. http://www.senate.gov/members/ks/browback/general/FinalDocs/MediaViolence/000321ste.pdf (accessed July 28, 2004).

Steinmetz, Suzanne K. 1977. *The Cycle of Violence: Assertive, Aggressive, and Abusive Family Interaction.* New York: Praeger Publishers.

Stone, M. David, and Alfred Poor. 2001. "Troubleshooting Your PC." Redmond, Wash.: Microsoft Press.

Stoner, James A. F. 1961. "A Comparison of Individual and Group Decisions Involving Risk." Master's thesis, MIT, Cambridge.

Stout, David. 2002. "9 Hijackers Drew Scrutiny on Sept. 11, Officials Say." *New York Times*, March 3, International section, 20.

Strahley, David. 2002. "Welcome to the Straight Talk Program." Dr. Strahley's medical Web site. http://drstrahley.com/prevention_teens.htm (accessed April 30, 2003).

Substance Abuse and Mental Heath Services Administration. 2001. *National Household Survey on Drug Abuse.* http://www.samhsa.gov/oas/NHSDA/2k1NHSDA/vol1/Chpter3.htm (accessed June 28, 2003).

Sutherland, Edwin H., and Donald R. Cressey. 1974. *Criminology.* 9th ed. Philadelphia: J. B. Lippincott.

Swidler, Ann. 1984. "Culture in Action." *American Sociological Review* 51, no. 2:273–86.

———. 2001. *Talk of Love: How Culture Matters.* Chicago: University of Chicago Press.

Swift, E. M. 2001. "Blind Ambition." SI Adventure. *Sports Illustrated*, April 23. http://sportsillustrated.cnn.com/features/siadventure/2001/blind_ambition/ (accessed October 4, 2001).

Szinovacz, Maximiliane E., and Lance C. Egley. 1995. "Comparing One-Partner and Couple Data on Sensitive Marital Behaviors: The Case of Marital Violence." *Journal of Marriage and the Family* 57:995–1010.

Taber's Cyclopedic Medical Dictionary. 2001. Ed. D. Venes and C. L. Thomas. Philadelphia: F. A. Davis.

Tagarinski, Mario. 2000. "Y2K: The Problem Which Bound Us Together." Report of the Y2K Coordinator for Central Europe, Eastern Europe, and Central Asia. http://ry2kcc.org/htmls/sitemap.htm (accessed January 13, 2004).

Takooshian, Harold, and H. Bodiner. 1982. "Bystander Indifference to Street Crime," In *Contemporary Criminology*, ed. L. Savitz and N. Johnston, 486. New York: Wiley.

Taylor, Humphrey. 2005. "Who Do We Trust Most to Tell the Truth?" Harris Inter-active. http://harrisinteractive.com/harris_poll/index.asp?PID=145 (accessed November 10, 2005).

Taylor, Susan L. 1995. *Lessons in Living.* New York: Anchor Books.

Tennis Masters Series. 2002. "An Interview with Serena Williams." ASAP Sports. http://www.asapsports.com/tennis/2002itopen/051902SW.html (accessed July 1, 2003).

Teno, Joan M., Brian R. Clarridge, Virginia Casey, Lisa C. Welch, Terri Wetle, Renee Shield, Vincent Mor. 2004. "Family Perspectives on End-of-Life Care at the Last Place of Care." *JAMA* 291:88–93.

Tetlock, Philip E., Randall S. Peterson, Charles McGuire, Shi-jie Chang, and Peter Feld. 1992. "Assessing Political Group Dynamics: A Test of the Groupthink Model." *Journal of Personality and Social Psychology* 63:403–25.

Thoits, Peggy A. 1989. "The Sociology of Emotions." *Annual Review of Sociology* 15:317–42.

———. 1990. "Emotional Deviance: Research Agendas." In *Research Agendas in the Sociology of Emotions,* ed. T. Kemper, 180–206. Albany: SUNY Press.

———. 1996. "Managing the Emotions of Others." *Symbolic Interaction* 19:85–109.

Tierney, Kathleen J., Michael K. Lindell, and Ronald W. Perry. 2001. *Facing the Unexpected: Disaster Preparedness and Response in the United States.* Washington, D.C.: Joseph Henry Press.

Tierney, Lawrence M. Jr., Stephen J. McPhee, and Maxine A. Papadakis, eds. 2004. *2004 Current Medical Diagnosis and Treatment.* New York: Lange Medical Books/McGraw Hill.

TIPP. 2002. "Economic Optimism, June 2001–2002." http://www.tipponline.com/ n_index/eoi/eo_602.htm (accessed July 8, 2002).

Toland, John. 1976. *Adolf Hitler.* New York: Ballantine Books.

Tomita, Susan K. 1990. "The Denial of Elderly Mistreatment by Victims and Abusers: The Application of Neutralization Theory." *Violence and Victims* 5, no. 3:171–84.

Trump, Donald. 1987. *The Art of the Deal.* New York: Random House.

Turgut, Pelin. 1998. "Loss of Honor Means Death in Turkish Regions." *Middle East Times.* http://www.metimes.com/issue98%2D17/reg/honor.htm (accessed July 26, 2001).

Tyler, Patrick E. 2002. "Feeling Secure, U.S. Failed to Grasp bin Laden Threat." *New York Times,* September 8, A1.

U.S. Administration on Aging. 2002. "A Profile of Older Americans." http://www .aoa.dhhd.gov/aoa/stats/profile.l.html (accessed July 9, 2003).

U.S. Bureau of the Census. 2002. *Statistical Abstracts of the United States,* 122nd ed. Washington, D.C.

———. 2004. *Statistical Abstracts of the United States.* 124th ed. Washington, D.C.

U.S. Central Intelligence Agency. 2003. "SARS: Lessons from the First Epidemic of the 21st Century: A Collaborative Analysis with Outside Experts." Posted by

Stark County Health Department, Canton, Ohio. http://www.starkhealth.org/ pdfs/CIA%20SARS%20Report.pdf (accessed January 13, 2004).

U.S. Congress. 1986. *Investigation of the Challenger Accident: Summary Report.* http://www.gpoaccess.gov/challenger/64-420.pdf (accessed February 18, 2004).

U.S. Department of State. 2000. "International Y2K Cooperation Center Final Report." http://usembassy-australia.state.gov/hyper/2000/0217/ep1414.htm (accessed January 13, 2004).

———. 2003. "U.S. Health Agency Pursuing SARS Preparedness Strategy: Congressional Testimony of HHS Official Jerome Hauer." http://usinfo.state.gov/gi/ Archives/2003/May/30-004908.html (accessed January 10, 2004).

U.S. Department of Transportation. 2001. "Alcohol." Washington, D. C.: National Center for Statistical Analysis.

———. 2002a. "Safety Belt Use in 2002—Demographic Characteristics." Washington, D.C.: National Highway Traffic Safety Commission.

———. 2002b. "Safety Belt Use in 2002—U.S. Rates in States and Territories." Washington, D.C.: National Highway Traffic Safety Commission.

U.S. Surgeon General's Office. 2000. *The Surgeon General's Call to Action to Prevent and Decrease Overweight and Obesity.* http://www.surgeongeneral.gov/ topics/obesity/ (accessed July 3, 2003).

USA Today. 2003. "Powell: U.S. Would Assist Saddam in Exile." January 29. http://www.usatoday.com/news/world/2003-01-29-us-iraq_x.htm (accessed August 27, 2003).

Van Til, Henry R., Richard J. Mouw, and Cornelius Van Til. 2001. *The Calvinistic Concept of Culture.* Grand Rapids, Mich.: Baker Book House.

Vance, David. 2001. "Toward a Professional Information Systems Ethic (Cyberethics)." Baylor University. http://hsb.baylor.edu/ramsower/acis/ papers/vance.htm (accessed October 18, 2001).

Vaughan, Diane. 1986. *Uncoupling: Turning Points in Intimate Relationships.* New York: Oxford University Press.

———. 1996. *The Challenger Launch Decision: Risky Technology, Culture, and Deviance at NASA.* Chicago: University of Chicago Press.

———. 2002. "Signals and Interpretive Work: The Role of Culture in a Theory of Practical Action." In *Culture in Mind: Toward a Sociology of Culture and Cognition,* ed. K. A. Cerulo, 28–54. New York: Routledge.

Veatch, Robert M. 1975. "The Whole Brain Concept of Death: An Outmoded Philosophical Formulation." *Journal of Thanatology* 3:13–30.

———. 1988. "The Definition of Death: Problems for Public Policy." In *Dying: Facing the Facts,* H. Wass. F. M. Berardo, and R. A. Neimeyer. New York: Hemisphere Publishing.

Veysey, B. M., and Steven F. Messner. 1999. "Further Testing of Social Disorganization Theory: An Elaboration of Sampson and Groves' 'Community, Structure, and Crime.'" *Journal of Research in Crime and Delinquency* 36:156–74.

Viders, Hillary. 1991. "It Can't Happen to Me." *New York Sub Aqua Journal* 1, no. 6:4.

Viorst, Milton. 2002. "The Wisdom of Imagining the Worst-Case Scenario." *New York Times*, September 12, A27.

Virginia PTA. 2003. "Mandatory Bicycle Helmet Use Ordinance." http://www.vapta .org/Committees/Legislati . . . olutions/01resolutions/bicyclehelmets.htm (accessed July 1, 2003).

Von Drehle, David. 2000. "World Celebrates Joyously as Y2K Worries Dissipate." *Washington Post*, January 1. http://www.garone.com/writing/2000.html (accessed January 13, 2004).

Walker, A. Earl. 1974. "The Death of a Brain." *Johns Hopkins Medical Journal* 124:190–201.

Walton, D. N. 1979. *On Defining Death.* Montreal: McGill–Queens University Press.

Ward, Robert R. 2001. "The Banishment." Ableza Native American Arts and Film Institute Web site. http://www.ableza.org/ward/ban.html (accessed August 29, 2002).

Wasswa, Henry. 2000. "Relatives Shunning Ugandan Ebola Survivors." Report on Canoe, a Canadian news site. http://www.canoe.ca/Health0011/10_ebola-ap .html (accessed March 29, 2001).

Weber, Elke U., Ann-Renee Blais, and Nancy E. Betz. 2002. "A Domain-Specific Risk Attitude Scale: Measuring Risk Perception and Risk Behaviors." *Journal of Behavioral Decision Making* 15, no. 4:263–90.

Weber, Eugen. 1999. *Apocalypses.* Cambridge: Harvard University Press.

Weick, Karl E. 1995. *Sensemaking in Organizations.* Thousand Oaks, Calif.: Sage.

Weil, Andrew. 1995. *Natural Health, Natural Medicine.* Boston: Houghton Mifflin.

Weinstein, Neil D. 1989. "Optimistic Biases about Personal Risk." *Science* 246:1232–33.

Whitehead, Barbara DeFoe, and David Popenoe. 1999. "Changes in Teen Attitudes toward Marriage, Cohabitation and Children." National Marriage Project, the Next Generation series. http://marriage.rutgers.edu/pubteena/htm (accessed July 17, 2002).

Whyte, G. 1993. "Escalating Commitment in Individual and Group Decision-making: A Prospect Theory Approach." *Organizational Behavior and Human Decision Processes* 54:430–55.

Will, George. 1999. "Gambler Nation." *Washington Post*, June 27.

Williams, Serena. 2001. "Aussie Sports-Lovers Ignore Injury Risk." Report for the Australian Government Department of Health and Ageing. http://www .health.gov.au/mediarel/yr2000/mw/mw20001.htm (accessed June 30, 2002).

Winfrey, Oprah. 2001. "What I Know for Sure." *O Magazine*, April, 232.

Winseman, Albert L. 2004. "Americans Maintain Love-hate Relationship with TV, Movies." Gallup Organization. http://poll.gallup.com/content/default.aspx ?ci=12961 (accessed November 8, 2005).

Winter, Arthur, ed. 1969. *The Moment of Death: A Symposium*. Springfield, Ill.: Charles C. Thomas.

Winters, Michael Sean. 2002. "The Betrayal: How to Save the Church." *New Republic* 555, no. 4 (May 6): 24–27.

Wise, David. 1999. "Assassination: The Thin Red Line between Diplomacy and Murder." *Los Angeles Times*, April 25, Opinion section, M2.

Wittgenstein, Ludwig. 1953. *Philosophical Investigations*. Trans. G. E. M. Anscombe. Oxford: Blackwell.

Woodford, Charles M., Layle D. Lawrence, Lisa Fazalare, and Jennifer Martin. 1996. "Hearing Loss and Hearing Conservation Practices among Agriculture Instructors." *Journal of Agricultural Education* 37, no. 2:34–39.

The World Almanac and Book of Facts. 2003. William A. McGeveran Jr., ed. dir. New York: World Almanac Books.

World Health Organization (WHO). 2003a. "Severe Acute Respiratory Syndrome (SARS): Status of the Outbreak and Lessons for the Immediate Future." WHO Epidemic and Pandemic Alert and Response, Geneva, May 20. http://www.who.int/csr/saes/en/ (accessed January 13, 2004).

———. 2003b. "Update 53—Situation in Singapore and Hong Kong, Interpretation of 'Areas with Recent Local Transmission.'" WHO Epidemic and Pandemic Alert and Response, May 12. http://www.who.int/csr/sarsarcmve/2003_05_12/en/ (accessed January 10, 2004).

Wuthnow, Robert. 1998. *Loose Connections: Joining Together in America's Fragmented Communities*. Cambridge: Harvard University Press.

Zerubavel, Eviatar. 1997. *Social Mindscapes: An Invitation to Cognitive Sociology*. Cambridge: Harvard University Press.

———. 2002. "The Elephant in the Room: Notes on the Social Organization of Denial." In *Culture in Mind: Toward a Sociology of Culture and Cognition*, ed. K. A. Cerulo, 21–27. New York: Routledge.

———. 2006. *The Elephant in the Room: Silence and Denial in Everyday Life*. New York: Oxford.

Zimmerman, Dean R. 1999. "Linex for eBusiness." Orem, Utah: Caldera Systems.

Zimmerman, Gertrude. 1971. "Concise Treasury of Popular Quotations." *The Webster Encyclopedic Dictionary of the English Language*. Chicago: Consolidated Book Publishers.

Zoglin, Richard. 1996. "The News Wars." *Time*, October 21, 3–4.

Zuckerman, Marvin. 1994. *Behavioral Expression and Biosocial Bases of Sensation Seeking*. New York: Cambridge University Press.

Index

Page numbers in italics indicate illustrations.

North Korea, 79, 150. *See also* Korea
NRA (National Rifle Association), 153–55
NSA (National Security Administration), 227, 228
nuclear power generators, 125–26
nuns, 161
nursing homes, 89
nutrition. *See* diet and nutrition

obesity, 50–51, 256n97
objectivity (claims of), 121–38
occupations. *See* workplace
O'Donahue, Maura, 161–62, 270n71
Oedipus (Greek mythological figure), 74–75
Of Mice and Men (Steinbeck), 81
Oklahoma City bombing, 262n39
On Becoming Baby Wise (Ezzo and Bucknam), 30
O'Neill, John, 275n42
Onizuka, Ellison, 212
optimism. *See* positive asymmetry
"organizational culture," 57–60
organizations and small groups: ancient Jewish, 90–91; cultural practices of, 72–121; emancipating structures as freeing, from perceptual asymmetry, 16, 193–232, 242–43; positive asymmetry in, 54–60, 206–16, 234; symbolization by, 217. *See also* power; structures; "thought communities"
original sin, 143–44
O-rings, 59, 213, 214, 216, 227
Oscars, 110
Ottoman Empire, 148
Owensboro (Kentucky), 86–87

Packwood, Robert, 157
Paine Webber (investment firm), 107, 135, 136
Palestine, 147
Palm Springs (Florida), 162
Panama, 150, 205
parenting, 26–34
Parkinson's disease, 119
Passover, 75
Patient Self-Determination Act, 42–43
Paul (Biblical figure), 67, 99
Paxil (drug), 64–65
Payr, Sabine, 247n26
PBS, 18
PCs for Dummies (Gookin), 180–81
Peale, Norman Vincent, 258n131
Pearl Harbor attack, 17, 55, 246n15

pedophilia, 162
penitentiaries, 83
Pennsylvania, 85–86
Perfect Storm, The (movie), 196
Perot, Ross, 155–56
Perrow, Charles, 58–59, 244
Persian Gulf War, 112, 113. *See also* Iraq War
pessimism. *See* negative asymmetry
Petty, Adam, 48
Pew poll, 63
Pfenninger, John L., 165
pharmaceutical companies, 64–65
Philadelphia (Pennsylvania), 85–86
"Phoenix Memo" (FBI), 16, 18, 193, 206–12, 216, 225–30, 233, 235
physical exams, 175
physical seclusion. *See* seclusion
Pinelli, Bartolomeo, 101, *104*
Pinto automobile, 57
Piven, Joshua, 70
plague, 116–17, 237
Poindexter, John, 256n94
"point horizons," 11
police, 159–60
Pol Pot, 149, 150
Poor, Alfred, 179, 184–86
poor, the (homeless): in an open class system, 142–43, 267n6; police violence against, 160; recasting of, as werewolves, 152; seclusion of, 82–85; shunning of, 92
porous boundaries. *See* boundaries: porous
"portholes" (described), 11–12
positive asymmetry (focusing on best-case scenarios; optimism; positive thinking), 1; in the brain, 6–10, 12, 234; costs and benefits of dominance of, 16, 236–37; cultural practices' role in sustaining, 1–2, 5–6, 10–14, 54–60, 72–121, 164, 234, 236, 253n60; definition of, 6, 10, 234; and disaster-preparedness, 16, 17–20, 57–60, 193, 206–16, 230; dominance of, in sociocultural practice, 6–14, 17–71, 233, 234; as emotional recovery tool, 32; exceptions to, 15, 64–71, 164–93, 235; as feeling "natural," 6, 10–11, 236; possibility of transforming, 16, 236–44; as skewing measurement and science, 121–38, 234; structure of sites of, 225–30; as a U.S. characteristic, 19, 60–71, 233, 237. *See also* best, the; worst, the
positive thinking, 1, 258n131. *See also* positive asymmetry